10-7-17

To Richard with thanks !

David Hildebrand
& Ginger Hildebrand

Musical Maryland

A History of Song and Performance
from the Colonial Period to the Age of Radio

DAVID K. HILDEBRAND & ELIZABETH M. SCHAAF
With Contributions by William Biehl

JOHNS HOPKINS UNIVERSITY PRESS   BALTIMORE

This book was brought to publication with the generous assistance of the Johns Hopkins University Press Regional Fund.

© 2017 Johns Hopkins University Press
All rights reserved. Published 2017
Printed in the United States of America on acid-free paper
9 8 7 6 5 4 3 2 1

Johns Hopkins University Press
2715 North Charles Street
Baltimore, Maryland 21218-4363
www.press.jhu.edu

Library of Congress Cataloging-in-Publication Data

Names: Hildebrand, David. | Schaaf, Elizabeth M. | Biehl, William
Title: Musical Maryland : a history of song and performance from
    the colonial period to the age of radio / David K. Hildebrand and
    Elizabeth M. Schaaf, with contributions by William Biehl.
Description: Baltimore : Johns Hopkins University Press, 2017. |
    Includes bibliographical references and index.
Identifiers: LCCN 2016040200| ISBN 9781421422398 (hardcover : alk.
    paper) | ISBN 9781421422404 (electronic) | ISBN 1421422395
    (hardcover : alk. paper) | ISBN 1421422409 (electronic)
Subjects: LCHS: Music—Maryland—History and criticism. |
    Music—Social aspects—Maryland—History.
Classification: LCC ML200.7.M25 H55 2017 |
    DDC 780.9752—dc23
    LC record available at https://lccn.loc.gov/2016040200

A catalog record for this book is available from the British Library.

Special discounts are available for bulk purchases of this book. For more information, please contact Special Sales at 410-516-6936 or specialsales@press.jhu.edu.

Johns Hopkins University Press uses environmentally friendly book materials, including recycled text paper that is composed of at least 30 percent post-consumer waste, whenever possible.

CONTENTS

Prelude

"THE HISTORY OF A COUNTRY," wrote the local bookseller Meredith Janvier in an early twentieth-century account of old Baltimore, "is largely written in its songs, since they record and reflect not only the spirit of the times but tell what its people did, how they lived and what they thought about."[1] We began this project convinced, with Janvier, that music means a great deal to musicians and their audiences and that, indeed, music lays bare the soul of a community. It entertains men and women but also comforts them in their sorrow, expresses hopes but also fears, celebrates love but also lifts up the disappointed. Music helps people worship their God and express the timeless; it stiffens soldiers to march in formation and gives them strength on the eve of battle. No history of a people can be complete without attention to its music.

At the beginning of the twenty-first century, music in Maryland encompassed the established symphony in Baltimore, which made its home in the impressive Meyerhoff Symphony Hall and also played regular concerts at Strathmore Hall, between Bethesda and Rockville; the renowned Peabody Institute, then a part of the Johns Hopkins University; the active and distinguished Choral Arts Society in Baltimore; jazz and blues at places like An die Musik in Baltimore and in cabarets outside Washington as well as in old Annapolis; ambitious and ever-morphing "garage bands"; barbershop singing groups of national and international prominence, made up of both men and women; bluegrass and county music at hangouts in the rural counties but also in the suburbs of Baltimore and Washington; and, especially in Baltimore, persistent ethnic musical groups like klezmer bands.

Technology and commercialization, it must be noted, have tended to homogenize American sounds, styles, and venues. CDs replaced LPs and then faced the threat of downloads off the Internet; likewise, iPods and mixed media available via on-line television subsumed MTV and conventional radio broadcasts. Live concerts in Maryland—whether featuring Yo-Yo Ma or Sting or Ice T—sounded just like those in Connecticut or Nevada. A praise-band service in a Protestant church in Annapolis featured the same rock-influenced instruments and musical selections as one in

Michigan or Texas. After about 1965, one can argue, a new generation, born soon after World War II, came of age and expressed its own musical taste. Technology changed yet again, making music literally portable; and music marketing, funding, and business models adapted accordingly, so that one musical chapter closed and another one opened. Only with care and circumspection can one speak of a peculiarly Maryland music after that.

This book explores the music Marylanders made through the mid-twentieth century, offering the first survey of the development and social function of music in the state. It makes the case that music in Maryland, that is, of the Europeans and others who established and settled Maryland (this book is not a study of the music of Native Americans who lived here first, however fascinating), began with music imported and adapted from the Old World but soon embraced original music that reflected Marylanders' passions and interests. Eventually, by the first half of the twentieth century, black and white artists born and mostly raised in Maryland had made significant contributions to American music, both formal and popular.

When we look at Maryland's contributions to America's musical history, we find more than a few choice stories to tell. In Upper Marlboro in 1752 some enterprising thespians and musicians staged the earliest American opera with orchestral accompaniment. After the Revolution, Baltimore provided a home to the first resident professional theater company in the United States. Exactly thirty-three years later, and only a few miles away, Francis Scott Key crafted the lyrics that would become our national anthem. As the country's fastest growing city in the nineteenth century, Baltimore stood in the vanguard in both sheet-music publishing and piano manufacturing. Sidney Lanier, Eubie Blake, John Hill Hewitt, Colin McPhee, Mabel Garrison, John Charles Thomas, Chick Webb, and Cab Calloway, among other influential composers and performers, called Maryland home. Billie Holiday, whose career owed heavily to radio and who enjoyed a base of admirers all across the country, had Baltimore connections and cultivated them.

We divide the long history of music in Maryland into episodes that reflect the region's emerging cultural and musical traditions over a span of more than three centuries. Extensive unpublished resources make possible a reasoned selection of some of the finest music created and performed in the state from colonial days to about twenty years after the end of World War II. The chapters that follow devote due attention to the lives of Maryland's African Americans, women, and middle- and working-class citizens, both native and immigrant, who together made up the greater part of the population. Like Janvier, we see music in Maryland as a richly melodious reflection of the varied people themselves.

Musical selections from this book are available online so that readers can listen to historical and modern versions of various pieces. Go to jhupbooks.press.jhu.edu/content/musical-maryland for the appropriate links.

Not long ago, two performers of historical American music presented an assembly program on the music of colonial Maryland at a school for dyslexic children. Part of the way into the question-and-answer period, a child raised his hand and asked, "Was music really important back then, or was it just for entertainment?" This book offers an extended answer to that excellent question.

CHAPTER ONE

Drawing Rooms, Taverns, Churches, and Tobacco Fields

MUSIC IN EARLY MARYLAND

MUSIC IS INTEGRAL to human experience. It may have been especially so during the colonial period in Maryland, when life was limited and difficult for many people regardless of their manner of living. Music expressed the colonists' thoughts, feelings, fears, and hopes, but it also played a role in many other aspects of their lives.

One must try to imagine the sounds to be heard in the mainland British colonies in, say, 1750. Philadelphia Quakers speak quietly and worship without music, while Anglicans in churches as far south as Savannah absorb the colorful sounds of fine organs. Indentured servants in Williamsburg sing old ballads while working; later they dance reels and jigs for pleasure. While a studious Moravian settler in North Carolina quietly copies the musical score for a Mozart string quartet, a French dance master in the city of New York fiddles minuets for wealthy young students. Georgia slaves craft homemade banjos and add African touches to Wesleyan hymns, airing a far more emotional plea than those expressed in the staid psalms that third-generation Puritans sang in Massachusetts churches. Such musical expressions flourished in the varied colonies of early British America. In Maryland, all sounded at once.

African music came to Maryland along with slaves, German music through its Lutheran and Moravian colonists. French music arrived, as did Catholic settlers and dance masters, and of course British music came with the many immigrants who sang psalms and ballads in English. Wealthier colonists imported refined Italian compositions and collections of popular Scottish songs. Maryland's musical history grew out of these varied streams as colonists adjusted and adapted to their new land. In microcosm one finds in Maryland nearly the whole scope of musical activity that characterized colonial British America, the British Isles, and much of western Europe.

Early in the colonial period, Maryland became dependent upon tobacco and the associated plantation system. Perhaps a hundred years after the settlement at St. Mary's City in 1634, a divergent culture emerged as farming communities in Maryland's piedmont region took root. In contrast to the tidewater region, with its older, slave-supported plantations, the piedmont attracted German settlers and British immigrants who could not afford the rising land prices near the Chesapeake. A more egalitarian society evolved inland, based on the labor of landowners and families rather than servants and slaves. So while the wealthy tidewater planters kept up with British fashion, following current tastes in theater, social dance, and amateur music-making, the austere piedmont farmers focused on work, family, church, and less refined sorts of entertainment. By 1750 one could almost consider Maryland two provinces, such were the differences between the tidewater and piedmont cultures.

Constant change characterized Maryland's colonial period, which lasted some 140 years. Musical practice reflected not just the colony's growing population but the increased role played by evangelical religion and the economics of cash-based trade (as opposed to tobacco credit). The growth of cities like Baltimore and Frederick paved the way for the establishment of music as a business and the gradual erosion of homemade music, the staple of the colonial period.

Overture: Toil and the Music to Lighten It

For many decades after the establishment of St. Mary's City, life in Maryland proved difficult and unstable. The first colonists, largely men from the southeast of England, laboriously cleared the forest in preparation for planting. Cultivation soon dispersed the population and kept many planters on the move, for the tobacco weed quickly depletes even the richest soils. Because Maryland's economy hinged on the value of this single crop, which almost everyone planted, tobacco prices eventually declined. Some indentured servants who remained healthy and served out their time often found ways to rent land and grow enough tobacco and corn to climb into a small middle class of lesser landowners and even serve in public office. But the annual drudgery of growing, tending, packing, and selling tobacco denied seventeenth-century colonists much leisure time.

Even so, music consoles the illiterate poor just as it ornaments the wealthy, and it is clear that tobacco planters and their families sang and danced. First-generation immigrants came largely from poor villages in which traditional ballads and dance tunes flourished. Few who emigrated knew the refined music of the English court or cathedral; instead, they grew up in the English countryside hearing dance music played on fiddles and ballads sung *a capella*, meaning without instrumental accompaniment. Maryland vestry records from the early 1700s include accusations of dancing on the Sabbath and of singing lewd songs in public.[1] Wealthier planter families had an especial fascination with dancing.

The English Dancing Master: Or, Plaine and easie Rules for the Dancing of Country Dances, with the Tune to Each Dance, an important English publication, included the sorts of melodies brought to early Maryland. John Playford compiled and published this book of music and dance instructions in London in 1651, and later editions remained in print through 1728. *The English Dancing Master* contained ballad tunes and country-dance melodies that Playford had adapted for middle- and upper-class use, thus casting current folk music into print. Country dances like "Stingo, or the Oyle of Barley," which involved line dancing in rows, flourished among the English and American upper classes for some 150 years. Many tunes collected by John Playford, his son Henry, and other compilers, such as Thomas D'Urfey, remained popular among Maryland's populace well into the eighteenth century. Fixed in print by these English publishers, such melodies formed a part of the unwritten culture that accompanied Maryland's earliest immigrants.[2] Ballads like "Chevy Chase," "Jockey and Jenny," and "Lilliburlero" enlivened spirits at tavern gatherings and perhaps helped planters pass the hours as they worked alone in the fields or sang for one another. Guests sang ballads in the way we share good stories today: in private homes, at weddings, on election days, or on feast days. Settlers danced almost anywhere. And many melodies could be used for both dancing and ballad-singing. The particular versions of tunes set by Playford give us a strong sense of Maryland's music during the 1600s, especially if allowance is made for variation and selection over time.

One of the earliest references to musical instruments

Tobacco is but an *Indian* Weed,
  Grows green in the Morn, cut down at Eve ;
    It shows our decay,
    We are but Clay,
Think of this and take Tobacco.

The Pipe that is so Lilly-white,
Where so many take delight ;
    Is broke with a touch,
    Man's Life is such,
Think of this, &c.

The Pipe that is so foul within,
Shews how Man's Soul is stain'd with Sin ;
    It does require,
    To be purg'd with fire,
Think of this, &c.

The Ashes that are left behind,
Does serve to put us all in mind ;
    That into Dust,
    Return we must,
Think of this, &c.

The Smoak that does so high ascend,
Shews you Man's Life must have an end ;
    The Vapour's gone,
    Man's Life is done,
Think of this and take Tobacco.

"Tobacco is but an Indian Weed." From Thomas D'Urfey, Songs Compleat, Pleasant and Divertive; set to Musick by Dr. John Blow, Mr. Henry Purcell, and other Excellent Masters of the Town (III, London, 1719), from series entitled Wit and Mirth: or Pills to Purge Melancholy, compiled by D'Urfey. This sober indictment of tobacco seems more puritanical than other, lighthearted songs on the topic. Archives of the Peabody Institute of the Johns Hopkins University.

in Maryland appears in the 1676 probate inventory of William Crouch. Crouch lived in Anne Arundel County, on the north side of the Severn River, where he kept a "hoe boy pipe," or oboe.[3] Other inventories of the period refer to violins and military instruments such as trumpets and drums. The only instruments known to survive from this period survive as remains. Jew's harps have been unearthed at the Drew family site, near Annapolis, which dates from 1670. Perhaps the Drews traded them with local Indians or gave them to their children. Jew's harps, as well as fiddles, trumpets, and oboes, could produce simple melodies for dancing, which made the harsh, primitive conditions of the seventeenth-century Chesapeake a little more bearable. Seventeenth-century Maryland sustained neither theaters nor public dance halls, and no evidence of music teachers or music publishers survives. Nor do we know of any professional musicians or makers of musical instruments. Lutes, citterns, guitars, virginals, and harpsichords do not appear in Maryland's earliest

records. Expensive and delicate, these instruments were better suited to playing more refined music in wealthier households under tame and stable circumstances, such as in New England, where they were in use around this time.

A series of English collections of ballads entitled *Wit and Mirth: or Pills to Purge Melancholy* first appeared in London in 1698. Its compiler, Thomas D'Urfey (1653–1723), gathered some one thousand popular ballad melodies and dance tunes, many of which doubtless resounded in seventeenth-century Maryland. One of them began by calling attention to the noxious qualities and possibly harmful effects of the principal Chesapeake export, tobacco, as a way of reminding listeners of the brevity of human life. The ditty went on in the same vein for four more verses, supplying a kind of companion to Ebenezer Cooke's well-known epic poem about early Maryland, *The Sot-Weed Factor* (1708). *Sot-weed* was slang for tobacco, and Cooke composed in a satirical style, expressing his frustration that colonial culture lagged so far behind that of the mother country.

Complete Gentlemen and Agreeable Women

Early in the eighteenth century a fortunate few Maryland settlers broke free of the limitations of small-scale tobacco planting. Intermarrying and diversifying into lending, land speculation, and merchandising, these families established large, stable plantations and succeeded in consolidating impressive holdings of land and other property. Beginning in the late 1600s, when English whites found more work at home and several factors made more Africans available to the mainland colonies at a lesser cost than before, these lawndowners shifted from indentured white to African slave labor. In the 1660s, lifetime servitude for African people became codified in Maryland law, and statutes against miscegenation and black liberties like gun ownership were also enacted. Racially, economically, and socially stratified, this new tidewater economy supported a small upper class that dominated the rest of society, most of which remained poor. By around 1720 this wealthy minority had built increasingly splendid homes on vast properties, and they wielded considerable political power. For them, the Maryland wilderness had become a sylvan retreat, and they sought to emulate the leisure recreations of the English manor.

The English concept of hierarchy was so entrenched that there was little questioning by the ordinary people that a well-born minority would be blessed with wealth, intelligence, and leadership and thus control society. In eighteenth-century Maryland, social class utterly defined a person's identity, and this distinction factored heavily in the practice of music. The wealthiest colonists pursued certain musical activities from which all others could be excluded, the best example being dancing a minuet to the sound of a hired fiddler in the privacy of a great plantation home.

In England, the nobility had monopolized formal music-making and concert life during the decades of Maryland's early settlement. Only toward the close of the seventeenth century could English music lovers outside the court attend public concerts and purchase music published for their use. By 1725 music had become an integral part of an English "polite" education, an aspect of the rising vogue for self-cultivation. It was around this time that Maryland's wealthy tidewater planters began to copy Georgian clothing fashions and architectural patterns, hold thoroughbred-horse races, and pursue both practical and polite education. They read English books on social etiquette and fashion magazines, such as *Complete Gentleman* and *London Magazine*, which stressed the importance of music and regularly included songs and dances. In 1744 a Virginian visitor to Annapolis observed, "The Ladies was so very Agreeable, and seem'd so Intent on Dancing that one might have Imagin'd they had some Design on the Virginians, either Designing to make Tryal of their Strength and Vigor, or to Convince them of their Activity and Sprightliness."[4] So Chesapeake planters vigorously embraced music as a pleasant means for improving moral character and impressing their peers. They imported fine music books and instruments. They practiced and performed in the drawing room before an audience of friends or family; occasionally guests or professional musicians would join in.

The sounds made in colonial Maryland's private drawing rooms perhaps were at times at odds with the elegant paintings and silver that graced the eye, since students far outnumbered teachers and performance standards were clearly below those in London. In the colonies, relatively simple solo and duet music predominated because of the shortage of instruments and highly trained players. Only the most advanced could do justice to trio sonatas and other chamber pieces. Except among the talented Moravians in Pennsylvania, Maryland, and North Carolina, large choral works, true concertos, and full symphonies lay outside the capabilities of wealthy amateurs. The leading families of Maryland, such as the Carrolls, the Lloyds, the Ridouts, the Dorseys, and the Chews, imported solos and duets for the German flute; violin music by Corelli, Vivaldi, and others; and lessons and sonatas for the harpsichord by Pasquali, Alberti, and a host of other Italian composers. Colonial amateurs rarely played Haydn and Mozart, being more attracted to Thomas Arne and other

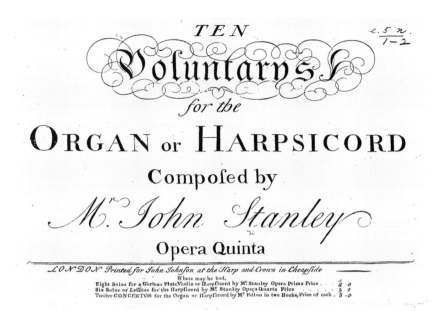

The title page from *Ten Voluntarys for the Organ or Harpsicord Composed by Mr. John Stanley, Opera Quinta* (London, 1745). Charles Carroll of Carrollton possessed one of the few personal libraries in colonial Maryland for which specific musical items are listed. His choices were typical of the late colonial upper-class repertory, except that he avoided Handel. Library of Congress, Music Division, M11.s case.

English composers who are less well known today. By the 1770s and 1780s, Johann Christian Bach and Carl Philipp Emanuel Bach enjoyed popularity, while the music of their deceased father, Johan Sebastian Bach, was forgotten and yet to be rediscovered. For lessons, colonists bought instruction books such as Robert Bremner's *The Harpsichord or Spinnet Miscellany* (ca. 1765) and similar publications for guitar, flute, voice, and violin.[5] They also purchased blank music paper and special pens for ruling music lines. Nearly all of the trappings of music then fashionable in London found their way to the colonial Chesapeake. Yet despite their vast resources and their desire to buy the best, just how well Maryland's wealthy amateurs performed remains unclear. While some of the drawing-room repertory remained exclusive to the elite, much of it was enjoyed by those on other levels of society as well. Handel's operatic overtures and marches, as well as selections from his *Messiah*, enjoyed widespread popularity in eighteenth-century Maryland, being played at public celebrations and in theaters, as well as at gatherings of social clubs and even on musical clocks. Psalm tunes, heard by most colonists in church, sounded on drawing-room spinets for entertainment and edification. Libraries of the wealthy included collections of favorite theater songs and stylized Scottish folk songs. Different social classes danced to many of the same dance tunes, except that

the minuet was reserved for the elite. The terms *classical*, *popular*, and *folk* had not yet been coined to segregate or layer tastes. In a sense, elite amateurs wanted the best of both worlds: they sought out the refined music that distinguished them from the lower classes and also appropriated the more appealing lower-class ballads and dance tunes for their own use.

Drawing-room etiquette required differing musical roles for men and women. The "Ode to Delia, playing on the harpsichord, with her gloves on," which appeared in the *Maryland Gazette* of February 13, 1772, focused on the upper-class ideal image of a woman gently playing music at home. Such a fine, well-educated lady should be musically expressive, and her proper suitor would be vulnerable to her musical charms. She could play for others of her own station or above, though never in public. Such a skill was both practical and ornamental. Reputation paramount, a fine woman never risked the appearance of promiscuity by associating herself with lewd songs. Women did not play the violin, long associated with lower-class dancing and "fiddling about," nor did they play wind instruments, because of the unladylike puckering required to play them. Women's repertory, presented to a select audience only, reflected polite, chaste themes. Ornament had its practical side too. Music served as a pleasurable and creative outlet for girls and young women that they often carried into marriage, despite the rigorous demands of managing the manor house, directing servants, and raising children.

Ladies of wealth most commonly played the harpsichord or the smaller, generally simpler and less expensive spinet. A spinet was designed to take up less space than the "grand" harpsichord, much like upright pianos today. Both types of harpsichords qualified as ideal status symbols and fine pieces of furniture, featuring delicate, costly ornamentation. Itinerant teachers advertised to instruct female students in their own homes, since it was unthinkable for a lady to go to a strange man's rooms. One Annapolis student, Ann (Nancy) Faris, "soon found t'was money and time thrown away" to study with her teacher, Harry Woodcock, the organist at St. Anne's Church. Frustrated, she "picked out a tune here and there by herself."[6] Men too played harpsichords, though more commonly they studied violin or flute.

A few early Maryland harpsichords survive, one of them an instrument Charles Carroll of Carrollton ordered in 1785. Carroll spared no expense when he commissioned a grand harpsichord, presumably for his eldest child, Mary. He requested "a harpsichord of the best maker, with two unisons and an octave stop and row of keys with the movement for a swell and octave [opening]."[7] Such specifications duplicated harpsichords of the kind Washington and Jefferson ordered (statesmen must have discussed things musical as well as political). The London firm of Shudi and Broadwood filled Carroll's commission promptly, and the exquisite instrument remained in use by the family well into the nineteenth century. John Ridout, who lived across Duke of Gloucester Street from the Carrolls, arrived in Annapolis as Governor Sharpe's secretary in 1764. Ridout soon married the Annapolitan Mary Ogle. For her wedding present he ordered from England an elegant Kirkman double-manual harpsichord costing 30 guineas. A man of wealth and high office, Ridout purchased another harpsichord in the 1780s (it survives in playing condition to this day). In 1781 he also bought a pianoforte made by the Londoner John Houston, the earliest piano known in Maryland. Harpsichords remained more common than pianos in Maryland until around 1800.[8]

Besides harpsichords, colonial women played English guitars. Most commonly referred to simply as the *guitar*, or *guittar*, this instrument truly descended from the Renaissance cittern. Citterns appeared commonly in late seventeenth-century England and New England, falling out of fashion around 1700. Some fifty years later the cittern reemerged, with its ten metal strings now in an open-C tuning, and for the rest of the eighteenth century it helped define feminine gentility in England and America. Unlike the true Spanish guitar, English guitars were generally played with a plectrum in order to protect the woman's fingernails; a later version owned by Nelly Custis had a keyed mechanism that allowed one to pluck the strings without touching them. Women in the Jefferson family owned and played these guitars, as did young Moravian women.[9]

Less expensive and less prestigious than keyboard instruments, English guitars were in good supply in Maryland. Between 1764 and 1774 Annapolis merchants imported hundreds of them, along with sets of strings and guitar music. Imported lesson books for the guitar contained popular songs from the English stage, instrumental selections by Italian and German composers, and country dance tunes, minuets, and livelier gigs and reels. Although less versatile than keyboard instruments, English guitars were easy to learn to play and made genteel musicianship available to many women, not just the extremely wealthy.

Colonial portraiture commonly featured objects that symbolized wealth, success, and vanity. The Maryland-born portraitist Charles Willson Peale painted English guitars in the laps of several prominent colonial women, including Mrs. Edward Lloyd IV, mother-in-law of Francis Scott Key. The inclusion of an instrument in the Lloyd family portrait suggests the importance of music to Mrs. Lloyd, who is seated at the focal center of the family grouping. Peale painted Mrs. Lloyd at home, where her prerogative as matron of the house was to play music in her spare time.

Men played a greater variety of instruments than did women, and societal expectations were less limiting.

The Edward Lloyd Family, Maryland, by Charles Willson Peale, 1771. A prolific painter, Peale focuses this portrait of the wealthy Lloyd family upon the matron, who is playing an English guitar. Peale was the son of a dancing teacher, and all his children enjoyed music, a family interest perhaps secondary only to painting. Winterthur Museum, Garden and Library, 64.124.

Thomas Jefferson, Patrick Henry, and Daniel Dulaney Jr. all played the violin, and so did some of their male slaves. Other notable musicians included Benjamin Franklin, who invented the glass armonica, and Francis Hopkinson, an accomplished composer and performer on the organ and harpsichord. The names of Maryland's amateur male musicians do not stand out in colonial American history, yet they played a critical role in the colony's unfolding musical life. Whether rich, middling, or poor, these men carried on the greater part of the musical activity during a time when professional musicians were few.

Governor Charles Calvert played the flute and also the violin. A decade after Calvert's death in 1734, Dr. Alexander Hamilton described a performance upon Calvert's violin at a Philadelphia concert:

I paid a visit to Collector Alexander in the afternoon, and at night going to the coffee-house, I went from thence, along with Messrs. Wallace and Currie, to the Musick Club, where I heard a tolerable concerto performed by a harpsichord and three violins. One Levy there played a very good violin; one Quin bore another pretty good part; Tench Francis played a very indifferent finger upon an excellent violin, that once belonged to the late Ch. Calvert, Governour of Maryland. We dismissed at eleven o'clock, after having regaled ourselves with musick, and good viands and liquor.[10]

Colonel Edward Lloyd III, who owned a harpsichord and a violin, earned honorary membership in the musical Tuesday Club of Annapolis. Upon the death of Edward Lloyd IV in 1796, the family owned a fiddle, a German flute, a drum, and two pianofortes, valued at £22 and £75. Other gentlemen amateurs included Edward H. Calvert, the Reverends Thomas Bacon, Alexander Malcolm, and Jonathan Boucher, and various members of the Dulaney, Brice, Galloway, Warfield, and Watkins families. William Faris, an English watchmaker and silversmith who settled in Annapolis around 1757, also built musical clocks and later a pianoforte. He owned a chamber organ and a music copybook, and he hosted actors and musicians in his tavern. The Annapolis painters Just Inglehart Kühn and Daniel Wolstenholme played their flutes in social gatherings, as did Jonas Green, publisher of the *Maryland Gazette*, his French horn. Green, Faris, Kühn, and Wolstenholme held considerably less wealth and status than did the Calverts, the Lloyds, and other gentlemen amateur musicians of the landed gentry. Among other lines of evidence, the prices of musical instruments reflected the varied means of those using them. While some violins sold quite cheaply, occasionally by the gross, others were quite dear, commanding prices of £50 and upwards.[11]

Not limited to playing in drawing rooms, as their wives and daughters were, Maryland men periodically formed social clubs. Such groups convened at private homes, at taverns, or, as in the case of the South River Club, in their own private clubhouses. At various times in colonial Maryland, dozens of gentlemen's clubs flourished, promoting almost anything from debate to horse-racing. Music, especially group singing, had a natural place in such convivial gatherings, and at times club members paraded the streets of Annapolis singing or playing instruments such as fiddles and drums. In 1771 a disgruntled Annapolitan complained publicly that members of the Independent Club, "flushed with wine," would "sally forth at a seasonable hour, preceded by minstrelsy."[12] Perhaps verses 2 and 5 of the "Song for the Homony Club," composed by Reverend Jonathan Boucher around 1771, best expressed club members' reasons for gathering "in the Anacreontic Taste":

Let the heart-frozen drone
Sit moping alone,
    A Stranger to Life's better Joys;
In Mirth's social Bowers
We pass the gay hours
    And boast ourselves merry and wise.
        Chorus—Then join hand in hand,
        And our bosoms expand
            Obedient to friendships decree,

Whilst freely we pass
The heart-cheering glass
    To Homony, Humour and Glee.

In festive delight
Thus let our Club night
    Still cheerful and social be found,
With loyalty sing
To our Country and King
    And pass the gay Chorus around.
        Chorus—Then join &c.[13]

The Tuesday Club of Annapolis clearly served as an impressive and significant forum for amateur music-making in colonial Maryland, predating and perhaps even rivaling the St. Cecilia Society of much wealthier Charleston, South Carolina. The immigrant Scottish physician Dr. Alexander Hamilton (1712–1756) formed and largely maintained this group, modeling it after clubs he had observed in Edinburgh and later when touring America's Eastern Seaboard. Hamilton hosted many of the Tuesday Club's 252 meetings in Annapolis, held roughly every other Tuesday from 1745 to 1756. Twelve regular members, several honorary members, and numerous invited guests included educated professionals, physicians, ministers, merchants, mariners, and even portrait painters. With its emphasis on wit and creativity, Maryland's Tuesday Club was less exclusive and class conscious than its European counterparts. In 1754, Dr. Hamilton commenced his lengthy "History of the Ancient and Honorable Tuesday Club of Annapolis"; these hundreds of manuscript pages remained unpublished until 1990, although the musical compositions had been studied and published and some recorded before then. The club at one meeting hosted Benjamin Franklin, perhaps its most distinguished guest, and granted him the pseudonym Electrico Vitrifico.[14]

In addition to speeches, mock lectures, punning, eating, smoking, drinking, dancing, and a great deal of general fooling around, Tuesday Club activities included singing songs, playing instrumental music, and marching in musical processions through town. Dr. Hamilton's extensive writings, both factual and satirical, preserve colorful descriptions of music-making. At

Grand Rehearsal of the anniversary ode.

"Grand Rehearsal of the Anniversary Ode," an illustration within the handwritten "History of the Ancient and Honorable Tuesday Club of Annapolis," depicts club members making music in mid-eighteenth-century Annapolis. The Tuesday Club included genteel immigrants who brought with them a strong heritage of British and Continental music and social life. Music became vitally important to the club over time. Members owned and played enough instruments to form a small orchestra; in addition to the violins and flute here depicted, club members also played the French horn, 'cello, and harpsichord. Garrett Library Manuscripts Collection, Sheridan Libraries, Johns Hopkins University.

meetings members performed popular songs from the theater, folk songs and dance tunes, catches (specialized rounds), and instrumental works by Handel, Corelli, and Vivaldi. Hamilton and other members from Edinburgh frequently performed Scottish songs. The club's records also preserve a rich body of new compositions, such as the Reverend Bacon's instrumental Overture to the *Anniversary Ode of the Tuesday Club for the year 1750.* Such works employed alternating vocal and instrumental sections, scored mostly in three parts. Though not exceptional by European standards, any American polyphonic composition at this time was extraordinary, and these works survive as a tribute to the high level of culture in Annapolis around 1750. The club performed some of Reverend Bacon's compositions in public concerts, perhaps America's earliest featuring compositions by a colonist. The prolific and creative Tuesday Club is perhaps Maryland's most impressive single contribution to America's colonial music.

Some Tuesday Club members also belonged to another musically active organization, the Free and Accepted Masons. Throughout the colonies Masons met, sang, and danced at their private and somewhat secretive meetings, and they encouraged public concerts, balls, and theatrical performances (as they had in Europe). Masons also paraded in public and had some of their songs published.

Playing by Heart

Eighteenth-century Maryland colonists, like their predecessors, continued to sing songs and play dance tunes by heart, leaving occasional written traces of such activities. Written lyrics and tunes date from as far back as 1729.[15] Thereafter words to ballads appeared in unexpected places, such as in the blank spaces of a merchant's account book or on the back of a map. (Wealthier amateurs used a special music book or even ruled music paper.) There is no telling how many unrecorded ballads, popular songs, and dance tunes were played from memory by servants, slaves, middling planters, tradesmen, housewives, and even gentlemen amateurs themselves.

At the time, both in England and in the colonies, the words to some ballads and common songs circulated on penny sheets called broadsides. (Besides songs, broadsides featured poems, advertisements, playbills, sermons, and official announcements.) In order to keep the prices down and because everyone knew the tunes anyway, song-related broadsides lacked musical notation. Benjamin Franklin as a young man printed several such broadside ballads, including one of his own composition about the capture and killing of the pirate Blackbeard (Edward Teach) in 1712. Most of the cheap imprints that appeared in Maryland had been imported from Philadelphia, New York, and Britain and then were sold to the public at county fairs or other events that brought people to town.

Music enjoyed a close relationship with the tavern, one of the chief meeting places in early America. Maryland needed taverns from the earliest times, for both social and practical reasons. Regulations governed the prices for accommodations, for keeping horses, and for food and drink. Most Maryland taverns were licensed to respectable men, the sort who served on parish vestries and as county justices of the peace. The records of the venerable Tuesday Club include a detailed poetic description of a gathering at Middleton's Tavern in Annapolis in 1752, when members drank, danced, and made music until dawn. After the first 463 lines, the lengthy poem penned by Tuesday Club member Jonas Green continues:

> To dance and to frisk it Six Champions arose
> and heads, Shoulders, arses, arms, Elbows and Toes
> By Sympathy mov'd in each Caper and leap,
> Whilst Orrock and Belt on two fiddles did Scrape
> Scotch reels and brisk Jiggs, they danc'd out of hand
> Whilst Dorsey and Jennings led up the Brisk band,
> And Middleton frisk'd on one leg Such a rate
> You'd Swear that it stood in no need of its mate.

By the end of the evening the tavern keeper was left amid the rubble:

> Now when all these heroes and dancers were gone,
> Poor Middleton, he lay in the field all alone,
> For the Drowsy god Morpheus had made him his prey
> and knock'd him asleep, Just at break of day,
> Eyes shut, and mouth open, he loudly did Snore,

> his arse on one Chair, and his legs on two more,
> and round him were Strow'd many bottles & Glasses,
> and piles of old fiddles and old fiddle cases,
> Some books lay in heaps, & Some Scatter'd abroad,
> The Great table Seem'd to groan under its load
> Of Corelli, Vivaldi, Alberti and others
> of the Tweedle-dum Twadle-dum, fiddle-dum brothers
> The drum and the Colors lay Sad and forlorn,
> and high on a peg hung the now Silent horn,
> Here the Empty punch bowl So capricious & wide
> and a mighty Bass fiddle lay close by its Side.[16]

Typical tavern gatherings probably did not, however, feature works by Corelli followed by "Scotch reels and brisk Jiggs."

While many early colonial taverns were in fact rooms in private homes rented out to guests, later in the period more specialized taverns appeared, especially in towns and cities where the population swelled during meetings of county courts or the General Assembly. Eventually urban taverns included ballrooms and musicians' galleries. Tavern keepers sponsored horse races, moving their wares out of doors and selling food and drink to onlookers. By the 1760s some ordinaries, as they were officially known, lured customers with gaming tables, especially backgammon and billiards. But music remained a powerful attraction. The Annapolis tavern keeper George Downey owned musical instruments that he most likely used to accompany his dance classes. Peter Kalkoffer advertised lessons on the German flute and clarinet "at Mr. Mills' tavern."[17] James McMordie reportedly sang for his Annapolis customers at the "Sign of the Blue Ball." A tavern keeper in Joppa played a crywth, a Welsh harp. The Maryland Coffee House in Annapolis, modeled after similar upper-class establishments in London, opened in 1767. It hosted meetings of the Homony Club in the early 1770s.[18]

Maryland's musical legacy of the colonial era formed a composite: folk ballads and dance tunes of England, Scotland, and Ireland, new sets of topical lyrics that evolved in the colonies and occasionally surfaced in written form, and of course the magical spice that later flavored the entire dish, African music. Most slaves came from West Africa, where musical culture varied

HEARING.

Hearing, hand-colored engraved print by John Nixon published by William Wells in London in 1784. The hammered dulcimer, seen here with a violin accompanying a puppet dance, is a folk instrument that dates from medieval times. It became newly popular in the late seventeenth century when a German musician, Panteleon Hebenstreit, played it on a tour of Europe. It had arrived in colonial Maryland by 1752, when Thomas Richison played his at a meeting of the Tuesday Club. Paul M. Gifford, The Hammered Dulcimer: A History (Lanham, MD: Scarecrow, 2001), 165–68, 241. The Colonial Williamsburg Foundation, Acc. No. 1964-472,1, Museum Purchase.

from tribe to tribe yet shared certain major features. Music and dance played critical roles in every tribe's social rituals. Rhythmically driving and complex, African music involved improvisation and a musical scale unlike that of western Europe in the seventeenth and eighteenth centuries. Certain African scale notes, notably the 3rd and 7th degrees, defied reproduction on instruments of discrete intonation, such as keyboard and fretted string instruments. Voices, fretless banjos, primitive flutes, and violins all shared the ability to shade intervals and reproduce African melodies that did not easily fit the standard do-re-mi scale. The combination of primordial rhythms, unfamiliar language, and an alien scale seemed strange, barbaric, and even frightening to non-Africans.

The musical culture of the slaves was introduced, passed on, and preserved entirely through oral tradition. They made their own instruments, which they based on those that had evolved in Africa. In 1774 Nicholas Cresswell, visiting Nanjemoy, Maryland, described a slave banjo there as having four strings stretched across a hollowed-out gourd and being strummed much like a guitar. Cresswell described the music as "rude and uncultivated." "Their Dancing," he went on, "is most violent exercise, but so Irregular and

grotesque. I am not able to describe it. They all appear to be exceedingly happy at these merry-makings and seem as if they had forgot or were not sensible of their miserable condition."[19]

African American slaves made drums and crude trumpets, but slave owners often confiscated them for fear that they would be used to signal insurrection. Many of the runaway-slave notices published in newspapers mention instruments—stolen fiddles most frequently, though banjos, fifes, and the ability to sing or dance are at times mentioned. The Maryland Gazette of 15 June 1748 announced: "Ran away from Cornelius Harkins of Kent County . . . a Negro fellow called Toby; . . . he took with him a canoe, a new fiddle, a Bonja [banjo], on both which he sometimes plays." A similar Maryland Gazette advertisement, of July 6, 1772, described a runaway from Soldiers Delight, in Baltimore County, noting that a "dark mulatto slave" had taken refuge in Baltimore, where he had learned "to read and write and to play on the violin."

African music was in a sense preadapted to the slaves' life of forced labor and limited leisure time on New World plantations. African call-and-response-style singing provided both rhythm and welcome distraction that lightened work, as the caller improvised creative, at

The Old Plantation, attributed to John Rose, Beaufort County, South Carolina, probably 1785–90. A paucity of written records hampers our understanding of the role of music in the lives of enslaved people in early America. In this watercolor a slave man and woman jump over a stick or broom handle to mark their marriage (and begin the celebration). The painting may be the only surviving illustration of slave music from eighteenth-century America. Abby Aldrich Rockefeller Folk Art Museum, The Colonial Williamsburg Foundation. Gift of Abby Aldrich Rockefeller.

times humorous verses. Cresswell described such songs as droll and satirical, embodying cryptic complaints of hard work and bad overseers.[20] Yet plantation masters encouraged such an innocuous outlet, and they dared not curtail the dancing and singing that took place after sundown, on Sundays, and on holidays. Then fast-paced leisure songs and dances allowed for some release of tension and aggression. Although African American dancing seemed violent and grotesque to Cresswell, it was clear that the slaves enjoyed it and needed it.

White colonists encouraged some slaves to learn to play Anglo-Irish-Scottish dance tunes on the violin, which they apparently did with much enthusiasm at plantation house balls. As early as 1690 in Accomac, Virginia, the Reverend Thomas Teackle was shocked to learn that his daughter had hired an African American boy to play dance music in his absence, especially since guests had danced all night in his rectory. Slave fiddlers were hired out to other plantations. A 1671 law encouraged slaves to be baptized and attend church, a challenge that some missionaries urged with great zest. Thereafter white missionaries taught some slaves psalms and hymns, along with the skills of reading and writing. The white man's music—dance tunes, church music, and even more formal European music—soon formed part of the traditions of the African slaves.

Playing Music for a Living

Although amateurs dominated the musical scene in colonial Maryland, a small group of professional musicians had a significant impact. These men clearly struggled to earn a living, needing to travel and offer a wide variety of services. Professionals taught lessons, played at dances and theatrical presentations, and sold music and instruments. Their way was not easy. At times, gentlemen amateurs competed with them, giving public concerts and playing in theater orchestras at no charge. Professional musicians in the Chesapeake in any event depended on patrons who lived scattered throughout the countryside. The cities of Philadelphia and New York offered considerably better prospects, including audiences large enough to support public concerts.

By the mid-eighteenth century, Annapolis attracted more commerce through its ideal harbor, and stores, taverns, and townhouses accommodated visitors during the late autumn and winter legislative season. At this time, an annual low point in the tobacco cycle, the landed gentry left their outlying plantations and went to Annapolis to foster their interests and socialize. While larger cities to the north had constant year-round populations, Annapolis's population swelled during the legislative season, when there was a flurry of horse races, theater performances, dinners, card parties, and public and private balls. A visitor recorded in 1774 that "at set Times, nothing but Jollity and Feasting goes forward: Musick and Dancing are the everlasting Delights of the Lads and Lasses."[21] The demand for professional musical services in Maryland's political, social, and cultural capital fluctuated with the rise and fall of the city's population. Some itinerant professionals arrived on the coattails of visiting theater troupes, who also timed their visits to coincide with the legislative season.

Daniel Thompson and George Downey appear as both musicians and innkeepers in their Annapolis estate inventories of 1724 and 1750, respectively. Both owned musical instruments. Downey advertised to play his fiddle for hire, and he also held public dance classes. Johannes Schley and Frederick Victor drew salaries as organists in Frederick and Annapolis, respectively. John Ormsby and John Lammond were others active in mid-eighteenth-century Maryland. John Schneider, who appeared at concerts in Fredericksburg, Virginia, and Philadelphia, left a fiddle, a French horn, and a trumpet in his room in Annapolis at his death there in 1771. Thomas Wall taught guitar and mandolin and performed for hire, while his colleague George James L'Argeau offered daily performances on the "musical glasses" in 1774. Both Wall and L'Argeau figured prominently in Maryland theater orchestras, especially after the Revolution.[22]

Itinerant professional musicians did not lead an easy life. There was ever a shortage of currency, and Marylanders often settled their accounts with promissory tobacco notes—which were not very useful to a musician on his way to New York, for instance. A musician's income fluctuated both seasonally and according to the competition, as even during the social season only one or two fiddles might be needed for a ball, while three or more fiddlers might be in the area looking for work. After 1768, theater orchestras provided more regular work, but touring troupes kept trim budgets, at times using volunteer gentlemen amateurs and perhaps employing only a handful of musicians at the busiest of times. In the late spring and summer, when tobacco crops required close attention, there was less demand for musicians. And the life of a musician must have been lonely, given the many hours spent on horseback going between towns or off to distant performances. Even if a professional musician had skipped meals and traveled through cold rain, nearly drowning at a ferry crossing, he had to play his best and be polite—a good reputation was essential, as few would associate with a man of questionable behavior. Musicians had few opportunities to play "serious" music for concert audiences, instead playing at any opportunity and taking on any available student. It was a trade, and not necessarily one commanding respect and dignified treatment.

Out-of-town professionals tended to keep moving. The Alexandria-based musician Charles Leonard traveled to Upper Marlboro in 1769 to mount a charity concert "by a number of the best hands."[23] John Beals, who taught and performed on violin, oboe, German flute, common flute (recorder), and hammered dulcimer in New York and Pennsylvania, last advertised in

Maryland in 1764, when he took on stocking manufacturing, apparently having retired from music.[24]

To make ends meet, most professionals taught music, despite limited opportunities. Music did not appear as part of the curricula of Maryland's county free schools or the curriculum of King William's School, later St. John's College. Students, or more likely their well-to-do parents, watched the *Maryland Gazette* for notices advertising willing teachers. Such advertisements appeared most regularly between 1760 and 1773 and normally mentioned other musical services, such as performing, instrument selling and repair, and even classes in fencing and foreign languages.

A Passion for Theater

Marylanders from virtually every level of society attended the theater—although ticket price and social convention dictated whether they sat in boxes, pit, or gallery. Annapolis served as colonial Maryland's theatrical center, and troupes mounted occasional performances in Upper Marlboro, Baltimore, Chestertown, and purportedly in Piscataway and Port Tobacco. Dancing became an increasingly important component of formal theater. Actors danced minuets and hornpipes presentationally, either as part of the drama, as interpolated by choice, or as miscellaneous inter-act entertainment. Theater audiences frequently danced upon conclusion of the show, once the chairs had been taken up. Theater and dance were the main public social diversions in tidewater Maryland.

Despite various attempts at presenting plays in 1716 and before, not until the 1750s did organized English theatrical groups began to develop an American circuit, which notably included Charleston, Williamsburg, Annapolis, Philadelphia, and New York. These troupes encountered strong moral opposition from the Quakers in Philadelphia and the Puritans in Boston, although creative troupe managers at times circumvented their official decrees. Less beholden to church leaders, southerners welcomed theater with open arms, and players developed a special fondness for appearing in the tobacco colonies. Annapolitans showed great support not only by attending plays but also by purchasing copies of plays, ballad-opera scores, libretti, theater histories, and collections of theater music. Eager anticipation preceded the arrival of stars and the opening of new theaters; even mere puppet shows and lesser acts drew crowds. Freemasons sponsored specific productions, parading to the Annapolis theater "in their proper cloathing."[25] The Homony Club, a gentleman's group that flourished in Annapolis in the early 1770s, arrived at the new brick theater en masse and to solid applause on one particular occasion, the club president offering a spontaneous speech in praise of drama. Yet while theater provided a sophisticated and highly social public entertainment, it could only be enjoyed in Maryland when itinerant companies came to town, which before 1769 meant waiting years between appearances.

Three different itinerant companies presented nearly a hundred documented evenings of theater in Maryland in the twenty or so years after 1750.[26] These visiting troupes were made up of roughly half a dozen to fifteen versatile actor-singers who traveled from town to town, playing a changing repertory night after night until dwindling box-office receipts suggested it was time to move on. These lengthy performances usually began at 6:00 or 7:00 p.m. Some planters secured the best box seats for themselves by dispatching their servants or slaves an hour or two in advance of performances. Their delegates then stayed on to watch from the gallery. This mixed audience saw a main piece of serious drama or lengthy comedy followed by a lighter, shorter afterpiece, often referred to as the "farce." Opening with the obligatory prologue and closing with an epilogue, an evening at the theater also included interspersed topical songs, presentational dances, and variety acts.

Maryland Gazette advertisements offered evidence of a full theater calendar in Annapolis. An advertisement appearing on March 16, 1769, began with a notice of permission or authority to perform and concluded with a full list of cast members and notice of special, inter-act entertainments:

> By Authority, At the New Theatre in Annapolis,
>   by the new
> American Company of Comedians,
> On Friday the 17th instant,

Illustration from George Bickham Jr., *Musical Entertainer* (London, 1737–39). This image, printed above the song "Moore's Engagement to Margery," shows the dramatic posturing of the early eighteenth-century stage. This static approach had fallen out of favor by the late 1740s thanks to the realistic innovations of the English actor, playwright, and manager David Garrick. Collection of David Hildebrand.

... End of the Play, a Dance, by Mr. Godwin, and
     Mr. Malone.
With Singing, by Mrs. Parker....
With a Minuet, by Mrs. Parker, and Mr. Spencer....

Playbills provided even greater detail than did newspaper advertisements.

Colonial theater repertory closely followed that in vogue at Covent Garden and Drury Lane in London. Managers made much ado when a play came to America fresh after its London debut, even though the New World renditions were typically scaled down. The works of Shakespeare, especially *Richard III* (1593) and *Romeo and Juliet* (1594), often served as main pieces, as did full-length comedies and ballad operas like George Farquhar's *The Constant Couple* (1700) and John Gay's *Beggar's Opera* (1728). Afterpieces included such farces as David Garrick's *The Lying Valet* (1742) and *Lethe, or Aesop in the Shades* (1748), the two most frequently performed works in colonial Annapolis, as well as works by Isaac Bickerstaffe, Henry Fielding, and other fashionable playwrights. The Annapolis spring season of 1760 featured twenty-nine different works.[27]

Excepting a few favorite tragedies, colonial Marylanders preferred light humor and familiar music. Producers shamelessly altered Shakespeare's scripts for itinerant productions. They allowed actors to improvise lines, while cutting slow-moving sections and inserting unrelated popular songs and dances. In response to a heated letter to the editor appearing in a 1769 *Maryland Gazette*, the manager assured the insulted patron

that his troupe used only alterations by David Garrick, Esq., and that such adaptations found acceptance in England.[28] Nonetheless, tragedies as main pieces fell out of demand over time as troupes adjusted repertory to suit the American taste for light ballad opera and farce.

It was the accessible, familiar music that made afterpieces and ballad operas especially popular. Unlike the composed operas in Italian that dominated London's elite theaters, less serious works such as John Gay's *Beggar's Opera* appealed to the average audience. Gay had set, to familiar folk melodies, new lyrics in English, and he even put sarcastic words to a march from George Frederick Handel's opera *Rinaldo* (1710), as if to pour salt on a musical wound. For ballad opera originated in reaction against Handel's complex, fluttery, foreign-language opera. Benjamin Franklin attended such a performance in London in 1765. He described it in a letter to his brother Peter as "*Stuttering*; or making many syllables of one" and "*Screaming*, without cause."[29] English ballad opera appealed, in format and ticket price, to middle- and lower-class patrons in England and to all classes in the colonies. It featured simple plots, spoken dialogue, lively dancing, slapstick comedy, and familiar songs that enjoyed popularity well beyond the stage. Ballad opera proved easily adaptable to performance under crude circumstances, and it caught on even better in the colonies than in England. Later in the eighteenth century, ballad opera would have competition from other genres, for example, pastiche, such as Thomas Arne's *Love in a Village* (1762), in which newly composed music was intermingled with old favorite melodies. Thus, in colonial America the success of popular theater depended upon recycled familiar tunes, or at least those that masqueraded as such, and it lasted well into the nineteenth century.

In 1769 the New American Company set a trend by planning a more extensive theatrical season to coincide with the fall legislative season, when social life flourished in Annapolis. At such times, wealthy visitors crowded the streets seeking diversion when they were not involved in legal matters. George Washington, who loved music, dance, and the stage, supported these arts and participated in some of them. In September 1771 he attended four plays in five evenings when in Annapolis, dining one day at the home of John Ridout, secretary to Governor Sharpe.[30] It would have been most appropriate for Mrs. Ridout to play a few pieces for Washington on the Ridout family harpsichord. The legislative season provided theater troupes with convenient access to the rich and powerful, whose patronage allowed for extended seasons during the early 1770s.

Colonial audiences held players to their own immediate standards and did not hesitate to express approval or disapproval. As back in London, happy audiences shouted for encores, in extraordinary circumstances showering money upon the stage for favorite stars. At other times, audience members talked loudly during the show, threw edible objects to express disapproval, freely hissed, or interrupted singers in mid-song to request preferred pieces. When provoked by a vocal or physical audience, colonial theater musicians could only claim that they had no control over production choices. Gallery patrons became the best projectile hurlers—perhaps this is why after 1760 the Annapolis theater no longer sold gallery seats. In all, and especially after the Revolution, as patriotism rose to a peak around 1814, American theater audiences freely offered feedback to shape the dramatic and musical repertory in the New World.

Itinerant theatrical troupes showed ingenuity in adapting structures for use as theaters. An English journalist described the theater at Upper Marlboro in 1760 as "a neat, convenient tobacco-house, well fitted up for the purpose."[31] Similarly, two of the three structures used as theaters in Annapolis before the Revolution were converted barns or warehouses; patrons complained of their inconvenient locations in town.[32] Managers advertised various improvements to these makeshift theaters, such as insulation during the winter, and they hoped patrons would pay more attention to expensive scenery and novel entr'actes than to the small, unattractive, makeshift spaces.

In 1771 David Douglas, the ingenious manager of the New American Company, constructed in Annapolis one of the earliest permanent theaters in colonial America. Financed through a subscription publicly supported by Governor Sharpe and other city notables, this handsome brick structure flourished at a convenient site on West Street, next door to Reynold's tavern, on land leased from St. Anne's Church. This new theater became the pride of the town, being "as elegant and commodious, for its size, as any theater in America," and the seasons of 1771–73 reigned as the golden years of colonial theater in Maryland.[33] That at the very same time St. Anne's Church, across the street, crumbled in disrepair eloquently spoke to the city's priorities.

Maryland audiences clearly appreciated the acting and singing skills of stars like Nancy Hallam, who received poetic praise in the *Maryland Gazette*. The Homony Club composer Jonathan Boucher, rector at St. Anne's, appears to have composed one such poem published in her honor on September 6, 1770. The author wonders in the eighth stanza:

> Do Solemn Measures slowly move?
> Her looks inform the Strings;
> Do Lydian Airs invite to Love?
> We feel it as she sings.

Such enthusiasm for Hallam about this time motivated several ardent Annapolis gentlemen to take up a collection and commission Charles Willson Peale to paint her portrait. Two other poems to Hallam soon followed, as did "An Ode Inscrib'd to Miss Storer," to a rival star, Maria Stoner, in 1773.[34]

Despite the great impact of itinerant theater on Maryland's colonial culture, uncertainty shadows the musical instruments used, who played them, and from what sources they played. Theater orchestras sometimes used local amateur players, while at other times they used paid company musicians or a mixture of the two. The harpsichord, despite its traditional role in European theater orchestras, did not regularly accompany itinerant productions in Maryland; the logistics of transporting large and delicate instruments on the primitive roads and the dangerous ferries of the early Chesapeake proved formidable. Occasionally a local harpsichord was offered up for use by a wealthy amateur, but more commonly troupes employed a violin or two and some smaller accompanying instrument, perhaps a guitar or mandolin. To have additional fiddles, a flute, an oboe, and a 'cello was less common in Annapolis than in Philadelphia, New York, or Charleston. Although resident theater orchestras shortly after the Revolution included perhaps a dozen or so instruments, the number of available professional musicians had greatly increased by then. Far from standardized, then, colonial theater orchestras were small ensembles that varied greatly according to the instruments and instrumentalists available for the season.

Not only did colonial gentlemen amateurs contribute their talents and even instruments to theater orchestras, they also acted and sang. The public considered it honorable and genteel for local gentlemen to appear as Romeo or Hamlet or to play the flute or harpsichord in support of Thesbia. As long as a man's name did not appear in print and he did not accept money, he could play for the fun of it alongside actors and musicians of a lower class. Itinerant companies welcomed such free labor. When the Murray and Kean Company traveled from Annapolis to perform *The Beggar's Opera* at the new theater in Upper Marlboro in 1752, the *Maryland Gazette* announced, in the earliest notice of an orchestra being used in a colonial American theater, that instrumental music to each air would be provided by "a Set of private Gentlemen." The musicians drew upon the Free and Accepted Masons but also the Tuesday Club of Annapolis. Jonas Green apparently played the French horn solo, while Dr. Alexander Hamilton contributed 'cello, flute, and/or oboe parts. Other club am-

ateurs probably included the Reverend Thomas Bacon (viola da gamba, violin, or harpsichord) and the Reverend Alexander Malcolm (flute or violin). That these gentlemen played in public is no great surprise, for they owned scores to ballad operas and regularly sang songs from the stage at Tuesday Club meetings. Two such songs were "Whilst I Gaze on Chloe Trembling" and "Come Jolly Bacchus," both from the farce *Devil to Pay* (Coffey, 1732), a favorite of the Maryland stage. Hamilton and Green encouraged the Murray and Kean Company to hold a benefit theatrical performance to raise funds for the Talbot County Charity School.[35] Twenty years later, in 1772, local amateurs played in a Baltimore stage orchestra under the director of Mr. Hallam,[36] by no means an unusual occurrence. Local musicians, both professional and amateur, helped fill out theater orchestras for later visiting troupes.

Although the Tuesday Club had disbanded in 1756, the Annapolis area continued to host an impressive pool of musicians from which a decent theater orchestra could be culled. Gentleman amateur musicians continued to purchase and practice on their violins, flutes, oboes, harpsichords, and other instruments. Opera scores and collections of theater songs were readily available for purchase by 1760, when Annapolis hosted its second visiting troupe and city amateurs enjoyed playing the hits of this season in their private drawing rooms. Theater tickets could be purchased at city taverns such as that of the clockmaker William Faris, who, himself musical, knew which other local musicians might be interested in playing. Especially during theater seasons from 1769 through 1773, when Annapolis swelled with visitors, assembling a local theater orchestra may have been almost easy. Many county seats and the town of Baltimore shared this lively artistic climate. Visiting troupes could depend on local, mostly amateur musicians to make up their orchestras as they moved from city to city.

Even so, professional musicians typically had better training than amateurs and, though fewer in number, offered versatility and dependability—assets worth paying for as seasons wore on and amateurs lost interest. Both Thomas Llewellyn Wall and George James

L'Argeau visited Annapolis as part of the New American Company for its 1769 season. Wall acted comic roles and accompanied solo songs on his guitar and mandolin, and he later taught music privately after the company disbanded. Later, Wall's career took him to New York, Philadelphia, and Charleston; he returned to Maryland only for brief stays before the Revolution and later for a longer stint in Baltimore. L'Argeau had also acted minor roles and performed in the New American Company orchestra, playing the violin and harpsichord. Like Wall, he also freelanced offstage, showing off his ability on the musical glasses, in particular. He offered lessons on several instruments but seems to have focused on teaching dancing. L'Argeau apparently settled in Maryland in 1769. As a professional musician he figured in the city's general musical life beyond the stage, perhaps even playing for other troupes that came to Annapolis from 1770 to 1773. L'Argeau stayed in Maryland for a time after the theater ban of 1773; his last pre-Revolutionary advertisement dates from November 1774. He resumed musical activities in Annapolis and Baltimore during the early 1780s. The actress-singer-dancer Henrietta Osborne also arrived in 1769. She made her Drury Lane debut in 1759, but she decided to retire in Annapolis and open a store near the Market House sometime before 1770. Playbills from 1772 list her as a performer; Annapolitans were proud to see their own talented citizen on stage.[37]

Theater musicians played variously from published scores, from hand-copied manuscripts, and from memory. London publishers issued full orchestral scores, as well as simplified versions of melody and bass lines from which needed parts could be extracted. Popular operas and farces also appeared in settings for solo violin, German and common flutes, harpsichord, or guitar. No actual music used in a colonial American theater survives, which is understandable as theaters were very prone to fires. Players found accompanying theater songs by memory to be easy, since many of these stage melodies were used and reused from play to play. For example, the "Over the Hills and Far Away" melody appears in *The Recruiting Officer* (Farquhar, 1706), *The Beggar's Opera, The Devil to Pay,* and *The Fashionable*

Lady or, Harlequin's Opera (Ralph, 1730)—all but the last of these presented in colonial Annapolis. In fact, people from all levels of society knew by heart many tunes like this one. The pit musician's job involved merely playing a brief introduction, then doubling the melody or improvising a harmony, basic skills for any trained eighteenth-century musician. Overtures and some song accompaniments, however, required multi-part scores.

While colonists enthusiastically welcomed itinerant troupes to Maryland, the brief and sporadic seasons must have been frustrating to aficionados. An impressive amount of theater music circulated for private consumption, including music to popular comic operas and song collections such as the *Friskey Songster; or, The budget of mirth laid open: containing the most favorite Songs, now singing at all the places of public amusement* and, most impressively, *The Humming Bird or, A compleat collection of the most esteemed Songs, containing above 14 hundred of the most celebrated English, Scotch, and Irish songs, in which are included all the favourite new Songs Sung at the Theatre Royale, Vauxhall, Ranleigh, and polite concerts, in the last season.* Both of these English publications were available in Annapolis in 1783.[38]

Theater music so dominated popular music in England that few collections or instrumental tutors went to print without some. The Annapolis firm Wallace, Davidson and Johnson imported many theater-related materials between 1771 and 1774, including works performed in the city such as *Conscious Lovers* (Steele, 1723), *Suspicious Husband* (Hoadly, 1747), *Love in A Village, Beggar's Opera, The Padlock* (Bickerstaffe, 1768), and *Maid of ye Mill.* Similar titles showed up in private libraries like those of Charles Carroll of Carrollton and Edward Lloyd IV. Both men had issues of *Gentleman's Magazine* and *London Magazine,* which routinely included theater music, as well as dozens of volumes of comedies, tragedies, and other books relating to the stage. Carroll's and Lloyd's libraries, like those of Washington and Jefferson, would have been unfashionably spare without plays and theater music.

The *Maryland Gazette* itself helped to stimulate

theatrical life in colonial Maryland, for it contained news and gossip about the stage—from Europe and her colonies—and otherwise kindled popular interest. Well before Jonas Green and his family took over this newspaper in 1745, the *Gazette* editor Edmund Hall in 1730 published what seems to have been the earliest American report of the stage, including the prologue and epilogue from a gala night in London. After Green began publishing, references to theater became common fare, not just in poetry and extended letters to the editor but through reviews and reprinted lyrics to stage songs as well. Importers took out *Maryland Gazette* advertisements and offered a host of dramatic works for sale, many of which had been performed in Annapolis before 1774. Jonas Green also sold related music, tickets, and playbooks at his printing office—in all, he published more theater news than any other colonial editor of the time. Anna Catherine Green carried on the tradition after Jonas's death by publishing in 1772 *The songs in Lionel and Clarissa or the School for Fathers, a Comic Opera shortly to be performed at the Theatre in Annapolis, by the American Company. (Price, one shilling).*[39] The *Maryland Gazette* faithfully reported on the early Maryland stage, its music, and the colonists' love of it.

Dance and Dance Music

Marylanders from the richest to the poorest shared a love of the theater, but it was with even greater passion that they danced. Of all social activities, public and private, dancing played the most important role in early Maryland, mostly because opportunities to dance vastly outnumbered occasions to attend the theater. Dancing varied widely, from formal assemblies to spontaneous tavern dancing to the everlasting jig of the slave quarters. Some popular melodies served stage and dance floor alike, such as the country dance tune "Rural Felicity" and its vocal setting as "Come Haste to the Wedding," which derived from Sheridan's farce *The Elopement* (1767).[40] Dancing offered one a chance to claim male prowess or display feminine charm. The violin, or fiddle, as it was commonly called when used for this purpose, played a central role in colonial dancing. This preference crossed social lines, although contemporary

accounts also mention the banjo in rustic situations and the harpsichord in refined ones.

Elite dance assemblies clearly served a variety of social purposes: they offered a chance to exchange gossip, admire one another's clothing, discuss business, and, it was hoped, to have some good plain fun. For the gentry, dancing, along with their fine clothing, fine furniture, and better education, reinforced their social status among their peers. Further, for eligible young men and women a well-danced minuet showed off the balance, control, and seeming effortlessness that aided in the courtship process. Accounts of elite gatherings emphasize exclusivity and the expected attendance of all the leading gentlemen and ladies in town. Dr. Alexander Hamilton's satirical description of an Annapolis ball sponsored by the Tuesday Club in late 1745 indicates that those who "chose to dance, danced, and those that chose not, looked on; and drank a bumper now and then to expand the animal spirits, . . . There were danced many minuets, country dances & jiggs, and there was much bowing, cringing, complimenting, curtsying, oggling, flurting, and smart repartees, as is usual on such occasions."[41]

The minuet, a complex couple's dance developed in the French court of Louis XIV, played a defining role for the colonial upper class. To dance a minuet well required instruction and much practice, and the sequence of subtle steps and postures left room for neither improvisation nor error. Social duty required keeping up with the latest new dances; demand for instruction kept dance teachers active.

Marylanders of all classes crammed into theaters, where actors danced between-acts jigs, in this setting often called hornpipes. A Mr. Godwin danced double hornpipes with a Mr. Malone, who, being a typically versatile showman, also performed rope vaulting, headstanding, pipe balancing, and various other acrobatics. The dancing of two men in public suited such a context, since they appeared doing presentational, theatrical dances rather than courtship dances like the minuet. Yet staged minuets caught the public eye, such as when Mrs. Parker and Mr. Spencer danced "a Minuet in Character" in the Annapolis theater in 1769.[42] Presentational dances later became especially popular in theater settings.

Few plantation homes or townhouses had rooms big enough to allow more than a few to dance at a time, so the elite made do by dancing in central hallways and dancing in turns rather than all at once. The midstair landings found in finer period homes, such as the Chase-Lloyd House in Annapolis, served as convenient musicians' perches. Children of elite families or even entire families paid lengthy visits to friends or relatives for weddings, baptisms, or just getting together. Dancing was a favorite activity at such times, often limited only by the availability of musicians or the stamina of the guests.

Maryland gentlemen's clubs faithfully featured dancing, and Tuesday Club records preserve some of its members' favorite dance tunes. Given the lack of women and the emphasis on drinking at Tuesday Club meetings, their accounts of dancing include only the presentational sort—hornpipes or jigs, and minuets solo. One evening in Annapolis in 1750, the club member Reverend Alexander Malcolm played the fiddle for another to dance, then danced together with him, and finally played and danced simultaneously. It must have been a curious sight to see the minister of the provincial capital's main church so relaxed. Maryland's Jockey Club and Free Masons sponsored dancing assemblies, both public and private. The tavern keeper William Faris, whose account books frequently list charges for club expenses, recorded that his visitors "drank Tea & after Tea they had the Fiddle & danced till ½ after 9 o'clock."[43]

Most organized dancing took the form of the ball or assembly. Maryland governors threw invitational balls both at the statehouse and at the armory nearby as early as 1710.[44] The *Maryland Gazette* mentioned ten such exclusive gatherings between 1729 and 1759. These generally occurred on special holidays, such as the birthday of Lord Baltimore or the king, to celebrate military victories, on feast days, or on election days. Weather permitting, organized dancing could be held outdoors. While convention excluded the middle and lower classes from attending assemblies, on special occasions

they received free alcoholic beverages outdoors and made their own merriment. By 1764 governors' balls and other special assemblies in Annapolis took place in a new, specially constructed building on Duke of Gloucester Street, which continued in use for dancing well into the nineteenth century. (Now it houses the mayor's office.) A public lottery financed construction of these assembly rooms, and the layout of the interior space reflected the intended use for dancing, card playing, and socializing. Some time before 1777 the proprietors added an elevated musicians' gallery, accessible by stairs. Dinners and various other entertainments took place in the Annapolis assembly rooms, or council chambers, as locals called this space when it served a more practical function while the new statehouse was being built. William Eddis described this building as follows in 1775: "During the Winter there are assemblies every fortnight; the room for dancing is large; the construction elegant; and the whole illuminated to great advantage. At each extremity are apartments for the card tables, where select companies enjoy the circulation of the party-colored gentry without having their attention diverted by the sound of fiddles and the evolutions of youthful performers."[45]

The gentry also held dances in Baltimore, Chestertown, and towns like Upper Marlboro, where subscribers maintained an assembly room for monthly events as early as 1760. In 1774 managers there sought to enlarge the hall, presumably because of demand. In all these locales, an appointed assembly manager regulated membership and enforced rules, commonly including one strictly requiring men to dance with the ladies at least part of the evening, rather than simply talking, drinking, and playing cards.

It is unclear exactly when public, that is, non-invitational balls were first held in Annapolis, but in 1767 James Brice paid £3 for his subscription to a series of dances.[46] Such a prohibitively high cost, about what a carpenter could earn in a month, suggests that the gentry dominated public as well as invitational balls. By 1772 tickets for public assemblies could be purchased at Mrs. Howard's Maryland Coffee House; within three years such assemblies occurred fortnightly. The demand

"A Minuet by the Rever^d Mr Bacon," from a handwritten collection whose title page reads, "Ex Libris Johannis Ormsby Annapolis January the 30th 1758." This minuet also survives among the papers of the Tuesday Club of Annapolis, of which Reverend Bacon was a member. Among the others Ormsby wrote out are two of local interest, "Miss Chase, her Minuet" and "Col. Tasker's Minuet." Reverend Bacon actively worked to achieve social justice for the poor, including African Americans, although his fundraising for a school in Easton, Maryland, was insufficient for the school he planned there. Among other activities in this cause was a benefit concert Bacon and others presented in Williamsburg. Carole Lynne Price, "Bacon, Thomas (1700?–1768)," Oxford Dictionary of National Biography, accessed October 2007, http://dx.doi.org/10.1093/ref:odnb/5916. Library and Museum of the Performing Arts, MUS RES Amer *MNZ, Lincoln Center, New York.

for musical accompaniment at regular dances stimulated the colony's musical life.

Dance teachers advertised in Maryland newspapers as early as 1724. More than a dozen known by name, mostly men, are known to have plied their trade in Maryland during the colonial period. Few of these teachers worked outside Maryland, where, at least to the north, denser population centers seemed to support more stable careers. Those who succeeded in teaching dance in the colonial South also depended upon their musical skills. They accompanied their own lessons and fiddled for assemblies, played out for hire, offered music lessons on the side, and even taught fencing as the opportunity arose. The versatile dance teacher George Downey, in a fashion similar to that of fellow Annapolitan Daniel Thompson, advertised "2 penny hops" in 1746 and 1747 at which young ladies and gentlemen would learn dancing and deportment. Apparently Downey provided his own music on the fiddle, as two fiddles show up in his estate inventory and he advertised to play out at "Gentlemen's Balls."[47]

John Ormsby lived in St. Anne's parish and taught dance in Annapolis, Baltimore, and Upper Marlboro during 1757. His surviving dance-music manuscript offers a representative sample of pre-Revolutionary dance music of Maryland, at least as heard by the gentry. Ormsby's music book, dated 1758, includes fifty-five minuets that he used for both balls and dance lessons. Though copied in Annapolis, it is unclear whether he wrote out the tunes from memory or copied them directly from one or more written sources. Especially significant is his selection of music: it represents that in vogue at the time, including tunes by Handel, Corelli, and other Italian composers, as well as many yet to be traced. In deference to his patrons, he composed or simply renamed some of these tunes for prominent Annapolitans, and he included one by Maryland's Reverend Bacon.[48]

Colonial dance teachers convened their schools in various places, mostly in rooms rented in taverns. Such tavern keepers included Mrs. Meroney, Samuel Johnson, and John Brewer, the last of whom had a harpsichord in his tavern and may have played for dance practice or allowed others to play it for that purpose.

George Downey taught in his own tavern. George James L'Argeau taught for a time at the assembly rooms, and Anthony Smith used the clubhouse of the South River Club. We know little about dance classes outside what *Maryland Gazette* advertisements tell us; no class lists nor descriptions of actual lessons survive. Men dominated the field, although in 1753 an escaped-convict servant woman posed as a dance mistress. Irregular income and competition perhaps explain the brevity of most known instructors' careers.[49]

Like music of the theater, dances and dancing instructions survive in a wide variety of period sources. Printed dance collections appear by title for sale in the *Maryland Gazette*, as well as in merchants' books and in private libraries. Aficionados could purchase minuet books in Annapolis as early as 1730, and a typical advertisement by William Rind in 1762 included a collection titled *Twenty-four new Country Dances*, possibly referring to *Twenty four country dances for the year 1762* (London: Thompson & Sons, 1762). Dance tunes appear also in tutors for guitars, harpsichords, flutes, and other instruments, as well as in song collections and magazines. Hand copies of such tunes often notated the melody in the treble clef only, although occasional manuscripts and published sources include a bass line as well. Dance tunes could be heard throughout colonial Maryland—in a drawing room on the harpsichord and the German flute, on the tavern green on a solo fiddle, in the formal assembly room, and in plantation quarters as sounded by ebullient slaves.

The colonial dance teacher typically represented the artisan class in terms of wealth and background, yet he had to dress up and defer to his upper-class patrons. When visiting the homes of the wealthy and politically powerful, dance teachers behaved as servants, not equals. The very language of newspaper advertisements shows the requisite deference. Deferring to the children of the wealthy held particular challenges, since some children, then as now, took advantage of being away from their supervising parents. Adalbert B. Ebert closed his Annapolis school in frustration, admitting publicly that "some complaints have been made, in relation to order observed in his dancing-school" because of "an

extraordinary Indulgence generally granted them by their Parents, aided by their own natural Forwardness, . . . as any child, under such unlimited restrictions, is capable of spoiling a whole school . . . how hard it is to please both Parent and Child."[50] Ebert no doubt left town quickly, having publicly insulted his patrons. Even worse than losing one's personal reputation, dance teachers as a group incurred the distrust of the masses as the Revolution approached, for they represented English aristocracy and its powers and privileges. Along with theater troupes, many dance teachers left America for England or the Caribbean islands in 1773 and 1774.

Liturgical Music

Music eventually became an integral part of worship in most denominations, but in colonial Maryland few churches could afford organs, organists, and/or choir leaders. Even if churches could afford them, they were in short supply. Some denominations discouraged music because of the Protestant urge to purify the religion of Rome. While Presbyterians and Congregationalists sang, they preferred the *a capella* style, that is, voices without instrumental accompaniment. Quaker doctrine simply forbade music in the meeting house.

Shortly after settlers landed at St. Mary's, a Jesuit priest reportedly sang the "Litany of Loreto to the Virgin Mary" at the baptism and marriage of Chief Tayac of the Piscataways.[51] But in this originally Catholic province, religious intolerance soon had a muting effect on music. Cecil Calvert's instructions to the first settlers asked that they practice their faiths quietly, avoiding ostentation, which might irritate the peace he hoped would prevail. Passage of the Act Concerning Religion in 1649 codified this reticent manner just as a flood of Puritans accepted an invitation to settle in Anne Arundel County and threatened to overwhelm the Catholic minority. Music apparently played little role in the Anglican service before 1696. After 1704, when Protestants legally established the Anglican Church as the official church of the colony and made the open practice of Catholicism illegal, priests had no choice but to say Mass in stark simplicity—much in the manner of Protestants. Wealthy families like

Plate XI from Kellom Tomlinson, The Art of Dancing (1735)

A minuet always marked the opening of a formal ball. The foremost man and woman present "opened" the assembly by dancing first as the only couple. Next, other couples took the floor in order of descending social status, each pair using the limelight to impress those gathered with their poise, controlled movement, and fine clothing.

The order of dance types within a formal assembly became a matter of convention. After minuets came the country dances, which had evolved somewhat since those of seventeenth-century Maryland. The number of tunes appropriate for eighteenth-century country dancing had grown considerably, with melodies such as "Fisher's Hornpipe," "Flowers of Edinburgh," and "Irish Washwoman" becoming favorites. Country dancing remained mostly an upper-class activity in Maryland nearly until the Revolution, although by 1750 the rising middle classes of New York and Philadelphia enjoyed simplified country dances at public dance halls. Unlike these larger urban centers, Maryland's rural landscape failed to produce a middle class with money to spare, leisure time, and social proximity, so country dancing remained an elite practice. Cotillions, like country dances, involved some difficulty and required practice; they came into fashion among the Maryland gentry only late in the colonial period. Reels, long associated with Scottish dancing and less formal gatherings of the middle and lower classes, occurred

only later during a "polite" assembly when the punch had been flowing freely. This standard progression of dances—first minuets, then country dances, perhaps cotillions, then reels—characterized elite dancing assemblies throughout the colonies. In a sense, as the evening wore on, the gentry progressed through the dances appropriate to each class, from highest to lowest, except that they dared not condescend to dancing the jigs of sailors and slaves.

The middle and lower classes danced spontaneously, being less dependent upon order, control, and restraint. Deprived of access to large indoor spaces and dependable, hired musicians, the ordinary people of Maryland danced outdoors or in cramped houses or taverns when a fiddler was handy—more or less spontaneously. They enjoyed reels, with steps most likely called on the spot as opposed to being danced from memory. Jigs, also called "hornpipes" at this time, involved free-form, improvised solo dancing—sailors had long done these to show off in a competitive manner. Such were the favorite steps of slaves and nonelite whites, and their gatherings sound like considerably more fun than those of the wealthy.

Accounts of plain folk's dances, which only the literate left for posterity, used terms like frolic and barbaric and made easy reference to the influence of drink. In 1760 two Anne Arundel County men got into a fistfight after "some bickerings about their skill in

dancing a jigg." One of them was killed (Maryland Gazette, August 21, 1760). The court showed mercy to the dancer who survived. Chesapeake masters encouraged their slaves to come up to the manor house to play the fiddle and accompany formal dancing, but whites who could draw upon the skills of African American musicians, whatever their station, eagerly did so. The journal of a visitor to Maryland, Nicholas Cresswell, describes less privileged whites having a barbecue in the mid-1770s and dancing "to some Negro tunes under a large Tree. A great number of young people met together with a Fiddle and Banjo played by two Negroes, with Plenty of Toddy" (The Journal of Nicholas Cresswell, 1774–1777, ed. Lincoln MacVeagh [New York: Dial, 1924], 30). Cresswell also witnessed a promiscuous "reaping frolic. This is a Harvest Feast. The people very merry, Dancing without either Shoes or Stockings and the Girls without stays" (26).

the Carrolls maintained priests in residence, but any music beyond a simple chant would have been unusual. In the 1750s, St. Thomas Manor, near Port Tobacco, purchased a Philadelphia organ and paid its organist twenty pounds a year to play it.[52]

In 1755 Maryland officials offered French Catholic Acadians from Nova Scotia a safe haven in Baltimore. Commercial development apparently took priority over the enforcement of old laws. The Acadians soon estab-

lished a chapel, which was served by the Carrolls' priest from Dourghoregan Manor. "French Town" grew substantially over the coming decades and exerted a strong musical influence over the city well into the Federal period. The Carrolls also assisted the Catholic cause in 1764 by virtually donating a Baltimore city lot to Reverend George Hunter, the Jesuit superior in Maryland. On this lot in 1770 the Jesuits began St. Peter's Church. Though small, plain, and incomplete even three years later, St. Peter's had a choir loft in the rear, with space for an organ. By 1791 the organ ordered by Bishop John Carroll had been installed, a choir formed, and music had begun to flourish at St. Peter's Church in Baltimore.[53]

Anglicans, meanwhile, allowed only the singing of the Psalms of David during services. They viewed chanting in Latin, as well as complex, flashy music, as "Popish," that is, too similar to Catholic music. Especially after English Puritans under Cromwell destroyed so many church organs, psalms were usually sung without accompaniment. Anglicans in the British colonies, like other Protestant settlers, brought with them a heritage of psalm-singing based on metrical settings using simple, memorized tunes. In other words, they were dependent on neither trained singers nor the reading of musical notation. Since colonists knew the melodies by heart, most psalmbooks (or psalters) included only the texts of the Psalms—quite different from traditional modern hymnals. So initially both southern Anglicans and Massachusetts Bay Puritans sang from the Sternhold and Hopkins translation, known widely as the "Old version of the Psalms."[54] In 1640 the Massachusetts Puritans published their own psalm translation, commonly called the "Bay Psalm Book." Printed on the press at Harvard, it was the first book printed in colonial British America. A copy was among the contents of a Maryland library inventoried in 1785.[55] American Anglicans kept with English practice and used the Sternhold and Hopkins translation until 1696, when Nahum Tate and Nicholas Brady published *A New Version of the Psalms of David, fitted to the Tunes used in Churches* (London). In various editions, the *New Version* was the source of most Anglican church music for the rest of the colonial period.

It appears that before the end of the seventeenth century Americans were corrupting or simply forgetting the psalm tunes their ancestors had known by heart. As early as 1700, supplements with printed musical notation to the *New Version* psalms were separately published and bound together with psalters. These appeared first in two-part harmonizations and later in three- and four-part settings. By 1713 the Tate

and Brady version enjoyed widespread use within the colonies, and American publishers reprinted it along with its music supplements. The Tate and Brady version became more widely accepted in America than in England. Merchants imported many hundreds of copies of the *New Version* and its music supplements, *Maryland Gazette* advertisements offered them new and used, and they appeared in bookstores, as well as in estate inventories and parish and private libraries. There are occasional references to other psalm collections in Maryland, but they are comparatively insignificant.[56]

The idealistic English-born missionary Reverend Thomas Bray helped establish *New Version* psalmody in early Maryland. Although Anglican services were held on Kent Island even before the *Ark* and the *Dove* landed at St. Mary's City in 1634, there is little evidence of sacred music predating Reverend Bray's appointment as commissary for Maryland in 1696. That year he sent printed materials, including some psalms, with music to St. James Parish, Herring Creek (in southern Anne Arundel County)—perhaps the first appearance of *New Version* settings in America. Bray formed the Society for Promoting Christian Knowledge in England in 1698 and two years later arrived in Annapolis to convene a conference of Maryland clergy. Perceiving a need for improving psalm-singing, Bray supplied the colony with copies of the *New Version* to sell and to give away to poor children and servants. He also set up ecclesiastical libraries, some quite large, in all thirty Maryland parishes. Bray saw psalm-singing as an important part of worship, yet despite establishment of a Society for the Propagation of the Gospel in Foreign Parts in 1701, his efforts in Maryland met with only limited success.

Among those attending Bray's Annapolis conference was Reverend Edward Topp, minister at St. Anne's Church from 1699 to 1704. Reverend Topp owned a flute and a flageolet, as well as a small music library. More than likely he was the man chosen to work with young people every Sunday at the church to read, discuss, and "sing the New Version of the Psalms according to the best Tunes."[57] Reverend Topp probably led psalm-singing at regular services too. Later Maryland ministers also had musical skills, several being active in amateur music-making among friends, in public, or in clubs, notably the Tuesday Club. From 1714 to 1725, Reverend Samuel Skippon officiated at St. Anne's. He owned "a flute, fiddle, fiddle strings," and "a parcel of Pamphlets and some small musical books."[58] During Skippon's tenure, most services were prayer services; communion was offered only four times a year. A quarter-century after Bray's visit, the bishop of London decreed that psalms either be sung or said during services, at the minister's discretion. When psalms were sung, the minister or clerk would pick a psalm and sing it out line by line to the largely illiterate congregation. The congregation in turn would sing each line back, the whole process being known as "lining out." The result was often a slower, embellished tune that gradually evolved into a version unique to that congregation. Parishioners in churches lacking musical leadership simply spoke the psalms back as they were read out, line by line.

Between 1745 and 1749, when the Reverend John Gordon served as rector at St. Anne's, the Psalms were most likely sung outright rather than lined out. The musical Reverend Gordon, along with other Tuesday Club members, had composed the "Song of the Baltimore Bards," after all. The second of seven verses hints at why Bray's noble efforts were perhaps wasted:

> This too would resemble some clerks of our day,
>   Who act as absurdly as think,
> In the morning on Sundays they preach & they pray,
>   In the evening they sing and they drink.[59]

Reverend Gordon may have had in mind his fellow club members the Reverends Malcom and Bacon. And Reverend Jonathan Boucher fit this description when he served the same church years later. The future governor William Paca stated in the *Maryland Gazette*s of March 18 and 25, 1773, that Boucher had "mistaken the loud strains of [his] own pipe for the pleasing harmony of a general concert" and that rather than attending to his proper duties as minister, he "pipes softest musick" all day long.[60] Boucher eventually led the loyalist Homony Club, serving as club composer and bon vivant, before escaping back to England just before the Revolution.

Clearly, the most musical minister of colonial Maryland was the Reverend Alexander Malcolm, who officiated at St. Anne's from 1749 to 1754 and led St. Paul's in Queen Anne's County from 1754 until 1759. Malcolm held a master of arts in music and a degree in mathematics from Edinburgh University, and he wrote the influential *Treatise of Musick: Speculative, Practical and Historical* (Edinburgh, 1721), as well as other theoretical works. Malcolm came to the New World as a teacher around 1731, afterwards becoming an Anglican missionary in Massachusetts. There he met the Tuesday Club founder, Dr. Alexander Hamilton, who perhaps helped arrange Malcolm's invitation to become the minister at St. Anne's Church. The minister played flute and violin, actively performing both in public and in private. (At a Tuesday Club meeting in 1750 he proved that he could play the fiddle and dance upon one leg at the same time.)[61]

Despite the musical capabilities of ministers like Reverends Malcolm, Bacon, and Skippon and the appearance of skilled musicians who served as vestrymen, wardens, and members of congregations, Anglican services were surprisingly unmusical.[62] Part of the reason is that the Anglican Church itself did not flourish in Maryland, despite Dr. Bray's early efforts, which caused both anger and apathy among colonists. First, the governor's unabashedly political style of appointing ministers often alienated congregations, while it established some irresponsible men in positions of power. Further, clergymen earned a reputation for "worldly" pursuits, since little supervision could be exerted over them either by the bishop of London or by individual parish vestries. The construction of new churches lagged behind population growth, and few were large enough or kept in good repair on limited budgets. On average, one minister served a thousand people spread over a large area, which necessitated preaching in different parts of his parish on alternate Sundays in "chapels of ease." Church attendance suffered despite ministers' attempts to soften theology and shorten services. Increasingly, Marylanders joined up with the more vibrant Lutherans, Presbyterians, and other unsanctioned denominations, so the Anglican establishment declined further, in some cases being supported largely by the local wealthy planters, who could show off their fine clothes every Sunday from their private pews. So while Anglican ministers brought to Maryland a degree of musical sophistication enjoyed by few among the native-born, they practiced it largely outside of church.

Religious life in the colonial Chesapeake was thus inhibited and quite inferior to that in colonial regions to the north. Congregationalist churches in New England flourished town by town and supported group singing, sacred-music education, and even composition. A nascent American style of sacred music emerged there, one typified by the compositions of the Bostonian William Billings. Music by Billings and other New England "tune-smiths" circulated as far south as Maryland by the 1770s, yet it could hardly be considered popular in Maryland. In the Chesapeake tidewater, music found its place in drawing rooms, theaters, dancing rooms, and taverns. The independent, materialistic tobacco planters could easily have supported music in their officially established church, but they often simply chose not to do so.

The commissioning of an organ for St. Anne's Church in Annapolis late in the colonial period encouraged some improvement to the status of church music in Maryland. Prominent men in Annapolis—parishioners, vestrymen, and even a church warden—owned chamber organs before 1750.[63] By 1753 the Reverend Thomas Chase, at St. Paul's Church in Baltimore, had noted the value of having an organ in his church. Organs appeared in advertisements in the *Maryland Gazette* by 1754, yet the head church in the colonial capital did not acquire one until 1761. The St. Anne's vestry ran a subscription to purchase an organ, probably a small, freestanding chamber organ with one keyboard, no pedals, and only a few ranks of pipes. While London craftsmen fulfilled their 280-guinea commission, Annapolis carpenters constructed an organ loft, since pew space could not be spared. At first caretakers periodically tuned and repaired the new organ, but lethargy prevailed; after six years of use someone commented on the heavy dust that had gathered on the expensive instrument.[64]

In 1761, shortly after the installation, Frederick Victor became the first official organist at St. Anne's Church. Victor received £45 current per annum, a fair salary for the time, although he served only through 1764. According to vestry records, it took nine years to fill Victor's post after he left, even though a year earlier the Philadelphia organist (and signer of the Declaration of Independence) Francis Hopkinson had written to Samuel Galloway, of South River, that John Stadler would make a good organist at St. Anne's.[65] Good organists were clearly rare and in high demand in the colonies. *Maryland Gazette* advertisements for organists at the Piscataway and Port Tobacco parish churches ran for some time. The Port Tobacco organ was a gift of Dr. Gustavus Brown in 1758, offered on the condition that the church would pay the organist. It took a special act of the General Assembly to raise funds for the organist, a move repeated again in 1774 for King and Queen parish, St. Mary's County, after George Goldie donated £133 for its organ.

Not only did the St. Anne's organ sit silent after Victor left but the church structure itself fell into disrepair. A satirical poem by Reverend Jonathan Boucher described this decadence. Written as if the church herself were speaking, Boucher's poem ridicules the poor attendance and bemoans with envy the fine, brick theater just constructed in her view, concluding, "Here, in Annapolis alone, / GOD has the meanest House in Town."[66] By 1775 the St. Anne's organ had to be moved from the neglected church, with its leaky roof, into the brick theater, which the vestry leased yearly thereafter. Harry Woodcock received £30 per year as organist, considerably less than his predecessor, to play for these services in the theater. The vestry held off officially appointing Woodcock until 1779, perhaps because of decreased activity during the war (vestry records from that period do not exist) or perhaps because of Woodcock's dubious reputation as a spinet instructor. Woodcock served again from 1790 until his death in 1792, shortly before the new St. Anne's Church opened its doors and the thirty-year-old organ sounded again in its rightful home. The active immigrant musician Raynor Taylor then served as organist at St. Anne's for the next four years, to be followed by two of America's earliest known female organists. A Madame Pineau and Miss Margaret Marye served in succession at St. Anne's during the 1790s. Both Pineau and Marye were upper-class women who had escaped the slave insurrection in San Domingo and found themselves forced to earn some income from a formerly genteel but suddenly quite practical talent.[67]

Organists in early Maryland set the pitch and tempo for psalm-singing, and they played interludes between verses. Based on a description of duties by Francis Hopkinson of Philadelphia, the Anglican organist also played a voluntary before the reading of the lesson, most often one composed by George Frederick Handel, William Boyce, or John Stanley. The organist should play with restraint and dignity, and certainly without showing off.[68] Peter Pelham, longtime organist at Bruton Parish Church in Williamsburg, also offered public concerts of secular works.

By the time of the installation of St. Anne's organ in Maryland, Congregationalists in New England had been developing the art of singing for more than forty years. Starting around 1720, the Boston clergy encouraged participation in singing schools, in which church members learned to read music. The singing-school movement succeeded most impressively in that region, such that many congregations could sing from printed music and did so with gusto and great enthusiasm. The days of fumbling through the old psalm tunes were gone, replaced by the concerted singing of energetic fuging tunes, four-part psalm settings, and impressive, complicated anthems. The itinerant singing master, then a fixture of society in New England, was practically unknown in the South. Yet, in Philadelphia in 1761 James Lyon compiled and had printed a collection of psalms and hymns entitled *Urania*, and the list of subscribers included only one person from Maryland.[69] Once Annapolis could boast of an organ in the church and had books from which to sing, what the city needed next was a singing master to conduct singing schools.

Not surprisingly, the *Maryland Gazette* carried advertisements for no fewer than three singing schools in Annapolis after the St. Anne's organ was installed. Yet

none seemed to succeed. The first of these schools had roots going back some thirty-five years, to 1729, when John Conner, aboard the ship *Mary*, bound for Annapolis, copied out twenty two-part settings of psalms. Conner's elegant manuscript book fell into the hands of Anthony Smith, whose wife, Elisabeth Smith, was a teacher. In 1764 Elizabeth advertised the first singing school in Maryland since that decreed by Bray in 1700. She added various French lessons to the back of Conner's psalm-tune manuscript, as she taught that subject also. Whoever attended Elisabeth Smith's singing school in Annapolis worked with one of the earliest surviving colonial American sacred manuscripts.[70]

Another advertisement for a singing school in Annapolis appeared in the paper only three weeks after Mrs. Smith's, presumably under church sanction. The clerk at St. Anne's, Philip Williams, proposed "teaching PSALMODY, in all its Parts, Treble, Contra, Tenor and Bass, in the Parish Church on Wednesdays and Fridays, from V to VIII o'Clock in the Evening, provided he can meet with Encouragement."[71] While Mrs. Smith had used much older, two-part settings, Williams hoped to attract students by teaching them to sing in four parts. Considerably more advanced than two-part singing, the use of four parts suggests that children and/or women were to participate in this choir. Williams apparently did not meet "with Encouragement," for while his advertisements ran for four consecutive weeks, there is no evidence that a choir was actually formed or that if it was formed, it performed either special concerts or within services. Within a year, Williams's successor, Hugh Maguire, also tried to get a choir started at St. Anne's Church. He also seems to have failed.

In 1775 a New England–style singing master, or at least someone who claimed to be one, arrived in Maryland. James Digins that year advertised himself as a "Vocal Music-Master from Boston" and solicited "the young gentlemen and ladies of Baltimore town" to attend his vocal music school, to be held at "Rev. Mr. Allison's meeting house, or any other place that may be agreed on, for the term of one year."[72] Four months later the newspaper carried word of a large reward for the return of an escapee from the Baltimore jail—"a certain

Page from John Conner's musical manuscript, begun aboard the ship *Mary* en route to Annapolis. Conner began, logically enough, with the rudiments. On this page appear tenor and bass parts to two of the twenty psalms he transcribed, apparently from Nahum Tate and Nicholas Brady's psalter; someone else on ship may have carried the *New Version*. Conner seized the opportunity to copy the introduction and his favorite tunes. Notice the older-style, diamond-shaped notes and seventeenth-century clef signs for both tenor (melody) and bass. Collection of the Maryland State Archives.

James Digins' about 26 years of age, 5 feet 9 or 10 inches high, dark complexion, yellow skin, fierce eyes, much addicted to wrangling, and professes to be a singing master. . . . Pretends to be a gentleman, and is much conceited."[73]

Singing schools caught on in New England and to some extent in the middle colonies, as socially enticing events that significantly raised peoples' musical literacy. Yet they found little support in Maryland during the colonial period. Anglican churches then stood mostly silent, merely echoing the spinet tunes from elegant homes down the street, songs from the theater nearby, and ballads and dance tunes from the tavern around the corner.

While the older, tobacco-bound tidewater region of Maryland failed to encourage sacred musical life, Maryland's piedmont region excelled in it. Those who populated the piedmont region took matters of religious faith more seriously than did the tobacco planters. The first wave of German immigrants came from Switzerland and the Palatine area in 1732 and settled in what eventually became Frederick and Washington Counties; others came later to northwest Carroll County. Hardworking, sober Germans made for desirable settlers, so Maryland authorities lured them with land grants in western (including what later became known as central) Maryland. In the early to mid-eighteenth century these immigrants, having brought their Bibles, prayer

books, and hymnals along with them, set up German Reformed and Lutheran churches. West of Frederick, Jonathan Hager helped establish the German Reformed church in Washington County. Music held these Germanic immigrants together in worship, and it spilled over into other aspects of their lives as well.[74]

In sixteenth-century Europe, Martin Luther had preached widely that proper congregational singing would improve worship services; he had argued against the trained choirs and operatic music of the Catholic Church. Since then music has been an important component of the Lutheran faith and its offshoot, the German Reformed Church, both in Europe and later in America. Philadelphia became a center for publishing this music in America, with more than twenty-two Lutheran and German Reformed hymnals issued by 1770. One of these alone contained nearly a thousand hymns, and many found their way into towns like Frederick, New Market, and Hagerstown. For many decades Maryland's German immigrants spoke, sang, and worshipped in German. Henry Melchior Muhlenberg was a great organizer of Lutheranism in the middle Atlantic region. He preached in Frederick as early as 1747.

Johannes Thomas Schley shared Muhlenberg's view of the importance of education and organization to immigrants. Schley was born in Germany (Palatinate) in 1712 and came to the Chesapeake region around 1745. He helped establish and lead a German Reformed congregation in Frederick in 1747, by which time about one thousand Germans had settled in the area. Schley served as schoolmaster, teaching singing to children, and he also led prayers and singing at services. The German Reformed church in Frederick got its first permanent pastor in 1753, and had an organ by at least 1770, when Schley served as organist. Perhaps feeling competitive, the Frederick Lutheran church hired the Moravian craftsman David Tannenberg to build a magnificent five-hundred-pipe organ there in 1775.[75]

Schley's surviving music copybooks give some indication of his activities as organist, choir leader, and teacher. Two bound manuscripts that he apparently began in Germany contained numerous four-part chorales and psalms, as well as works by Handel, Corelli, and Lully. A surprising number of secular musical pieces—American patriotic and English theater songs, some with lyrics—were added later, along with country dance tunes that show up in other eighteenth-century American manuscripts. Three pieces were unique to Schley's manuscripts, one entitled "Williamsburg Serenade" and "A Favourite Minuet" and "Giga," both by Mr. Leonard, probably the one already mentioned as being active in Alexandria and tidewater Maryland. Totaling some eight hundred pages, these manuscripts also included compositions by Schley himself, such as sonatas, lessons, and organ preludes. These works are nearly all copied for keyboard, many specifically marked for pianoforte, harpsichord, or organ. His manuscripts also include some sections on music theory and keyboard fingering, which reflect dedicated musicianship on Schley's part over a long and productive life. Not surprisingly, Schley's son, John Schley Jr., carried on the family profession and perhaps contributed to his father's manuscripts. He managed a concert in Hagerstown in 1794 and had settled there as a music master by then. The elder Schley had died in 1790, leaving behind an important artifact of early American music history.

German immigrants also settled in Baltimore, some directly from the Old World and others, disenchanted farmers, from Western Maryland and southern Pennsylvania. By 1758 a German Reformed church had been built in Baltimore, and by 1770 then Lutheran Reverend Philip William Otterbein had come to Baltimore, soon to head a separatist reform congregation called the United Brethren. Dr. Charles Frederick Weisenthal, who founded the first medical school in Maryland, came to Baltimore in 1755 and helped build a Lutheran church there in 1762. By 1775 there were some thirty Lutheran and German Reformed churches throughout Maryland, many struggling with the pressure to hold services in English instead of German. The urban churches generally adopted English sooner than country congregations.[76]

The most musically significant Germanic immigrants were the Moravians, or Unitas Fratrum, who arrived in Georgia in 1735 and later settled mostly in Pennsylvania and North Carolina. This religious sect emphasized music both for worship and as an important part of its strict communal lifestyle. Their music involved disciplined training, and they had both the will and the resources to flourish. Among the talented Moravian performers and composers active in America were Johannes Herbst, Johannes Peter, Jeremiah Denke, and John Antes. In addition to their own sacred and secular compositions, Moravians also performed Haydn, Mozart, and other European composers' works with sophistication seen nowhere else in the colonies. Yet, living communally, and with their strongest ties to the Old World, they did not generally influence the development of music in America.[77]

In the mid-eighteenth century a group of Moravians settled in Maryland at a place they called Graceham, near what became Thurmont. They built a church there, brought fellow Moravian David Tannenberg in to build an organ, and maintained an impressive musical life for decades. An organ book copied at Graceham in 1830 survives today, preserving a selection of hymns and anthems in vogue at that time. In the larger Moravian towns in Pennsylvania and North Carolina, one could hear trombone choirs, concerted vocal music, chamber music, and orchestral music—some of which reverberated at Graceham.

Aboard the same ship that transported the first Moravians to America were two Anglican missionaries, John and Charles Wesley, who found their German shipmates' enthusiastic singing of hymns and the emotional power of their music to be profoundly impressive. The Wesleys came to question their own church's prejudice against hymns and dependency upon the old psalm tunes. Over time, and with much theological wrangling, Methodism, a new denomination that espoused emotionalism and personal salvation, gradually emerged as a variation on Anglican worship. For the many Marylanders who in the mid-eighteenth century found the established Anglican church uninspiring, the time was ripe for religious change. This was true especially for the ethnically British middle- and lower-class colonists in both tidewater and piedmont Maryland. They welcomed pioneering Methodist ministers with open arms. The established Anglican gentry feared this rising tide of evangelism as potentially dangerous to the social hierarchy they dominated. Thus the powerful Methodist preacher George Whitefield met with scorn in Annapolis yet found unbounded encouragement in the countryside as he sowed early seeds for a religious fervor eventually known as the Great Awakening.[78]

Music contributed immensely to the Methodists' ability to lure spiritually bereft Marylanders away from Anglicanism. The Wesleys had brought with them to America both a Tate and Brady psalter and a hymnal by the Englishman Dr. Isaac Watts. As early as 1707 Watts's hymns appealed to people eager to listen to tunefully pleasant church music. Watts's music was soon imported, sold, and reprinted in the colonies. The Wesleys also composed a large number of their own hymns, publishing the first of them in Georgia in 1739. Together with Watts's music, that of the Wesleys ultimately appeared in the hymnals of many denominations, not just the Methodists'. Though chastised by the Church of England for composing new, unapproved music for service, the Wesleys knew the value of singing well-crafted, tuneful hymns, as opposed to lining out the old, worn psalm tunes. Music-making became an inspirational, personal experience central to the grass-roots Methodist movement, far more appealing than the dry Anglican Church and its scant music.

Carroll County, Maryland, became the "cradle of American Methodism" when Irish-born Robert Straw-bridge settled at Sam's Creek in the early 1760s. A "melodious singer" who preached in Baltimore, Frederick, and parts of Pennsylvania and Virginia, Strawbridge formed the first Methodist Society in Maryland in 1765 and established "Union churches," which served several congregations and also functioned as schools. Methodists were holding services in Baltimore by 1773. Methodism truly flourished on the Eastern Shore, thanks to circuit riders like Francis Asbury, who worked diligently throughout Maryland during the 1770s. Later, Mason Locke Weems, "the Parson of the Island," helped cement Methodism as the dominant denomination of the Eastern Shore. Though the Wesley brothers never officially broke with the Anglican Church, their musical and theological efforts helped Methodism emerge as a separate denomination in America—in Baltimore—in 1784.[79]

Music and Independence

While no one can say exactly what effect music had on Maryland political debates in the 1770s, familiar tunes permitted savvy adaptation. With new lyrics and politically pointed choruses, singers could arouse listeners in a tavern or around a liberty tree with tales of rights and wrongs, gallant patriots, and villains in red uniforms. Newspapers ensured that lyrics spread far and wide. During the French and Indian War, Marylanders and other colonists had enjoyed a musical tribute to Admiral Edward Hawke following his victory over the French at Quiberon Bay late in 1759—"A New Toast. Tune, God save our Noble King."[80] Sentiment shifted after the war, when the British tried to recoup some costs of the conflict by taxing or levying new fees on their American subjects. On July 14, 1768, the *Maryland Gazette* joined other colonial newspapers in publishing "The Liberty Song," a call for resistance to new trade restrictions penned by John Dickinson. Dickinson, whose public life included service in both Delaware and Pennsylvania, wrote with much spirit against tyranny and the prospective loss of liberty but closed by praising the king and "Britannia's Glory and Wealth" (he later refused to sign the Declaration of Independence). To accompany his lyrics, Dickinson chose the melody from a song in praise of British sailors, "Hearts of Oak," a popular air in London theaters in 1759. The tune appeared in an Annapolis manuscript from the late colonial era under its original title. Dickinson's first verse and chorus read:

> Come join hand in hand brave Americans all
> And rouse your bold hearts at fair liberty's call
> no tyrannous acts shall suppress your just claim
> or stain with dishonour America's name
>
>> In freedom we're born and in freedom we'll live
>> Our purses are ready
>> Steady, friends, steady
>> Not as slaves but freemen our money we'll give[81]

The number of parodies this song inspired testifies to its wide popularity then. After the outbreak of hostilities in 1775, patriot newspapers continued to publish words one could sing to common melodies. On November 2, 1777, *Dunlap's Maryland Gazette; or, the Baltimore General Advertiser* published "A New Song," whose lyrics mercilessly satirized "Gentleman Johnny" Burgoyne, the flamboyant British general who, after the Battle of Saratoga, had surrendered his army to the Continentals. Francis Hopkinson's "British Valour Displayed: or, The Battle of the Kegs" (1778) followed the tactic of laughing at the enemy. Burgoyne's surrender helped persuade the French to enter the war on the Revolutionary side, so in 1781, when Queen Marie Antoinette bore a male child, patriots at Lower Marlboro celebrated with a "dance on the green" that attracted "thirteen couples of the younger ladies and gentlemen."[82] Perhaps they danced to some newer American dance tunes of this era, such as "Stony Point," "Valley Forge," "Lady Washington's Reel," or "Burgoyne's Defeat."

"Yankee Doodle" circulated in the oral tradition by the late 1760s, when words to it first appeared in print in Philadelphia. No one knows who composed the melody, yet it was disseminated widely in both printed sources and hand-copied manuscripts in a variety of versions. By 1775 various sets of lyrics appeared in broadsides and newspapers, mocking patriots and loyalists alike. A well-crafted song could be a powerful

rhetorical weapon. Playing "Yankee Doodle" as a march could not fail to evoke strong patriotic (or antagonistic) feelings.[83]

Because declaring independence meant nothing unless the colonies could win it on the battlefield, Marylanders during the Revolution paid close attention to the forces they organized for the war, and not surprisingly, men under arms paid close attention to music. The military and music of course had a long experience together. Some of the first musical instruments to appear in Maryland records had military functions or symbolism. In Anne Arundel County alone, estate inventories dating from between 1676 and 1776 included seven drums, six trumpets, two oboes, and a pair of French horns.[84] Though considered orchestral instruments today, trumpets, oboes, and bassoons were long associated with military music ensembles. In early Maryland many such instruments were owned by men with ranks such as captain and major. Some of these instruments may have been held merely as family heirlooms or status symbols, yet all were necessary for functional military music. In late 1754, following the defeat that summer of General Edward Braddock near Fort Duquesne and the onset of the French and Indian War, some verses to inspire recruitment appeared in the September 19 *Maryland Gazette* as "A Recruiting Song, For the Maryland Independent Company. (By an Officer of the Company)." The implied tune was clearly "Over the Hills and Far Away," well known from *The Beggar's Opera*, the ballad opera presented in Annapolis, Chestertown, and beyond. Due to the difficulty of printing musical notation and a relatively undeveloped publishing business, war songs rarely appeared as sheet music, that is, with both text and musical notation. Instead, lyrics appeared in broadsides and newspapers, as well as being copied by hand into tune books, diaries, and other places. Standard ballad melodies, unlike psalm tunes, came readily to the popular mind in the oral tradition that prevailed in Maryland. Ballads popular in 1759, such as "The Lillies of France" and "Death of General Wolfe," lifted the spirits of Maryland soldiers far afield, and the inclusion of these two ballads in the two-volume *Baltimore Musical Miscellany or Colum-*

bian Songster (1804–5) attests to their longstanding popularity.

General Washington recognized the practical value of field music, but he also understood the ceremonial function of a *band of musick*, which catered to officers. A band of music was a military wind band ensemble based on the German *Harmoniemusik* ensemble. The *South-Carolina Weekly Gazette* of July 5, 1783, offers a report on the previous day's Fourth of July festivities, in which "the Continental Artillery, with five field pieces, and the militia of this town, paraded in Meeting-Street, attended with a Band of Music, Colours, Drums, and Fifes." The dignitaries "went in front of the Artillery and Militia, who received the procession with Presented Arms, Music, Drums and Fifes, Colours Flying, . . . after which the following toasts were given, accompanied with 13 guns, vocal and instrumental music performing God save the Thirteen States, after the first toast, and particular pieces of music after every other, the last consisting with a solemn Dirge of Music.[85] Bands of music played concerts for officers and guests, and they provided background music during dinners and at public and private dances. They played at military funerals and even at executions. They performed divertimenti and arrangements of other works by Mozart, Haydn and lesser-known composers, even settings of simple songs and dance tunes.[86] Works like the *Monthly Military Concertos*, imported to Annapolis in 1772, had been composed for such a use. Military balls were a common treat for officers during wartime, thrown to honor recent victories or holidays or for just about any excuse to summon the ladies from near and far to dance and socialize. Sometimes lavish, these gatherings featured dances with titles like "Philadelphia Minuet" and "Successful Campaign." Common foot soldiers must have envied, or resented, the fine food, dress, and company of fine ladies, since their camp life by contrast was poor and dreary.

The players in bands of music were professional musicians hired directly by the officers. They were not commissioned by the army and therefore had no other duties. The status given the band of music reflects the importance of ornamental music to the gentlemen officers themselves. In the same way that American officers copied English manners and fashion, American bands of music emulated the crack British units that had paraded in Boston, New York, and Philadelphia during the French and Indian War. By the middle of the Revolutionary period the bands of the Third and Fourth artillery regiments of the Continental army had developed great reputations and served in turn as models for other American bands to follow. In this sense, Revolutionary-era bands of music were the true precursors of the United States Marine Band, formed in 1798 and still active today.

By contrast, field musicians were enlisted men who sent signals to other soldiers, relaying orders and duties. As soldiers paid from public coffers, they could be ordered to gather firewood, dig trenches or graves, and perform other nonmusical duties. Field musicians defined daily camp routine, with drums and often fifes playing reveille, tattoo, troop, and other calls that signaled the soldiers to wake up, bed down, and assemble for roll call. In addition to providing music for military duties, field drummers set the cadence for marching and beat commands during battle, such as attack, retreat, and parley. Fifes provided color to the drums' rhythmic patterns, and the use of familiar song and dance tunes for marching often eased tired soldiers' steps. Fifes seem to have gradually replaced trumpets, which had been in use earlier. When in 1737 Thomas Cresap attacked German settlers in a border dispute with the Penn family, he reportedly did so "with 300 men in arms . . . with Drums and Trumpets."[87] Drums had been used as signals in civilian life from earliest times, announcing market days, special meetings, even church. Town drummers were among America's earliest civically employed musicians.

The Continental Congress standardized the preferred use of one drummer and one fifer per company, although sometimes a lone drummer had to suffice. Field musicians drew pay of about eight dollars per month, like that of a private, and the army provided their instruments. Early in the Revolution, uncoordinated drum signals and confusion in interpreting them proved deadly. In 1778 Washington appointed Lieutenant John Hiwell inspector and superintendent of music, and the following year Baron von Steuben insisted on the standardization of field-signal music. Fife and drum majors now trained and led other field musicians, using imported instruction books for the drum patterns and associated fife tunes. As American fifers made their own copies from such publications, they added American favorites like "Yankee Doodle" and "Road to Boston."

Maryland's Revolutionary drummers and fifers came from surprisingly diverse backgrounds, including Irish and Scottish convict servants as well as local recruits. An English convict servant runaway in Anne Arundel County "play'd the fife for Col. Dorsey's battalion of militia."[88] These field musicians were generally grown men, although occasional reports give ages as low as 11 and 8. Nace Butler, who served as a fifer in the Second Maryland of the Continental army, was an African American. In 1777 Virginia enacted a law allowing "free Negroes or mulattoes" to serve as field musicians, and other colonies soon followed suit. A Baltimore newspaper described Lord Dunmore's Royal Regiment of Black Fusiliers as being formed of both "runaway and stolen negroes" who played the "sprightly and enlivening barrafoot."[89] This is a rare reference to an African instrument similar to a xylophone, likely fabricated to mock and degrade these loyalist soldiers and make them appear foolish.

Field music carried much meaning. A fifer marching with Massachusetts militia to meet the British at Concord Bridge in 1775 reportedly played a tune entitled "The White Cockade," recalling the emblem of the Scottish separatists in their uprisings against the English. Conditions of surrender often dictated whether drummers would beat or silently carry their instruments while exiting; either way, drums had to be present. Allowing the defeated army to play its favorite march gave the prisoners added dignity. To deny it increased the insult of defeat. The winning side's musicians could taunt the losers by playing "Yankee Doodle" when they marched by. According to an old story, British field musicians played "The World Turned Upside Down" when Cornwallis's army surrendered at Yorktown in 1781. Such a strong musical message would have

been quite appropriate; after all, an underequipped assortment of colonists, along with French allies, had defeated the most powerful military in the world. This myth, however, took root in 1828, long after the event—at about the same time Americans started reading Parson Weems's story about young George Washington cutting down a cherry tree. Neither of these endearing stories can be proven true with historical documents. In any case, drums and fifes propelled men into action. They also appeared symbolically in poetry and song lyrics. Though merely a couplet, the following lines a young lady sent the editor of a Baltimore newspaper convey it all:

> Hark! the drum beats To Arms—to your girls bid adieu,
> The proud foe is advancing on the plain,
> We'll presently humble this blood-thirsty crew,
> And come home to our sweethearts again.[90]

The Continentals' capture of the Hessians at the Battle of Trenton on Christmas Day 1776 proved to be of musical as well as tactical significance. The fine brass drums used by the Hessian band of music were soon sounded instead by American drummers against the British cause. The captured Hessian musicians themselves, later imprisoned at Frederick, Maryland, found their talents useful to the American cause. Just the following year, in 1777, they performed as a group in Philadelphia, and in 1782 they played in the theater orchestra in Baltimore. The following year the Hessian bandsmen worked overtime in celebrating formal American victory as word spread about the Treaty of Paris. In one instance at the Montgomery County courthouse "a military band in faded Hessian uniform played marches and gavottes," and the celebrants danced until midnight.[91] The Hessians contributed greatly to American musical life, especially after the war, when many decided to stay and even intermarry. One Hessian corporal, Philip Phile, settled in Philadelphia after the war and established himself as a composer, conductor, and instrumentalist. Phile wrote "The President's March."[92] This melody shows up in Johannes Schley's manuscript, and it is possible that Schley and this Hessian musician knew each other, as they shared a common language and the prison lay only four miles from the musical minister's house. After Schley died, another Hessian, William Peter Hardt, became the organist for the German Reformed congregation in Frederick.

French bands also played mightily for the American cause—in camp and in town. The Count de Charlus's regimental band accompanied a theatrical production in Annapolis as French troops passed through from Rhode Island, on their way to engage Cornwallis at Yorktown.[93]

Music mattered to Maryland militiamen, riflemen, camp followers, officers, and enlisted men. It played a role in recruiting them, organizing their daily camp life, enlivening special events and ceremonies, and passing weary or boring hours by means of singing and dancing. Perhaps most importantly, it voiced the cause one fought for. Loyalists sang verses of "God Save the King" and "Britons strike home . . . vociferated at taverns, over porter, punch and wine, till the imagination is heated and the blood in a ferment." Patriots sang "the sweet lullaby of Liberty to the people to keep them quiet."[94] In a 1715 songbook after the fashion of Thomas D'Urfey's *Pills To Purge Melancholy*, it is asserted that the political ballad "Lilliburlero" was "highly instrumental in singing out a Bad Monarch."[95] More constructively, music underscores the success of a hero, as when George Washington came to Annapolis to resign his commission in late 1783. The owner of the Maryland Coffee House, George Mann, made it a point to hire musicians to play and honor the general, who departed public life then to return for good, he thought, to Mount Vernon.

CHAPTER TWO

Something for Everyone

MARYLAND MUSIC FROM INDEPENDENCE

TO THE 1850S

AFTER THE AMERICAN REVOLUTION and especially after 1815, when a second war for independence ended, musical activities in Maryland reflected a rapidly changing society. Mass production and industrialization brought not only railroads and steamboats but also pianos and improved brass-band instruments. Partisan politics and social issues such as abolition and temperance found expression in sheet music as well as in stump speeches. As immigration added to natural increase, Maryland's working classes clamored for humorous and patriotic songs, as well as ethnic folk songs and dance tunes. Prosperity led to more urbanization and improved living standards, especially for people in the middle and upper income levels. Leisure activities, such as circuses, parades, and theatrical entertainments, attracted the rich, the poor, and many in between. Other gatherings, such as minstrel shows, barn dances, private balls, and domestic musicales, segregated the classes. Opera played a changing role, bringing different classes together before around 1850, then serving the upper class exclusively thereafter. Church congregations grew, split, and multiplied, hiring composer-conductors who purchased or published and sold their own hymnals, formed choirs, and oversaw the commissioning and construction of fine organs. Professional musicians competed for newly emerging opportunities to perform, teach, compose, and publish.

Human nature dictated that despite rampant growth and change, certain colonial themes remained constant. The possibility of elevating themselves through lessons and domestic music-making drove wealthy amateurs and those aspiring to gentility. Prominent men still led Maryland's militia groups, upon which the public so often called to supply band music at parades and civic celebrations. Social mores still limited women's musical outlets, both at the amateur and professional levels. European musical styles and forms continued to dominate after independence, although each decade brought increasingly "Americanized" material. As early as the 1820s, touring white entertainers blackened their faces and mimicked African music and gestures. Thereafter a uniquely American genre emerged, reflecting social and racial tensions despite the superficially humorous lyrics and sprightly tunes. American sheet music, at times more serious and otherwise more sentimental but now wrapped in a simpler, more accessible style than that of the preceding century, answered diverse needs.

From Cathedral to Camp Meeting

After the Revolution, Baltimore supplanted Annapolis as Maryland's social and cultural center. More importantly, it quickly emerged as a center for countless enterprises. The coupling of artistic and commercial growth sent the city into a musical ascendancy that continued for decades. Families that profited from shipping, manufacturing, and railroading found recreational outlets in singing clubs, public dances, concerts, and private soirées. The hardworking laborers who made them rich, whether from Maryland or neighboring states or newly arrived from Acadia, Saint-Domingue, France, Germany, or Ireland, filled a wide variety of ethnic neighborhoods, all of them ringing with diverse folk songs, dances, and hymns. Driven by rapid industrialization and technological innovation, Baltimore, no less than New York and Philadelphia, typified nineteenth-century urban developments.

Church music flourished in Baltimore. Throughout the new nation, religious groups after the Revolution worshiped freely under constitutionally guaranteed religious liberty. Church-building increased significantly, especially in larger cities, where wealthy congregations constructed grand, imposing structures. Competition over physical size spilled over into the realm of music, as seen in the trend toward ever-larger choirs, fancier organs, and more flamboyant music directors, who composed hymns, anthems, and sacred instrumental works. Such enthusiasm packed singing schools, and it fed the demand for sacred-music publishing. In Baltimore, swelling Lutheran, German Reformed, Methodist, Catholic, Presbyterian, Episcopalian, and Jewish congregations set ever-higher musical standards.

Maryland Catholics in particular thrived following more than a century of repression. By papal decree Baltimore in 1784 became the seat of the Catholic Church in the United States, and in 1789 John Carroll,

nephew of Charles Carroll of Carrollton, served as the first Catholic bishop in the United States. Significantly, Bishop Carroll approved the first American book of Catholic service music, *A Compilation of the Litanies, Vespers, etc.* This collection, published in Philadelphia in 1787, included materials in both German and English, with some lyrics, of course, in Latin. Bishop Carroll encouraged the use of vernacular hymns, and Masses in Baltimore's Catholic churches were celebrated sometimes in English, sometimes in German or French. (Neither Carroll nor the pope himself, however, encouraged German Catholics to form separate congregations.)

Baltimore Catholics in 1795 began planning the first cathedral in America. The architect Benjamin Henry Latrobe, himself a clarinetist and careful observer of musical activities, located the organ to reflect the primacy of music during service. The 1806 cornerstone-laying ceremony included lavish musical display, and the prededication concert at the cathedral in 1821 featured one of America's earliest full performances of Haydn's oratorio *The Creation.* An audience of nearly two thousand attended this grand performance, which featured the Holliday Street Theatre's orchestra and a chorus of about two hundred amateur and professional singers. By then the New York organ builder Thomas Hall had installed America's largest and most expensive organ at the cathedral; it had 2,213 pipes, one stretching thirty-two feet. The instrument cost six thousand dollars. A French-born woman, Florine de Chateldun, served as organist there for twenty-three years, the first cathedral organist in the United States.[1]

Adventurous city musicians contributed to the cathedral's lively music program. As early as 1798 the Reverend Jean Baptiste Moranville composed hymns that he had published locally. For nearly thirty years he encouraged lavish music. Moranville oversaw the interior design of the cathedral organ and choir lofts and also directed the choir. For about a decade, ending in 1834, Henri-Noël Gilles served as leading tenor, oboe soloist, and occasional choirmaster for the cathedral. His four-part mass received favorable reviews as far away as Boston. Gilles figured prominently in Baltimore's secular musical life also, notably as Eliza Ridgely's harp teacher. The German violinist John Nenninger, who conducted the 1821 *Creation* performance, served as the cathedral's first official music director. Nenninger also taught music at Baltimore's St. Mary's Seminary from 1815 to 1839, challenging his choirs with the first American performances of Beethoven's Mass in C Major and Pergolesi's *Stabat Mater*. Whatever their background, Maryland Catholics zealously pursued superior music programs, thereby supporting professional musicians and associated tradesmen. Though the French outnumbered other Baltimore Catholics early on, the German presence grew steadily. Eventually the city's huge Irish Catholic population controlled musical tastes.

Other denominations, notably Baltimore's Episcopal, Unitarian, and Presbyterian congregations, also emphasized musical display. These churches likewise offered stable employment to musicians well known and admired in other musical circles. Christopher Meinecke served at St. Paul's Protestant Episcopal, as did Thomas Carr, who also worked at First Presbyterian. Yet city church leaders at times considered talented musicians to be a mixed blessing, questioning the unbounded enthusiasm that music directors, organists, and sometimes indecorous amateur choir members brought to their jobs. In 1840 a critic pointed out that rather than serving the needs of worship, Meinecke's music had grown to sound "rather like overtures and interludes to a melodramatic entertainment than the chastened expression of devotional feeling."[2] Several denominations issued rubrics, pastoral letters, and resolutions specifying that the minister had ultimate control over music and that "flashy" playing by organists and "operatic-style" singing were forbidden. Church superiors demanded that music be participatory and less ostentatious, rarely acknowledging that just such lavish display inspired choir members and helped to keep the pews filled.

The interest in what was becoming known as "classical" sacred music fueled a movement to form music clubs in Baltimore. Better-educated parishioners in particular reasoned that the finer sacred music of Handel and Haydn, though not welcome immediately within the worship service, should be performed. These associations ostensibly stemmed from the urge to support and improve church music. A Baltimore Harmonic Society practiced as early as 1799 and contributed some sixty singers to the 1821 *Creation* performance at Baltimore's cathedral. This group predated by some sixteen years the better-known and still active Boston Handel and Haydn Society. Baltimore's Handelian Society, having established itself at Christ Church in or around 1803, also predated its Boston counterpart. Baltimore's Handelian Society owned an organ but remained active only fifteen years.[3]

The Baltimore Musical Association stood out as especially successful. This formal amateur chorus met regularly from 1835 to at least 1839. Rial Shaw, who taught psalmody both privately and later in the city's public schools, apparently founded and helped run the organization. He had just suffered the devastating loss of an organ valued at one thousand dollars, which perished when the Baltimore Athenaeum burned. Immersing himself in running the Baltimore Musical Association, Shaw called frequent rehearsals at the First Presbyterian Church. Baltimore's prominent music publisher John Cole directed the chorus, assisted at times by John Nenninger and Henry Dielman. The exclusive membership of some sixty-four men, later joined by a few women, paid the accompanists' salaries and helped fund an association library. The group printed its own tickets and programs, notably a fourteen-page libretto to Mendelssohn's oratorio *The Conversion of St. Paul* for a special performance in May 1839. The group also presented lighter "monthly soirées" of sacred solos, duets, and favorite choruses.[4]

Only a wealthy few could afford the hefty dues or meet the social requirements of Baltimore's elite music groups. Less prestigious were the many informal singing schools, which offered inexpensive, readily available instruction. Visiting singing-school masters, largely from New England, took a self-conscious approach to "proper" training, one that stressed reading standard musical notation and working only with "approved" church music. The New Englanders Noah Webster and Andrew Law actively taught early nineteenth-century Baltimoreans the conservative European style of sacred music then in vogue in Boston. Webster arrived in Baltimore in 1785. He immediately gained the support of the First Presbyterian Church, where he formed a choir and showed off its newfound skills. Webster's future fame lay outside the field of music, in lexicography, and yet the ease with which he could come to town and successfully teach music suggests strong demand and little competition. Soon the outspoken Andrew Law arrived in town, also opening a singing school. Law copyrighted one of his many sacred publications in Baltimore, and he hired several assistant teachers to fan out into the countryside to hold classes and sell his books. Several of these underlings exceeded Law's expectations: they went out, sold the books, and absconded with the proceeds.[5]

Rinaldo Pindell, a storekeeper in West River, Anne Arundel County, strove to elevate his skills by attending a singing school. In his copy of the 1822 edition of John Cole's *The Seraph; A New Selection of Psalm tunes, Hymns, and Anthems*, Pindell noted the two singing-school sessions he had attended and that he had sung from this book in 1823. Pindell's attempts to learn singing in four parts, using an approved singing book, suggest that he aspired to the genteel urban church music of his day. Perhaps his favorite tunes from the *Seraph* included "Baltimore," "Annapolis," and "Meinecke's," for he marked those titles with stars.[6]

While city churchgoers largely championed European-style church music led by professionals, a heartfelt, less trained approach to singing flourished in Maryland's countryside. Most rural congregations sang humbler music—old psalms and fuging tunes, folk hymns, and white and black spirituals. Such less pretentious genres were evolving as peculiarly American forms of sacred music, being disseminated through oral tradition, in hymnbooks with or without musical notation, in farmers' almanacs, and even as simple broadsheets sold at Sunday schools and camp meetings. Much of the sacred music published in America between 1770 and 1850 adhered to this simpler style. Just after the Revolution, the Baltimore compilers Samuel Dyer and Wheeler Gillet and the firm Cushing & Jewett issued collections designed for rural use. However primitive and simple sounding, sacred folk music evolved through a complex interplay of oral transmission and non-European notation.

Middle- and lower-class people attended sacred singing schools too, though the subject matter and manner of performance differed considerably from those taught by Webster and Law. Even before Maryland's state constitution granted religions freedom in 1776, Maryland's rural Methodist and Baptist evangelists had struggled to convert and educate the poor and illiterate, especially outside the major cities. They depended upon a totally different sort of church music that had descended directly from colonial psalm- and hymn-singing traditions, especially those of New England. Such folk hymnody evolved through a curious mixture of oral and written practice, yet congregations as a whole practiced it rather than delegating the singing to choirs as in many city churches. New, religious texts to familiar secular folk melodies began to show up before 1800 in crude hymnbooks, and since the undereducated found standard musical notation difficult to learn, leaders came to depend upon a simplified form of musical notation known as shape-note, or Sacred Harp, music.[7] Shunned by snobby urbanites as "dunce notes," shape notes in fact gave rural singers a genuinely simplified way to read music. Stylistically, the music that appeared in shape-note hymnals tended toward simpler, primitive melodies and harmonies. Yet, as heard in shape-note singing still practiced today, the ancient-sounding sonorities and straightforward rhythms gave rural congregations a solid, driving kind of music that faithfully embodied their tangible, fervent beliefs.

Marylanders obtained their sacred hymnbooks in various ways. Many immigrants who settled in Western Maryland and further south had first landed at Philadelphia and then worked their way westward through Harrisburg, Pennsylvania. John Wyeth, of Harrisburg, sold thousands of shape-note tune books to these migrating people, especially to Methodists and Baptists. John Cole, in Baltimore, generally catered to more sophisticated congregations. His Methodist hymnal *David's Harp* (1813) included his own compositions of local flavor, such as "Light Street" and "Eutaw" (street

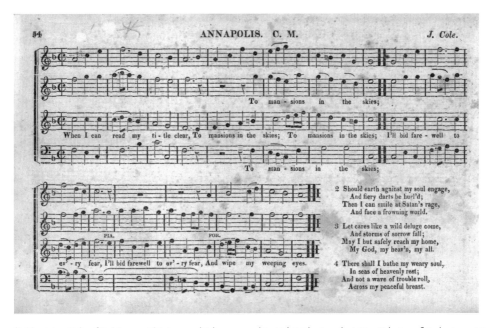

Music for "Annapolis," by John Cole of Baltimore. This tune, which appeared in Cole's *The Seraph; A New Selection of Psalm tunes, Hymns, and Anthems, from Favorite and Celebrated Authors; . . . As Performed by the Choir of St. Paul's Church, Baltimore* (Baltimore, 1822), exemplifies the music that flourished in modest rural Maryland churches, both in regular notation and in shape notes. Cole was long active in Baltimore as a composer, publisher, and performer. William Hauser's *The Hesperian Harp* (Philadelphia, 1848) contained a very different sacred work entitled "Annapolis," in shape notation, and the New Englander Daniel Read composed and published yet another piece with the same title, as a fuging tune, in 1785. Mrs. Worth B. Daniels Collection, Collection of the Maryland State Archives, MdHR MSA SC 557.

names still used in modern Baltimore), and older, familiar hymns by John Wesley and Isaac Watts. Cole catered to both arriving immigrants and established farmers, but in regular notation, not shape notes. At first a condescending classicist, Cole called shape notes "new fangled block-headed notes" in the preface to *David's Harp*; he clearly preferred standard musical notation.[8] Native-language hymnals were available in Maryland for the many German immigrants and residents of Germanic descent.

Shape-note hymnody and other rural forms were appropriate not only in country churches but at camp meetings as well. Camp meetings by design were social, emotionally charged experiences. Indeed, to some degree they served as an alternative to secular ballad singing and dancing, which the Methodists preachers particularly abhorred. Anywhere from a few hundred to ten or more thousand lower- and middle-class people would gather in a large clearing and erect giant tents and open-air grandstands for preaching. Such meetings, held during the summer, lasted from a couple days to

a full week. They featured virtually round-the-clock preaching of the fire-and-brimstone variety, as well as huge bonfires at night and inescapable mass singing. Energetic and loud hymn-singing was the natural way for common people to participate and spread the evangelical theologies of the day, which preached salvation as a direct, heartfelt experience only possible through an emotional moment of realization, or conversion. In many cases Methodists, Baptists, and more evangelical Presbyterians shared the same tune books and repertory. In addition to singing, outdoor camp-meeting converts were seen shouting for joy and writhing or "jerking" uncontrollably on the ground as they grappled with the devil and sought the aid of Christ. An 1806 Methodist camp meeting near Baltimore attracted four to five thousand participants, nearly six hundred of whom experienced conversion. Trumpets announced daily prayer times, and "guards" were posted to minimize disruptions; boys were paid to chase off dogs and pigs.[9]

While revival hymns and spiritual songs sold widely,

the music itself was stylistically simple and redundant, so that camp-meeting participants could sing by heart if neither songbook nor shape-note tune book was in hand. A preacher might take a well-known Wesleyan hymn and sing out the first line solo, with the crowd answering back, "Halleluia! Halleluia!" as a simple, brief reprise. The preacher would then sing the next line, the crowd answering again "Halleluia!," and so on. Camp meetings were major public events during the first half of the nineteenth century, not just for participants but for spectators as well. Some spectators came from restrained, well-to-do urban churches, and they wrote with awe, even disgust about such raw emotionalism.

Camp meetings at times included both whites and African Americans (many of them free), though the races slept in separate tents and held smaller, separate prayer meetings. While the term *spiritual* today usually suggests a kind of song and style of singing exclusive to African Americans, traditions for both white and black spirituals coexisted and shared much in common. Both types of spirituals flourished in rural nineteenth-century Maryland, but that of African Americans has survived as a living tradition. There was much regional variation in both tune and dialect lyric. The first organized congregation of African American Methodists formed in Baltimore in 1785, and in 1816 it incorporated as Bethel A.M.E. (African Methodist Episcopal) Church. A.M.E. churches in Baltimore advertised concerts of sacred music before midcentury. In 1801 Richard Allen published the first A.M.E. hymnbook, and through various editions it remained in use for nearly a century and a half. Unlike hymnals that had printed music as well as words, this collection of words no doubt served as a point of departure for a largely oral tradition. The A.M.E. service emphasized singing and praying bands reminiscent of African ring-shout dancing.[10] John Wesley himself had used the term *band societies* for inner circles within Methodist congregations. Organizers held camp meetings in Maryland seasonally. In rural churches, emotional, enthusiastic hymn-singing was routine year-round.

Baltimore Theater at the Dawn of the New Republic

Public entertainment after independence evolved considerably, because urban theaters became the focus of musical life. By the 1790s the old days of an amateur-dominated music scene had given way to a fledgling music industry. Talented immigrant professional musicians like James Hewitt in New York, Gottleib Graupner in Boston, and members of the Carr family in Philadelphia and Baltimore led theater orchestras, produced concerts, composed, and established the nation's first large-scale music publishing firms. Such pioneer musical entrepreneurs in turn encouraged other professionals to emigrate. Soon America hosted hundreds of well-trained Italian, English, and German musicians who taught, performed, directed, arranged, composed, and published music and built musical instruments. America's incipient music industry centered on large newly built theaters, structures that put to shame the small, mostly makeshift theaters of colonial times. Maryland played a leading role in this musical revolution.

The new nation's first resident repertory theatrical company chose Baltimore as a home. In the year of Cornwallis's surrender at Yorktown, 1781, the musician Thomas Wall and the actor Adam Lindsey formed the Maryland Company of Comedians. Wall and Lindsay chose George James L'Argeau as their company musician. An itinerant professional who had been musically active in Annapolis before the Revolution, L'Argeau around this time opened a dancing school and served as organist at a Baltimore church. The Maryland Company of Comedians offered programs much like those presented before the war, including comic operas, afterpieces, entr'acte music, and presentational dance. The company appeared at Baltimore's "Old Theatre," a stone house at the present-day intersection of East and East Baltimore Streets with a small pit area and only ten box seats. L'Argeau accompanied and entertained on harpsichord, violin, and musical glasses, while Wall acted and played guitar and mandolin. In 1782 the company enacted "Articles to be strictly enforced by the Managers and Performers belonging to the Maryland Company of Comedians." It comprised a daily time-table for stage and music rehearsals and a set of rules that included a fifty-shilling fine for showing up drunk for a performance. The 1782 season included eighteen performances of five different operas. Four years later the company disbanded, having played mostly in Balti-more but touring as far away as Charleston.[11]

Wall and Lindsay's failure to establish a permanent, healthy theater in Baltimore probably reflected the city's small size and difficult economic times during the 1780s. The older, larger city of Philadelphia had come to embrace and support theater, dance, and concert music despite Quaker opposition. Over time the City of Brotherly Love drew off much of Maryland's raw musical talent, including the gifted Raynor Taylor, who felt mistreated as organist at St. Anne's Church in 1792 and promptly left. In 1793 the Philadelphia musician Alexander Reinagle and the actor Thomas Wignell simultaneously constructed two theaters that became long-lived institutions. One was the Chestnut Street Theater in Philadelphia, the other, a long-distance at-tempt to fill the void left by Lindsay and Wall, the Holliday Street Theatre in Baltimore.[12]

The full-time company of the Holliday Street The-atre, which served as a satellite of Philadelphia's two-thousand-seat Chestnut Street Theater, mounted more than four hundred Baltimore performances between 1794 and 1803. The two theaters hosted many of the same productions in turn, though Baltimore's was open only a few months of the year. Successful Philadelphia-based composers and instrumentalists came to Bal-timore, including the English immigrant George Gillingham, a violinist who had been brought over as the Chestnut Street Theater's first concertmaster and conductor. He significantly improved orchestral stan-dards in both cities, and several of the twenty players in his orchestra tarried in Baltimore to ply their trade. For a time, Gillingham and his talented orchestra played extended seasons in Baltimore, occasionally performing at the popular outdoor socializing spot, Gray's Gardens, and also in Annapolis. In addition to the requisite songs, marches, and dances within the show, theater or-

chestras typically played a half-hour before curtain and between acts. Audiences clamored for patriotic tunes and favorite songs of the day, while orchestra members preferred concertos and operatic overtures, even sym-phonic movements by Haydn and Stamitz, as well as their own compositions. Described in 1796 as "a neat little playhouse, consisting of a pit capable of contain-ing about 300 persons and two rows of boxes, but no gallery," the two-story Holliday Street Theatre saw a major renovation and enlargement in 1813.[13]

Alexander Reinagle, a cofounder of the Holliday Street Theatre, dominated Baltimore theater music at the turn of the nineteenth century. Born in England in 1756, this pianist-conductor-composer performed extensively in London and befriended J. C. Bach there. In 1786 Reinagle arrived in Philadelphia, where he established himself as one of the country's leading musi-cians. He managed Philadelphia concerts from the late 1780s into the 1790s, and he established a superlative reputation by composing and publishing piano sonatas, string quartets, songs, and also the first four-hand piano music composed in America. In addition to manage-ment duties at the new theaters in Philadelphia and Baltimore, he had the honor of teaching George Wash-ington's step-granddaughter Nelly Custis when the president and his family lived in Philadelphia. In 1803 Reinagle relocated to Maryland to manage the Holliday Street Theatre, soon thereafter marrying Anna Duport, daughter of the dance master Pierre Landrin Duport. Reinagle's duties in Baltimore included arranging, conducting, and composing overtures and incidental music to accompany dances and songs within dramas. His patriotic tunes, as well as those composed for local interest, were widely published.[14]

The Holliday Street Theatre hosted visiting specialty acts in addition to the brief seasons mounted by its own stock company and its parent Philadelphia company. French dramatic groups appeared at various times, as did circuses and individuals like William Priest, then touring America playing a seemingly impossible com-bination of instruments at the same time. Audiences sought sheer spectacle, visual and aural, and for gen-erations the Holliday Street Theatre was the primary

"The Maryland Hornpipe," by Alexander Reinagle, from *Mr. Francis's Ball Room Assistant . . .*, by William Francis (Philadelphia, 1801), 11–12. Published along with other pieces of local interest, "The Maryland Hornpipe" appeared in a series of dance books by Francis, who served as the ballet master to theaters in Philadelphia and Baltimore. Reinagle also wrote marches for Jefferson and Madison, patriotic songs like "America, Commerce, and Freedom" (1794) and "The First Baltimore Hussars," which appeared in 1807 with lyrics by John H. Pratt. Reinagle was an immigrant composer of immense talent and skill whose tightly crafted piano sonatas, which he performed in Baltimore as early as 1791, proved exceptionally advanced, beyond the reach of most players. Indeed, audience demand for easier music hampered formal "classical" composing on the part of Maryland musicians in the new republic. Lester S. Levy Collection of Sheet Music, Sheridan Libraries, Johns Hopkins University, box 3, item 77.

place to find it. They wanted to be thrilled, entertained, humored, romanced, and emotionally stimulated—subtlety and reflection were not profitable ingredients. Johann Maelzel, the European who patented the metronome, demonstrated his puppet trumpet player and left Baltimore with some hefty profits; less convincing was "Maelzel's Chess-Player," which Edgar Allan Poe publicly debunked in the *Southern Literary Messenger* in April 1836. In addition to exotic acts, audiences enjoyed melodramatic plays with simple, repeatable songs and lyrics that stressed feelings and situations with which the common person could identify. A little emotional exaggeration went over well too. Within the plays and operas, good music helped fill the house and determine economic life or death. Managers grew particularly sensitive to audience shouts for interspersed popular and patriotic songs like "Hail, Columbia!" and "Yankee Doodle." Local favorite singers like Mrs. Oldmixon would risk continued employment, not to mention becoming a target for fruit and other projectiles, if she failed to comply.

The Holliday Street Theatre served as a base for a few individual performers, one of them John Durang, who was born in Lancaster, Pennsylvania, and first performed in Baltimore in 1787, at the age of 19. A self-taught stage dancer, he later studied with Alexander Roussel and collaborated with another dance master, William Francis, in Baltimore and Philadelphia. Durang excelled in pantomime and horsemanship. He also sang, played the fiddle, choreographed, and painted scenery. He purportedly could dance and play panpipes or the German flute simultaneously. His specialty was dancing the hornpipe, frequently doing the popular "Durang's Hornpipe" to a tune a friend had composed for him in his youth. He occasionally danced at the Peale Museum, Bryden's Fountain Inn, and Baltimore's Layman's Gardens, as well as in Annapolis and on the Eastern Shore. During each summer from 1806 through 1816, Durang assembled his own family company—incorporating his wife and sons Ferdinand and Charles—and performed in Frederick and Hagerstown as well as towns in south-central Pennsylvania. Locals once sabotaged his wagon so that he had to stay in town longer and perform more. In these areas heavily populated by Germans, Durang adapted plays and songs to that language, and for country folk Durang offered a peek at city-style entertainment of the time. His company performed scaled-down productions of English operas like *The Poor Soldier* (London, 1783), as well as comic and tragic plays, and also offered acrobatics and presentational dancing.[15]

Unfortunately, Baltimore could not sustain its burst of musical activity beyond the first decade of the nineteenth century. The threat of war with Britain slowed an already stagnant economy, and recurring epidemics of yellow fever, beginning in the 1790s, closed the theater during the summer. Irregular productions and unpredictable demand could not support the cost of a live orchestra. Reinagle himself—directing and arranging the music, playing variously at the piano, violin, 'cello, trumpet, or flute—found himself painting scenery and performing other menial tasks as well. Shortly after his death in 1809, the theater in Baltimore needed to be sold in order to pay off debts owed by Reinagle and Thomas Wignell, who had died in 1802. Falling further into decay, the Holliday Street Theatre came under the management of William Warren and William Wood, who in 1813 completely rebuilt it, installed gas lighting, and rejuvenated activity to some extent. John Pendleton Kennedy, a Virginia-born lawyer who traveled in high social circles, wrote that the theater "had something of the splendor of a great barn, weatherboarded, milk white, with many windows, and looked with a hospitable, patronizing, tragicomic greeting down upon the street."[16] Yet just one company of actors served both Philadelphia and Baltimore stages, and seasons were quite short—three shows a week for only a few weeks a year.

Dancing

Maryland's upper and middle classes, especially urbanites, enjoyed a wide variety of social entertainments at theaters and commercial dance halls in the late eighteenth and early nineteenth centuries. Whether in Easton, Georgetown, or Baltimore, the fashions of dance and dance music evolved considerably. In the Federal period, social dance still drew heavily on colonial practice, and one could purchase dance-music collections such as *Mr. Francis's Ball Room Assistant*, issued from 1798 to 1804, "a collection of the most admired, cotillions and country dances with their proper figures annexed. Including a variety of marches, minutes [*sic*], reels, gavots, hornpipes, &c. The music composed and selected and the whole arranged for the piano forte by Mr. Reinagle."[17]

The English-born William Francis served as ballet master of the theaters in Philadelphia and Baltimore beginning in 1794. He taught, directed, acted, choreographed, and danced professionally at the Holliday Street Theatre for the next thirty-two years. Beyond the theater, Francis was quite active at Baltimore's assembly rooms for dancing. A group known as the Baltimore Assembly, which held dances elsewhere as early as 1787, built this structure in 1796. Designed by Colonel Nicholas Rogers and built by subscription at the corner of Fayette and Holliday Streets, the structure hosted fortnightly dances. Baltimoreans considered it on a par with the best dancing rooms in Europe.[18] Yet, through his long career Francis witnessed a continuing decline in organized dance as a specifically upper-class activity. The middle class, so intrusive, was seeking gentility as well.

Among the colorful dance masters of early Maryland, Baltimore's Pierre Landrin Duport played a significant role by introducing ballet to the new state. Active between 1783 and 1841, Duport was also a musician and composer who played on the public's demand for patriotic music during the War of 1812.[19] While early on he helped prolong interest in French minuets and gavottes, later he fueled the fad for formal classical ballet, as popularized on the Maryland stage in 1791 by

Alexandre Placide's traveling troupe. Audiences appreciated the sheer beauty and control exhibited by such visiting ballet stars as Thomas Cooper in 1804 and Fanny Elssler, who visited Baltimore first in 1832. Elssler swept the nation as a star who presented exotic and enticing character dances; her Baltimore fans reportedly got so carried away that they unhooked her horses and hand-carried her carriage out of town.

By the 1820s the urban middle classes had truly become a serious market force in the field of dance. The exclusive, upper-class minuet had gone out of fashion for good by this time, replaced by the simpler and considerably less subtle waltz. The waltz carried no overtones of elitism, while the cotillion became simpler over time and thus within reach of participants with little training. The wealthy also danced waltzes and cotillions, but in nicer settings and to more polished dance bands. William Frick, a long-tenured judge on Maryland's supreme court, composed his "Baltimore Waltz" of 1822 for just such a setting. Able to skirt older barriers regarding skill and social acceptance, middle-class urbanites gathered by the hundreds in large, commercial dance halls where the old-school dance masters no longer ruled. The newer dances represented a variety of national, ethnic, and religious traditions by midcentury. Polish immigrants brought their polkas, mazurkas, and other round dances to social gatherings. Likewise, Russians danced to the sounds of balalaikas. Sheet-music publishers cashed in on the growing popularity of these exotic dances among the people at large. The music for John Hill Hewitt's "Magnolia Polka" (Baltimore: George Willig Jr., 1851) included a notice on the title page that it was "danced by the pupils of Mr. Cadel's Academy."

Marylanders danced in both private and public settings. Molly Tilghman, relatively isolated in Chestertown during the 1790s, wrote of dancing at home with just a few friends. In 1796, William Faris, as part of the festivities surrounding his daughter Nancy's marriage in Annapolis, "spent the Evening [and] Genl. Davidson Plaid the fiddel and they Danced." At a private party in Baltimore in 1825 a visiting German duke noted the quality of the hired dance band and that "the ladies

sung well." Julia Latrobe, daughter of the architect Benjamin Henry Latrobe, preserved her dance instructions in a personal notebook.[20]

On some special occasions, such as Benjamin I. Cohen's fancy dress ball (a private masquerade party) in 1837, professional musicians were hired to play. Guests including Brantz Mayer, John Pendleton Kennedy, Mrs. Richard Caton, Mr. and Mrs. Robert Gilmor, Severn Teackle Wallis, John H. B. Latrobe, and Madame Jerome Bonaparte (Betsy Patterson Bonaparte) danced to the music of Mr. Murray and his band. The host, an amateur violinist, masqueraded as a fiddler in his hired orchestra.[21] The great demand for dance-band musicians helped stimulate music of other sorts also.

Baltimore sported large, commercial dance halls with hired professional bands and low admission prices. Dance halls also sprouted up in other cities around the state, where bands ranged from competitive professional ones to those filled out by local amateurs. After Francis Johnson's successful Philadelphia band played in Baltimore, band instrumentation became flashy and full of flourishes. Johnson's newfangled keyed bugle, brighter horns, and other military instruments replaced the stringed instruments of dance bands of the previous era. Dancing and dance music, like other aspects of popular music in early nineteenth-century Maryland, evolved to meet the needs of a middle class growing in size, economic impact, and ethnic diversity.

Nineteenth-century dance-tune titles consequently reflected middle-class life. The "Fireman's Grand March and Gallope: (performed at the Fireman's Grand Fancy Ball, 3d March, 1835, composed & respectfully dedicated to the Baltimore United Fire Department) by John H. Hewitt" is a good example. The "Crow Quadrilles," of 1837, cashed in on early public interest in solo blackface performances even before the organized minstrel show evolved as a genre. Some dances took on place names, such as "The Annapolis Galoppade, Composed & Respectfully Dedicated to the Ladies of Annapolis, Maryland Composed by Julius E. Muller" (Baltimore: Sam'l Carusi, 1841).

As the nineteenth century unfolded, distinctions between urban and rural life deepened, especially among the less wealthy. Maryland rural culture changed little over the decades. People in the country continued to enjoy singing and dancing at barn raisings, country weddings, husking parties, and quilting bees. Performed by single fiddlers or small string-based ensembles, traditional dance tunes as well as newly composed melodies in that style lived on as homemade entertainment. Tunes like "Soldier's Joy" and "Flowers of Edinburgh" enjoyed popularity in contradancing for generations. Rural dance music belonged to a mostly unwritten tradition, although in 1839 the Baltimore publisher George Willig Jr. issued America's first published collection of rural dance tunes, entitled *Virginia Reels, Selected and Arranged for the Piano Forte by G. P. Knauf.* This important publication codified the oral and aural traditions of the time, thus preserving not just the names of the tunes in use then but their melodic contours as well.[22] For rural fiddlers, playing these tunes over and over at dances made it comparatively easy for young fiddlers to learn the old-timers' music by ear, without the benefit of musical notation. That Willig perceived an urban market for these tunes underscores the importance of dance gatherings for socializing, courtship, ethnic solidarity, and community cohesion in the countryside.

Effusion: Societies of Gentlemen

"Baltimore," declared the nineteenth-century musician and memoirist John Hill Hewitt, "has always extended encouragement to music. Her concerts have been well patronized and her teachers well sustained."[23] History supports this view. For one thing, music-making offered an excellent pretext for socializing, as was apparent in clubs like Baltimore's Anacreontic Society, which local gentlemen founded in 1820. They named it for the licentious ancient Greek poet Anacreon and doubtless after the original Anacreontic Society in London, formed in the mid-1760s. These English gentlemen contrived and published their theme song, "To Anacreon in Heaven," to which Francis Scott Key would set his famous lyrics. The later Anacreontic Society of Baltimore originated when a few amateur musicians met at the home of the publisher Edward J. Coale. For a

time the group met in private homes, such as that of the founder and lead musician, Arthur Clifton. They later met and performed at Barnum's City Hotel. Some gatherings grew quite large, with ladies attending as guests. Clifton kept charge of the society's music books and served for a time as musical conductor. Club meetings proved vastly popular, lively and fun; why the organization folded in 1826 is unclear.[24]

In its heyday the Anacreontic Society limited its membership to fifty-five, requiring annual dues of ten dollars for weekly meetings. Honorary members included the prominent city musician Christopher Meinecke, who regularly led singing from the piano, Henri-Noël Gilles and John Nenninger, who shared musical duties at the Baltimore Cathedral, and the composer and publisher John Cole. Visitors and guests, including women, came from as far away as Spain, Mexico, and England. Charles Carroll of Carrollton attended at least one meeting as a guest, as did John Pendleton Kennedy, who in 1819 wrote that in Baltimore "music is portrayed by those who have the least *ear* and the most *money* (which is another name for discord)."[25] Kennedy mocked the society because it focused on singing music for fun, just simple songs for light entertainment rather than deeper music for moral edification or respectful worship. A list of sixty-eight songs from the society's first season includes "Drink to Me Only" and "Three Blind Mice." Society members sang glees (songs with choruses sung by the society), solos, and duets and trios in German and Italian, as well as catches of the period. Robert Gilmor, one of the city's wealthiest merchants, was a member who referred to club meetings with affection. Of a meeting in 1827, Gilmor wrote in his diary, "We had some delightful music from Meinecke at the piano, Nenninger on the violin, Gilles on the Oboe, and charming glees, catches and single songs from the singing members of the Club. At 11 o'clock Barnum gave us a splendid supper." A couple of months later, Gilmor wrote: "The ladies of the family went in the evening to hear Mr. Smith play on the grand harmonicon, an instrument of his own invention. I was too unwell to accompany them."[26] In addition to Smith, a French ballet troupe performed at a meeting in 1822.

The Baltimore publisher George Willig Jr. issued various songs in honor of the Baltimore Anacreontic Society, including texts by G. W. Reeve and John Pattison, Esq. Other club songs featured music borrowed from Beethoven, and a Mr. Nichols was credited as prime vocalist in some such publications.[27]

Soon after the demise of Baltimore's Anacreontic Society, the Baltimore Glee Club attracted its own prominent city musicians. Among them were John Hill Hewitt and Henry Dielman (also spelled Diehlman), an outstanding violinist, pianist, organist, flutist, and composer and reputedly popular with the ladies. Dielman arrived in Baltimore in 1830 to lead the Holliday Street Theatre orchestra. Born in Germany in 1811, Dielman received the first doctorate in music granted in the United States. He later directed music in various Baltimore churches, and for some forty years after 1843 he taught music and played the organ at Mount St. Mary's College in Emmittsburg, Maryland.[28]

Some of Maryland's leading antebellum musicians belonged to the Free and Accepted Masons, whose member formed societies in Maryland cities large and small. John Cole and Christopher Meinecke composed works for their fraternity and led performances at special Masonic events. As they had done in the colonial period, Masons supported theater, musical processions, dances, and songs. They gathered to march in grand processions on state occasions, notably during the Marquis de Lafayette's visit to Baltimore in 1824, as well as twenty years earlier, on the Fourth of July, when the *Baltimore American & Commercial Advertiser* published their invitation to meet before the grand city parade that day. Masons formed their own bands and published their own music. *The Maryland Ahiman Rezon, of Free & Accepted Masons*, running some 272 pages, was published in Baltimore in 1797 and contained many Masonic songs, such as "Let Masons be Merry each Night when they Meet."

Many other organizations enjoyed secular music-making. Most of them sponsored formal concerts of works by local composers. Locally published sheet music names such groups; for example, the sheet music for "Vive La Compagnie" (Baltimore: Benteen, ca.

1840) included the description, "Solo and Chorus as sung by the Maryland Cadet's Glee Club composed and arranged for the piano forte." Other musically active groups in Baltimore included the Robert Burns Society, the Delphian Society, the St. George's Society, the Hibernian Society, and the Dorcas Society. Group singing enlivened gatherings ranging from elite hunt clubs to temperance societies.

Musical Entrepreneurship

Maryland's first full-scale music-publishing operation began business in 1794, when Thomas Carr and his father, Joseph, formed a branch of the business established by Benjamin Carr a year earlier in Philadelphia. The Carr family assured Baltimore a competitive place in the rapidly developing music-publishing business. The Carrs supplied teaching materials, music for church organists and choirs, printed dance music, and, most importantly, parlor music for use by amateurs. They also sold instruments, such as harpsichords, barrel organs, pianofortes, and guitars. The Carr family's city-based businesses depended heavily upon the success of local theaters, since after hearing songs in the theaters, audiences demanded sheet-music copies of them.[29]

Joseph Carr ran the Baltimore shop until his death in 1819, after which his son Thomas carried on. Thomas had served as organist at Christ Church in Baltimore from 1798 to 1811, despite Bishop John Carroll's view of him as "fiery" and "ungovernable." For nearly thirty years the Carrs published, imported, and sold contemporary European music in Baltimore—Mozart piano variations, arias from English operas, and works by Handel, Rossini, and Clementi. The firm also issued American dances, popular ballads, sacred music, and a tremendous number of American patriotic pieces. Many of these appeared in arrangements for voice and keyboard, though some had extra parts for flute, guitar, or violin—a practice carried over from the colonial period. The Carr's Baltimore branch issued the nation's first music magazine to survive more than a year, *Benjamin Carr's Musical Journal for the Piano Forte*, which appeared from 1800 to 1804. The family placed Baltimore at the forefront of publishing in the new republic,

Sheet music for "Bee'swings & Fish, A Humourous Glee in Three Parts," lyrics by John Hill Hewitt, music by Henry Dielman (Baltimore: Geo. Willig Jr., n.d.). Hewitt, who was active in so many aspects of the city's musical life, combined forces with Dielman to compose this curious song at a meeting of the Baltimore Glee Club. The club organized around 1830 and never grew as large as the Anacreontic Society. The title of this glee honored Frederick Reglin, whose Baltimore oyster house served as a meeting place for the glee club. "Beeswings" was the nickname for a port or other wine in which small shiny flakes of tartar float to the surface, resembling insect appendages. Reglin apparently sang professionally around Baltimore, doing benefit concerts and working regularly at St. Martin's Church. Hewitt, *Shadows on the Wall*, 78–79. Lester S. Levy Collection, Sheridan Libraries, Johns Hopkins University, box 46, item 31.

issuing much of Maryland's earliest music, including, in 1796, the first piano instruction book printed in America. Francis Linley, a blind English organist who spent three years in Baltimore, compiled a volume of keyboard exercises and sonatas that he entitled *A New Assistant for the Piano-forte or Harpsichord containing the necessary rudiments for beginners with twelve airs*. The title page of this 1796 imprint noted that the music cost $1.50 and could be purchased in "Baltimore, printed and sold by J. Carr at his music store Market street and by B. Carr at his musical Repositorys Market Street Philadelphia & William Street New York."[30]

Published music addressing Maryland's provincial heroes and local institutions of course held great appeal. Francis Scott Key's choice of a popular tune for

his lyrics "The Defence of Fort M'Henry" reflected a common practice in eighteenth- and early nineteenth-century America. His dramatic words favorably fit the intended tune, and the combination truly resonated with the inflated patriotism of Baltimore and the country after militia forces turned back a British land assault on Baltimore and weathered the fierce naval attack on Fort McHenry on September 13–14, 1814. Otherwise this song would have fallen into the oblivion that befell so many briefly popular songs. While drafting his lyrics, Key had in mind the Anacreontic Society's original club song, "To Anacreon in Heaven."[31] Key's genius lay in coupling a very popular tune with extraordinarily apt lyrics and having the work sung in public while Baltimoreans were still giddy about their narrow escape.

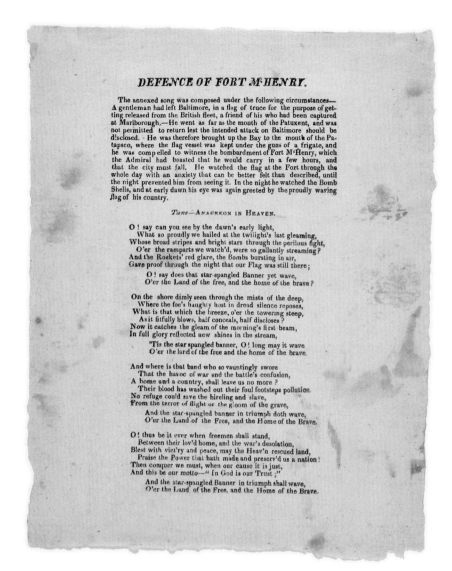

DEFENCE OF FORT M·HENRY.

The annexed song was composed under the following circumstances—
A gentleman had left Baltimore, in a flag of truce for the purpose of getting released from the British fleet, a friend of his who had been captured
at Marlborough.—He went as far as the mouth of the Patuxent, and was
not permitted to return lest the intended attack on Baltimore should be
disclosed. He was therefore brought up the Bay to the mouth of the Patapsco, where the flag vessel was kept under the guns of a frigate, and
he was compelled to witness the bombardment of Fort M'Henry, which
the Admiral had boasted that he would carry in a few hours, and
that the city must fall. He watched the flag at the Fort through the
whole day with an anxiety that can be better felt than described, until
the night prevented him from seeing it. In the night he watched the Bomb
Shells, and at early dawn his eye was again greeted by the proudly waving
flag of his country.

Tune—Anacreon in Heaven.

O ! say can you see by the dawn's early light,
    What so proudly we hailed at the twilight's last gleaming,
Whose broad stripes and bright stars through the perilous fight,
    O'er the ramparts we watch'd, were so gallantly streaming?
And the Rockets' red glare, the Bombs bursting in air,
Gave proof through the night that our Flag was still there;
    O ! say does that star-spangled Banner yet wave,
    O'er the Land of the free, and the home of the brave?

On the shore dimly seen through the mists of the deep,
    Where the foe's haughty host in dread silence reposes,
What is that which the breeze, o'er the towering steep,
    As it fitfully blows, half conceals, half discloses ?
Now it catches the gleam of the morning's first beam,
In full glory reflected now shines in the stream,
    'Tis the star spangled banner, O ! long may it wave
    O'er the land of the free and the home of the brave.

And where is that band who so vauntingly swore
    That the havoc of war and the battle's confusion,
A home and a country, shall leave us no more ?
    Their blood has washed out their foul footsteps pollution.
No refuge could save the hireling and slave,
From the terror of flight or the gloom of the grave,
    And the star-spangled banner in triumph doth wave,
    O'er the Land of the Free, and the Home of the Brave.

O ! thus be it ever when freemen shall stand,
    Between their lov'd home, and the war's desolation,
Blest with vict'ry and peace, may the Heav'n rescued land,
    Praise the Power that hath made and preserv'd us a nation!
Then conquer we must, when our cause it is just,
And this be our motto—" In God is our Trust ;"
    And the star-spangled Banner in triumph shall wave,
    O'er the Land of the Free, and the Home of the Brave.

Defence of Fort M'Henry, the first printed version of "The Star-Spangled Banner," 1814. This first version of the song by Francis Scott Key emerged in broadside form on Saturday, September 17, 1814, the day after Key returned to Baltimore after witnessing the bombardment of Fort McHenry on September 13–14. His name did not appear in this first edition, but the second edition added, parenthetically, "Francis S. Key, Esq. of Georgetown, District of Columbia." Courtesy of the Maryland Historical Society.

Key's lyrics appeared almost immediately in broadsides, newspapers, and songsters. Within a month or two, the Baltimore publisher Thomas Carr issued the first sheet-music arrangement, and the title evolved into "The Star-Spangled Banner." The melody of "To Anacreon in Heaven" proved so catchy that by 1818 eighty-five other sets of lyrics had been set to it and published. A lawyer with an affinity for music, Key also wrote several hymns and a setting of the Lord's Prayer for St. John's Episcopal Church, Georgetown.[32] The words to our national anthem came from the pen of a Marylander in Maryland, and the song's first public performances and first publication occurred in Baltimore. Moreover, the Maryland chapter of the US Daughters of 1812 more

than a hundred years after the fact petitioned their Maryland congressman, John Charles Linthicum, to submit the legislation that would eventually become law and deem "The Star-Spangled Banner" the national anthem. Perhaps this is the state's single most notable contribution to American music.

Along with this outpouring of local compositions and music publishing, Maryland craftsmen, largely German immigrants in Baltimore, capably answered the rising demand for pianos. Though pianos were initially quite expensive, their prices gradually fell due to competition and plentiful labor; simultaneously, consumer buying power rose as the nineteenth century progressed. Baltimore-made pianos graced parlors in Maryland and also to the south and west, the city's prime advantage over makers to the north being its proximity to these markets. Piano makers offered varying styles, options, and price ranges to satisfy a range of consumers with discretionary income.

The first Maryland-made piano probably emerged from the shop of John Harper in 1802, although one by James Stewart may have preceded it by a couple of years.[33] Until the financial downturn known as the Panic of 1819, more than a dozen small shops in Baltimore produced pianos, notably the brothers Adam and James Stewart, whose instruments in 1812 started at $175. For a time in 1814, Rembrandt Peale showed off a Stewart piano at his famous museum near the Holliday Street Theatre. The Stewarts went out of business in 1819 or 1820.[34]

Parlor Music: Songs of Sentiment and More

In the fledgling United States, the piano replaced the harpsichord as a musical symbol of upper-class gentility. By the middle of the nineteenth century pianos decorated the parlors of the upper middle class as well as the rich. Baltimore manufacturers designed and priced pianos to meet the demands of both these groups. For the same reason, inexpensive sheet-music arrangements of songs and instrumental pieces for piano appeared in increasing quantity. While prices for pianos, piano music, and private instruction fell over time, nineteenth-century American popular music grew to reflect a casual, recreational approach to music-making. Antebellum publishers consciously churned out undemanding music for an increasingly middle-class market. Performing popular music at home became a prime amusement in everyday life. All these changes made it easier for women, who dominated the domestic household, to carry on the colonial drawing-room music tradition. A shift occurred during the first half of the nineteenth century that left women generally in charge of music-making in the home.

Mary Dorsey's beautiful hand-copied music book survives as an excellent example of music for home use by a woman. Dorsey failed to date her copybook, but the contents strongly suggest that she began compiling it in 1799 or 1800. Many of her thirty-eight pieces are patriotic in nature, such as the Federalist songs "Adams and Liberty," "The New Yankee Doodle," and "The Federal Constitution and Liberty for Ever," as well as the conciliatory "Hail, Columbia!"[35] Dorsey also included fairly difficult instrumental keyboard solos and duets by Ignaz Pleyel, Valentino Nicolai, and Samuel Arnold. Virtually all of the pieces she copied could have been purchased at the time at Carr's music store in Baltimore, and many later appeared in *The Baltimore Musical Miscellany or Columbian Songster*.[36] She must have played a harpsichord rather than a piano, since she left out the dynamic markings found in many of these early piano publications. Such a refined, polite collection of music included some operatic selections and sacred songs as well. The contents and the worn page corners suggest that Mary Dorsey, like her ancestors in pre-Revolutionary Anne Arundel County, took her music seriously.

Other wealthy Maryland women partook in keyboard music and dance as socially significant activities. Sophie Gough took her piano with her from Perry Hall to Mt. Clare, outside Baltimore, when, in 1787, at the age of 15, she married James Carroll. In 1806 Rosalie Stier Calvert, the mistress of Riversdale plantation in Prince George's County, wrote her niece back in Belgium, "I rarely play [the harpsichord] anymore. I have so many other occupations, but even more because there is no one in my circle who is musical. Still, here as there, music is an indispensable talent for a young lady. Dancing is even more essential. We start children dancing here at age five."[37] Along with this letter, she sent some popular music, yet two years later she would lament, "I never hear music—not even the violin our old servant plays."[38] The daughters of Charles Carroll of Carrollton entertained guests upon a variety of instruments, including harp, guitar, harpsichord, and piano. The Carroll family music library grew considerably, accumulating an impressive mixture of lessons and sonatas, marches, variation sets, and arrangements of orchestral compositions, as well as operatic airs and popular songs. Items like William Shield's comic operas *Rosina* (London, 1782) and *The Poor Soldier* remained in

"Tune of Alknomook" and the first part of "A Sonata by Nicolai," from Mary Dorsey's manuscript copybook, ca. 1800. The rise of music publishing undermined the hand-copying of music. Mary Dorsey copied this music from a song published in both New York and Boston entitled "Alknomook (The Death Song of the Cherokee Indian)." "Alknomook" is the only surviving song from the earliest opera composed in America with an Indian theme, Tammany; or the Indian Chief (1794). James Hewitt, father of John Hill Hewitt, composed the music for this opera, and the libretto was by Anna Julia Hatton. While Dorsey copied the musical notation exactly, the lyrics she inserted appear in Nightengale of Liberty: or Delights of Harmony. A Choice Collection of Patriotic, Masonic, & Entertaining Songs (New York: John Harrison, 1797), 24–25. She gave credit for the text to "a Gentleman of Col. McPherson's Blues," a Frederick militia regiment famous for its band. Collection of the Maryland State Archives, MSA SC 5879.

vogue from the 1780s into the 1830s. When visiting the Carroll family at their Annapolis home in 1811, David Bailie Warden fully enjoyed his evening, being "much entertained by Conversation, and Charming little airs, which the youngest [Miss Carroll] sung, and played on the Piano." On the same visit Warden attended a dinner honoring William Pinkney at which the governor, Edward Lloyd V, sang "some fine songs, and presided with much dignity."[39] A visitor from abroad at this time summarized the effect of this feminine attention to music.

"There is much vivacity," he testified, in the appearance and language of the women of Baltimore; "they seem very fond of music and have the credit of singing and playing well; their society is most pleasant."[40]

Although women excelled in domestic music-making, they rarely entered the male-dominated world of publishing and composing. A Madame LePelletier broke the norm by compiling some European piano music along with a few of her own compositions. Her periodic Journal of Music, with its lovely pages engraved

Published by J. COLE & SON, Baltimore.

An idealized image of two sisters playing piano duets adorned the title page of "The Sisters. A Selection of Popular & Esteemed Airs Arranged as Duets for Two Performers on the Piano Forte by Various Authors," a collection of several pieces of music that John Cole published in Baltimore in 1828. Maryland had a long history of images of the idealized woman seated at a keyboard. A close look at the keywell of the piano in this etching reveals that the sisters are playing a Chickering piano from Boston rather than a Baltimore-built Knabe or Stieff. Archives of the Peabody Institute of the Johns Hopkins University.

in Philadelphia yet published under her own name in Baltimore, lasted only from 1810 to 1811. She was perhaps the nation's first female publisher, as well as Maryland's first female composer. It would be nearly a century before the American performer and composer Amy Beach was accepted into the man's world of professional music, and even then her acceptance was partial and qualified.

By the 1830s, most popular songs could be characterized as comic or sentimental. Both types resounded in theaters and concert halls, where performers exaggerated the humorous and the emotional. Elite-level drawing-room music once had featured refined lyrics, often thick with allusion and simile; composers of popular parlor music now employed unabashedly simple texts. Lyrics increasingly presented flatly sentimental situations, many of which seem trite to the modern ear. The direct language of parlor song lyrics expressed a newfound romantic ideal in music and poetry, an ideal that rubbed uncharitably against residual eighteenth-century balance and order. Nonetheless, the older concept of achieving gentility through the performing arts carried over into parlor practice. Popular music, in terms of both melody and lyric, not only became easier for the average person to play and sing but also became easier to understand. Music students displayed their skills at recitals and parlor gatherings.

Sheet Music and Civics Lessons

Parlor music inspired thousands of composers, arrangers, and publishers nationwide to churn out sentimental lyrics and sweet tunes on just about every subject imaginable. They invoked unrequited love and tragic death, incited patriotism by celebrating war heroes and battles won, marveled at inventions like the railroad and the telegraph, and drew attention to important public buildings and a host of exotic and unusual things. Publishers marketed the songs that star performers had sung and thus publicized. Money was to be made, and therefore hack composers scrambled to be the first to publish songs focused on political campaigns, great events, and visiting dignitaries. Such commercial competition also inspired a proliferation of artwork for sheet-music covers. Attractive illustrations boosted sales and, in the days before photography, gave people their first visual impression of many new and interesting things. First engraved, by the 1820s lithographed, and by the 1840s lithographed in color, sheet-music covers offer a valuable view into the temper of the times. Beyond the music and the lyrics, then, parlor song-sheet covers provide valuable historical evidence.[41]

Baltimore's composers and publishers contributed enormously to the output of sheet music. They simplified and reprinted arrangements of songs and dances by European composers such as Hook, Pleyel, Arnold,

Louisa Catherine Adams at the Harp, by Charles Bird King, ca. 1824. Louisa Catherine Johnson, whose father was born in Calvert County, in 1797 married John Quincy Adams, who won the hotly contested presidential election in 1825. Her fine, European upbringing included music lessons. An outspoken abolitionist and women's-rights advocate, Mrs. Adams at the White House enjoyed playing the piano from her own music albums. Elise K. Kirk, Music at the White House: A History of the American Spirit (Urbana: University of Illinois Press, 1986), 42, 45–48. Adams-Clement Collection, Smithsonian Institution.

Dibdin, and Shield, as well as Haydn, Mozart, and Beethoven. Huge collections of Scottish and Irish songs, such as *The Minstrel* and *The Harp of Erin* (both published in Baltimore in 1812) answered the public thirst for traditional Gaelic music as adapted by Robert Burns and Thomas Moore. Works like "Music, Love & Wine, Sung at the Anacreontic Society, Baltimore, arranged by Beethoven" (Cole, ca. 1824) referenced well-known composers' names. Continuing the trend, American publishers borrowed tunes and created new titles and lyrics, such as John Hill Hewitt's "Oh! Soon Return. Original Words Adapted to an Air of Mozart" (Baltimore: Geo. Willig Jr., 1829). Side by side with

Europeans, American composers like Benjamin Carr, Raynor Taylor, James Hewitt, and Alexander Reinagle wrote their own music in both popular and more serious styles. Such early hits included Carr's "The Little Sailor Boy" and James Hewitt's "The Wounded Hussar." Patriotic music by immigrant composers enjoyed especial popularity. Maryland composers and publishers participated in the national evolution of parlor music toward exoticism, as in Swiss airs, a "Celebrated Spanish Serenade," Greek dances, and even an "Indian Polka."

The self-appointed bard of Baltimore music in the period, John Hill Hewitt, provides a window into com-

"Le Désir," by Beethoven, guitar arrangement by Henri Noël Gilles. Gilles hand-copied this guitar arrangement while teaching in Baltimore. A French-born performer and songwriter, Gilles and his younger brother, Peter, settled in Baltimore. Henri played an active role on the local music scene from the early 1820s until his death in 1834. According to John Hill Hewitt, in his *Shadows on the Wall*, 68, Gilles was "the greatest hautboy [oboe] player of the times," and his brother was a very good cellist. Both "taught according to the Italian system of vocal music, then much in vogue, and were very popular with the upper classes of society." Besides being involved in the musical program at the Baltimore Cathedral, Gilles published many songs with guitar accompaniment, both individually and in his collection *The Vocal Cabinet* (Baltimore, ca. 1825). Among the most ambitious arrangers of music for the guitar at this time in the entire country, Gilles also issued an instruction book titled *Improved Method for Learning the Guitar, or Lyre* in 1827. He composed songs in French and Italian. Archives of the Peabody Institute of the Johns Hopkins University, rare books M1.A15G7.

posers' relationship to Maryland society and the importance of parlor song in nineteenth-century America. Son of James Hewitt, an influential publisher and composer active in both New York and Boston, the younger Hewitt (like Edgar Allan Poe) attended but dropped out of West Point. He then spent long segments of his varied and prolific life in Baltimore, arriving first in 1828 to edit the literary magazines *The Baltimore Minerva and Emerald*, *The Minerva and Saturday Post*, and the *Baltimore Saturday Visitor*. At one point he gave Poe a bad review and carried on a public dispute with him over a literary prize.[42]

Hewitt's first love was music. He composed, arranged, published, wrote lyrics of his own, and set those of others. He taught privately and sang publicly. For a time also captain of a local militia unit, Hewitt in 1837 founded a short-lived Baltimore Musical Institute, an optimistic name for a program he launched with just one other teacher. His considerable output, including works issued under the pseudonym Eugene Raymond, totaled some 176 compositions that appeared in Baltimore alone between 1828 and 1865. He enjoyed the support of major Baltimore publishers of the time. George Willig issued half of Hewitt's works; Benteen, about a quarter; and Miller & Beacham, Carusi, and others, the remainder. "The Minstrel's Return from War" (ca. 1829) won him wide attention early in his career. His autobiography, *Shadows on the Wall*, preserves valuable details about Baltimore's social and cultural life in the early to middle nineteenth century.

Hewitt—along with Christopher Meinecke, John Cole, Henri-Noël Gilles, and John B. Gauline—excelled in composing regional favorites. All but Hewitt being first-generation immigrants, eager to make an impression in their new country, they frequently dedicated works to prominent men, women, and organizations in Maryland and beyond—besides their students, to local Oddfellows, the Whig Ladies of the United States, or the Academy of the Visitation in Georgetown. Hewitt especially seemed to understand and hone the practice of employing flattering song dedications.[43]

Maryland composers also set to music the poetry of local talent, for example, the works of R. Horace Pratt, Esq., and John Pattison, Esq., who celebrated the laying of the foundation stone for the Masonic lodge in Hagerstown in 1822. Baltimore composers embraced national subjects, composing presidential marches and music to accompany boisterous political parades. They excelled at commemorating museum and lyceum openings, groundbreaking ceremonies, commencement exercises, and Independence Day celebrations. Few significant mid-nineteenth-century events, people, or places escaped being the inspiration for a march, a waltz, a quickstep, or the like. Many such works first found an audience as band music, then appeared in keyboard arrangement.

Some of the state's most prominent musicians directed, composed, and marketed music for militia bands. In 1798 Generals Smith and Swan composed "The Baltimore Volunteers, on the occasion of a grand review of the Baltimore City and County Volunteers." These militia units, as in earlier times, transcended their function of preparedness and played an important social role in public display and solidarity. During the War of 1812 John Cole played the clarinet and led a small ensemble of violin, Kent bugle, serpent, bassoon,

and bass drum. The group's quick marches were usually "The Girl I Left behind Me," "Marlbrook," "Road to Boston," and "Monymusk." "With these they made the militia boys tramp briskly through the streets, and never failed to gather a motley escort of ragged urchins and grinning negroes," Hewitt recalled.[44] Christopher Meinecke, who led Baltimore band concerts as early as 1809, composed military marches and dance tunes. Apparently involved with both the Baltimore Yaegers and the Maryland Fifth Regiment, Meinecke composed several works in honor of their heroes of the Battle of North Point and later armed conflicts. Mostly published in piano score, the title pages to such patriotic marches often carried credits like "as performed by the band of the 5th Regiment, MM[Maryland Militia]."[45] Meinecke also wrote pieces to celebrate Commodore Oliver Hazard Perry's 1813 victory on Lake Erie and General Andrew Jackson's triumph at New Orleans in January 1815. The grand visit of the Marquis de Lafayette in 1824 inspired a slew of musical works, including "Lafayette's Welcome" and "The Champion of Freedom, written by Miss Eliza L. Hening," which Meinecke arranged for piano. Meinecke also wrote "The Chivalrous Knight of France, with words by Col. W. H. Hamilton" and "General Lafayette's Grand March and Quickstep." Gilles, Clifton, and others also jumped on the Lafayette musical bandwagon, and few missed the opportunity to celebrate Baltimore's centennial celebrations just eight years later.

Bands of this era permeated civic life. Music at the funeral for the renowned Federalist Robert Goodloe Harper in January 1825 involved no fewer than three full bands. The groundbreaking for the Baltimore and Ohio Railroad on July 4, 1828, inspired several compositions. Baltimore's popular composer Arthur Clifton wrote "The Carrollton March" to honor Charles Carroll of Carrollton, who at the age of 90, the last living signer of the Declaration of Independence, presided at the climactic laying of the cornerstone during this huge public spectacle. Some five thousand people paraded, watched fireworks, heard numerous orations, and enjoyed a full public holiday with copious free liquor.

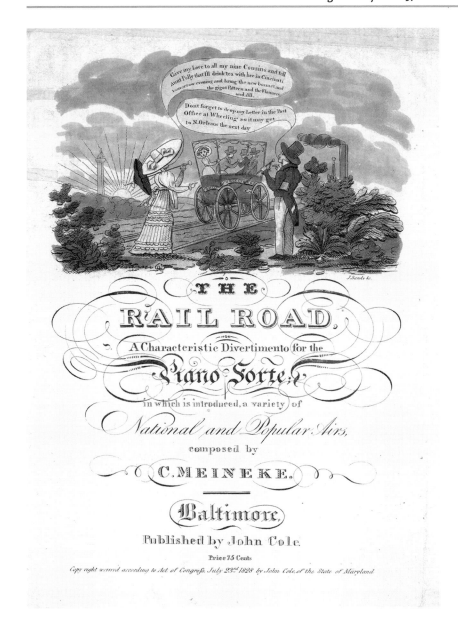

Sheet-music cover for "The Rail Road, A Characteristic Divertimento for the Piano Forte; in which is introduced a variety of National and Popular Airs," composed by Christopher Meinecke and published by John Cole, of Baltimore in 1828. This composition, like W. Broadbent's "Railroad Quickstep," marked the 1828 groundbreaking of the B&O Railroad. Many people's first images of early trains came from sheet-music covers such as Meinecke's "Rail Road March for the Fourth of July, Dedicated to the Directors of the Baltimore & Ohio Rail Road," which was really just a medley of "Yankee Doodle," "Hail, Columbia!," "The Star-Spangled Banner," "Polly Put the Kettle On," and other tunes. Lester S. Levy Collection of Sheet Music, Sheridan Libraries, Johns Hopkins University, box 59, item 9.

"The Carrollton March" survives as an arrangement for piano, although at the time audiences typically heard it conducted by the popular bandleaders George Walter and William Roundtree.[46] The *Baltimore American & Commercial Advertiser* of July 4, 1828, resorted to verse in reporting on the laying of the first stone for the B&O:

> See Roundtree with his band,
> Take an elevated Stand,
> And the Carrollton March re-echoes to the skies.
> We shall play it, whistle it, and sing it,
> We shall all play it here in Baltimore.

Among other verses printed that day was the following:

> O we're full of life, fun, and jollity,
> We're all crazy here in Baltimore.
> Here's a road to be made,
> With a pick and a spade,
> 'Tis to reach to Ohio for the benefit of trade.

Arthur Clifton's tremendous output included hymns, anthems, songs, duets, glees, and a vocal instruction book. He also taught vocal music, ran a music store, and served as organist at Baltimore's First Presbyterian Church for some fifteen years, until his death in 1832. The composer's involvement in Baltimore's Anacreontic Society resulted in several compositions dedicated to that group. Clifton also wrote a lyric song "The Maryland Line," which was used in a play called *The Railroad*. Such multifaceted involvements in city society supported Clifton and a handful of other professional musicians in Baltimore.[47] (Clifton's involvement in composing opera are discussed further below.)

Music to Work By

Hymns and camp-meeting songs helped sustain hope among enslaved African Americans. So did work songs. Frederick Douglass's recollections of slave life on the Lloyds' Wye River plantation made it abundantly clear that the lyrics of slave work songs often disguised tremendous pain and anger. White listeners mostly mistook such singing as an expression of happiness. Slaves sang while planting, tending, and packing tobacco; they sang using regular, chanteylike rhythms when rolling hogsheads of tobacco or loading heavy cargoes onto ships. African American women sang hymns and spirituals during long hours of toil. Whites who kept diaries and observed African Americans at work frequently referred to their singing; a young slave girl carrying water in Baltimore around 1830 was described as "singing in the soft rich voice peculiar to their race."[48] Rarely were work-related folk hymns or songs accompanied by instrumental music; everybody worked, and with both hands.

Under altogether different circumstances, music accompanied the toil of white workers and helped them find solace. From Easton peddlers' street cries to menhaden fishing songs of the Patuxent River, from Allegany miners' work songs to Ukrainian lullabies in Baltimore row houses, secular folk music of many sorts abounded in nineteenth-century Maryland. Music served important functions. It preserved a sense of heritage for ethnic minorities, eased the strain and tedium of countless laborers, and provided welcome diversion through ballad-sharing and informal dance. Maryland's varied people sang folk songs in city and country, in factories and taverns. Nineteenth-century diaries and letters occasionally mentioned the scenes that appear in sketches, drawings, and paintings. People played fiddles at barn dances and sang while husking corn, packing tobacco, and shucking oysters.

Folk practices reflected original regional settlement patterns well into the nineteenth century, when most Marylanders still lived in the countryside. English ballads survived among lower Eastern Shore watermen (as do certain old-English linguistic traits on Smith Island into the early twenty-first century). Scottish and Irish recreational dancing in Western Maryland retained much of the flavor of colonial times. Instruments like fiddles and banjos became associated with rural life at the same time that urban musical tastes became more sophisticated. Though referencing the same instrument, people differentiated between fiddle and violin well before the nineteenth century, associating fiddles with rustic, less refined uses, and dancing especially, and reserving the term *violin* for more formal circumstances.

Banjos—in whose manufacture Baltimore rose to prominence—became wildly popular in the 1800s. Whites first associated them with slave music, but by the 1820s a growing number of white musicians were playing the banjo, while mimicking and mocking slaves and slave life.[49] Folk instruments generally reflected country people's need for sturdiness, simple construction, portability, and low price.

Following its arrival on the East Coast in colonial times, the hammered dulcimer enjoyed popularity as an American folk instrument in the Great Lakes region and the central Appalachians, including Western Maryland. Men played it for dances, and women reportedly used it in church to accompany singing; dulcimers showed up at circuses as well. Most early dulcimers were home-built, although makers from New York State by midcentury were sending salesmen south with instruments and method books that featured patriotic melodies, dance tunes, and even opera airs. The Appalachian dulcimer developed on its own, south and west of Maryland. Folk instruments in the city of Baltimore, by contrast, reflected the broad cultural diversity of an immigrant-rich seaport. There were Italian mandolins,

67

85.   JUST NOW.

1. Sanc - to - fy   me,   sanc - to - fy   me,   Sanc - to -

- fy   me,   sanc - to - fy   me,   Sanc - to - fy   me,   just

now;   Just now;   just now;   Sancto - fy   me just now.

2 Good religion, good religion, etc.
3 Come to Jesus, come to Jesus, etc.

[This, which is now, in a somewhat different form, a Methodist hymn, was sung as given above, by the colored people of Ann Arundel Co., Md., twenty-five years ago.—W. A. H.]

Music for "Just Now," transcribed around 1842 in Anne Arundel County, later to be published in *Slave Songs of the United States* (1867), compiled and edited by William Francis Allen, Charles Pickard Ware, and Lucy McKim Garrisson. Along with a corn-shucking song and another religious song from Maryland, the volume included the earliest notated spirituals in America, collected in several southern states. Archives of the Peabody Institute of the Johns Hopkins University.

Russian balalaikas, and various traditional Old World instruments like zithers and hurdy-gurdies, instruments that would have puzzled Maryland's rural populace.

White laborers sang folk songs, work songs, and favorite hymns as they worked. The rigors of building railroads invited a brusque, chanteylike vocal music that differed greatly from the romanticized images of railroads and great factories adorning sheet-music covers. Accounts of Irish laborers singing ballads, drinking heavily, and dancing jigs after hours abound. Even hymns helped pass the hours. Work songs sung *a capella* emerged from the process of driving spikes, constructing bridges, and running steam locomotives, especially ballads of famous train wrecks or working-class heroes like John Henry. The transient nature of track-laying crews provided for dispersal of musical ideas and lyrics; it led to some standardization of these songs over time.

Immigrant Irish laborers also had a hand in digging Maryland's canals and running the longboats on them. Both the Patowmack Company canal (1785–1819) and the more successful Chesapeake & Ohio canal (begun 1828) required the grueling labor of thousands to construct and staff. Eventually men piloted eighty-foot longboats that hauled coal and other heavy goods between Cumberland and Alexandria, a four-day trip during which they often sang and drank whiskey to pass the hours. A song popularized by minstrel troupes explains how canal pilots passed their recreational hours:

De boatmen dance, de boatmen sing,
de boatmen up to ebery ting
An when de boatmen gets on shore
He spends his cash and works for more
Den dance de boatmen dance, dance boatmen dance
They dance all night till broad daylight
An go home wid de gals in de morning[50]

When in 1834 fights between rival canal-construction crews broke out and the governor called on state militia to intervene, an Irish fifer cunningly warned his camp of approaching authorities by playing telltale jigs on his tin whistle.[51]

Women in rural nineteenth-century America sang ballads while gardening, washing, cooking, sewing, and performing other domestic tasks. Chosen for diversion, such music ranged from old English ballads to nursery songs and simple ditties. Some lyrics focused on the dark side of life, venting anger and frustration over a life that held little hope for improvement. In contrast to the published parlor songs of the period championing commerce and freedom, for example, women's folk songs recounted the woes of the downtrodden as well as thinly veiled fantasies of revenge against the husbands who mistreated them. Many rural women spent countless hours with little or no adult companionship while their husbands were off hunting or working. The use of music to soothe one's sorrows and pass long hours is found the world over and indeed seems timeless.

While canals and railroads tied Maryland commercially to the North, the South, and the West, the Chesapeake Bay remained a busy water highway, connecting both shores and also connecting Maryland's bayside and riverside towns with those in Virginia. The Chesapeake also led to rich markets in the Caribbean, Latin America, and Europe—as well as the China trade.[52] Work music of the sea and of the Chesapeake Bay shared certain traits with that of the land, especially the variation in repertory according to social class. During the nineteenth century, upper-class officers enjoyed refined, romanticized sea songs aboard ship. "Sit by the Summer Sea, with lyrics by Mrs. Hemans and music by G. F. Cole," published in Baltimore in 1834, features the typically ornate tune and poetic lyrics that also satisfied elite amateur musicians on land. For the middle and upper classes, music about the sea offered romantic material for recreational music-making.

On the other hand, the mostly lower-class men who worked the water sang both during and after work hours, and distinct types of sea music evolved for each time, namely, chanteys and forecastle songs. The crew's place of rest and leisure aboard ship, the forecastle, or fo'c's'le, naturally led to the fo'c's'le song, or forebitter. Fo'c's'le songs were lively, rustic tunes with seafaring language that bluntly portrayed sailors' daily lives, fears, and fantasies about wealth and female companionship. Topical sea ballads understandably were long and varied, as sailors sought to speed the tedious hours in cramped quarters. They sang unaccompanied or perhaps backed by fiddle, penny whistle, or squeezebox (a concertina or button accordion). Sea battles and heroes like John Paul Jones, life at sea, storms and shipwrecks, even disguised female sailors and cannibalism, made these musical tales vivid and memorable. English broadsheets of forebitters circulated in the late eighteenth century. Eventually publishable versions appeared in the United States, one of them being *The Nautical Songster* (Baltimore, 1798). Small and inexpensive, sea songsters enjoyed great popularity during the War of 1812, including ballads of decisive military engagements like "Constitution and Guerriere," "The Battle of Plattsburgh," and "The Shannon & the Chesapeake."

The "Star-Spangled Banner" appeared quite frequently, first in *The National Songster* (Hagerstown, 1814). Songsters lacked musical notation, as their many sets of lyrics were to be sung to familiar tunes—such as "The Battle of Baltimore," intended for the melody "Yankee Doodle," the familiar chorus slightly altered:

> Yankee Doodle beat the drum,
> Yankee Doodle dandy,
> And if by day or night they come,
> They'll always find us handy.[53]

Few forebitters that directly relate to the Chesapeake Bay survive. Maryland's watermen used shallow-draft boats to drudge oysters, haul goods, or fish; only those on the larger punks or schooners worked in crews approaching the size of those on oceangoing vessels. Rarely would watermen spend nights or leisure hours on the water; instead, they lived on land with their families and worked by daylight in small groups. Only a few hauling songs and gentler menhaden chanteys survive, such as "Joanna and Rhodie," "Roseanna," and "See You when the Sun goes Down." The first of these seems to have descended from Afro-Caribbean sources, its calm, bluesy melody contrasting markedly with those of standard sea chanteys. These songs survive through oral traditions alone. African Americans who worked the water, many on oyster-dredging skipjacks, sang their land-based spirituals and camp-meeting songs, especially the Methodist ones.[54]

True sea chanteys, straightforward work songs that evolved aboard larger vessels on the open ocean, helped men in larger groups to coordinate strenuous labors. Chanteys had strong accented rhythms and simple melodies, and they varied according to the task being performed. Gradually, whole families of chanteys evolved to accompany walking the capstan to raise the anchor, making sail, and other burdensome tasks. Sailors on the Baltimore clippers of the 1840s and 1850s sang such internationally popular chanteys as "Jackie Tar," "Blow the Man Down," and "Leave Her, Jonny." Like Liverpool and other thriving seaports, Baltimore has its place in songs such as "The City of Baltimore" and "Bound for Baltimore," in which the singer boasts of his great skills

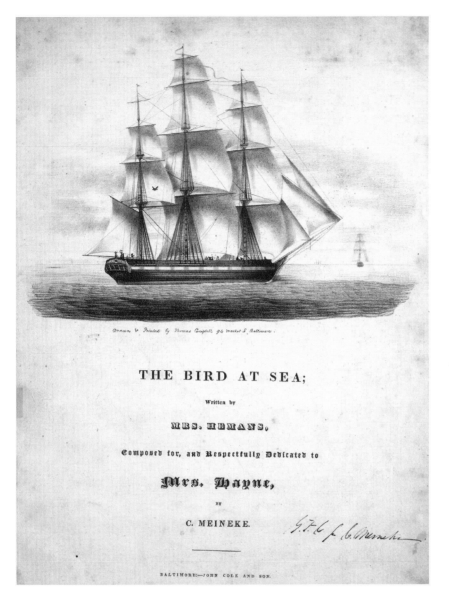

Cover for Christopher Meinecke's popular parlor song "The Bird at Sea," published by John Cole & Son, of Baltimore. There were four Baltimore editions from 1834 to 1836. Nineteenth-century parlor music often glorified life at sea, rarely drawing upon the songs and dance tunes that watermen and seagoing sailors actually used. The carefully composed melody and poetic lyrics of "The Bird at Sea" dealt only superficially with nineteenth-century seafaring. Mark Twain mentioned this tearjerker by name among other works appropriate for the genteel parlor in *Life on the Mississippi* (New York: Harper, 1917), 319. Lester S. Levy Collection of Sheet Music, Sheridan Libraries, Johns Hopkins University, box 181, item 36.

at creative kissing. Given that sailors from many nations plied the seas, chanteys had diverse sources, including the music of England, Ireland, Scotland, Holland, and beyond. Over time the words and melodies became fairly standardized.[55]

Chanteys generally employed a call-and-response structure, much like that of slave work songs. African Americans and Irishmen, both representing downtrodden yet innately musical cultures, had special talents for leading chanteys, which were mostly sung *a capella*. Chantey leaders improvised verses with creativity and humor, keeping the men motivated, if not distracted, from the hard work. Chanteys like "Run Right Round

to Cubay" served both to ease work at sea and to coordinate the heaving and hauling of cargo at docks on the Chesapeake Bay, largely done by African American stevedores. Chantey-singing truly eased the labors at sea during the heyday of nineteenth-century merchant sail, roughly 1815–60. The heartiest singing was perhaps heard on the homeward voyage.

Sailors in the navy had their own songs and instrumental music. The US Navy surgeon Jacques Gershom preserved some 450 dance tunes, marches, and other melodies for flageolet and German flute in a manuscript he copied in 1803 aboard the schooner *Nautilus*. Many of Gershom's tunes also appear in other hand-copied sources and printed songsters. Another naval surgeon, Thomas van Dyke Weisenthal, composed and had published numerous songs and dance arrangements. While not intending these for common sailors, he set lyrics by Thomas Moore, Lord Byron, and personal friends, including fellow naval officers. Perhaps his bestselling song, "Take This Rose," appeared in an arrangement for harp, clarinet, violin, and German flute, as well as a standard piano-vocal score. Enlisted sailors used chanteys and fo'c's'le songs aboard US Navy vessels, much as did their commercial counterparts aboard privately owned ships.[56]

Sailors at sea, whether civilian or naval, needed more than chantey-singing and forebitter-swapping to relieve the tension of shipboard duty and long confinement. The dancing of hornpipes met this need and became quite popular. A fast dotted, duple-meter rhythm characterizes the hornpipe, a brisk, energetic dance of solo display. All-men crews welcomed this opportunity to show off their talents. Given the limited recreational space available to sailors (above or below deck), a solo dance had to be performed in a small space with little arm movement yet lots of fancy legwork. Sailors danced to fiddles, penny whistles, and other instruments, the same instruments that accompanied fo'c's'le songs. The civilian stage dancer John Durang, who widely performed his "Sailor's Hornpipe," demonstrated that landlubbers too could appreciate hornpipe dancing.

Although the literate and the well-to-do generally subscribed to more sophisticated musical activities than those of laborers, the prominent lawyer and politician Henry Stockbridge took appreciative note of an everyday bit of music in Baltimore, the calls of a street vendor he knew only as Moses. Moses likely belonged to the community of slave or free black street merchants in the city at midcentury. He was an "itinerant oyster and ice cream vendor," Stockbridge recalled; "his whistle was an institution that lingered in the memory of all who ever heard it, but which none can describe. It could be heard squares away in snatches between the cry of his oysters or ice cream—a curious medley the likes of which we may not hear again. I would give more to recall for five minutes old Moses' whistle and

cry, than for a half hour of the best orchestra we have heard since he passed away in 1847."[57] By the time scholars began to take interest in oral, unwritten musical traditions, many such songs had slipped away.[58]

Off Hours

Meantime, industrialization had the effect of introducing more commercially produced entertainments to Maryland's white urban laborers. Their leisure hours, once filled with creative storytelling and the singing of handed-down ballads, were now open to the consumption of music performed by others, now for a fee. Factory jobs and other stable employment allowed workers to set aside modest sums to spend on amusements on weekday evenings and weekends. Unsympathetic observers complained that people drank too much on the Fourth of July and other civic occasions,[59] which began to swell in number as immigrants celebrated Saint Patrick's Day, Robert Burns's birthday, and a Welsh festival called an eisteddfod. Promoters of urban entertainments strove to make their shows more exotic than those of their competitors. Money was to be made, so Maryland's commercial entertainment industry, based initially in city theaters, rose to meet this demand.

Theatergoing grew enormously in popularity in the mid-nineteenth century. Established theaters increased their seating capacity, and new theaters offered audiences a wide choice of spectacles. Baltimore in 1798 had only one theater, one library, a circus, and one assembly hall. People of differing economic stations paid graduated ticket prices to sit in separate sections of these same places. But by 1840, reflecting the growth of population and economy, the city sported four theaters, several dance halls, and many private clubs that featured bands for dancing, concerts, or background music. The Holliday Street Theatre remained the premier theater of the wealthy—it was the "best," according to Tyrone Power. Baltimore's official fete for the Marquis de Lafayette in 1825 was held at Holliday Street. The Front Street Theatre, opened in 1829, was a larger and, by its own claims, more democratic public theater. Though not so fashionable in decor or repertory, it welcomed audiences for more than seventy-five years. In 1833 seats

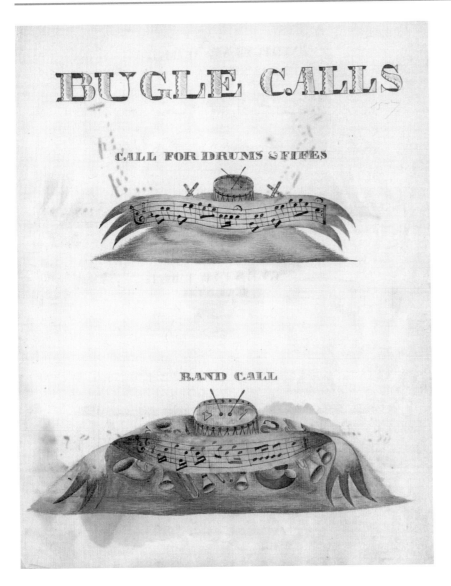

Page from a music book, hand drawn and hand colored, copied aboard the USS Concord ca. 1831. Fifes and drums and even bugles were used to signal orders aboard ship, much as in the army. Unlike land-bound field musicians, naval bands were culled from regular personnel aboard ship whose primary duties were those of a sailor. These men also played for ceremonies and special entertainments. Special Collections & Archives Department, MS 55, Nimitz Library, US Naval Academy.

there ran twenty-five and fifty cents for pit and box, considerably cheaper than at Holliday Street. Throughout the state, other such theaters sprang up to serve the middle and lower classes. Because investors built few structures explicitly for musical presentations, most Baltimore concerts took place in theaters, hotels, taverns, or even, on occasion, churches. The leading library and lecture hall, the Baltimore Athenaeum, hosted concerts beginning in the 1820s. Views on what was appropriate for which class depended on wildly fluctuating economic and social forces. "Drama was the major form of public entertainment available to all classes . . . it became an unusually sensitive barometer of the least common denomination of our age's attitudes and concerns."[60]

Of the entertainments catering to Maryland's working classes, circuses and museums predominated. In 1794 Rickett's circus, the first in America, offered a mixture of entertainments in Baltimore—pantomime, acrobatics, horsemanship, magic, presentational dance, popular operatic airs, and ballads. Circus clowns sang comic songs, and bands played patriotic airs. John Durang combined musical and acrobatic skills. Though initially appealing to all, circuses like that of Pepin & Brechard, which first appeared in Baltimore in 1800, eventually catered to middle- and lower-class customers alone because of their reliance less on artistic performance and more on the hyped-up presentation of strange animals and freaks of nature. Early museums also tried to attract and retain a broad clientele and were somewhat successful in keeping their elite customers. Rembrandt Peale's museum employed musicians to enliven exhibitions. Sporting a music gallery with an organ, it hosted concerts and oratorios. In 1830 Peale moved the museum from Holliday Street to much larger quarters on the northwest corner of Baltimore and Calvert Streets. There, in the upstairs theater he regularly sponsored a wide variety of acts, ranging from violin and harp duets to the remarkable Signor Hillenne, who simultaneously played violin, Pandean pipes, Chinese bells, Turkish cymbals, and a drum.[61] Over the first half of the nineteenth century, the shows at circuses, museums, and theaters diversified and specialized, and their offerings, once competitive, became complementary.

The same forces that encouraged the social stratification of public entertainments also created social tension. Frustrations had long simmered in theaters, as the elite sought classically leaning programs, while managers could only fill their seats by offering plebeian productions. Just as in colonial times, theater musicians were torn between their own artistic aspiration to play more challenging music and the audience's roaring for simple patriotic songs like "Yankee Doodle." That people of differing classes would have different musical tastes is understandable, since they lived in dissimilar houses, worked in different settings, and came from varied families, means, and cultures. Elite music critics openly questioned the value of popular music, while comic performers lampooned elitist behavior and pretense. Heroes from the underside of life, such as "Mose the B'howry B'hoy," had become popular idols in some quarters. At Baltimore's Adelphi Theater, already an unruly place known as the "mud theater," friction between working men and better-dressed patrons led to a riot in 1826 that left several dead. This event prefigured the more deadly scuffle at New York's Astor Place Theater two decades later, in which dozens of lives were lost. The musician Robert Bunyie once had a rock thrown through his bass fiddle while the Adelphi's

manager tried to quiet the raucous audience by singing and dancing a hornpipe. Such disorder finally forced American theater managers to give up trying to serve multiclass audiences. The performing arts thus became more socially stratified at about midcentury.[62]

Classical Taste

The upper class claimed their leisure territory, maintaining exclusivity through high admission prices. They patronized outdoor pleasure gardens, steamship cruises, and railroad excursions. Some traveled to fancy springs in Virginia or York Springs, Pennsylvania, to take comfortable hotel rooms, enjoy polite dancing, and hear evening concerts at places too distant and too costly for most citizens.

The parting of popular and elitist audiences paved the way for several important developments, among them the rise of Italian opera, not "Englished" (i.e., translated) but actually sung in Italian. Involving higher production costs, a florid presentational style, and a mystique of musical superiority, opera sung in Italian offered wealthier Americans a distinctive, exclusive form of entertainment. While audiences of all classes had long enjoyed works by Rossini and Bellini in English translation, the rise of Italian opera in Italian represented a critical shift that polarized audiences. Despite its shaky start, opera in Italian had become the rage by 1850, first in New York City. The impresario William Niblo almost single-handedly fostered the development of this art form, deftly dodging criticisms of elitism while capitalizing on the scandals that surrounded the Italian companies and singers themselves. He managed to keep ticket prices low enough to attract upper-middle-class patrons while still selling expensive box seats to wealthier patrons—an excellent marketing coup. People flocked to theaters, at least partially attracted to theatergoing as a social event, yet also curious about the highly publicized squabbling and in-fighting that came to characterize Italian stars, managers, and musicians, greedily and often dishonestly vying for fame and profits.[63]

Baltimore's exposure to this new fashion began in 1843 with visits from the Havana Company and the

Seguin Opera Company, the latter of which returned again in 1845 and 1848. The Holliday Street Theatre hosted runs of about two weeks each. The Havana Company presented Bellini's operas *Norma* and *I Puritani* and Donizetti's *Gemma di Vergy* and *Lucia di Lammermoor*. This was a full touring company of thirty members, including stars, chorus, and orchestra, the first such group to tour America successfully. Baltimore's acceptance of Italian opera as a more classically inspired form of entertainment relates to several important developments at this time, including the general increase in wealth within the city and the rise of the term *classical* as applied to music.

Eventually *classical* came to refer to the chamber and orchestral music of European composers such as Beethoven, J. S. Bach, and Mozart, as well as solo instrumental music, formal church music, and opera. Yet in the formal study of music history the term refers to just the so-called classical era, which lasted roughly from 1745 to 1790. J. S. Bach belongs more specifically to the earlier baroque era, and Beethoven to the later romantic one; neither one is strictly classical, a term associated with the discovery of remains from classical antiquity. The style in which Mozart and Haydn composed in the mid- to late eighteenth-century embodied the true classical ideals of symmetry, proportion, and rationalism— all characteristic of the Enlightenment. By contrast, the baroque and romantic styles of Bach and Beethoven involve heavier, more complex, and more emotional elements.

Some argue that classical music, in the general sense of the term, is inherently better because its creation involves genius, and its performance and appreciation require education (or "taste"). Some lovers of less pretentious, popular music label classical music lovers as elitist snobs because of just such claims. The association of musical taste with social class was not new in mid-nineteenth-century America, but the claims about implicit value and the coining of the term *classical* were. Music critics of the larger Eastern Seaboard cities, such as Boston, New York, and Baltimore, consciously used this new term to distinguish what they saw as a morally superior type of music from "lower," popular forms.[64]

By 1840, elite music critics began to write openly about "good" and "bad" music. They used these words not just to distinguish between what they liked and what they disliked but as labels for composers, performers, and listeners themselves. Around this time America's upper classes welcomed such a musical distinction. They felt both put off by the decadent state of public entertainments and threatened by the intrusion of the middle class into both domestic and public music-making. The classical-popular dichotomy emerged as an elite counterattack, defining certain types of music that purportedly elevated and improved both the listener and the performer, while scorning all other types as superficial and designed merely to entertain the "lower sorts." This move was not immediately and widely successful, but its effect continues to be seen in Maryland's cultural landscape to this day.

Proponents of classical music at first encouraged publications that championed a critical perspective. Maryland's first periodical devoted strictly to music news and criticism, the *Baltimore Olio, and American Musical Gazette*, survived only from January to December 1850, but it registered the rise of a sensibility. Its mission, stated on each title page, was to be "a monthly parlor companion for the ladies: devoted chiefly to music, the arts, and musical intelligence generally." Earlier Baltimore journals—the *Baltimore Weekly Magazine and Ladies' Miscellany* (1818), the *National Magazine or Lady's Emporium* (ca. 1830), and the equally short-lived *Baltimore Literary Monument* (1838–39)—all had included occasional articles on music, even songs and piano works by local composers. But the *Baltimore Olio* espoused the cause of musical classicism, featuring reviews, biographical sketches, printed music, and essays, especially those pointing out how classical music surpassed popular forms. The *Olio*'s editor, the out-of-towner William Peters, chastised Baltimoreans for allowing their musical life to lag behind the city's flourishing architecture, visual arts, and sculpture. Critics writing for the *Baltimore Olio* noted with envy the thriving classical musical activities in Boston, New York, and Philadelphia. Though nearly on a par in terms of net publishing output, Baltimore, before (and after) the *Olio*, lagged well behind these other cities when it came to music criticism and commentary.[65]

Another mark of the new classical musical ideal was the creation of exclusive groups like the Baltimore Harmonic Society and the Baltimore Musical Association, as well as the city's Bach Society, Mozart Association, and Handel Society. Most propitiously, an eighty-member Monumental Music Society invited the Massachusetts-born Baltimore banker George Peabody to a concert series at the Maryland Institute in 1857. This group had been "formed for the practice & cultivation of the Classic Music of the best composers."[66] Tickets to classical-music concerts were expensive, and elite amateurs attempted to play more demanding classical compositions on their own lavish instruments at home.

While the espousal of classicism encouraged the performance of works by great European composers, the impact on American composers was profoundly harmful. Composers of formal music in Maryland felt doubly hampered: even if they could get a work performed, its reception would likely be negative lest the audience or critics offend good taste by praising a non-European's composition. As a result, neither immigrants nor native-born musicians composed much beyond conservative church music and the more marketable parlor songs, marches, variation sets, and dance pieces of a simpler, pedestrian nature. Such compositions were played at home on parlor pianos, sung between acts at the theater, and heard at Fourth of July celebrations, but they were not featured in formal concerts at concert halls. An exception was the opera *The Enterprise*, composed by Baltimore's Arthur Clifton in 1822. Colonel W. H. Hamilton, of Baltimore, contributed to the libretto. Clifton apparently thrived in Baltimore's music scene, and he wrote many popular songs, though what was probably the first opera composed in Maryland did not succeed beyond a short run and the printing of several songs from it, such as "O Steal Not the Ray, Sung by Mrs. Burke in the Opera of *The Enterprise*" (Philadelphia: Willig Jr., n.d.).

Few could bear the thought of an American creating a symphonic or operatic masterpiece at this time. Besides, the supply of music by more viable European composers had steadily increased after independence. While Chopin and Liszt were flourishing in Europe, formal composition in antebellum America was really a rather watered-down affair. Americans attending concerts in early nineteenth-century Maryland heard a wide variety of music in a rather piecemeal fashion. Programs included a mixture of opera arias from Weber, Mozart, or Bellini (still mostly in English), perhaps interspersed with overtures, Scottish or Irish sentimental songs, and shorter symphonic movements. Virtually all programs included some patriotic marches and current popular songs. Rare at this time would be performances of string quartets, concertos, or entire symphonies, not to mention songs or opera selections in a foreign language. Church-sponsored performances of Handel or Haydn oratorios with volunteer choruses and small orchestras had been going on for years, but there was neither the supply nor the demand for hiring enough professional players to rehearse and perform an all-Beethoven symphonic program.

The performance of full symphonies and significant larger classical works uninterrupted by popular offerings came into fashion in America largely due to a visiting European group called the Germania Orchestra, led by Charles Lenschow. The orchestra's twenty-five talented young performers left Germany for America in 1848 with great hopes and a large repertory of pure symphonic music. Its initial concerts in New York met with some encouragement but inadequate receipts, so the group moved to Baltimore, hoping that that city, with its large German population, might be welcoming and supportive. At midcentury more than twenty-five thousand Baltimoreans spoke German, and Zion Lutheran Church was active in supporting new immigrants. In early 1849 the orchestra performed at the inauguration of President Zachary Taylor in Washington, DC. Afterward, Zion Lutheran hosted the Germania for a series of ten subscription symphony concerts—the first in the country—held in Baltimore at such places as Carroll Hall, the Law Building, the assembly rooms, and various churches. The city became the Germania Orchestra's southern home base for touring America. In 1850 Lenschow turned over his baton to

Carl Bergmann and returned from touring to settle in Baltimore.[67]

Lenschow became a central figure in the musical life of his adopted city. Under Lenschow, Baltimoreans enjoyed first American performances of Mozart's Symphony no. 35 and Mendelssohn's Concert Overture no. 3 in D, op. 27. Many people in Baltimore were in turn musically inspired, from its immigrant-dominated musical community to the upper-class citizens eager to sponsor something lofty and classical. Hence the successful Baltimore appearance of the violinist Ole Bull in 1852, accompanied by the Germania Society, and that of the soprano Henrietta Sontag, who was only eighteen when she sang solos in the first American performance of Beethoven's Ninth Symphony. With the continuing support and encouragement of Maryland's Germans, the Germania Orchestra gave more than nine hundred concerts in the United States, introducing many Americans to the heavier classical and romantic instrumental music of Beethoven, Mendelssohn (especially his *Midsummer Night's Dream*), Haydn, Mozart, Liszt, and Wagner.

Piano Making and Musical Instruction

Baltimore piano making increased in volume and reputation as the nineteenth century wore on. It also served as an index to various musical activities. Coming to Baltimore in 1819 was Joseph Hiskey, later joined by Louis Fissore and other pioneer builders who helped establish the trade in the city. When Henry Hartye opened a shop in Baltimore in 1826, and a decade later he patented a new technique of metal plate bracing, the city took on a higher level of prestige. The next year, Hartye hired William Knabe, who had just arrived in Baltimore from Germany. The name Knabe would soon overtake that of Hartye and loom large in this industry, when William Knabe partnered with Henry Gaehle in 1839. By the early 1850s some ten Baltimore factories were turning out more than twenty-five pianos per week, while Baltimore-trained makers like James Stewart and Conrad Meyer moved on to forward the development of piano-building in Boston and Philadelphia, respectively.[68]

Baltimore' piano-making firms Knabe and Stieff eventually both rose to great prominence. Knabe pianos won gold medals at Maryland Institute exhibitions during the 1850s. John Hill Hewitt believed that the "peculiarities" of Knabe pianos were owing to "their strength of construction, the sweetness, power and purity of their tone, and durability; besides, the touch is pleasant and elastic."[69] Charles M. Stieff left his native Germany for Baltimore in 1837, where he taught music and led a church choir. He began importing pianos in 1842 and by 1852 had given up other musical activities to focus on making his own pianos. Stieff would survive the setbacks of the Civil War and continue to make fine pianos well into the twentieth century.[70]

Pianos evolved considerably in the mid-1800s, from small, delicate square pianos and uprights to colossal metal-framed squares and grands weighing up to nearly a ton. Such achievements resulted from refined production techniques, improved design, and wide distribution gained through aggressive advertising and marketing. Increasing sheet-music sales fueled demand for pianos, as did the growing availability of lessons and people's desire to play the hits of the theater and concert hall at home.

Not only did Maryland's music businessmen manufacture and import instruments and compose, compile, and publish music to be played upon them, but, of course, they also taught people how to play those instruments, especially young women. Teaching music became a brisk business. Professional musicians taught part time to supplement their income from performances. Organists and choir directors, band and theater instrumentalists, composers, and even publishers offered lessons, as did accomplished artists like Christopher Meinecke, Arthur Clifton, Henri-Noël Gilles, and the popular opera singer Miss Eliza George. Frederick Lucchesi, who had once played piccolo in the West Point band, also performed on the flute but taught vocal music and counterpoint in Baltimore for three decades beginning in 1840.[71] Competition for students, coupled with lesser wages for female teachers, combined to make inexpensive lessons readily available, especially in cities but nearly throughout the state.

Square pianoforte, manufactured by Joseph Hiskey, Museum Department, ca. 1825–35. Hiskey, an Austrian immigrant, crafted perhaps the finest pianos in Baltimore for a quarter century after 1820. Within the prevailing Empire style, he built distinctive painted instruments like the one shown here. It featured a hand-colored landscape engraving above the keyboard. For a detailed description of the piano shown here, see Gregory R. Weidman, *Furniture in Maryland, 1740–1940* (Baltimore: Maryland Historical Society, 1984). 144. Courtesy of the Maryland Historical Society, 1962.6.1.

Teachers offered lessons on a wide variety of instruments, mostly piano, guitar, harp, and violin, as well as voice lessons, although less common instruments such as the zither also appear in advertisements.

Women clearly played an increasing role in musical instruction as the nineteenth century progressed. In about 1840, after the death of Charles DeRonceray, his wife and daughter carried on his private musical tutoring. Young women from wealthier families studied music while attending academies like the Thorndale Seminary for Young Ladies (founded ca. 1837), Friendship Academy (1839), or the Patapsco Female Institute (1837), whose headmistress, Mrs. Almira Lincoln Phelps, composed some songs and generally emphasized music in her curriculum. Students at the institute studied a variety of instruments and performed at commencements and annual examinations. A few teachers, such as Rial Shaw, specialized in sacred vocal music instruction for group classes. A founder of the Baltimore Musical Association, Shaw also compiled and published pedagogical materials. Teachers commonly sold sheet music to their students; some wrote arrangements for hire.[72]

Musically German

German immigrants to the state maintained tight social bonds, and religion often served as the glue. A poem that appeared in the *Baltimore Sun* in the spring of 1848 characterized German piety while commenting on a meeting of a German society in Baltimore: "Where'er is heard the German tongue / and German hymns to God are sung." Early Lutheran and German Reformed hymns often did resound in German. Although congregations bickered over whether to sing and worship in their native or their adopted tongue, English slowly became the norm both in Baltimore and in the countryside. While German Catholics still made up only a minority of Maryland's Catholic population, the German Jewish community in Baltimore grew after restrictions were lifted on their political activity in 1826. By the 1840s and 1850s trained cantors were singing in city synagogues.[73]

Maryland Germans of whatever faith shared some degree of practical, business, and social cooperation, largely through the Deutsche Gesellschaft (German Society) of Maryland, whose purpose was to aid German immigrants. The society, as part of its benevolent mission, sponsored singing sessions and social outings that aimed to reinforce German American solidarity. The *Baltimore American* opined on February 2, 1838, that German songs like "Was ist des Deutchen Vaterland?" (What is the German's fatherland?) and "Die Wacht am Rhein" (The Watch/Guard on the Rhine) made Maryland Germans feel at home, and their numbers increased after the failed European revolutions of 1848. Along with German-language newspapers, benevolent societies, churches, and schools, familiar music offered immigrants a sense of ethnic community in the New World.[74]

Baltimore Germans at Zion Lutheran Church in 1836 founded the nation's second German singing society, the Liederkranz, which flourished under the direction of Zion's Reverend Heinrich Scheib. In the late 1830s and 1840s, the group mounted the state's first performance of a full Beethoven symphony, as well as Carl Maria von Weber's opera *Der Freischütz* (1821) and works by Haydn. The Liederkranz did the country an important service in 1849 by hosting the visiting Germania Orchestra. It sponsored a performance of Mozart's *Magic Flute* in 1852. Then a new director took over and redirected the group's repertory toward German part-songs.[75]

Singing groups maintained much of the class consciousness of Old World German society. In 1851 Baltimore Germans formed the Arion Singing Society, which for generations was one of the country's finest. It sang common hymns and folk songs appropriate to its working-class membership. The Arbeiter-Gesangverein (Workers' Songfest) merged with Arion in 1855, but it was the Turner movement that truly united working-class Germans in Baltimore. Founded in 1849, the Baltimore Sozialdemokratische Turnverein (Social-Democratic Gymnastic Union) espoused personal discipline and gymnastic exercise as the path to liberty. The city's most prominent Turner, Carl H. Schnauffer, wrote songs, including the official Turner song "Der Turnerbund" in 1852. That same year, Baltimore Turners hosted an interregional Bundes-Turnfest (Gymnastic Gathering) during which lay Germans, members, and the Turner-Liedertafel and Liederkranz singing societies all raised their voices together in solidarity. Baltimore became the headquarters for the Turner movement in the United States in 1859, when some sixty German clubs or societies flourished in Maryland. With their own distinctions between elite and middle class, they met social, intellectual, and entertainment needs. They staged dramas and concerts based on German musical traditions, preserved folk and ethnic dances, and played the music that accompanied them. They formed military music corps, such as the Deutsche Jäger and the Erste Deutsche Baltimore Garde. In 1856 they organized a *Männerchor* (men's chorus) for the performance of secular and sacred music at festive gatherings—*Sängerbunds* and *Sängerfests*. Maryland Germans were not alone in savoring their ethnic musical heritage, but few other groups organized this impulse as well.[76]

Celebrity Singers and the Clamor for Opera

Especially after turnpikes and then railroads made long-distance travel more feasible than it had been in the days of creaking wagons and rough roads, American impresarios regularly sent celebrity singers, alone or in small groups, around the United States to star in operatic performances and occasional concert presentations. The masses clamored for these well-promoted stars.

Opera then was in fact vastly more popular and widespread than in the twentieth century. People enjoyed opera in English for its entertainment value, not as a vehicle for self-enhancement or "classical" improvement. Favorite airs and overtures found their way into brass-band concerts, amateur piano playing at home, and music boxes. Melodramas featured parodies of operatic plots and music. From a production standpoint, opera was big business, attracting far larger and more diverse audiences than did formal symphonic concerts of the time or, for that matter, opera today.

The star system drove the passion for opera to a near frenzy, as audiences clamored for big-name singers. It played havoc with local actors and musicians, who were at the mercy of touring star performers' irregular schedules, limited rehearsal time, and repertory choices. Local managers also disliked this arrangement, but the public supported it wildly, eager to see exotic actors and singers whose reputations in some cases were well earned and in others rested entirely on hired clappers, exaggerated handbills, and contrived newspaper "puffs." A natural outgrowth of industrial development, the evolution of advertising, and commercialization of the arts, the star system depended on a powerful press not averse to accepting bribes and kickbacks.[77]

In larger cities like New York and Philadelphia, the star system supplemented otherwise active performing-arts venues. Those cities could absorb the vicissitudes of itinerant troupes' irregular schedules and offerings. But in smaller cities like Baltimore and Washington, DC, this arrangement took a great toll, forcing stages to stand dark much of the year and depriving residents of regular entertainment. Local companies faltered, while touring companies breezed through and made tremendous profits. The actor Edmund Kean made five hundred dollars each night during a Baltimore stint in 1821, while the house and staff received little more than pocket change.[78] Underpaid, local actors, musicians, and managers struggled and often gave up. Over time, independent Baltimore musicians like Robert Bunyie and Augustus Metz adjusted to the system and learned to juggle sporadic theater work with teaching and other performing. Such was the impact of nineteenth-century

Americans' natural fascination with visiting stars, singers mostly, on Baltimore's music scene.

For many stars, exoticism served as a standard calling card. Marylanders gathered to see and hear anything new and different, from a guitarist claiming to be "Laureate of Paris and Madrid" in 1824 to the famous Norwegian violinist Ole Bull. The nationally known British opera star Charles Horn first appeared in Baltimore in 1827. He was followed by the singers Joseph Philip Knight and John Braham, who toured America quite late in his career. The prominent English composer George K. Jackson lived briefly in Baltimore, publishing several works there, and both Henrietta Sontag and the socially minded, sentimental Henry Russell performed in Baltimore as well. The German-born composer Anthony Philip Heinrich visited Maryland as early as 1825, when he composed a patriotic song and dedicated it to a local German militia group.[79] A quarter century later, in February 1850, the *Baltimore Olio* ran a biographical sketch of Heinrich, who was known then as the Beethoven of America.

Exoticism fueled certain folkloric, primitive themes, such as those embodied in Carl Maria von Weber's romantic German opera *Der Freischütz*, which debuted in Baltimore in 1824. The critics praised its highly supernatural, German folk-like character. Quintessentially exotic and romantic, *Der Freischütz* introduced a freer, more emotional and dynamic interpretation of dance as well as drama, conveniently connecting with the current fad for formal ballet. Weber's opera also spawned interest in European folk art as well as romantic music, paving the way for visits from the Tyrolese Minstrels, an Austrian touring group also known as the Rainer Family. Their renditions of "Ranz des Vaches" and "Schweizerbache" in Baltimore embodied these folk and exotic Germanic elements.

The English opera singers Jane Shirreff and John Wilson typified the successful stars who visited Maryland. Appearing first in Baltimore in 1839, they sang lead roles in operas at the Holliday Street Theatre nearly every night for a two-week stretch, bringing their own complete company of lesser roles, chorus, and even an orchestra. Upon their return visit in the fall of that year they used local Maryland choristers and instrumentalists. Typical of small opera-star troupes, Shirreff and Wilson toured America with their families for nearly two years, having major runs at the main theaters in New York and Philadelphia, then touring to lesser theatrical cities as far afield as Savannah, Detroit, and Quebec.[80]

Shirreff and Wilson enjoyed warm receptions in Baltimore from the press and the many people who came to hear them, often more than once. Much of their repertory is unperformed today, yet Bellini's *La Sonnambula* earned great praise and achieved wild popularity. Auber's *Fra Diavalo*, Rossini's *Cinderella*, and Mozart's *Marriage of Figaro* also were performed frequently. Singers often inserted arias from these popular operas into concerts or interpolated them into other operas. Rarely did visiting stars perform opera as written; rather, they freely shortened and adapted it, using English translations of the original Italian, French, or German libretti. They spoke recitative rather than sang it, simplified or dropped complex music, even streamlined plots. These "Englished" productions were light, accessible, and entertaining for American audiences, much in the style of the ballad operas that flourished in colonial times. The local stock company presented a lighter afterpiece, perhaps a melodrama, when the stars had finished the main attraction. The incredible popularity of opera in America at the time was owing to its middle-class appeal.[81]

As a kind of apogee for the star system, Phineas Taylor Barnum carefully plotted the blazingly successful American tour of the opera singer Jenny Lind in 1850–51.[82] A ruthless capitalist, Barnum created an exotic yet virtuous character image for Lind, the Swedish Nightingale, as the best opera singer in the world. Lind did indeed bring grace and pristine poise to American stages, having already enjoyed a successful career as an opera performer in the Old World. Yet her fame in Europe never approached the fame she achieved through Barnum's groundbreaking promotional techniques, which were based on sheer hype and calculated, controversial stunts. He exploited the dupable American public through exaggerated statements spread via newspapers, handbills, and posters. Thus induced, the nation yearned for the exotic Lind, and Barnum delivered.

Barnum arranged for five of Lind's nearly one hundred concerts to take place in Baltimore, where, as throughout the country, a crowd of people pushed to catch a glimpse of her arrival. During one such visit in 1850, Barnum and his daughter attended a Sunday church service, while Lind stayed at the hotel. Some people in the congregation recognized Barnum in the congregation and presumed the woman with him was Jenny Lind herself. Everyone strained to hear the woman sing along in the hymns, claiming afterward that she had the most beautiful voice they had ever heard. Barnum's daughter, Caroline, apparently went along with the misapprehension, afterwards smiling and shaking hands and leaving many people quite pleased, even though she had a terrible singing voice.[83] Of the hundreds of thousands of tickets sold nationwide to see Miss Lind, many were auctioned in public; a Maryland man purportedly paid one hundred dollars for the first Baltimore ticket sold at auction. Regular tickets were not cheap, costing from three to seven dollars apiece. Marylanders clamored to see Lind, hear her, and even sing "Hail, Columbia!" along with her, only to sit mesmerized by selections from Handel's *Messiah*, operatic arias by Bellini and others, and, of course, popular favorites like "Home, Sweet Home."[84]

Other visiting artists achieved some degree of success. The touring Rainer family, from Austria, served as a model for the Hutchinson Family Singers, a group from Vermont that got its start by imitating the Tyrolese visitors. Homespun and unpretentious, the Hutchinsons soon billed themselves as exemplars of down-to-earth values and moral consciousness. Far more humble than the exotic, well-trained European concert performers of the day, they enjoyed enormous popularity among America's middle and lower classes. From their first concert in 1842, the group appeared in church halls, warehouses, and even outdoors, vocalizing fervent support for causes like temperance and abolition. The Sons of Temperance had established its national office in Baltimore, so the city's reform-minded

Cover for a collection of sheet music entitled *The Songs of Jenny Lind* (Baltimore and New Orleans, n.d.). During the mid-nineteenth century, Baltimore reigned as the musical capital of the Chesapeake. Visiting performers included Jenny Lind, "the Swedish Nightingale," the most famous and most highly paid singer of her day, here portrayed in the title role in *The Daughter of the Regiment*, a very popular opera by Gaetano Donizetti. In 1850 Lind held a special concert for some six hundred Baltimore schoolchildren, who serenaded her with a performance of "The Star-Spangled Banner." Lester S. Levy Collection of Sheet Music, Sheridan Libraries, Johns Hopkins University, box 187, item 16.

middle class needed little prodding to attend these concerts.[85]

Not all Marylanders welcomed the Hutchinson stance on abolition, which the Vermonters voiced in a signature piece, "Get off the Track." After the appearance of Harriet Beecher Stowe's *Uncle Tom's Cabin* in 1852, John Hill Hewitt and another Baltimore resident, Charles Soran, took the trouble to write an antiabolition minstrel song, "Aunt Harriet Becha Stowe," which a Baltimore firm published in 1853. Later, when the Hutchinsons came to Maryland and performed songs in favor of abolition, citizens greeted them with catcalls and a near riot. The group vowed never to appear in the South again.[86]

Popular Song and Racial Prejudice

Most of the music one heard in Baltimore was truly popular in nature—songs and marches about political conventions, famous people, or recent inventions. Hewitt later described the musical taste of the city in the 1830s and 1840s as "elevated, the Italian being the fashionable school." "It is now happily blended with the solid German," he went on, "the light beauty of the one mingling nicely with the classic grandeur of the other."

He testified approvingly that in that earlier, halcyon day, "negro minstrelsy was unknown, except through the grotesque posturing and husky warbling of Tom Rice, the original 'Jim Crow.' Our native ballads were pure; no mongrel off-spring of Scotch jigs and plantation refrains."[87] Of all the popular musical forms classicists assailed, the favorite target and worst offender was the minstrel show.

The singing of comic songs about African American slaves and even the blackface impersonation of them by white performers dated from the eighteenth century. Lewis Hallam adopted this pose in New York in 1769 and probably elsewhere in the colonies. In 1801 "A Negro Song" appeared in Benjamin Carr's *Musical Journal for the Pianoforte*, which was sold in Baltimore. By the mid-1830s American publishers in every major city issued "Zip Coon," "The Cork Leg," and other comic solo songs of this emerging genre.

The minstrel show as a group presentation, rather than a solo rendition, first emerged in New York in 1842, when Dan Emmitt collaborated with three other soloists. Following their success, literally hundreds of minstrel troupes appeared. Their shows had a standardized routine, with an Interlocutor at the center and Brother Tambo and Brother Bones at either side. A truly American construct that only prejudiced whites living amid blacks could conjure and support with enthusiasm, the minstrel show depended on "plantation" dialect songs, caricatured dances, and slapstick humor. Minstrel troupes stereotyped African Americans as either dull yet happy plantation slaves or stupid yet aggressive city dwellers, imposing the character names Uncle Ned and Zip Coon, respectively. Yet stump speeches and one-act skits poked fun not just at slaves but also at pretentious whites, politicians, the clergy, and especially opera. The music of Stephen Foster, whose "Oh! Susanna" appeared in 1848, hastened the minstrels' jollity.

Baltimore had its full share of minstrel troupes, among them George Kunkel's Nightingale Minstrels. Active in Baltimore and touring as far off as Cumberland, Maryland, and Richmond, Virginia, Kunkel's group pushed songs like its 1853 hit "Maryland, My Home." Kunkel wrote music for the troupe, as in fact did John Hill Hewitt. John T. Ford handled bookings for the group starting in 1851, when he also managed Baltimore's Holliday Street and Front Street Theatres (as well as the theater in Washington that bore his name).[88] While Kunkel's minstrels and most others during antebellum times were white, the Baltimore-born Jim Sanford referred to himself as "The Celebrated Negro Singer and Dancer." His song "Lucy Neale" inspired many parodies and enjoyed great popularity in its own right. Walking through the streets of Baltimore and other Maryland cities at midcentury, one would have noticed hundreds of posters announcing the performances of Kunkel's troupe and others, such as The Ethiopian Serenaders. The *Baltimore Olio* reported wrongly in 1850 that "the days of triumph of Ethiopian melodies are numbered."[89]

CHAPTER THREE

Intermission

THE SOUNDS OF CIVIL WAR

BRASS BANDS, CIVIC AND MILITARY, performed not only dance music but also public ceremonial music and commercial music of various sorts in antebellum Maryland. People heard bands play on steamship cruises along the Chesapeake, at private resorts like Old Point Comfort and Betterton, and even on trains that employed excursion bands to attract pleasure riders. In addition to concerts, bands performed at public fairs, taverns, circuses, horse races, and Fourth of July celebrations, to which admission was either free or priced to suit the leanest pocketbook. The sounds were bright, energetic, and flashy, as by the 1850s bands had dropped most woodwind instruments and were made up mostly of brass and percussion instruments.

Home of the Brave

All Americans knew of such music, but in Maryland as in a few other places it had special distinction because it reminded people of local military glory. In September 1814, besides providing the backdrop for Key's "Star-Spangled Banner," Baltimore had equipped regimental bands, including one led by Captain Jacob Deems. Sponsors later sent Captain Deems's son, James, born in Baltimore in 1818, to Europe to study music. The younger Deems became an excellent player of the cornet-à-piston and for a long time served as director of the Independent Blues Band. After 1848 he spent ten years as an instructor in music at the University of Virginia. He was "a theorist of the highest order, and has composed many heavy works; some of his lighter productions have been given to the public," recalled Hewitt. Another longtime leader of the Independent Blues Band was Albert Holland, a native Baltimorean who taught music from about 1845 to 1887. Holland arranged and composed military music for his own group to perform, such as the "Fillmore Quick Step" (1856) and "The Blues Band Reels" (1858), both published by Miller & Beacham. He also wrote a "Sun Quickstep" (Henry McCaffrey, 1854), dedicated to the readers of the Baltimore newspaper. Holland's wife often sang with him, to much acclaim.[1]

On the Origins of Music in Rohrersville (1858)

Rohrersville owes much of its musical fame to an early employee of the C&O Canal, Washington McCoy, who organized McCoy's Cornet Band in 1837 and then opened a marble business in Rohrersville. He became the band's first director and arranger. McCoy would send away for a single-cornet melody line of music and then score the necessary parts for others in the band. He gave both vocal and instrumental instruction, often without charge. The town rewarded him with warm appreciation, which surfaced in a steamy report in a local paper in late 1858:

"The Ladies' Fair, for the benefit of McCoy's Cornet Band opened on Christmas Eve," the male reporter wrote,

> as has been previously announced. Early had the throng assembled, anxiously awaiting the salutatory, which was displayed by Prof. Mc-Coy's Band in soul-stirring strains of Grafful-lar, which passed along with eager gaze, when my attention was drawn by the fascinating smiles of a fair damsel. . . . [The orchestra] is composed of flutes, violins, guitar and violin-cello, under the direction of Prof. McCoy, whose delight it is to instruct all who desire a

knowledge of music. He is a gentleman who elicits the highest encomiums for the position he has attained in the science. The music was delightful. The plaintive sounds of the flutes harmonizing with the shrill chords of the violins, mingling with the vibrations of the guitar and deep toned bass, form[ed] one sublime strain of melody. (*Hagerstown Herald and Torch,* January 20, 1858)

McCoy, so fondly remembered, seems to have founded the oldest community band in Maryland. Except during the Civil War—when it fell inactive, perhaps also divided in sentiment as important battles raged nearby—it has played inspiring music ever since.

Patriotic melodies and march tunes resounded at Maryland public events, as had become American custom. Familiar titles included "Hail, Columbia!," "Washington's March," "The Star-Spangled Banner," and "Yankee Doodle." George Willig Jr. issued Charles Grobe's "The Battle of Buena Vista" during the Mexican War, in 1847, perhaps one of the pieces a brass band played in Cumberland when the C&O Canal opened for traffic between the Queen City and Washington in

1850. Ironically, the Baltimore musicians arrived by railroad, the C&O Canal and the B&O Railroad having begun their race to reach that city back in 1828.

When full military bands were not available, smaller groups of fifes and drums brought these tunes to life. Indeed, upon establishment of the Naval Academy at Fort Severn, Annapolis, in 1845, a single fifer and drummer constituted its band. The two men signaled daily commands, impervious to the existence of the army garrison band, which remained on station. The Marine Band from Washington came to Annapolis for special events, such as the first grand naval ball in 1846. In late 1852 the secretary of the navy, John Pendleton Kennedy, then of Baltimore, decreed that "the want of Music at the Naval Academy is so evident that I deem it necessary to invite your attention to the organization of a Band to consist of not less than twelve instruments to be directed by a leader or Master."[2] The first academy bandmaster, John Philip Pfeiffer, recruited German musicians on a trip to Boston and shipped them to Annapolis, where they joined his two young sons. At times as enlisted men, other times as civilians, early band players donned Marine Band attire and lived on academy grounds. The initial monthly pay for the bandmaster was eighteen dollars, and for the others, ten to twelve dollars. Though each player had bugling duties, they doubled on other brass, woodwind, and string instruments provided by the government so that they could play dance and concert music indoors as well as ceremonial music outdoors. Pfeiffer supposedly played melodeon for Sunday services as well. From 1853 to 1861 the Naval Academy Band performed actively and may have accepted private work in town to supplement its meager pay; in the mid-1850s the band threatened to quit because of low pay. Commodore Goldsborough, who loved dancing and music and believed in the military value of both, levied essentially a per capita tax on the midshipmen to raise the musicians' pay. In February 1861, when the USF Constitution—Old Ironsides— docked in Annapolis, the band gave a concert on the main deck.[3]

Meanwhile, midshipmen earned a reputation for their singing and ribaldry, often on display in Annapolis taverns. The song "Rosy-Gosy, Oh!," to the tune "Benny Haven, Oh!," frequently resounded at Rosenthall's tavern in Annapolis. The tavern keeper Harry Matthews regularly hosted midshipmen, who also sang the "Spirit Song" in the first decade after the academy's founding. The chorus called for another drink:

Then fill, fill yet once again,
And as we pass the merry jest,

Be each sparkling cup we drain,
To her we love the best.[4]

Midshipmen staged their first play, *The Lady of Lyons*, in 1846,[5] when Congress declared war on Mexico. The treaty ending that conflict vastly increased the size of the country but also badly aggravated the question of slavery versus free soil in the western territories. After the failure of various attempts at compromise, Abraham Lincoln and his party, recognizing the right to slave property within the existing slave states but firmly opposing the extension of slavery further into the West, won the presidential election in 1860. Soon the country divided and went to war.

Parlor to Patriotism

The Civil War prompted a massive outpouring of poetry and song. Composers embraced war-related themes, adapting them to the parlor song and minstrel styles, which had sold so well during the 1840s and 1850s. Aggressive marketing resulted in Civil War sheet-music sales in the millions of copies, spreading a vast body of inspirational and sentimental song throughout the countryside. Additionally, newspapers provided a natural outlet for wartime prose, poetry, and song lyrics, as did broadsheets and songsters.

Music filled a variety of functions during the war, some overlapping. Parlor songs for home use portrayed an idealized camp and battlefield, their lyrics playing on the emotions of soldiers' families, friends, and sweethearts at home. The bloody, horrible truth of war rarely intruded into the refined and sentimental lyrics that people sang at home from printed music. Sheet-music publishers between 1861 and 1865 focused on creating new hits and keeping popular prewar songs like "Lorena" in demand and available for sale.

Wartime parlor music came from pens beyond those of influential composers like George F. Root, Henry Clay Work, and John Hill Hewitt.[6] These men at times composed their own tunes and at other time borrowed folk and popular melodies, as had ballad-opera compilers during colonial times. All told, Civil War melodic sources included minstrel tunes, earlier parlor reper-

The Naval Academy Band on the banks of the Severn River, ca. 1860. This is apparently the earliest known photograph of this group of fourteen musicians and, for some reason, a child. The band, along with all loyal midshipmen, relocated from Annapolis to Newport, Rhode Island, upon the outbreak of the Civil War. Five years later, numbering twenty-eight, plus the bandmaster, the band returned to Annapolis. The band never went to war, however. Michael Mrlik, "Some Facts and Assumptions Relative to the Origin and History of the U.S. Naval Academy Band," 3, typescript, n.d., US Naval Academy Archives. Special Collections & Archives Department, Nimitz Library, US Naval Academy.

tory, hymns and camp-meeting songs, white and black spirituals, and European material such as Irish and German songs. Lyrics too could be borrowed; composers set poems like "All Quiet on the Potomac Tonight" to their own tunes. The soldiers themselves informally sang bawdy songs, as well as those of love, glory, pain, and foolishness, echoing around campfires and beyond. Rather than sheet music, soldiers commonly carried printed songsters or broadsheets, and they also composed and sang lyrics preserved in their diaries. Singing mostly by ear, soldiers welcomed any sort of accompaniment by those willing to haul a fiddle, flute, or banjo over many miles of the march.

The more popular Civil War songs circulated in print and by oral means, soon inspiring parodies such as the new words to the melodies of "John Brown's Body," "Dixie," and "The Battle Cry of Freedom." Most parodies ridiculed; others answered songs that posed questions, such as "Who will take Care of Mother?," for which "God will take care of Mother" and "I will

take care of Mother" served as responses. Mother was perhaps the most widespread theme of sentimental war songs, next to dying soldiers' last words, wounded drummer boys, and brother fighting brother. Other themes included commemorations of great battles, the ennoblement of officers and statesmen, and lighter aspects of camp life in songs of complaint like "Goober Peas." The rich, varied musical legacy of this war runs much deeper than the few popular titles remembered today might suggest.

Most optimistic Civil War songs dated from early in the conflict and functioned primarily to sound the patriotic call to arms, each side believing that victory would come quickly and heroically. Yet as the war dragged on, demoralizing both sides, music of the war came to reflect not only nationalistic hopes but also the wrenching losses and emotional fatigue of a people torn by prolonged struggle. Soldiers and families both blue and gray eventually sang of death and loss, while de-emphasizing glory and righteousness. Outright antiwar songs like "Tenting Tonight," "Weeping Sad and Lonely," and "The Bonnie White Flag" appeared.

In any case, the formidable Northern music industry eagerly perpetrated the propaganda war against the Southern cause. It closely followed evolving sentiment. Its music enriched loyal publishers at the expense of those in Maryland and the seceded South.

My Maryland

Maryland's peculiar wartime position as a divided state, more or less garrisoned by the Union to ensure its loyalty, only heightened tensions among its polarized citizenry. Some people who spoke out freely in favor of the South found themselves jailed. Union authorities shut down newspapers and sheet-music shops that expressed pro-Confederate views. Secession seemed most appropriate to tidewater tobacco growers, who had depended on slavery for some 150 years and wanted to protect their property and way of life. Baltimore's gentry had much in common with the South socially and culturally. Yet businessmen with commercial ties to markets in Europe and the North, along with skilled workmen who cherished the concept and value of free labor generally, logically supported the Union, as did Maryland Germans, from Baltimore to the western counties. Illustrating this strong tendency, members of Baltimore's German singing societies happened to be in New York at the frightful moment when shells fell on Fort Sumter, rehearsing for the ninth national *Sængerfest*. Many of them had taken part in, or been sympathetic to, the revolution of 1848 in Europe. As citizens of the United States, they tended to stand strongly against slavery. Many German Americans thus answered Lincoln's call for troops.[7]

Maryland's Civil War music thus expressed both Union and Confederate sentiments. So some citizens issued Union-sanctioned publications and attended public events featuring stars and stripes and the singing of patriotic tunes, while others surreptitiously printed Confederate song sheets and defiantly sang songs of Confederate sympathy. Baltimore, which hitherto had supplied music to the South, found its southern market largely blocked at war's outbreak, and the role of that

city in American music publishing waned markedly. New York, Philadelphia, Chicago, Cincinnati, and other Union cities easily absorbed the lost business.

With so many able-bodied men fleeing to join the rebels or enlisting with the Union army, Maryland's instrument manufacturing also fell off considerably. The federal government took over the Stieff piano factory in Baltimore and used it as a hospital. The Knabe Piano Company barely survived the war years, shifting its market from the South to the West. Erben's Baltimore organ factory closed in 1863.[8]

Maryland Sings for the South

Despite Union-imposed martial law, pro-Confederate sentiment did find a musical voice. Confederate composers apparently tried to avoid American minstrel tunes or lyrics, however popular they were in the South, wishing to downplay slavery as an issue, at least among themselves. Instead they focused on chivalry and the "Spirit of '76." Southern lyricists justified secession as necessary to preserve liberties and property rights, comparing the war between the states to the American and French revolutions. Early Baltimore titles like "Chivalrous C.S.A.! Air 'Vive la Compagnie!'" (n.p., 1861); "God Save the South, words by a Baltimorean" (Benteen, 1862); "The Baltimore Rebel Song. 1776 Versus 1861" (a great example of an underground publication, as it was printed as a simple broadside with neither date nor publisher given); and "The Volunteer; or, It is My Country's Call" (McCaffrey, 1862) rang with hope. Others made fun of Lincoln and his advisers. In 1861 Charles Denstedt composed "The Maryland Guard Galope," which the publisher "respectfully dedicated to the Battalion." The Maryland Guard, aligned with the Democratic Party, supported the racial status quo and after Fort Sumter largely went south to join the Confederate army.

In Baltimore such expression caught the attention of Union authorities, who shut down the pro-Southern presses. Maryland's Confederate publishers recognized the inferior grade of paper available and foresaw the consequent decline in production quality. With a smaller, impoverished consumer base, many rebel songs appeared in mere broadsheet form, something rarely seen in the North, where sheet-music profits were pumped into fancy new publications. Lyrics sympathetic to the South also evolved over the course of the war, with the most exuberant Confederate songs dating from the first year of conflict. Later music reflected an increasingly depressed spirit. The pro-Southern music industry, like the confiscated houses of Confederate Marylanders, fell apart over time.

Yet, Maryland's awkward position as a Confederate-leaning state under martial law became a rallying point for Southern poets and lyricists. Forced underground, Confederate publishers and composers in Baltimore wisely left their names off sheet music and broadsides. Their provocative song titles during the occupation of Baltimore included "Are We Free?," "The Debt of Maryland," "There's Life in the Old Land Yet," "Song of the Baltimore Rebels," and "Down-Trodden Maryland," the last of which carried the initials N.G.R. Perhaps these were the initials of Dr. Nicholas G. Ridgely, of the slaveholding family that owned the Hampton mansion and estate north of Baltimore. Butler Brayne Minor boldly attached his name to "The Baltimore Greys." When in 1863 the Baltimore Daily Republican published a paean to the Confederacy, "The Southern Cross," mocking "The Star-Spangled Banner," it brought down the wrath of the authorities, who closed the paper. Some songs revealed a local focus, as did "Smallwood's Infantry Song" (Westminster) and "Maryland Zouaves Own," about a regiment mustered in Richmond, set to the tune of "Dixie." Southern lyricists memorialized Confederate prisoners at Fort McHenry, called on Maryland to secede, praised the Old Line troops, expressed resentment of the occupying forces in Baltimore, and hoped that the Confederate army would rescue the state. Music was clearly the voice of these people.

While such songs were especially dear to Maryland soldiers fighting far from home, they also captured the tragic situation that fueled other Confederates' general frustration, anger, and determination as only music can, as in the lyrics of one song: "My sword shall not ingloriously rust! / Exiled, I swear to die, or set thee free."[9]

Out-of-state publishers also issued songs lamenting Maryland's plight, including "Hark! O'er the Southern Hills," by "A Southern Lady." Other states in both the South and the North had their own songs, but Maryland may have been the most frequently mentioned state in the Civil War repertory.

James Ryder Randall's emotional poem "Maryland" became the state's most widely recognized Civil War song; indeed, it currently serves as Maryland's official state song.[10] The son of a Baltimore merchant, Randall was teaching English at Poydras College in Point Coupée, Louisiana, when war broke out. He penned his nine stanzas upon receiving the news of the blood shed in Baltimore on April 19, 1861, blood spilled when citizens sympathetic to the Confederacy fired upon Union troops as they passed through the city. Randall's poem first appeared in the New Orleans Delta, and soon thereafter it appeared in print in Baltimore, where it was seen by a young woman whose family lived in Mount Vernon Place, Jennie Cary. Cary proposed setting Randall's words to the melody of the German melody "O Tannenbaum," which Charles Ellerbock adapted. The Baltimore firm of Miller & Beacham straightaway published it as sheet music. Ellerbock expanded the original poem's refrain from "Maryland" to "Maryland, My Maryland!" In July 1861, Cary slipped across the Potomac into Virginia and sang it to Confederate troops shortly after the First Battle of Bull Run (also known as the Battle of First Manassas). From then on Ellerbock's setting became a rallying song, reprinted by nearly as many publishers as "Dixie" and parodied under the titles "Delaware, My Delaware" and "The Union Maryland," among many others.

In addition to resounding in thousands of Confederate parlors, "Maryland, My Maryland!" held special meaning for many rebel soldiers. John H. Stone, a Catholic farmer from Charles County, served as a first lieutenant in Company B, Second Maryland Infantry. He referred to the song in his diary and also wrote to his sister Sallie from Camp Maryland, Richmond: "At night we were entertained by General A. P. Hill's wife," he wrote, "who played & sang for our benefit. My Maryland being the piece most enjoyed."[11] In late June

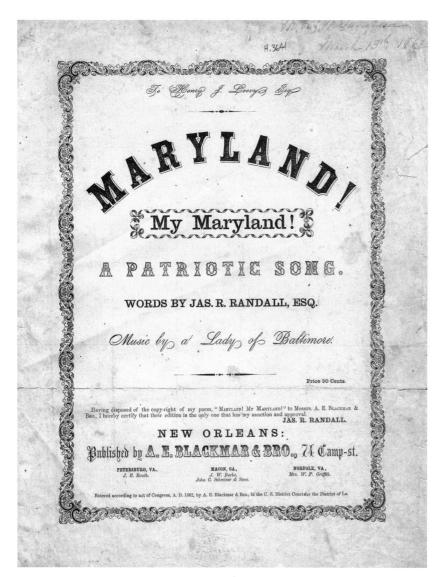

Sheet-music cover for "Maryland! My Maryland!" Based on a poem later set to the tune widely known as "O, Christmas Tree," James Ryder Randall's song appeared commonly as "Maryland, My Maryland!" or even just "My Maryland!" It became a war cry throughout the South. This cover gives a sense of where some Confederate music was published once the presses in Baltimore were silenced: New Orleans; Petersburg and Norfolk, Virginia; Macon, Georgia. Lester S. Levy Collection, Sheridan Libraries, Johns Hopkins University, box 93, item 135.

1863, Stone's regiment crossed into Maryland, fording the Potomac during a heavy rainstorm in waist-deep water and rapid current. When the Maryland troops crossed the C&O Canal, General George H. Steuart, known as "Maryland Steuart," "dismounted & kissed the ground, at sight of which the men sent up one long loud shout for My Maryland."[12] Other rebel diaries refer to regimental bands playing "Maryland, My Maryland!" when crossing the Potomac into Washington, Frederick, or Montgomery County. John Hill Hewitt, who left Baltimore at the onset of war to run the theater in Richmond, Virginia, remembered that this song "kept alive the drooping spirits of the battle-worn sol-

diers. . . . I have heard [Randall's] 'Maryland' sung with stirring effect by upwards of 5,000 men. The Marylanders, in particular, claimed it as their battle-song."[13] Randall's poem "Maryland" took on a new life not just as an American parlor song but as a band piece and a rally song of tremendous significance.

Hewitt also recognized the power of another poem, "All Quiet on the Potomac Tonight," by Ethel Lynn Beers of Boston. The Bard of Baltimore now turned Bard of the Confederacy, Hewitt produced the most popular of several musical settings of Beers's poem. Her powerful, mock-sarcastic lines concern a "mere" enlisted man dying unnoticed, and Hewitt's creation of a

The Rebels Dream in Prison, by John Jacob Omenhausser. Omenhausser, a Confederate prisoner of war, sketched this fantasy of a better life during his confinement at Point Lookout, Maryland. The unusually shaped guitar that the woman strums was likely drawn from memory and not an actual model, yet the opulent scene of courting a wealthy woman remains timeless. Maryland Manuscripts Collection, item 5213, Special Collections, University of Maryland.

happy, giglike melody heightens the poem's ironic message. As the Potomac served as both a literal and a symbolic dividing line between North and South, this song went beyond local to national significance. Hewitt's setting of "All Quiet" ranks along with "Dixie," "The Bonnie Blue Flag," and "Maryland, My Maryland!" among the favorite songs of all Confederates, not only those from Maryland.

Other war songs, many by amateurs, offered colorful Confederate viewpoints. A series of verses survives in J. H. Steever's plane trigonometry notebook. He copied some verses from the popular broadside titled "The Exiled Soldier's Adieu to Maryland," including the following:

> Adieu my home! Adieu dear Maryland!
> for honor calls me now away from thee!
> To end my days within my native land.
> Had ever been sweetest hope to me.[14]

Later in Steever's book, someone copied out the "Maryland Boys Camp Song" and dated it September 27, 1862

(ten days after the Battle of Antietam, also referred to as Sharpsburg). It made the author's views clear in its five powerful verses, one of which follows:

> From hill to hill, exultant shrill,
> Our battle cry sings forth:
> Freedom or death on every breath,
> And hatred to the north.[15]

Subtlety has its place in some lyrics but clearly not in these.

Maryland's Songs for Union

During the war, exercising what one might call a musical advantage, Northern publishers issued some ten times as many pro-Union song sheets as their counterparts printed in support of the Southern war effort. Union presses in both the East and the Midwest published handsome sheet music of ever-increasing quantity and quality. Firms in Chicago and St. Louis competed successfully with those in New York, Boston, and Philadelphia. George F. Root, based in Chicago, churned out hits like "The Battle Cry of Freedom,"

MOST RESPECTFULLY DEDICATED TO PRESIDENT
JEFFERSON DAVIS.
CONFEDERACY MARCH.

Jeff'n Davis
Miss

BY
ALFRED F. TOULMIN.
OF PATAPSCO INSTITUTE.

Lithographed cover for "Confederacy March"—"Most Respectfully Dedicated to President Jefferson Davis . . . by Alfred F. Toulmin of [the] Patapsco Institute." This pro-Confederate composition was issued by the Baltimore publisher George Willig in 1861, before Union forces seized control of the presses. A women's finishing school founded in 1837 in Ellicott City and a favorite among some leading Southern families, the Patapsco Female Institute for years under the direction of its headmistress Almira Lincoln Phelps had encouraged music-making. Toulmin taught music at the institute. E. Sachse & Company, of Baltimore, created this cover. Celia M. Holland, Ellicott City, Maryland—Mill Town, U.S.A. (Chicago: Adams, 1970), 147. Lester S. Levy Collection of Sheet Music, Sheridan Libraries, Johns Hopkins University, box 94, item 17.

"Tramp, Tramp, Tramp," and "Just Before the Battle, Mother." Legend has it that rebel officers said after the war that if they had had the music of the Union army, they "would have won in a flash!"

Baltimore presses leaning toward Lincoln published a smattering of music, but they produced no Union songs of broad popularity. Of more local interest were songs directly attacking two allegedly Southern-leaning officials, Baltimore's mayor, George William Brown, and the city's police marshal, George P. Kane, both of whom Union authorities had jailed for their roles in

handling the Pratt Street riot of April 19, 1861.[16] Much of the officially condoned sheet music published in Baltimore carried obvious titles like "Help us Save the Union," "Union Ode," and "Cling to the Union."

Like the Confederates, Union composers within and outside the state capitalized on Maryland's tenuous position between North and South. "The Slain at Baltimore" (Philadelphia, 1861) served as a formal Yankee response to "Maryland, My Maryland!" An especially cutting song referring to those Baltimore women who tried to aid the Confederate war effort took the title

"The Ladies of Baltimore, God Bless Them, they have beautiful Turned up Noses." The intended melody for this song eluded no one:

> Our father's Flag, it waves once more,
> In Maryland! my Maryland!
> Secession's dead in Baltimore,
> Through Maryland! my Maryland![17]

Meanwhile, "A Lady of Baltimore" composed "Our Union Flag" (Baltimore: Thomas G. Doyle, n.d.), which was sung to the popular tune of "Nellie Grey." The song sheet noted that this new work parodied "Our Southern Flag." The fifth verse proclaimed:

> And the North will meet them bravely, with her wisest and
>   her best;
> Frank and warm will be the greeting of the free,
> And the glory and the honor of the vast and chainless
>   West,
> Shall be offered at the shrine of liberty.

Northern songs ranged from those praising the Union cause and its victories and leaders to attempts to turn pro-Southern songs on their heads. Indignant over secession, Oliver Wendell Holmes in 1861 added to Francis Scott Key's original four stanzas a fifth, which appeared in songbooks of the era.

> When our land is illumined with liberty's smile,
> If a foe from within strikes a blow at her glory,
> Down, down with the traitor that tries to defile
> The flag of the stars, and the page of her story!
>   By the millions unchained,
>   Who their birthright have gained
>   We will keep her bright blazon forever unstained;
>   And the star-spangled banner in triumph shall
>   wave,
>   While the land of the free is the home of the brave.[18]

Music Encamped

The romanticized images of destruction, heartbreak, and death that appeared in parlor songs barely conveyed the true experience of war. Quite apart from the horror of battle, soldiers' daily lives were harsh, boring, and mostly inglorious. As the rigors of marching and camp life settled in, most men adopted crude and simple music to blow off steam. They parodied their enemies' most cherished music; they roughed up—concocted new words for—the delicate parlor songs they knew from home. Since some soldiers could read lyrics, pocket songsters, including John Pendleton Kennedy's *American Songster* (Baltimore, 1836), became popular in camp.

Amid the booming of cannon and the rattling of musket fire, through the din of confused shouts and painful screams, punctuated by awful silences, field musicians were the army's principal means of communication during battle. Descriptions survive of whole military bands, not just fifes and drums, playing patriotic music in the midst of battle, inspiring soldiers to fight rather than flee, to rally through sheer will and spirit rather than run in plain terror. In addition to its crucial role on the battlefield, field music served a functional role in camp. The playing of duty signals on drum, fife, and bugle or trumpet ordered a typical soldier's day in camp. Some fifers and drummers studied at the army music school in New York. The English-born Frederick Nicholas Crouch served as a trumpeter in the Confederate army, having made his home in Baltimore for years. A composer, scholar, and lecturer, Crouch had studied at the Royal Academy of Music. He wrote two operas and some two thousand songs, the best remembered of which is "Kathleen Mavoureen" (London, 1838).[19] Talented musicians like Crouch at times cheered up their fellow soldiers in camp, adding hope to the otherwise unglamorous, dirty, and alternately terrifying and boring hours between fighting and marching.

While ceremonial bands functioned in the Civil War largely as had those during the Revolution, instrumentation reflected the evolution toward brass and away from woodwind instruments. In the 1850s brass bands entered a golden age that lasted more than half a century under the batons of Patrick S. Gilmore and John Philip Sousa. Numerous amateur and professional groups played an abundance of European and Ameri-

A Bivouac Fire on the Potomac, by Winslow Homer, in Harper's Weekly, December 21, 1861. Music and dance improved Civil War soldiers' spirits and helped them blow off steam, offering emotional escape from the grisly realities of war. Many other wood engravings by Winslow Homer appeared in the popular Harper's Weekly magazine, and he painted a more realistic depiction of soldiers in a time of sadness, entitled Home Sweet Home. Archives of the Peabody Institute of the Johns Hopkins University.

can music composed and arranged for them. Civil War military bands decreased in size as the war progressed, especially Confederate bands, who received less training and had fewer supplies. Testifying to the severity of Confederate hardship, musicians from Maryland deserted Confederate service early in the war and swam across the Potomac from Virginia. Made up of professional musicians, regimental bands typically required members to "double" on two or more instruments each. The names of some Maryland military musicians survive in paymasters' records.[20]

The Bostonian Patrick Gilmore, the most celebrated bandleader of the day, served as the official bandmaster of the Union army. Gilmore claimed to have written "When Johnny Comes Marching Home," although its melody closely resembles an eighteenth-century Scottish song, "John Anderson, My Jo." While by 1862 regimental bands on both sides mostly had disbanded due to the rigors of war and a shortage of good soldiers, Union brigade and post bands played an important role in boosting the morale of both soldiers and civilians. A

description of the Union camp at Cumberland in 1861 speaks of "a fine band" that "discoursed sweet music in the camp and through the city, and every day became festive with military pomp and display."[21]

Music of the Maryland US Colored Troops

As the war ground on, Union spirits received a much-needed influx of musical energy as the first African Americans enrolled in service. All six Maryland regiments of the US Colored Troops, mustered in late 1863, had field musicians, and one regiment had its own band. This band had begun performing professionally in Hagerstown in 1854 as the Moxley Band. The former slave Robert Moxley, two of his brothers, and nine other civilian players proved quite competent as the First Regimental Band and quickly earned promotion to brigade band. Moxley's talented group served as a Union army showpiece in Maryland, Virginia, and then Texas after the war, building an impressive service record along the way. Upon honorable discharge and return to Hagerstown, Maryland's earliest African

Drum belonging to a Union drummer boy named James W. Sank. A silver plaque on the drum reads, "Presented to James W. Sank, by the officers and men of Camp A Purnell Legion Md. Vols. May 1863." The interior maker's label reads, "From the Union Manufacturing Co. 98 W. Baltimore Street, Corner of Holiday, Baltimore, Maryland Drums of all sizes from $1 to $50." Drummers, as well as flag bearers, were defenseless and utterly vulnerable to enemy fire. Many sentimental songs of the war years feature fallen drummer boys, the most famous being "The Drummer Boy of Shiloh." Sank, fortunately, survived the war and worked as a letter carrier in Baltimore. Other local drum-makers, William Boucher Sr. and Jr., active for a time at 38 East Baltimore Street, also made banjos. Courtesy of the Maryland Historical Society, 1995.18.1.

American military band briefly returned to performing in public, but war-inflicted health problems cut the venture short.[22]

The presence of African Americans in camp and on the march gave many Northerners their first exposure to genuine spirituals and plantation work songs, music more heartfelt and genuine than the demeaning minstrel-show songs so widely performed since the 1840s. Intense interest in this true African American music encouraged and supported publication of the first collection of spirituals, *Slave Songs of the United States*, in 1867.[23] African Americans' unofficial marching tunes and campfire songs helped relieve the tedium of military life, much as a good sea chantey or railroad work song helped relieve drudgery and distract strained spirits.

Sotto Voce: Music in a Divided City

During four years of war and despite the sharp social divisions the war caused in Maryland, private life went on, and music continued. Except, that is, at a Baltimore institution whose birth coincided with the outbreak of the conflict. As a partner in the firm of Riggs, Peabody & Co., George Peabody settled in Baltimore in 1815, and over the next two decades he built a lucrative dry-goods business. He also acquired a lifelong and useful circle of friends. Peabody maintained close ties to Maryland affairs, social, political, and mercantile, even after moving to London in 1837. Two of his most influential Baltimore friends—Charles James Madison Eaton, a patron of the arts and a staunch promoter of American talent, and John Pendleton Kennedy, a Virginia-born legislator and man of letters—corresponded regularly with Peabody and met Peabody in London during the 1850s. Peabody knew how poorly the musical life of Baltimore compared with that of London and the cities he had visited on the Continent. Determined to create an institution that would provide a setting in which art and music might flourish, and inspired by his discussions with Eaton and Kennedy, Peabody decided to establish a cultural center in the city where he had begun to make his fortune.

In February 1857 the merchant prince returned to Baltimore to see old friends and work out final plans. Mayor Thomas Swann presided over a sumptuous dinner party for more than eighty guests in Peabody's honor. During the course of the evening the wine list, rather than art and culture, seems to have dominated the conversation. The following day, Kennedy agreed to draft the letter outlining Peabody's new institution,

Band of the 107th US Colored Troops in November 1865, then stationed in Arlington, Virginia. Few of the instruments they hold, known then as saxhorns, remain in use today. Photo by William M. Smith. Library of Congress glass negative LC-B817-7861, lot 4190F.

which would include "a splendid music saloon." After some prodding, Kennedy produced an acceptable draft, and Peabody scrawled his name at the bottom of the revised document.[24] When the contents of the letter appeared in the Baltimore newspapers, his ship had weighed anchor for London.

The first of its kind in the nation, Peabody's institution promised to provide Baltimoreans and Marylanders with a scholars' library, a lecture series, an academy of music, and an art gallery. It promised to redirect development of the musical arts in the city. In mid-April 1859 a dozen Peabody Institute trustees gathered on the southeast corner of Mount Vernon Place to oversee the laying of a cornerstone.[25] Two years later, as trustees prepared to dedicate the completed building, Confederates fired on Fort Sumter and the Peabody trustees divided, having strikingly different views on the issues that had led to civil war. Union authorities soon arrested one trustee, Severn Teackle Wallis, for his Southern sympathies and eventually imprisoned him at

Fort Warren, near Boston. Another, Enoch Pratt, grew wealthy providing horseshoes to the Union army. John Pendleton Kennedy, despite his Virginia roots, warned Marylanders against leaving the Union. Peabody himself supported the Union from London. The east wing of the splendid building designed by Edmund G. Lind, an architect and musician, sat vacant and quiet in Mount Vernon Place. Delayed by the start of the Civil War, its doors would not open until 1866.

Even so, church music in Maryland thrived, and although theater and concert life dropped off considerably, Baltimore theaters occasionally offered minstrel shows, military dramas, English and French plays, operas, and concerts. In 1861 Kunkel's Ethiopian Opera House opened in Charles Willson Peale's old museum building. Professional actors and musicians received passes to travel unmolested across battle lines, since both sides sought entertainment. Most entertainers stayed in the North, where the pay was better. The soprano Adelina Patti, who commanded five thousand

A Musical Soirée, etching by Frederick Dielman, 1872. Dielman's good-natured caricature portrays his friends (left to right) Otto Sutro, Asger Hamerik, Professor Henry Allen, Kate Dieter (standing), Professor Bernard Courlaender, Henry Jungnickel, and Henry Wysham. Copy in Archives of the Peabody Institute of the Johns Hopkins University.

dollars in gold for her performances, made a Baltimore appearance in 1862. Earlier, at the White House, she had sung "Home, Sweet Home" for President and Mrs. Lincoln as they mourned the loss of their son Willie. That same year, the Norwegian violinist and composer Ole Bull first performed in Baltimore on his American tour. The University of Maryland commencement ball of 1863 featured a band, likely filled out with military musicians. On patriotic occasions like Washington's Birthday and the Fourth of July, Marylanders sang songs and enjoyed band concerts with wartime gusto. They also attended wartime military balls and fairs for soldier relief.[26]

As before, many Marylanders made music in their parlors and sent their children to music lessons. The unrest did impede the travels of touring musicians, but the pianist and composer Louis Moreau Gottschalk, a favorite of Marylanders, was an exception. Traveling tens of thousands of miles by rail, Gottschalk gave hundreds of concerts throughout the North in 1860–65. He repeatedly found his way to Baltimore in the war years, ignoring military restrictions to perform and enjoy the congenial company of friends and colleagues in

the city's "Latin Quarter," an area northwest of Mount Vernon Place that was a haven for musicians.[27] "I love Baltimore," he wrote. "I love its people. I am assured that they are Secessionists, but I do not wish to know anything about it, and have no right to speak but of that which they have let me know—the warmth of their friendship, and the constancy with which they keep their appreciation of me as an artist. Besides at Baltimore they love the arts. They sing more there, and better, than in many of the larger cities of the United States. The professorship of the piano is represented there by artists of great talent, who love me (*O rara avis!*), and whom I love. O Baltimoreans, my friends, may you some day forget our misfortunes!!"[28] Gottschalk left the country in 1865 after having a scandalous affair with a student in a California seminary, but Louis G. Curlett, a composer and organist at the Catholic cathedral, so admired him that he named a son for him.

One of the principal members of the wartime musical community in Baltimore, Otto Sutro, had sailed from New York to Baltimore in 1851. An organist, conductor, composer, and music store owner who had studied with Felix Mendelsohn,[29] Sutro had an engaging personality that quickly won him an extended circle of influential friends. His boundless energy and penchant for organization soon secured his place as the central figure in Maryland's amateur and professional music circles. On the occasion of his birthday in 1858, Sutro held a bachelor party to reciprocate a host of invitations he had received from friends and colleagues. The successful event began a tradition of regular evening entertainments at Sutro's residence on North Charles Street, above Saratoga.[30] These affairs quickly grew in size and popularity, attracting the city's leading musicians. At about ten o'clock they would begin gathering for a night of music and a rollicking good time, closing before dawn with a raucous performance of Verdi's "Anvil Chorus," with coal scuttles, andirons, pots, and pans substituted for the anvils. The group included the lawyer and flutist Henry C. Wysham and the violinist Henry A. Allen, members of the Peabody faculty, along with the musically gifted artists John R. Robertson, Dr. Adalbert Johann Volck,[31] and Leonce Rabillon. Composers drawn to these congenial surroundings performed their own works, which Sutro occasionally published.

Just a few blocks away, at the painter Frank B. Mayer's studio at Lexington and Charles Streets, a small group of Baltimore artists and art lovers that included the stonemason Hugh Sisson, George B. Coale, Hugh Newell, and the merchant William T. Walters, converged on the same evenings for their own informal gatherings.[32] Volck, a regular at these affairs as well as Sutro's Wednesday group, suggested that instead of monopolizing Mayer's time and studio, they should combine and rent a place for their gatherings. On March 14, 1859, the group organized under the name Allston Association. It met at 8 West Mount Vernon Place.

At the outbreak of the Civil War, Allston members generally sided with the South, Volck being conspicuous among them. He offered his home as a rendezvous for Confederate sympathizers and under the pseudonym "Blada" published cartoons and caricatures that lampooned federal and state officials.[33] Volck was arrested for sedition and served time as a prisoner at Fort McHenry. After his release he used his pen to make visual records of club performances—as long as they lasted. In 1863 the Union military commander in Baltimore closed down the Allston Association.[34]

HOMAGE TO THE LADIES OF BALTIMORE

ORIOLE

MARCH

SONG & CHORUS

Instrumental ◇4
With Vocal part ◇5

Separate
Vocal part ◇1

PUBLISHED BY

OTTO SUTRO

207 W. BALTIMORE ST.
BALTIMORE MD.

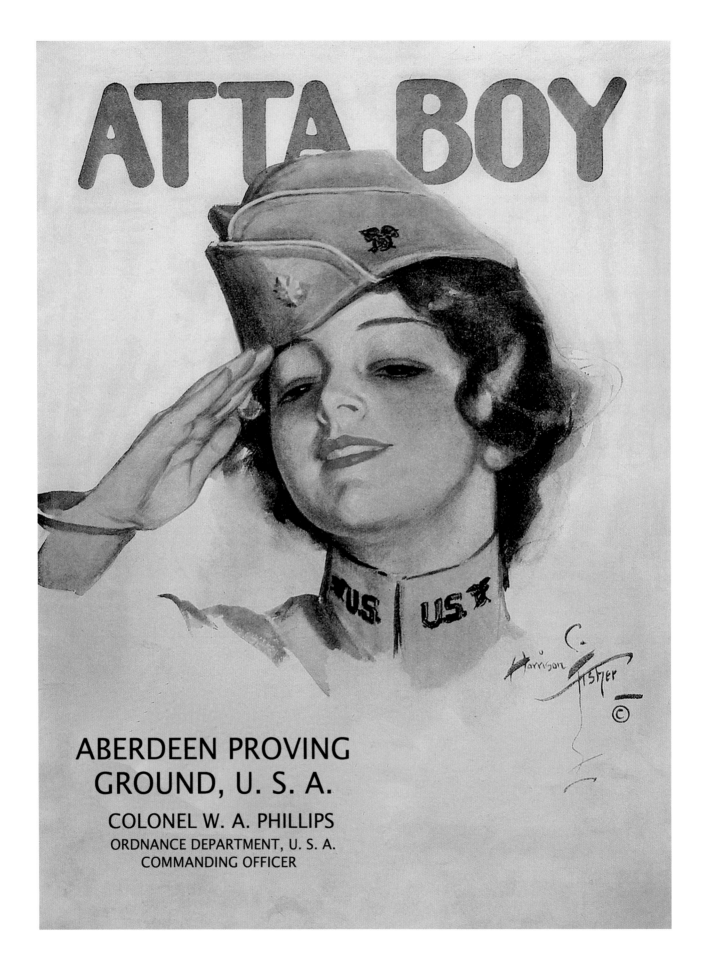

ATTA BOY

ABERDEEN PROVING
GROUND, U. S. A.

COLONEL W. A. PHILLIPS
ORDNANCE DEPARTMENT, U. S. A.
COMMANDING OFFICER

POPULAR EDITION
SAILING DOWN THE CHESAPEAKE BAY
SONG
WORDS BY
JEAN C. HAVEZ
MUSIC BY
GEORGE BOTSFORD
STARMER
5
JEROME H. REMICK & CO.
NEW YORK DETROIT

u

The Messrs. Shubert
present

My Maryland

A MUSICAL ROMANCE
BASED ON CLYDE FITCH'S FAMOUS PLAY
"BARBARA FRITCHIE"

BOOK & LYRICS BY
DOROTHY DONNELLY

MUSIC BY
SIGMUND ROMBERG

BOOK & ENSEMBLES
STAGED BY
J. C. HUFFMAN

DANCES BY
JACK MASON

Your Land And My Land
Silver Moon
Won't You Marry Me ?
Mother
Boys In Gray

SETTINGS BY
WATSON BARRATT
ENTIRE PRODUCTION
UNDER THE PERSONAL
DIRECTION OF
Mr. J. J. SHUBERT

HARMS
INCORPORATED
BY ARRANGEMENT WITH
M. WITMARK & SONS
NEW YORK

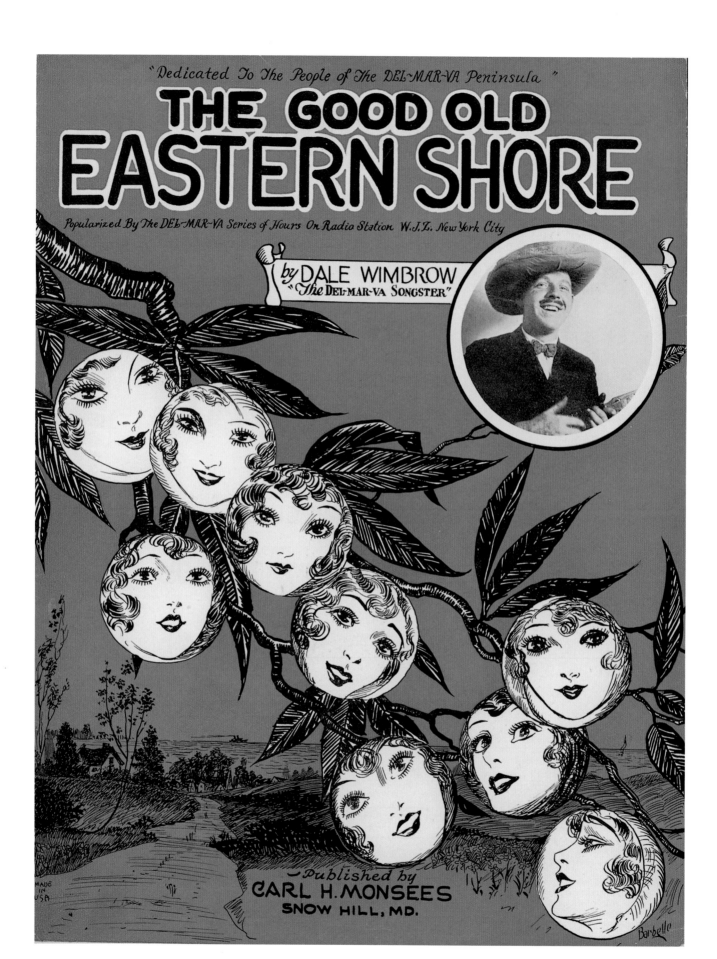

BALTIMORE
.VOCAL WALTZ.

2/- NET

CECIL LENNOX & C°
134. CHARING CROSS ROAD.
LONDON. W.C.2.

COPYRIGHT.

BY
HENRY. J
STAFFORD

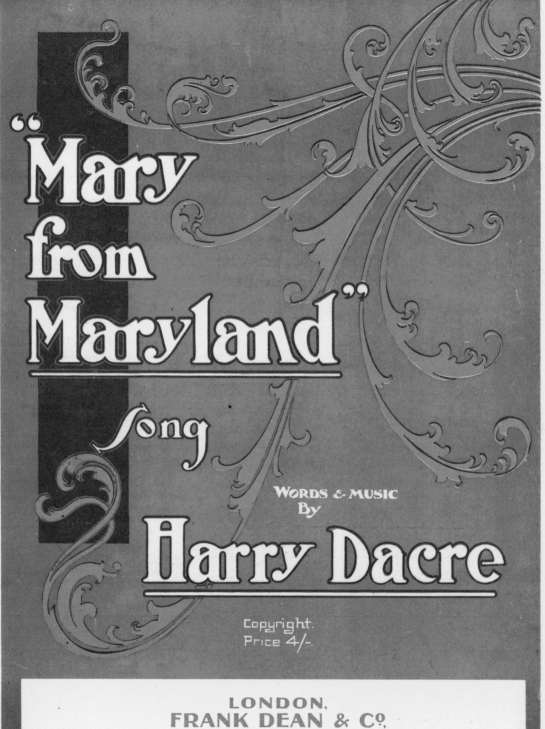

"Mary from Maryland"

Song

WORDS & MUSIC By

Harry Dacre

Copyright.
Price 4/-

LONDON,
FRANK DEAN & C?,
40, BERNERS S?, OXFORD S?, W.

U.S.A. SOL BLOOM, NEW YORK, CHICAGO, SAN FRANCISCO.   SYDNEY, W.H. PALING & C?, L?

LOWE & BRYDONE, LITH., LONDON. W.

CHAPTER FOUR

Toward Union and Concord

DURING THE LATE NINETEENTH CENTURY, when one could find amateur ensembles in many Maryland communities, Baltimore reigned as the musical capital of the Chesapeake. The city supported a large number of music publishers and instrument makers, especially piano manufacturers. In Baltimore as in other large American cities, people of means welcomed the traveling artists who played music for a living, whether orchestral or "popular," and benefited from resident theater orchestras.

Small groups made loud music. At the end of the war, still under the tutelage of Otto Sutro, the Allston Club reopened at 67 North Charles Street, and membership grew swiftly. A former soldier in Lee's army, Innes Randolph, came to Baltimore in 1868 to practice law and soon joined the group. Besides legal work, he devoted time to writing poems and sketches for city newspapers. At length he left the bar and became an editorial writer on the *Baltimore American*, a position he held for the remainder of his days. Highly respected as a critic of music and art, Randolph enjoyed a reputation as a poet, composer—mostly of humorous songs written chiefly for his friends—and sculptor.[1] He enjoyed entertaining them with satires of Italian grand opera. The artistic dentist Adalbert Volck sketched club members as they staged these events, which included *The Grasshopper: A Tragic Cantata* and a club favorite, Randolph's *Good Old Rebel*.

In 1869 Sutro's marriage to Arianna Handy threatened to put an end to Allston congeniality, but William Prescott Smith, along with others, including, eventually, the Sutros themselves, formed a new ensemble they called the Wednesday Club. For years it met for evening soirées and hosted visiting musicians at 207 West Baltimore Street. Members persuaded Sutro to preside over this club and chose other officers and a board. The bylaws called for a committee of five professors of music, who would take turns overseeing "the direction of music." The club carried on the tradition of celebrating Sutro's birthday. One of the original members, the piano industrialist Ernest Knabe, provided the club with a new piano. Unlike earlier musical groups of its ilk, the Wednesday Club welcomed ladies (as "auxiliary members") to its monthly evening sessions. As the club waxed, murmurs and then voluble cries of alarm went up as billiards and

Cover for The Grasshopper: A Tragic Cantata, by Innes Randolph, illustrated by A. J. Volck, facsimile ca. 1865. This fanciful satire of Italian grand opera, dedicated to the Wednesday Club, was originally published by Otto Sutro. Courtesy of John McLean, publisher of the facsimile.

cards threatened to displace art. Sutro led a revolt that produced yet another Wednesday Club, one made up of nearly one hundred music lovers. Their rules made their purposes clear. "The amusements and entertainments of the Club at the regular meetings on Wednesday evenings shall be Strictly Musical," they declared, "until ½ past ten o'clock. . . . Perfect Silence must prevail."[2]

The club's numbers reached two hundred, with a long waiting list of men clamoring for admission into the magic circle of seventy-five "active members." The Wednesday Club built a splendid new concert hall, seating 750, at the corner of Centre and St. Paul Streets. On January 31, 1877, it held its first gathering in the new quarters. "Crockery, glassware, furniture or other property of the club, broken or injured by a member must be paid by him" the governors warned.[3] With Sutro at the piano and Knabe's smiling face in the audience, harmony prevailed, and the club exerted a powerful influence on the musical life of the city for years to come.

Another musical society testified to the persistent German influence in Baltimore. Late in the war, with the city's Männerchor Singing Association performing at the ceremony, the Concordia German Association of Baltimore laid the cornerstone for Concordia Hall, a new building on the west side of Eutaw Street, south of German Street (now Redwood Street). Opening at about the time the war ended, and aptly named, the new hall seated nearly two thousand people and featured a garden with a pavilion for outdoor gatherings. Charles Lenschow himself wrote the *Concordia March* to mark the event.[4] He went on to form the Baltimore Amateur Orchestra and, as director after 1869, to breathe new life into the German Männerchor.

A New Birth of Music

For decades young American musicians had relied heavily on teachers with European training. Parents may have worried about exposing their talented and impressionable young children to the corrupting influence of the Old World, but in any event few American families could afford the huge expense of study at European conservatories and academies. So the region and the country took notice when, on a bright October day in 1866, long-postponed ceremonies opened the Peabody Institute in Baltimore. Judge George W. Dobbin, of the Wednesday Club, read remarks that John Pendleton Kennedy, the Institute's president, had written before departing on a trip to Paris: "The strife of five years, steeped in the carnage and desolation of a civil war of such bitterness as history never before recorded has come to an end, and the frightened propriety of national and social life is creeping back to the homesteads. We have invited our fellow-citizens to partake in the celebration of the opening of the Institute, and to add a new pleasure to the happy change in our public affairs."[5] The elderly George Peabody once again journeyed from London, using the cheerful occasion resolutely to defend his right during the late war to maintain friendships with men who had cast their lot with the Confederacy.[6] The opening of the Peabody Institute captured the interest of major newspapers on both sides of the Atlantic.

Nothing in the years following the end of the war had a more profound impact on American music than the introduction of the Peabody Institute's conservatory. American conservatories provided high-quality training for musicians and became a powerful force, raising the standards of musical performance and the average level of musical culture in the United States. The musical branch of the Peabody Institute, the Academy of Music, drew highly trained performers and teachers from all over the world. These men and women formed choral and instrumental ensembles, organized music festivals, improved the quality of music in places of worship, and enriched the cultural life in cities and towns in Maryland and the surrounding states.

Leadership of the new academy fell to a Civil War veteran, brevet Brigadier General James Monroe Deems, a Baltimore native who had commanded the First Maryland Cavalry at Gettysburg.[7] Director of the Lenschow Amateur Orchestra and the Haydn Amateur Orchestra, Deems had offered to provide music for the

Peabody's dedication. He began his musical career playing with the band attached to his father's militia company, receiving instruction from the band's conductor, Captain William Roundtree. Deems became proficient on the clarinet and the French horn before going on to master the piano, the organ, and later, after studies in Dresden, the cello. In 1839 he had sailed to Europe, as did many accomplished musicians of his day, to pursue his musical studies, and he achieved a respectable reputation as a composer. The transmission in 1844 of the first telegraph message, sent from Washington, DC, over wires covered with rope yarn to Baltimore's Mt. Clare Depot, inspired Deems to write his popular *Telegraph Quickstep*. Deems earned a lasting reputation as the composer of one of the first American oratorios, *Nebuchadnezzar*.[8]

Although the Academy of Music lacked teaching studios, Deems opened its first season on December 22, 1866, with three lectures and a series of twelve concerts. He recruited local musicians to form a small orchestra and presented concerts in the Institute's lecture hall on alternate Saturday evenings. The following February, a writer in *Dwight's Journal of Music*, a Boston publication of national pretensions, commented on the new academy with characteristic condescension: "Its design is too vast and utopian for realization, and I think, if it will confine itself to the formation, from local material, of a tolerably complete orchestra, and build up a thoroughly complete musical Library for use and reference, it will do all that can be reasonably expected of it."[9]

During its first years the Peabody Academy operated much along the lines suggested by the correspondent for *Dwight's*. The concerts found large and appreciative audiences, and the public soon took to complaining about the difficulty and inconvenience involved in obtaining tickets. Even the Academy's critics readily admitted that the concerts presented the best musical talent in the city. The Peabody provost, Nathaniel Holmes Morison, despite his preoccupation with the library and lectures, had to concede that the modest Academy of Music had done most to win over the public to the Institute.

When the Peabody Academy of Music finally

George Peabody, ca. 1865. George Peabody settled in Baltimore in 1815. The young partner in the firm of Riggs, Peabody & Company spent the next two decades building up his business. In 1837 he moved to London to establish George Peabody & Company, a merchant-banking firm that would eventually become the House of Morgan. Peabody enjoyed music. He loved to sing and held boxes at the opera and the Royal Albert Hall. In 1857 Peabody returned to Baltimore—his first visit in twenty years—to visit friends and to work out the final plans for an institution he hoped would dramatically alter the city. Photo by John Jabez Edwin Paisley Mayall. Collection of Elizabeth Schaaf.

opened its first teaching studios at 34 Mulberry Street in October 1868, the trustees replaced Deems with another war veteran, the Vermont-born and Boston-educated organist and composer Lucien Southard, who had served as a cavalry captain in the Army of the Potomac.[10] The Academy's first faculty comprised two instructors in addition to Southard. He organized an orchestra of forty-one musicians drawn from the various theater orchestras, who were paid for their services. On November 21 they presented the first of twelve regular concerts. During the next two years, instructors in voice and flute were added.

Musicians teaching privately found little to celebrate in the new academy, which drew away many of their best students. Southard had no interest in creating a pe-

culiarly American institution, hoping instead to pattern the school on European conservatories like those in Paris and Leipzig. Soon after Southard's appointment, controversy over his musical qualifications began to rage in city newspapers. Many of the difficulties at the Institute were beyond Southard's control. The trustees' decision to scale back the orchestra in a futile attempt to reduce the Academy's rising expenses stymied the development of the fledgling ensemble. As a consequence, attendance at concerts dropped. Southard's inability to rally his meager faculty left the Academy of Music in a shambles. Teachers arrived late for lessons or failed to show up at all.[11] The chorus class disbanded when its membership fell from eighty-eight to four. Unwilling to shoulder responsibility for the floundering school,

Cover of sheet music for James Monroe Deems, *Bell Gallop*. The composer is shown conducting the Haydn Amateur Orchestra. At the beginning of the Civil War, Deems enlisted in the First Maryland Cavalry and was appointed major. He led the First Maryland at Gettysburg and was made a brigadier general for his gallantry in the field. After the war, he returned to Baltimore and resumed his profession as a musician and composer. He wrote to the Peabody board of trustees in the spring of 1866 offering to provide music for the Peabody's dedication. The trustees engaged Deems to lead the Peabody's fledgling Academy of Music, and he opened the Academy's first season, in 1866, with a series of twelve concerts. Archives of the Peabody Institute of the Johns Hopkins University.

Southard complained to the trustees of the impracticality, for a city like Baltimore, of an academy of music of the scope and design outlined in Peabody's original letter. In June 1871 he learned that his contract would not be renewed.[12]

The trustees looked to Europe for a new director. In the summer of 1871, after a four-month search, they engaged Asger Hamerik. A young and highly respected Danish composer and conductor recommended by Dietrich Fehrman, the American consul in Vienna and a good friend of Charles James Madison Eaton's,

Hamerik had studied with J. P. E. Hartmann and Niels Gade in Copenhagen and later with Hans von Bülow in Berlin and Hector Berlioz in Paris. Still a bachelor in his twenties when he sailed into the August heat of Baltimore, Hamerik appeared to be a youthful version of the conductor and composer Leopold Damrosch. His arrival did much to enhance Baltimore's standing in the world of music. Hamerik's works had been performed in the capitals of the Continent. At the World Exhibition in Paris in 1867, Napoleon III presented Hamerik with a gold medal "for services rendered" after the performance of his colossal *Hymn of Peace*, a piece that required the entire musical resources of the Garde de Paris, fourteen harps from the Grand Opéra, two church organs, and four church bells. Hamerik received a warm welcome into the city's musical circles and became a frequent and enthusiastic participant in the Sutro soirées. He was undoubtedly pleased to find musically sophisticated colleagues well acquainted with European musical life. Hamerik's close friends soon included the English-born violinist Henry A. Allen, who had played under Mendelssohn in the first performance of *Elijah*, and a fellow Dane, Bernard Courlaender, formerly court pianist and teacher to King Christian VIII and Princess Alexandra. Regulars at the Sutros events, Allen and Courlaender were members of the original Peabody faculty.[13]

The prospect of a new concert hall just a few blocks away from the Peabody Institute caused great celebration on the part of Hamerik and his circle of friends. Having learned that the hall would be called the Academy of Music, in June 1874 the new director of the Peabody persuaded trustees to adopt the name Conservatory of Music for the Institute's conservatory, better to reflect this new seriousness of purpose.[14] The newly styled Conservatory of Music took off under Hamerik's direction. After acquainting himself with the students, many of whom were young women, Hamerik made it clear to the trustees that he had no interest in running a mere school for girls. "As now practiced music is an importation, or a weak imitation of Europe, and not a plant which has any permanent root in American soil," he wrote with the authority of an immigrant. "The object of an American Conservatory of Music should, therefore, be to educate gifted boys in the practice of all kinds of instruments, and give them a thorough education, always keeping in mind that the education of women, for art, has a drawback—marriage." That said, most of the Peabody pianists were women. "We have no student who has passed the examination for a diploma—and but one who has received a certificate. She has studied Theory for 3 years, Vocal Music 4 years, Piano 4 years."[15]

Hamerik insisted on the introduction of theoretical

studies, a first-rate series of concerts, and a proper music library. Classes began on time, and complaints about faculty ceased. Special classes encouraged musical interest among public-school children (who then did not receive training in instrumental music). He increased the number of orchestra rehearsals and made needed changes in the orchestra's personnel. At the end of his first academic year, he took off for Europe, where he acquired a full set of orchestral wind instruments, all built to one standard of pitch, from the celebrated Parisian instrument maker Adolph Sax, the inventor of the saxophone. A new Hamlin & Mason organ, replacing one that had been damaged by mice and the unskilled workmen attempting repairs, and a Chickering concert grand from Otto Sutro were installed in the concert hall. The choice of Boston instruments could only have vexed Baltimore organ builders and piano manufacturers. Wm. Knabe & Co. alone produced from fifteen hundred to two thousand grand, upright, and square pianos a year in its new factory on Eutaw Street. The growing Conservatory had outgrown its quarters on Mulberry Street, however, so Hamerik pressed the trustees to provide space in the Institute's building for classes, practice rooms, and access to the lecture hall for rehearsals. Hamerik established a music library with important new editions from Paris, Leipzig, and Copenhagen. Guest artists of the first rank performed as soloists. The Peabody Symphony became a nationally known professional symphony orchestra, hailed in 1871 as "the best orchestra which Baltimore has ever professed."[16]

Hamerik's sophisticated programs introduced many unusual works to Marylanders, including Beethoven's "Choral Fantasy" and Ninth Symphony, Brahms' First Symphony, and Tchaikovsky's *Pathétique*, as well presenting the first performance of any work by Antonin Dvořák in Baltimore. Performances of contemporary compositions dominated the orchestra's programs. Marylanders in the 1870s heard music from notable contemporary, as opposed to classical, composers. Hamerik not only improved the quality of the orchestra and its parent institution but took to heart George Peabody's hope that the Institute would substantially im-

Asger Hamerik. The Danish composer and conductor Asger Hamerik (1843–1923) sailed to Baltimore in 1872 to become director of the Peabody Conservatory. Many of his symphonic works received their premiere performance in Baltimore. Archives of the Peabody Institute of the Johns Hopkins University.

prove the city's taste in the arts. Concert programs were specifically designed to educate Peabody audiences. To familiarize his students and the general public with the contemporary works that dominated the programs, Hamerik introduced preconcert lectures devoted to the composers whose works were being performed. He scheduled daytime lectures to accommodate women, who, he believed, would be more likely than men to attend. The results of his efforts were sufficiently dramatic to inspire comment in the press on the rise in the level of sophistication of Baltimore audiences, attributing this phenomenon attributed solely to Hamerik.

Anton Rubinstein, then on a concert tour sponsored by Steinway & Sons, came to Baltimore to give his "Last and Farewell" concerts in March 1873. Rubenstein became one of the first of the Peabody's illustrious visitors. He shared the stage at the Masonic Temple with Henri Wieniawski (billed as the only rival to the memory of Paganini) and the celebrated London soprano Louise

Liebhart.[17] Rubinstein readily accepted Hamerik's invitation to hear the young musicians studying at America's first conservatory. Himself the founder of the newly established conservatory in St. Petersburg, the first such in Russia, Rubenstein naturally took this opportunity to weigh the accomplishments of American students and assess the progress of a sister institution.[18]

Hamerik arranged to have almost the entire student body assembled for the visit. Rubinstein, observing how few males were among the ranks of Peabody students, remarked to Hamerik that "America can never expect to be musical unless the sons of America devote themselves more to music and not only to business. The daughters must not be the only ones studying music."[19] Nonetheless, paying the ladies a compliment, Rubinstein composed a short piece that he dedicated to the Baltimore women who had performed for him. Afterwards the whole entourage trooped down to Barnum's Hotel for a lively affair that lasted until four o'clock in the morning. When Rubenstein staged the first Concours International de Musique in St. Petersburg in 1890, he invited Hamerik to serve as the sole American judge.

In December 1874 Hamerik attended the entertainment for the visiting Leipzig Conservatory pianist Constantine Weickert. The program opened in glorious fashion with Gounod's march *La Reine de Saba* arranged for sixteen hands, played on two Chickering and two Steinway concert grand pianos. After a varied program of solo and ensemble offerings, the evening closed with the overture from Weber's *Oberon*, played by "full Orchestra, consisting of all the leading musicians of the city," under the direction of Asger Hamerik.

The long string of distinguished visitors during the Hamerik years included foreigners such as Anton Rubinstein, Hans von Bülow, one of the most famous conductors of the nineteenth century,[20] and Sir Arthur Sullivan, of the illustrious writing duo Gilbert and Sullivan. The soprano Emma Thursby, the American Nightingale, made three trips to Baltimore to sing with the Peabody Symphony in 1875, a season in which works by new composers predominated. Hans von Bülow played with Hamerik and the Peabody Symphony at the Academy of Music that same year. On the morning of his performance, von Bülow stood at the back of the concert hall listening to the orchestra rehearse a Gluck overture. Overcome by his former pupil's performance, von Bülow rushed down the aisle and made his way to the stage. Threading his way through double basses, music stands, and trombones, he walked up to the podium and threw his arms around Hamerik. Spotting a sign resting on the grand piano with "Chickering" emblazoned in gilded letters, the volatile von Bülow next stormed over to the offending object and threw it onto the floor. When Hamerik was ready to rehearse the Beethoven Concerto in E flat, op. 73, von Bülow sat down quietly at the piano, completely absorbed in the music. During an orchestral interlude he rose up, kicked the sign under the piano, and returned to his place at the keyboard in time for his next entrance. At the end of the rehearsal von Bülow gave a courtly bow to the orchestra, thanked Hamerik, and

departed. Von Bülow's performance that evening was faultless. *Dwight's Journal of Music* reprinted the glowing review of von Bülow's performance in the *Baltimore Bulletin*, along with an account of his antics at the rehearsal.

The soloists engaged to perform in the 1880–81 season reflected Hamerik's stated intention to introduce contemporary artists with established reputations as well as provide opportunities for emerging talent. The remarkable Teresa Carreño returned to Baltimore to perform Grieg's *Norwegian Folk-Life, No. 19*, for piano and orchestra with the Peabody Symphony.[21] Several weeks later, Hamerik had the satisfaction of seeing three of his former students—Katie, Cecilia, and Emma Gaul—perform on the Peabody stage. The concert celebrated the return of Katie Gaul from Europe, where she had earned recognition as a concert pianist. Katie toured with Theodore Thomas and his orchestra the following season.

Hamerik began the process of gently steering the Peabody away from European models and prescriptions toward something notably American. One of the earliest champions of American composers, he regularly included their works in concert programs, which prompted a barrage of criticism in the press. Hamerik defended the practice, arguing that "there was evidently an intention on Mr. Peabody's part to give some opportunity, not only for American performers but also for native composers, and whatever might be of value in American music."[22] He introduced the use of English terms in programs in place of the usual Italian (a cause that would be taken up in the twentieth century by Percy Grainger). Acting on the suggestion of the Peabody pianist Nanette Falk-Auerbach, during the 1874–75 season Hamerik introduced the legendary Friday Afternoon Concerts for the convenience of unescorted ladies. Women from the surrounding countryside, arrayed in hats, gloves buttoned up to the elbows, and high-heeled shoes, took the train to Baltimore's Calvert Street station and trooped up the hill to hear performances at the Peabody. In June 1876, *Dwight's Journal of Music*, once so dismissive of the Peabody, recognized "the very high artistic standard which it has reached."[23]

Sidney Lanier, ca. 1874. A volunteer in the Confederate army, Lanier (1842–1881) served as a scout. A signal officer aboard the blockade-runner Lucy when he was captured in 1864, he was held as a prisoner of war at Point Lookout, in Southern Maryland, where he contracted tuberculosis. He described battle scenes, the prison, and the life of its prisoners in his only novel, Tiger-Lilies (1867). Photo by Kuhn & Cummins, in Poems of Sidney Lanier, Edited by his Wife (New York: Charles Scribner's Sons, 1884).

The Enchanted Flute

Having brought the Peabody up to the level he wished, Hamerick next turned his attention to building a first-rate symphony orchestra. He managed to lure a top-flight Georgia-born flutist, Sidney Lanier, to Baltimore. Curiously, Lanier earlier had spent time in Maryland incarcerated as a Confederate prisoner of war at Point Lookout. There, having smuggled in his flute, which he had tucked up his sleeve, he played music that he later claimed had helped him survive his confinement.[24] In February 1865, ill with tuberculosis, he won release in a prisoner exchange and set off for Macon, Georgia, traveling much of the way on foot. He went on to San Antonio, Texas, in a vain attempt to recover his health. During his south Texas sojourn, Lanier wrote his plaintive *Song of the Lost Spirit*, a song in "Negro" dialect. Returning to Macon, he obtained employment as a law clerk and finally completed a fictional account of his youth and war experiences, which a New York firm published in 1867 as *Tiger-Lilies*. Remembered today,

if at all, for his writing, Lanier thought of himself as a musician who dabbled in poetry.

His health broken by the war and keenly aware that he would not live a long life, in September 1873 Lanier left Georgia and his despised clerkship and headed for New York to try to make his mark as a professional musician. On his way north he stopped in Baltimore to see a fellow lawyer and flutist, Henry Clay Wysham. On September 22, the night before departing for New York, Lanier wrote to his wife, Mary, to tell her that Wysham had invited Hamerik "for a farewell session over duos." After Hamerik listened to the slender, gray-eyed musician from the South play *Blackbirds*, his freshly composed piece for unaccompanied flute, he offered him a post as solo flutist for the professional orchestra he planned to organize at the Peabody. Armed with a letter of introduction from Hamerik to Theodore Thomas, leader of the symphony concerts at Steinway Hall, Lanier set out to explore New York. In November, he received word that Hamerik had succeeded in forming the new orchestra, but it was to last only four months—

Henry Clay Wysham. Wysham, like Sidney Lanier, was a lawyer and flutist who worked primarily as a musician. One of the first flutists to write about flute tradition from Japan, China, and Egypt, Wysham is recognized for his *Evolution of the Boehm Flute*, one of the most extensive resources on American flute performance practice during the nineteenth century. Archives of the Peabody Institute of the Johns Hopkins University.

and each player would receive only sixty dollars a month, half what Hamerik had originally offered him.[25] It would occupy little of his time and would allow him to take full advantage of the Peabody Library. Knowing that he would be able to supplement his income by giving lessons and playing at balls and parties, Lanier packed up his belongings and departed for Baltimore to accept his first engagement as a professional musician.

A month later, weary, worn, and suffering from a cold, Lanier made his way through an early December snowstorm to the Institute's concert hall for his first rehearsal with Hamerik and the Peabody Orchestra. Un-

til then, his musical career had been devoted almost entirely to solo performances in congenial settings rather than to the routine, disciplined existence of an orchestral musician. Half dead with a cold complicated by his ongoing struggle with tuberculosis, Lanier straightaway marched to his place on stage, knowing that the seasoned professionals who were now his colleagues would be anxious to evaluate the worth of Hamerik's newest appointment. Next he learned that they would not, after all, play Beethoven's Fifth Symphony, which he had rehearsed the day before. Hamerik announced that the musicians would be rehearsing instead Niels Gade's

The Peabody Orchestra rehearsing in the Peabody Concert Hall, ca. 1880. The orchestra's conductor, Asger Hamerik, and Peabody's provost, Nathaniel H. Morison, found themselves at odds over the use of the hall. For Hamerik it was a concert hall, and for Morison it was his lecture hall. It is now known as Friedberg Hall. Archives of the Peabody Institute of the Johns Hopkins University.

Ossin Overture, which Lanier had never seen or heard. Surviving the ordeal, he wrote to his wife that he "got through it without causing any disturbance. Maestro had to stop several times on account of some other players. I failed to come in twice in the symphony."[26]

A week later, on December 9, the thirty-five-member orchestra played its first concert. Between works, introducing new musicians in the orchestra, Hamerik called on Lanier, who still suffered from his cold. Reluctantly, he rose and played without accompaniment his own *Blackbirds*. The *Baltimore Sun* praised his performance as one of the outstanding moments of the concert.[27] Hamerik's pleasure with his orchestra and his *flauto*

primo is evident in the outpouring of compositions from his pen, some of which Hamerik worked on during summer retreats to the shores of Nova Scotia.

Lanier brought his wife to Baltimore, set up house at 161 St. Paul Street, and happily fitted himself into the life of a professional musician. He set to work with Wysham on a method book for the Boehm flute and also threw himself into his own compositions. Lanier and Wysham frequently performed together and were among the Peabody Orchestra musicians hired by Old St. Paul's Church, at Charles and Saratoga Streets, to play on Christmas Day 1873. Lanier recounted the experience in a letter to his wife, Mary:

I am just home from St. Paul's Church, where ten musicians of our Orchestra (among them myself) were engaged to help make the music for the Grand services of the day. We were a 1st Violin, Viola, 'Cello, double bass, Clarinet, French horn, bassoon, two flutes (Wysham and I) and great organ: with a choir of about forty boys and men, and some female voices. The service was nearly three hours long: and Music, music, all the time. We opened with the Overture to Mozart's Magic Flute: (wh. was, I am free to say, a most abominably outré affair for a church service): and then played with the choir throughout the service. . . . Some of the pieces were magnificent: and the crash of the organ and voices and instruments rolled gloriously among the great arches. All of them wd have been fine: but some of the music was composed by the father of the rector, and was not properly phrased, though containing a few good ideas.

Lanier went on to lament the behavior of his fellow musicians:

And O these heathenish Germans! Double-bass was a big fellow with black mustache, to whom life is all a joke wh. he expresseth by a comical scowl: and viola was a young Hercules, so full of beer that he dreamed himself in heaven . . . and there they sat, Oboe, and Viola and double bass, and ogled each other, and raised their brows, and snickered behind the columns, without a suspicion of interest either in the music or the service. Dash these fellows, they are utterly given over to heathenism, prejudice, beer, they ought to be annihilated, if they do get control of the Age, life will be a mere barbaric grab of the senses at whatever there is of sensual good of the world.[28]

Hamerik took Lanier under his wing and helped him find solo engagements. The transplanted Georgian found himself in great demand. An ardent admirer of German music, he cultivated the vereins. He performed with the Germania Männerchor and with the orchestra at the Concordia Theater. Though fragile health forced him to turn away many invitations, in April 1874 Lanier toured with the soprano Jenny Busk, who had heard him play when she appeared earlier as a soloist with the Peabody Orchestra. The tour proved a trial. It began in Wheeling, West Virginia, where the usually buoyant Lanier recoiled from the odor of kerosene and showers of soot from the "the hell-colored smoke of the factories";[29] it included playing to sparse houses and working with a manager whom Lanier described as the world's

wonder of stupidity and heavy drink. Meantime, Lanier doctored pieces like Adolf Terschak's "Favorite de Vienne" with excerpts from his own composition "Swamp Robin." Performing Rubinstein's Trio for Violin, Cello, and Piano—Lanier had transcribed the violin part for flute—provided some compensation for the indifferent pieces that made up much of the program.

Despite worsening health, Lanier continued to write and to perform. He composed *Wind Song* for solo flute, a work that captures the caprices of the wind and luxuriates in the wide range of the flute, and a haunting piece called *Longing*. Back at the Peabody the following season, Lanier became acquainted with the vast resources of the Peabody Library, pouring over volumes on the acoustics of music. He attended Peabody lectures on the physics of music given by Prof. Alfred M. Mayer, of the Stevens Institute of Technology in Hoboken, New Jersey. Lanier became so completely absorbed by the subject that he contemplated a chair in the physics of music for himself at the Peabody. He wrote to the former Confederate president, Jefferson Davis, asking him to compose letters of introduction to wealthy Marylanders who might support his research. On January 24, Davis wrote to Lanier enclosing an introductory letter.[30]

Lanier put aside these hopes when he received a commission from the United States Centennial Commission to write a text for a cantata. The composer Dudley Buck set Lanier's text to music. Their cantata premiered at the Centennial Exhibition in Philadelphia in May 1876. A chorus of eight hundred men and women sang Lanier's lyrics, accompanied by an orchestra of 150 musicians under the baton of his idol, Theodore Thomas, listening to whose music the Georgian described as like bathing in sweet amber seas. A German-born conductor and violinist who emigrated to the United States in 1845, Thomas had toured with Jenny Lind and founded his own orchestra in New York in 1862. Thereafter he had begun a series of summer concerts in New York City and embarked on national tours. Thomas paired Lanier and Buck's Centennial *Meditation of Columbia* with John Knowles Paine's *Centennial Hymn*, based on a poem by John Greenleaf

Whittier. Despite record heat, humidity, and the threat of rain, Lanier's work, sung by the baritone Myron Whitney, was performed brilliantly, receiving an enthusiastic reception from an audience that included President Grant, members of Congress, and justices of the Supreme Court. The crowd demanded a repeat performance, and the press echoed Thomas's high regard for the work. The president of the new Johns Hopkins University, Daniel Coit Gilman, proclaimed the piece a triumph from overture to closing cadence. The only discordant note came from the reviewer for the *New York Tribune*, who swore that he could not remember hearing a more bewildering collection of rhymes. Lanier shot back a rhetorical question: "Can't good poetry be set to music?"[31] He left Philadelphia in triumph.

After three years in the Peabody Symphony Orchestra, Lanier's worsening health prompted his physician to order him to quit playing and go South to recuperate. Lanier complied—until December 15, 1877, when he was well enough to return to his chair in the orchestra. His fellow musicians, pleased to have him among their ranks once again, organized a benefit concert for Lanier at Lehman's Hall. He began teaching to bolster his finances and the following autumn delivered a series of lectures on Shakespeare. What time and energy he had left, he devoted to his music and literary pursuits.[32]

Out on the Town

Music lovers whose tastes ran toward popular fare had their choice of entertainments in late nineteenth-century Baltimore. At the Maryland Institute, a long and narrow hall situated above the market at the northwest corner of Gay and Baltimore Streets, a series of Promenade Concerts entertained audiences—with band members struggling to overcome the din from the floor below as they played. The Front Street Theatre reopened in 1870 under the management of William Seim, who operated it as a variety theater. Its offerings included the first Baltimore performance by the comic J. H. Milburn, famous for his Lancashire Clog Dance; C. A. Booth and the Comical Dwarfs; and Bettie Remmelsberg and the Baltimore Ballet Troupe. Seim billed the troupe as the most complete terpsichorean organi-

zation in the country.[33] Musical theater productions at Front Street drew huge crowds. During a splendid run in the spring of 1871, *Help*—featuring Irish sketches, Dutch characters, and Ethiopian specialties—filled the house to overflowing every night. Occupying the building that originally had housed the Peale Museum, Kunkle's Ethiopian Opera enjoyed a reputation that stood less on music, in fact, than on drinking and dancing. It was the site of at least one murder. To the relief of upright Baltimoreans, the place burned down in 1873.[34]

More respectably, Ford's Grand Opera House, on Fayette Street near Eutaw, opened its doors on October 2, 1871, with a performance of Shakespeare's *As You Like It*.[35] Its manager, John T. Ford, had been involved in the theater ever since he turned his back on the family's tobacco-manufacturing business at the age of twenty. Before opening his 2,250-seat Grand Opera House, he had operated the Holliday Street Theatre together with George Kunkel and Thomas Moxley. Ford also built the Washington house that became the scene of the Lincoln assassination. Ford's Grand Opera House in Baltimore was one of the largest auditoriums in the country. Its architect, James J. Gifford, modeled the three-story building with its mansard roof after the Booth Theatre in New York.[36] Gentlemen patrons enjoyed Ford's for its Smoking Salon, to which they happily repaired during intermissions for cigars and refreshments.

J. H. Mapleson chose Ford's Grand Opera House when he brought the Hess Grand English Opera Company to Baltimore in 1878. On a cold Christmas Eve, crowds flocked to Ford's to hear Gilbert and Sullivan's amazingly popular and profitable *H.M.S. Pinafore*. "It achieved the most remarkable success. The music is decidedly above the average of comic operas," wrote the critic for the *Sun*, who added that the opera, as it was presented that night, was "entirely free from vulgar phrase and immoral suggestion." The evening concluded with a pantomime of "Humpty Dumpty's Christmas."[37]

For the organist William Wallace Furst, the new Ford's offered a glamorous escape from the penury and monotony of a church musician's career. In 1878 he left his post as organist and choirmaster at St. Ignatius Catholic Church for the pit of Ford's. The following year he produced *The Electric Light*, which celebrated the introduction of arc lighting in Baltimore. He then left Baltimore for San Francisco, where he produced his first and only grand opera, *Theodora*, and New York, where in the 1890s he took up residence as conductor at the Empire Theatre and achieved considerable national recognition as a composer for the theater. His incidental music for plays included music for *Kismet*, starring Otis Skinner, and for the moving picture *Joan, the Woman*, starring Geraldine Farrar. In 1907 he returned to Ford's to conduct the orchestra for *The Christian Pilgrim*, starring Lillian Russell, Tyrone Power, and Henrietta Crossmann. Ford's became Maryland's premier venue for legitimate theater and a popular location for Broadway tryouts.

Over a long and illustrious history, the Academy of Music, an ornate and sizeable building on the west side of the 500 block of Howard Street, hosted a vast array of entertainments ranging from fully staged operas featuring the world's leading prima donnas to popular productions with maypole dancers and performing parrots. Designed by the architects John R. Niernsee and H. Crawford Nielsen, the Academy opened on January 5, 1875, with festivities that included a glittering ball and a concert featuring the United States Marine Band.[38] A removable jointed floor that could be stored in the catacombs below allowed the hall to be converted into a huge ballroom, on which Baltimoreans often waltzed beneath an enormous chandelier. On stage, lighted gas footlights made a crackling sound that could be heard throughout the hall. A great stage curtain portrayed a scene from medieval Venice. The always nattily dressed manager of the hall, Tunif F. Dean, appeared on streetcar placards, advertising twenty-five dollar made-to-order suits. Frank Borst's Rathskeller, located under the building, provided patrons a venue for after-concert refreshment and became a popular gathering place for artists, writers, and journalists. Between acts, patrons of Dean's establishment could dash across Howard Street to the Diamond, a popular public house with bowling alleys in the basement.

All the rage after its opening, the Academy of Music provided a stage for a wide assortment of talent, due in large measure to the energy and influence of its conductor, Adam Itzel Jr. As a youth, Itzel had played every orchestral instrument and performed with or guest-conducted local orchestras. In effect musical director at the Academy, the mature Itzel commanded respect among music lovers in the city. A Calvert Street resident, he would leave his house just before seven o'clock on performance nights and walk to the Academy, just a few blocks away, looking, wrote an admirer, like a bear in his astrakhan fur hat and coat.[39]

In its opening season the Academy hosted a series of performances by the Strakosch Italian Opera, featuring the first performance in Baltimore of Wagner's *Lohengrin* and starring Emma Albani. In the days that followed, Anna Louise Cary sang the role of Amneris, with Carlo Carpi as Radames and Sr. Del Puente singing the role of Amonasro in the company's performance of Verdi's *Aida*. The company's little season closed with *Rigoletto*, starring Albani. Emma Thursby appeared with the sixty-five "Distinguished Musicians" that made up Gilmore's Twenty-second Regiment Band, of New York. The Kellogg English Opera, starring Miss Clara Louise Kellogg, presented a brief season of English opera. Theodore Thomas, who became music director of the New York Philharmonic in 1877 and the next year conducted the first complete North American performance of J. S. Bach's *St. Matthew Passion*, brought his orchestra of sixty musicians to the Academy for a series of annual concerts in 1878. Ole Bull's "farewell" violin concerts threatened to become annual events.

The Academy also hosted performances of varying quality by local artists. One such event, "A Grand Tableau and Concert Entertainment," featured live re-creations of paintings at the Walters Art Gallery with musical accompaniment. For the replication of the grisly *Judith with the Head of Holofernes*, presented in *tableau vivant*, a Strauss waltz played merrily in accompaniment. The finale featured costumed players enacting the scene depicted in Jean-Léon Gérôme's famous *Duel After the Masquerade* to a rapturous accompaniment.

International artists touring the East Coast never

A grand ball at the Academy of Music in the spring of 1880. Engraving from a sketch by Walter Coates. The Academy's grand concert hall, with a jointed floor and a seating capacity of twelve hundred, opened its doors after the Civil War. In the 1920s the splendid building at 516 North Howard was torn down to make way for the Stanley, once the city's largest theater, seating more than three thousand. The Stanley was demolished in 1965, and the site became a parking lot. From Meredith Janvier, *Baltimore in the Eighties and Nineties* (Baltimore: H. G. Roebuck & Son, 1933), 37.

failed to schedule the Academy of Music. Pasquale Brignoli's troupe performed in 1878, presenting "One Night Only of Italian Opera," with Adelina Patti and Venezuelan-born Teresa Carreño. The playbill described Carreño as the finest lady pianist in the Americas. A perennial favorite for nearly four decades, she returned again and again to perform for Maryland audiences.[40] That same year the Academy hosted the Baltimore premiere of *Carmen*, with Clara Louise Kellogg in the title role. The new role suited Kellogg admirably, and she

dazzled the audience with her coquettish charm. Sadly, Adriano Pantaleoni, her Escamillo, had long passed his prime. *Dwight's Journal of Music* derided the company's "trashy cast, passable chorus and orchestra."[41] Kellogg and Anna Louise Cary alone escaped the scathing criticisms heaped on the rest of Max Strakosch's cast.

In 1882 Adam Itzel received one of the first Peabody diplomas, soon afterward serving under Hamerik as assistant conductor of the Peabody Symphony Orchestra. With both of his sons playing violin in the Academy orchestra, Itzel may have been destined to teach. He joined the Peabody faculty in 1890, tutoring in piano, music theory, and conducting. He also taught a class in composition, building on his considerable success as a composer. Reliably drawing large audiences, the Academy program often included Itzel's own work. In the mid-1880s the Academy orchestra performed his *The Swiss Swains; or, A Slip Upon the Alps*, based on a libretto by George A. Gardner.

In the summer months, when most concert halls closed their doors, the Academy of Music remained open. Its Summer Garden Concerts offered light orchestral fare on June evenings and, for a time, a summer opera season (two bits bought an evening of music). Members of the audience could purchase palm-leaf fans and sit in a hall decorated to make it appear cooler than it could possibly be.

This effort to overcome the Baltimore heat produced a collision with Ford's Grand Opera House in August 1885. Marylanders then exhibited—as they do now—a particular fondness for Gilbert and Sullivan. So locals readily lined up to buy tickets late that summer for the Baltimore premiere of *The Mikado*. John T. Ford had acquired the American rights from the author and composer and planned to give the operetta its first Baltimore performance on the night of August 25. Rights or no rights, the manager of the Academy of Music laid hands on the score, began rehearsals, and then opened the comic opera a week before the scheduled event at Ford's—accommodating the many patrons who discovered that Ford's was sold out. Programs at Ford's described its production as "The Real Mikado." Attendees there could pay fifteen cents and receive libretti of the text and two Sullivan songs. "Heart Do Not Break" and "Titwillow" resounded in Baltimore parlors and streets for weeks afterward.[42]

Chambers, Beer Gardens, and Festivals Fortissimo

As prima donnas sang and virtuosos played, private groups continued to make their own contributions to the musical life of the state. Baltimore-built Knabe, Stieff, and Weber pianos played in hundreds of Maryland living rooms. In the homes of the well-to-do, small orchestras entertained at evening parties. Enoch Pratt, founder of the library bearing his name, Ross Winans, a renowned builder of locomotives, and the brewer Gottlieb Bauernschmidt hosted concerts and musicales at their Baltimore homes after the Civil War. Besides teaching arithmetic, English, and spelling at Colonel Johnson's Pen Lucy School, Sidney Lanier gave lectures and recitals in the homes of prominent Baltimoreans. In the summer of 1878 the Academy of the Visitation in Baltimore mounted an ambitious musical program that included a performance of Mendelssohn's *Loreley*. The convent-school girls failed to generate any interest on the part of local press, but a misguided reporter from *Dwight's Journal of Music* attended the production. He could not help wondering why the music teachers at the Academy of the Visitation would take on such an ambitious work, when a program of lighter compositions would have exacted far fewer demands. Stunned by the artistry and technical skill of the young women, he called their performance a "triumph."[43]

Equally ambitious, Lucian Odend'hal, the premier voice teacher in late nineteenth-century Baltimore, presided over a studio with a long history and strong record of tutoring gifted students. In 1877 he organized the Beethoven Chorus Class, made up of 110 young women whose singing a leading musical journal of the day described as comparable to "Nikisch's Boston Symphony Orchestra in volume, finish and smoothness." Musicians from all over the world wrote choruses for them, and their two yearly concerts were *the* musical events of the season in Baltimore. Another Odend'hal group, the Johns Hopkins Glee Club, made its debut in Hopkins Hall in mid-February 1884. A graduate student in historical and political science at the university, Woodrow Wilson, sat on stage that evening in the first tenor section.

The Franco-Prussian War, though a German victory, persuaded many subjects of the kaiser that the future promised more war and continued compulsory military service. When the conflict ended in 1871, German immigration to the United States again increased, and a number of the newcomers landed in Baltimore. In the 1880s more than 250,000 registered immigrants arrived in the country, more than in any decade before or since, and many found their way to Baltimore. Before the end of the century one-quarter of Baltimore residents spoke German. Increased beer production kept apace of this growing population, and its consumption was considered a birthright, Sabbath laws notwithstanding. Baltimore Germans boasted more than a dozen singing societies, and they easily ran afoul of the law, as exemplified by the Arion Männerchor, a workers' choral group, at its Sunday evening meetings in 1872.[44] Picnic dinners, beer, some target shooting, and always plenty of music spelled a successful social event. Darley Park, on Harford Road at the end of the Baltimore and Hall Spring Railway, became a favorite site for these festivities.

Meanwhile, in the late 1870s Baltimore, the state of Maryland, and the rest of the rapidly industrializing country became enthralled with a form of musical gigantism—festivals typically featuring massed choruses and combined orchestras. Those governing the state's musical activities prevented the excesses of some of these spectacles. Nonetheless, they provided entertainment, and the successful ones proved a boon to local businesses, swelling hotel occupancy, driving up railroad and streetcar revenues, and pleasing the owners of beer halls. In one manifestation of the civic enthusiasm for music, in 1881 the Baltimore city fathers planned to mark the sesquicentennial of the city by celebrating the opening of the new municipal water supply, Loch Raven Reservoir, by staging a gigantic Oriole Festival. Problems sprang up from the outset, when locals objected to hiring out-of-town musicians. The incumbent mayor, Ferdinand C. Latrobe, spoke no German, complicating negotiations. The two men who could have smoothed over the conflict and make the festival work, Hamerik and Sutro, were both away from the city when planning got under way. The festival in September involved thousands of participants, hundreds of horses, and an endless stream of floats. Musical offerings included a concert at Druid Hill Park, with the enthusiastic participation of the city's best amateur musicians. A second Oriole Festival in 1882 enjoyed the cooperation of the city's professional musicians and the charms of a band of musicians from the Academy of Music led

by Adam Itzel, playing on a huge platform in front of the Washington Monument and again in Druid Hill Park.

Fired with the idea of musical festivals, in 1878 Itzel emerged as the guiding hand behind the Maryland Musical Festival at the Academy of Music on Howard Street. The first festival got off to an uncertain beginning when funding fell through. Instead of disbanding, the musicians agreed to play for a pittance, accepting "less than longshoremen on the wharf."[45] The ambitious programs made rehearsals fatiguing.[46] In late May the assembled mass of singers and musicians performed Gade's Symphony in C minor; Beethoven's "Choral Fantasy," with Madame Auerbach; and Hamerik's *Jewish Trilogy* for chorus and orchestra.[47]

Opinion about the success of the festival divided sharply. One observer denounced the whole thing as an egregious failure, criticizing everyone from Hamerik "down to the florist who decorated the stage." A local newspaper, anxious to find fault with the closing concert, overlooked a major substitution in the program. The astonished reporter for *Dwight's* observed that local critics "demolished to their heart's content the finest musical entertainment that ever took place in this city" and then vented their remaining spleen upon one another.[48] But everyone agreed that the festival offered impeccable fare and that Maryland musicians had scored a victory by demonstrating that they themselves could successfully mount and carry off a major music festival.

After years of discussion and failed attempts to organize a quality group capable of performing major choral works, Otto Sutro in 1880 took on the job of organizing the Oratorio Society, modeling it on Boston's Handel and Haydn Society. Sutro recruited Fritz Fincke, who had sailed from Wismar, Mecklenburg-Schwerin, to join the Peabody faculty as a teacher of voice, to conduct the ensemble.[49] Just after New Year's Day 1881, 350 singers gathered for their first rehearsal. Within weeks their numbers grew to 600. The Peabody board desperately looked for money to support the burgeoning organization, while Professor Fincke rehearsed the ensemble for its first presentation, an Easter performance of Handel's *Messiah*.[50] The Oratorio Society

The Baltimore Oriole Festival (1881)

In October 1881, just after the mourning period that followed the death of President James A. Garfield, a colorful three-day festival celebrated Baltimore's newest water supply. Engineers had dammed Gunpowder River and created Loch Raven Reservoir, which replaced Druid Lake and Lake Roland and, by means of modern pumping stations, sent its water to Lake Montebello and later Lake Clifton.

The event attracted some 150,000 people. To open it, the city on Monday afternoon turned on the "Water Witch," as the Gunpowder pumping works were nicknamed, providing a brilliant fountain display on Mount Vernon Place. There, in the afternoon, the famous Gilmore's Band played a concert.

The big parade, which was held at night and took five hours to pass by any given point along its eight-mile route, passed beneath ten triumphal arches. Bands of every description marched through the streets; strains of the "Oriole Quickstep" floated over the crowds. A three-thousand-pound bell, drawn by four horses, pealed to announce the procession. Tableaux, some more than twenty feet high, were steadied by streetcar tracks and serenaded by the Fifth Regiment Band at Howard and Baltimore Streets. African Americans, included in the event but relegated to a supporting role, carried torches and were dressed as dominoes.

The next day, five thousand people attended a spectacular fireworks display at Druid Hill Park. Chinese lanterns glimmered about the lake, and colored calcium lights lit up the water fountains as the Fifth Regiment and Grand Army of the Republic bands played. To cap it off, one hundred Japanese fireworks illuminated the heavens for miles around. On the last day, the Peabody Orchestra played for the closing ball.

The colors of the Baltimore Oriole and the lords Baltimore—orange and black—were prominently displayed throughout the city. "A city decked in holiday attire, and brave with flags, banners, streamers, breadths of colored bunting; and wreaths of flowers from end to end, and its streets and windows filled with crowds of merry pleasure-seekers is at any time a pleasant sight," reported Harper's Weekly; "but when a great city suddenly emerges from the deepest mourning and doffs the somber black worn for many days to don her most brilliant gala dress, the transition is most startling and effective."

French, German, and British visitors added much color to the occasion before they headed off to Yorktown, Virginia, and ceremonies marking the centennial of Cornwallis's surrender and American victory in the Revolutionary War. Baltimore's festival thus captured European attention. In New York a French visitor received an invitation to attend a ball in Baltimore. "I had heard even in France of the beauty of the Baltimore ladies," he said, according to the Sun of October 10, "and thought no better opportunity could be afforded than at a ball to ascertain if all we had heard was true."

The composer of the "Oriole March, in Homage to the Ladies of Baltimore," which Otto Sutro published in 1881, needed no persuading.

made its debut performance before a sold-out house. Outdoors, overflow listeners found places at windows, on the pavement, and on doorsteps. They were undoubtedly happier than the paying audience inside, for an early May hot spell had turned the hall into a Turkish bath. Even so, at the conclusion of the "Hallelujah Chorus" the wilted audience leaped to its feet, whoops and cheers following the final "Amen."

Theodore Thomas next organized a gigantic tripartite music festival that he planned to take place in New York, Cincinnati, and Chicago. The first part would be held at New York's Seventh Regiment Armory in May 1882, featuring an orchestra of 300 (all of whom had played in Thomas's orchestra at one time or another).

Thomas intended to create a monster chorus of 3,000, surpassing the forces marshaled by Leopold Damrosch in 1881. Thomas's own choral groups in New York and Brooklyn, with more than 1,000 singers, formed the nucleus. His extensive tours of other East Coast cities had familiarized him with their choral resources. From Boston came the Handel and Haydn Society, with 500 singers. The Philadelphia Cecilia Society brought an additional 350. Baltimore outdid Boston and Philadelphia, furnishing the largest out-of-town contingent with the Oratorio Society's 550 singers. The great choir also drew upon members of the Reading, Pennsylvania, Choral Society and the Worcester County, Massachusetts, Musical Association. The massed choirs performed Beethoven's *Missa Solemnis*; Handel's *Israel in Egypt*; Berlioz's *Fall of Troy*; selections from Wagner's *Nibelung Trilogy*; and a Bach cantata.

Success in 1882 inspired Thomas to launch an "Ocean to Ocean" festival, a tour that would begin in Baltimore and travel through twenty cities, from Minneapolis to Memphis, concluding in San Francisco. Individual festivals, ranging from modest concerts to extravagant events featuring a veritable galaxy of musical stars, would depend on the resources of the host cities. Thomas's orchestra would play seventy-three concerts in seventy-three days, with city size and level of audience sophistication determining the program. Each city would produce its own chorus. Thomas's entourage included Amalia Friedrich-Materna (soprano), Hermann Winkelmann (tenor), and Emil Scaria (bass), all from the Imperial Court Opera House of Vienna, as well as Emma Juch (soprano), Emily Winant (alto), Theodore J. Toedt (tenor), and Franz Remmertz (bass). The festival's board of management and list of guarantors included Maryland's most powerful business and professional people,[51] as well as three of the most powerful men in Baltimore music circles—Hamerik, the Peabody director; Otto Sutro; and the Oratorio Society's conductor, Fritz Fincke. An orchestra made up of Baltimore's best musicians, the 750-member Oratorio Chorus, and an organ played by Harold Randolph would join Thomas's orchestra.

Nearly two thousand people—Marylanders from all over the state, arriving by rail and coach—witnessed this extravaganza, which opened at the Academy of Music on Sunday, April 26, 1884. It began with the Oratorio Society and Thomas's orchestra performing Rossini's *Stabat Mater*; this was followed by the premiere of Hamerik's *Christian Trilogy*, which he had composed for the Oratorio Society. On Friday evening, Symphony Night, the audience heard Thomas's orchestra perform works by Bach, Handel, Mozart, Weber, Gounod, and Beethoven.[52] The festival was a critical success and, despite its substantial cost—nearly ten thousand dollars— the society managed to end up in the black.

In 1885 the Oratorio Society moved its concerts to the commodious Armory, the only hall in the city

large enough to accommodate the combined forces marshaled for the society's concerts and the huge audiences that attended them (the Drill Hall, measuring 300 × 200 feet, could seat 16,000). Sutro and Fincke scheduled two performances of Niels W. Gade's *The Crusaders* and Max Bruch's cantata *Fair Ellen*. Still, conditions were far from ideal. The audience braved seats crowded together, the room's dreadful acoustics, and the building's inadequate ventilation system, a source of complaint that defied remedy.[53] The ladies in the chorus glistened, and the men in the upper reaches of the stage roasted. Decorum vanished as the heat drove singers from their places on stage to the relatively cooler seats in the auditorium during solo and orchestral passages. The temperature and crowding in the Armory during Society performances prompted the city council to demand an official investigation.

In 1892, after resigning from the Peabody's faculty and leaving his post as conductor of the Oratorio Society, Fincke returned to Germany.[54] Sutro invited Joseph Pache to come to Baltimore to take Fincke's place. Born and trained in Germany, Pache began his musical career as a teacher of vocal music in Berlin at the music school founded by the pianist Xaver Scharwenka. Pache was still in his twenties when Scharwenka asked him to come to the United States to teach at his newly established conservatory in New York. What attracted Pache to Baltimore was not its musical offerings; rather, it was the recollection of an earlier visit during which a Baltimore resident had taken him through Lexington Market. Baltimore, he discovered, also had "the advantage of the societies in New York, Boston, and other Northern cities in having better voices in our chorus. There is something in the climate of Baltimore which allows the voice to come to its full perfection."[55] Irascible and sometimes difficult, the new conductor of the Oratorio Society had high expectations. His brooding eyes commanded the undivided attention of his musicians. Joseph Pache died on December 7, 1926.

Sturm und Drang at the Peabody

Sidney Lanier had hoped to engage Asger Hamerik in ambitious plans for musical festivals in Baltimore.

The Hills Are Alive (1886)

Beginning in the 1870s, the Baltimore and Ohio Railroad carried thousands of Marylanders and Washingtonians from the sweltering tidewater and piedmont to the cool hills of Garrett County. The traffic produced two notable resorts, Mountain Lake Park and Deer Park, which became outposts of classical music in a region traditionally associated with Appalachian folk music. Chautauqua conferences in the mountains near Oakland aimed to cultivate mind and spirit alike. Besides scholars, the movement imported theologians, among them Lewis E. Jones, who in 1899 produced his gospel song "There's Power in the Blood." Classical orchestral conductors and well-known soloists also catered to the discriminating audiences. William F. Thiede, H. M. Jungnickel, and

Jungnickel's son, W. Ross Jungnickel, led orchestras for the Deer Park and Oakland Hotels (as well as the Baltimore Symphony Orchestra).

Thiede, a member of the Germania Musical Society, had toured the United States from 1848 until the society disbanded in 1854. The first bassoon soloist in the country, Thiede settled into the strong German community in Baltimore, opened a music store, and in the summers directed orchestras in Oakland. He also founded the Haydn Musical Association.

The German-born Henry A. Rasche Sr. immigrated to the United States in 1842 and settled in Oakland. After the death of his first wife, he married Katherine Rowan, a local music teacher and the organist at the Roman

Catholic church. As the family grew and the children displayed musical aptitude, the parents cultivated it, and so within a few years, and for many years afterward, the Rasche Family Orchestra played at important functions in Oakland and nearby Garrett County. The ensemble included Katherine Rasche (piano), Leo (cornet), Harry (violin), Estelle (violincello), Dennis (French horn), Agnes (clarinet and piano), and Veronica (bass violin and saxophone). Katherine Rasche, meanwhile, achieved notoriety for her musical writing. In 1886, when President and Mrs. Cleveland visited Deer Park on their wedding trip, she composed and published a "Cleveland Grand March" to mark the occasion. (The president and his bride gave her an autograph album as a thank-you gift.) Her other compositions included "Mary O' Maryland," "My Maryland Home," "A Maryland Exile," and "Deer Park Waltz."

But in 1878, in the midst of a financial crisis, the beleaguered Peabody director faced the daunting prospect of moving the Conservatory of Music from its temporary quarters on Mulberry Street to Mount Vernon Place.[56]

The newly opened and impressive Peabody Institute building—its original design realized—provided elegant quarters for the library, generous space for the newly developing Gallery of Art, but perhaps compara-

tively limited room for the flourishing Conservatory. It certainly left the trustees with staggering debt. Various voices criticized them for neglecting the Conservatory of Music. *Dwight's Journal of Music* flatly declared that the Peabody's trustees "are not at present in a position to render much assistance to the Musical Department owing to the bad standing of the Tennessee bonds, smothering a considerable part of the Fund."[57]

In the ensuing financial crisis, the trustees threatened to discontinue Peabody Symphony concerts. They relented but declared that in order for the concerts to continue, they would have to become self-supporting. When this became public knowledge, an efficient group of musical ladies volunteered their services to dispose of a sufficient number of season tickets to make the concerts possible. Patrons soon bought some five hundred of the eight hundred tickets whose sale was deemed necessary to secure a full orchestra—a large increase over any previous year's sale.[58] Meanwhile, by eliminating complimentary passes for newspapermen, the trustees seemingly invited the press to ignore the concerts.

People flocked to performances all the same, and the musicians, whose pay depended on ticket sales, remained reasonably happy. Lanier's extraordinary performance of Emil Hartmann's G minor Violin Concerto, op. 19, in the spring of 1878 brought cheers from the audience. The prospect of a performance of Hamerik's own composition *Peace Hymn* at the Paris Exposition tempered the seemingly endless problems besieging the director.

In 1879 Hamerik took the Peabody Orchestra on tour, with performances in New York, Philadelphia, and Washington. The *Philadelphia Times* critic congratulated Baltimoreans on their good fortune, writing that "until we can get enough earnest interest in art in Philadelphia to maintain such an orchestra of our own, we may hope that they will lead us to it often."[59]

The orchestra's admirers did not, however, include the majority of the Institute trustees, who generally believed that it would be better to reduce the number of concerts and spend Mr. Peabody's money on books for the library. Reporting the decline in the use of the library, the Peabody's provost, Nathaniel Morison, countered that "the library is the great central department of the institute, around which the other departments are clustered."[60] The local press creditably came to the rescue of music. The Conservatory's programs, wrote the *Sun*, were far more beneficial to Marylanders than the untouched volumes on the library's shelves: "No better evidence could be given that a main objective of the founder has been achieved in the great elevation of

the musical standard in Baltimore, as well as the rapid cultivation of popular tastes. . . . It is at present the only institution in this country that substantially fosters and encourages American talent and American music, while at the same time the works of foreign masters are given and played which have not been produced in any other city in this country."[61]

Sidney Lanier, who also appreciated and made extensive use of the Peabody's research library, stood staunchly beside Hamerik throughout these skirmishes. Sadly, Hamerik lost this ally when Lanier, his health failing, had to give up his chair in the orchestra at the end of the Peabody Orchestra season of 1880. The *Sun* hired him to review concerts (including those by the Peabody Symphony); though unable to perform, he could capture the music of Rubinstein and Hartman in dancing prose. Perhaps looking back over the seasons of his own years, he wrote a symphonic work, *Life*, whose movements were named for the ages of man.[62] Desperately ill, in May 1881 he left Baltimore for the mountains of North Carolina to write a railroad guidebook. He died there the following September at the age of thirty-nine. His friends buried him in Greenmount Cemetery.

Expressions of support for Hamerik and his orchestra galled the Peabody provost and librarian, Nathaniel Morison. As the prestige of the Conservatory of Music grew, relations between Hamerik and Morison so deteriorated that Hamerik could not schedule a rehearsal in the Institute buildings without first seeking Morison's permission. The librarian's disdain apparently encompassed the Conservatory faculty, programming, and a student orchestra organized by Fritz Gaul. It came to an unceremonious end when Morison barred members from their rehearsal hall. He handled the whole affair in such fashion that many in the ensemble refused to return, despite having paid tuition.

Caught in the quarrel between books and music, Hamerik also faced criticism from some parts of the musical community. Cuts to his budget might force a reduction in the size of the orchestra, but a smaller group could still comfortably handle programs of Mozart and Haydn, which so many Baltimoreans loved, if not the difficult works of modern composers like Berlioz and Wagner, which many concertgoers found irritating. A correspondent for *Dwight's Journal of Music* contended that Hamerik's choice of repertoire was too adventurous and that general audiences were not ready for the music of the future: "We can well afford to do without the clashing innovations of Berlioz and Saint-Saëns . . . and turn with keener enjoyment to the pure simplicity, the passionate depth, and the sublime beauties of Haydn, Beethoven, and Mozart."[63] Guiding an institution whose business, as he saw it, lay in the future, Hamerik emphatically disagreed.

These unhappy circumstances notwithstanding, Hamerik scored a personal and professional triumph when the famed Russian composer Peter Ilych Tchaikovsky visited Baltimore in the spring of 1891. The maestro had agreed to conduct a mid-May concert at Baltimore's Lyceum Theater, one of six American appearances. After disembarking at the harbor, Tchaikovsky made his way to his hotel, where he met Ernest Knabe and the pianist Adele Aus-der-Ohe, a former Liszt student who was scheduled to perform Tchaikovsky's Concerto in B-flat Minor. After an afternoon rehearsal at the Lyceum with a small orchestra made up of Boston musicians, Knabe entertained Tchaikovsky with a lavish dinner and generous complement of wine. Besides Hamerik (recently knighted by the king of Denmark), the guests included the Aus-der-Ohe sisters and several members of the Peabody faculty—Fincke, Courlaender, and the pianist-composer Richard Burmeister.[64] After the celebrity guest toured the Peabody and inspected a Knabe piano, his host secured a warm Tchaikovsky endorsement.

Almost simultaneously Adam Itzel scored a remarkable success with his best-known work, a light opera titled *The Tar and the Tartar*, which opened on April 15, 1891, "for the first time on any stage," at the Chicago Opera House.[65] The opera had its New York premiere at Palmer's Theater on May 11, 1891, and then toured. A December performance in Toronto drew the theater's largest audience of the year. The opera had its New York premiere on May 11 (and created a bit of a stir when the actress Helen Bertram performed a sensu-

ous "barefoot" dance). The Peabody faculty member's work ran for an impressive 119 performances at Palmer's Theater; no fewer than six different companies played it, from New England to the Deep South and as far westward as Minnesota. Two years later, when Itzel suddenly died, only in his twenties, the *New York Times* saluted him as "the finest leader of light opera in the United States."[66] Thanks in large part to Hamerik and Itzel, the Peabody Conservatory and the Peabody Symphony Orchestra were known well beyond the boundaries of Maryland.

Regardless, the stars did not align for Hamerik. In 1895 Baltimoreans prepared to celebrate the centenary of the birth of George Peabody, the man who had single-handedly transformed cultural life in Maryland's largest city. The crowning moment of the centennial year was to be the premiere performance of Hamerik's *Requiem*. Disputes with the musicians' union over salaries soon soured things. Worse, the Peabody trustees decided once and for all to end the symphony orchestra concerts. Despite the circumstances, Hamerik managed somehow to pull off his *Requiem*. The fifty-member Peabody Orchestra—together with a chorus of 250 voices and the Boston soprano Julie Wyman—played its last concerts to capacity audiences.

Maryland would be without a resident symphony orchestra for more than two decades. The end of the orchestra not only represented a major loss to the concertgoing public; it undercut composers, who in the Peabody orchestra had had an ensemble dedicated to the performance of contemporary American music. Besides losing the orchestra he had struggled so long to build, Hamerik must have been troubled by the fact that American music still paled in comparison to that of Europe. He had built the Peabody Conservatory to be a distinctly American one, and though he wanted it full of American boys, he also enthusiastically trained and took pride in the accomplishments of dozens of talented female musicians.

Most Peabody trustees who had been sympathetic to Hamerik were gone by mid-April 1898, when Hamerik was in the midst of rehearsals for the premiere of his most recent (and last) American work, the Choral Sym-

Masters of Piano Making (1891–1893)

During much of the nineteenth century and well into the twentieth, piano manufacturing contributed heavily to Baltimore's national reputation for Old World craftsmanship, thanks in large part to Charles M. Stieff and William Knabe. Stieff emigrated from Germany and settled in Baltimore in the early 1830s. By 1842 he had begun importing German pianos and selling them from a warehouse on Liberty Street. Observing the popularity of the instruments, he returned to Europe in 1852 to study piano manufacturing. On his return to Baltimore, he and his sons began crafting Stieff pianos under the supervision of Jacob Gross, an expert piano maker of the old school (and Stieff's future son-in-law). The business grew steadily. Stieff eventually occupied a five-story factory in northeast Baltimore and opened sales offices in Washington, Norfolk, Harrisburg, Pittsburgh, Boston, Chicago, Charlotte, Toledo, and Philadelphia. Stieff pianos gained international acclaim. They received medals at the 1876 Philadelphia Centennial Exposition, the 1878 Paris Exposition, the 1881 Atlanta Exposition, the New Orleans Exposition of 1884–85, and the World's Columbian Exposition in Chicago in 1893. Steinway, in New York, may have offered more glamour at a higher price; Stieff pianos gained a reputation as "the poor man's Steinway."

William Knabe, born in 1803 in Kreutzburg, Germany, began working with a cabinetmaker at an early age and then apprenticed himself to a piano manufacturer. Knabe moved to America in 1833, settling in Baltimore, where he immediately went to work in the shop of Henry Hartje, the original inventor of iron piano frames. Within a few years Knabe had accumulated sufficient capital to begin business for himself, and in 1839 he formed a partnership with Henry Gaehle, making and selling Knabe & Gaehle pianos. Knabe later bought out his partner and formed Wm. Knabe & Company, which by 1860 practically controlled the southern trade in pianos of the highest grade. William died in 1864, but his sons, Ernest and William Knabe Jr., along with Charles Keidel, a relative by marriage, continued the firm successfully for many years. Before the close of the century, the Knabe factory and lumber yards covered more than three acres. The firm produced some three thousand pianos annually and held numerous patents. Eventually, Knabe workers made every part of the piano, including their own action and hammers. The Knabe instrument was known as "a singer's piano" because of its mellow tone.

In New York in early April 1889, after a performance at the Peabody Institute's Academy of Music, Hans von Bülow wrote, "The Knabe pianos, which I did not know before, have been chosen for my present concert tour in the United States by my Impresario and accepted by me on the recommendation of my friend Bechstein, acquainted with their merits. Had I known these pianos as now I do, I would have chosen them by myself, as their sound and touch are more sympathetic to my ears and hands than all others of the country" (Knabe Piano Catalogue, 1870).

Camille Saint-Saëns preferred Knabe pianos, and on May 5, 1891, Peter Ilyich Tchaikovsky helped to open Carnegie Hall playing one.

phony, op. 24. He then learned that the Peabody board had dismissed him, along with Henry A. Allen, one of two remaining members of the original Conservatory faculty. The other remaining member, and Hamerik's dear friend, Bernard Courlaender, died the same day. Hamerik soon boarded a ship for Copenhagen. Margaret Hamerik stayed behind to prepare the chorus, which Joseph Pache conducted on April 28 in Hamerik's absence.

Baltimore Builds the Lyric

A spark ignited the idea of a new music hall on Mount Royal Avenue. It was, quite literally, the fire that destroyed the Concordia Opera House in June 1891. The loss of the Concordia left visiting organizations at the mercy of the Academy of Music on Howard Street, which had booked its evenings solid with theatrical productions, leaving only daytime hours for musical performances. Long before the burning of the Concordia, Otto Sutro had been campaigning for a new and larger concert hall, even going so far as to formulate a formal recommendation that the city issue non-interest-bearing certificates to support construction.[67]

Baltimore musicians and music lovers clamored for a large, new performance hall. So did city leaders, who felt that Baltimore, not Chicago, would have hosted the recent political conventions if the city had been able to offer better facilities for large gatherings. In the autumn of 1891, a group of Baltimore's leading citizens—among them Frank Frick, president of the Board of Trade of Baltimore, the piano manufacturer Ernest Knabe, and Mayor Latrobe—convened at the Mount Vernon Hotel, on the north square of Mount Vernon Place, to discuss plans for a new concert hall. Frick proposed a building that could comfortably seat between twenty-five hundred and three thousand persons at a minimum cost of $150,000 (privately hoping that the committee would collect a far greater sum). Knabe argued in favor of a smaller hall, observing that a seating capacity of three thousand would more often be too large than too small for Baltimore audiences. The mayor favored a larger hall with a seating capacity of five thousand that could double as a convention center. Frick's proposal, backed by the local architect J. Noel Wyatt, provided a comfortable middle ground acceptable to all. A subscription committee organized and immediately raised $10,000 toward the project.[68] Incredibly, committee members maintained that they could construct a building as grand as New York's Carnegie Hall (which cost $1.6 million) for a mere $250,000—one day's operating expenses at the Chicago World's Fair.

The site chosen for the new hall lay on the main trolley lines and in close proximity to the Pennsylvania and B&O railroad stations, with service to downtown Washington, DC, and Philadelphia. The editors of the *Baltimore Sun* applauded the plans;[69] city curmudgeons disagreed, citing the very proximity of the trains as undesirable. Baltimoreans, they claimed, would never support the auditorium. Supporters of the new hall countered that the city's population had grown by fifty thousand since the last theater opened in Baltimore.[70] The project's supporters prevailed. Henry Randall, of the New York architectural firm Griffin & Randall, produced a design based upon the great music hall in Leipzig. The process of scaling back the project began almost at once: The exterior marble finish and the terracotta and yellow brick for the sidewalls were eliminated. The large lecture or rehearsal hall, with its comfortable dressing rooms, would never materialize (to the ever-

lasting regret of all the musicians who would spend the ensuing decades dressing and tuning amid trunks and harp cases). The final indignity came in April 1893, when for the sake of economy directors decided to jettison the hall's most striking characteristic, the grandiose curved facade with its carriage drives. Construction began in the summer of 1893, and by autumn the hall stood complete. It carried the name Music Hall but not long after became known as the Lyric. The Pennsylvania Railroad agreed to halt switching operations in the Bolton Street yards during performances.

On All Hallows' Eve 1894, the opening of the new Music Hall featured one of the most brilliant musical events Baltimoreans had seen in years. Still smarting over the loss of the city's only professional orchestra, Baltimore invited the Boston Symphony Orchestra to perform at the opening. The renowned Australian soprano Nellie Melba, the baritone Pol Plançon, the contralto Sofia Scalchi, and the tenor Mauriere, "all members of Messrs. Abbey, Schoofel & Grau's Grand Opera and French Opera Company of the Metropolitan Opera House,"[71] were engaged as soloists. Carriages, hired hacks, and hansom cabs clattered down the cobblestones to the hall's canopied and candlelit entrance on Mount Royal Avenue. Others arrived by streetcar. Concertgoers in their evening clothes passed beneath the striped canvas canopy and into the beautiful new hall softly lit with incandescent electric lights. Shortly after the audience was seated, the lights began to flicker and dim. Fearing that the hall would be plunged into total darkness, the hall manager quickly ignited the gaslights installed as backup lighting. The conductor, Emil Paur, made his way to the podium and picked up his baton. Hearing a loud murmuring in the audience behind him, Paur turned to find the hall's ushers struggling down the aisle beneath the weight of a huge floral music stand and baton. The ushers hoisted the botanical horror up onto the stage and placed it on the podium in front of the orchestra.

With an appropriate flourish, the good-humored Paur proceeded to conduct the evening's program with the floral baton. Dame Nellie Melba added to the color, sweeping onto the stage in her costume of tur-

The Lyric Theatre, ca. 1873. The architect Henry Randall produced a design for the Lyric based on the great music hall in Leipzig. Almost at once he had to scale back, beginning with the grand facade and entry inspired by the Paris Opera. On opening night, October 31, concertgoers in their evening finery made their way through a long striped tent stretching across the pavement that led to a yet unfinished lobby. Records of the Lyric Theatre, Archives of the Peabody Institute of the Johns Hopkins University.

quoise blue satin. Madame Scalchi performed Handel's *L'Allegro, il Penseroso* and works by Chabrier and Gluck. The famous quartet from *Rigoletto* provided a dazzling finale for the singers, and Paur closed the concert with the *Academic Overture* by Brahms, still conducting from the floral music stand.

All Baltimore seemed delighted with the hall's acoustics and its graceful and tastefully decorated interior. The building's exterior was another matter. An otherwise laudatory *Sun* article justifiably observed that without its semicircular front, the Music Hall was "but little more attractive looking than the storage warehouse a few blocks away."[72]

In 1896 the hall manager, Edgar Strakosch, made arrangements for a series of Promenade Concerts in mid-May featuring Schattof's Russian Imperial Tsekerkess Band. The band, made up of members of a Tartar tribe wearing uniforms designed by Alexander I, was attached to the Winter Palace, the official residence of the czar of Russia. The hall's cooling system, which employed forced air over tons of ice, received as much publicity as the musicians. The concerts, patterned after those at Madison Square Garden in New York and London's Covent Garden, were scheduled in the hope of enlivening what had become known as the "be-

tween period," when sultry evenings closed the doors of other theaters and put an end to most organized entertainments. The hall, cooled by overhead fans, was transformed into a flower garden with Japanese lanterns and an iridescent cascade of "live water over rocks and vines" built into the auditorium's organ loft,[73] with special lighting effects producing the illusion of a rainbow in the water. The orchestra sat on stage amid a jungle of potted palms. The Studio Hotel provided refreshments for patrons, who were seated at tables arranged to provide ample space for those wishing to walk about the hall and visit with friends. Baltimore's Promenade Concerts, with their air of informality and for which tickets were inexpensive, proved as irresistible as those in London and New York, and attendance grew with each performance, eventually forcing Strakosch to double the number of tables and extend the season. Entertainments booked into the Lyric had to be moved to the Lyceum Theatre.

The popularity of the concerts and the idea that large groups of Marylanders were enjoying themselves raised the ire of the Reverend W. W. Davis, superintendent of the Baltimore City Missionary and Church Extension Society. Davis called the fashionable Promenade Concerts a "bon-ton beer garden" and called on

When Warships Made Popular Songs (1890)

"The Cruiser Baltimore" apparently first appeared in the May 9, 1890, issue of the *Baltimore Sun's* illustrated supplement. Soon thereafter, George Willig published a version of the song as sheet music, its cover portraying the warship (the navy then, as now, named cruisers after American cities) and also picturing the Baltimore Sun building in Washington, DC, and the Sun Iron

Building in Baltimore. Adam Itzel Jr. wrote the music, which orchestras and bands in Baltimore performed in the weeks before the cruiser paid an official visit to the city in May 1890. Staying for almost a week, the warship welcomed visitors while officers and crew enjoyed receptions, dinners, excursions to horse races and the circus, and finally a grand banquet at the Hotel Rennert.

As the *Baltimore* sailed off, the *Sun* reported, "Although it was impractical for more than a small percentage to tread her decks, all could get a view of the handsome yet formidable warship as she lay at anchor in the harbor. There are probably very few persons in the city who are not now familiar with the appearance of the cruiser, which is destined, doubtless, to carry the name of Baltimore, as did 'the clipper ships of yore,' to the remotest corners of the globe."

the Maryland State Temperance Alliance to appoint a committee of businessmen to put a stop to the goings-on at the Music Hall. To the delight of Strakosch, Davis's rants stimulated interest in the concerts, and attendance dramatically increased. Capitalizing on the publicity, Strakosch declared Monday evenings "Gilbert and Sullivan Nights."[74] He scheduled Italian, German, Russian, and French nights and introduced vaudeville acts. The Great Stuart, a well-known vaude-

ville singer who had made his reputation with Frederick Innes's Band,[75] was engaged. A native Texan, Stewart took his operatic voice to music halls in the United States and Europe from 1899 to 1908. With a vocal range that extended from E below middle C to F-sharp above high C, he was known as the male Patti. Stuart's popularity had as much to do with his makeup and dazzling costumes as it did with his splendid voice. He was so enthusiastically received that Strakosch extended his

Ross Jungnickel
DIRECTOR
BALTIMORE SYMPHONY ORCHESTRA.

Ross Jungnickel placard, ca. 1880. The cellist and conductor Ross Jungnickel, who taught music privately in his studio at 672 West Saratoga Street, single-handedly organized and became conductor of the first Baltimore Symphony Orchestra in the 1890s. Later, he had a successful career as a composer and arranger. Archives of the Peabody Institute of the Johns Hopkins University.

engagement. The Promenade Concerts stretched on through June, until Strakosch was obliged to close the run to make time for repairs to the hall in preparation for the next season.

Over the years the Lyric became the scene of a host of diverse activities that included a bicycle festival with riders dressed as Hottentots, hypnotism demonstrations, passion plays, moving pictures, boxing matches, charity banquets, revival and temperance meetings, and debutante balls.[76] The Metropolitan Opera brought Sembrich, Gluck, Homer, Caruso, Plançon, and Rossi. Mary Garden, John McCormack, Charles Dalmores, and Nicola Zerola came with the Chicago Grand Opera. Anna Pavlova and Mikhail Mordkin danced on the Lyric stage with the Imperial Russian Ballet and Orchestra. The Strakosch Opera Company and the Milton Aborn Stock Opera Company gave extended seasons at the Lyric.

Prelude to an Orchestra

The Lyric provided the scene for Ross Jungnickel's attempts to establish a resident symphony orchestra in the city. As early as 1890, this enterprising cellist and

conductor had organized what he called the Baltimore Orchestra. "Now that we are assured of a magnificent Music Hall for the coming season," wrote Jungnickel in his proposal for an orchestra, "an impulse is given to all corporations to redouble their efforts. . . . One of the first steps in the advancement of musical art ought to be the organization of a superb permanent orchestra, which could take equal rank with like institutions in other cities."[77] Using local artists and serving as conductor, manager, press agent, and fundraiser, he put together a series of three concerts at the Academy of Music, presenting a lively mix of songs, overtures, and symphonic and ballet excerpts, all more lighthearted in character than the more serious fare the Peabody Symphony Orchestra offered. After a successful inaugural "season," the ensemble styled itself the Baltimore Symphony Orchestra and doubled the number of annual performances. After three seasons the little orchestra collapsed.

In 1897 Jungnickel resurrected the orchestra as the nucleus for "a Magnificent Permanent Symphony Orchestra," which he expected to replace the defunct Peabody orchestra while also drawing heavily from

The Heart of Maryland (1895)

Dedicated to WALTER B. ROGERS, Director of the Seventh Regiment Band, N.G.S.N.Y.

Heart OF Maryland MARCH. (TWO STEP) Composed by ISIDORE BURNS

Published by PETRIE MUSIC COMPANY.~
NEW YORK CITY, N.Y.   CHICAGO, ILL.
4 EAST 20TH STREET   4627 CHAMPLAIN AVE.
50

At the western foot of South Mountain lies the small town of Boonsboro, which the brothers George and William Boone, cousins of Daniel Boone, founded in 1792. In the fall of 1862, after the battles of South Mountain and Sharpsburg (called Antietam by the Union), the churches and public buildings of Boonsboro served as makeshift hospitals for wounded soldiers. Thirty-three years later, David Belasco chose Boonsboro as the setting for a Civil War drama he entitled The Heart of Maryland.

Belasco built his play around the painful divisions the Civil War imposed on many Maryland families. General Hugh Kendrick, a robust Confederate, has a son, Colonel Alan Kendrick, who remains loyal to the Union. Alan's sweetheart, Maryland Calvert, sides with the South and so has broken their engagement, while her brother Lloyd leans toward the Northern cause. When Alan sneaks through the lines to see her, he is captured by Colonel Fulton Thorpe, formerly a Northern officer, whom Alan once court-martialed and who now fights with the Confederates. Seeking revenge, Thorpe arranges to have Alan shot as a spy. Maryland then pleads for Alan's life, only to have Thorpe attempt to seduce her. She grabs Thorpe's bayonet and stabs him, giving Alan time to escape. The wounded Thorpe orders the church bell rung to announce a prisoner's escape, but Maryland climbs into the belfry shouting, "The bell shall not ring!" She then grabs the clapper and swings with it to prevent the bell from sounding. Alan returns with a force of troops and surrounds Thorpe. The villain finally lands in prison for being a dangerous double agent, Alan and Maryland reconcile, and everything ends on a happy note.

The famous scene in which Maryland swings on the clapper made the play a huge success. It toured for three consecutive seasons (and later resurfaced as a silent motion picture).

While not part of the Belasco play, the "Heart of Maryland March" (1895), written by Isidore Burns, capitalized on the play's wide popularity.

its remains.[78] Jungnickel hired the Peabody's concertmaster, J. C. Van Hulsteyn, ensuring not only that the orchestra had the best violinist in Maryland but that it would have access to the best of the Conservatory's string players. Jungnickel worked like a demon to find money to support the struggling ensemble and eventually managed to assemble an impressive list of contributors that included members of the city's leading families. He confidently moved the reorganized ensemble to the new Music Hall—the Lyric—on Mount Royal Avenue.

The Baltimore Symphony attracted a number of outstanding and colorful musicians. For example, the Boston Symphony's handsome virtuoso Xavier Reiter, who had played for Wagner in Bayreuth, became the orchestra's principal horn player. Reiter, a handsome bear of a man with a full beard and long coal-black hair, which he wore hanging down his back, was sought by artists as a model. He posed on several occasions for the head of Christ. Dressed in his fur coat and wearing a broad-brimmed Texas slouch hat,[79] the Bavarian horn player looked more like Buffalo Bill; or, when flying through the park on a bicycle wearing a cape, he could be mistaken for Count Dracula. On Friday, January 10, 1890, after four years in the first chair of the orchestra's horn section, Reiter failed to show up for a rehearsal. The following Tuesday, the New York Times reported that "Xavier Reiter, the great horn player, has disappeared."[80] He later explained that he could not live "in such an uncivilized city as Boston, where the beer saloons closed at 11 p.m."[81] It is also likely that his arrest in the Boston Commons for bathing his Russian wolfhound in a public fountain contributed to his decision to leave the city. Baltimore's German population, plentiful saloons, and welcoming musicians perfectly suited Reiter. An avid sportsman, Reiter rejoiced when he encountered Druid Hill Park. The day after this discovery, the police arrested Reiter for shooting squirrels with his shotgun in the park. Jungnickel bailed him out of jail in time for the evening's performance.

Hoping to extend the reach of his orchestra beyond the city, Jungnickel marshaled his musicians for tours in

Western Maryland and the District of Columbia. In the summer of 1883 the Baltimore Symphony's members boarded the Baltimore and Ohio train to Deer Park, in Garret County, where they played daily concerts and for a weekly fancy-dress ball for the well-to-do visitors to the cool mountains. Their performances in Washington, DC, constituted the only series of symphony concerts given there that year.[82]

In 1898, when the country went to war with Spain, the Lyric advertised Promenade Concerts that featured the Baltimore Symphony Orchestra under the direction of Ross Jungnickel. While the work certainly helped, financial shortages continued to plague Jungnickel, who often found himself unable to pay his musicians. A Friday evening performance that year came perilously close to being cancelled for the second time over a salary dispute. An angry timpanist who had not been paid for his last performance with the orchestra flatly refused to go on stage and threatened to take his timpani home. Jungnickel's frantic attempts to persuade the musician to relent went nowhere. Refusing to cancel the performance, Jungnickel went to the podium and led his musicians through the Beethoven Eighth, without the timpani.[83]

Jungnickel opened the Symphony Orchestral School at the Mechanics' Hall, which stood on Fayette Street across from Ford's Theatre. Jungnickel staffed it with members of his orchestra in an attempt to supplement their meager income and provide young musicians an opportunity to experience "the pleasure and routine of orchestral work."[84] Students paid five dollars a year to rehearse on Monday evenings under his watchful eye.

The following year, Jungnickel assembled the combined choirs of the Eastern and Western High Schools and an assortment of grammar schools for a grand concert with J. Harry Deems as guest conductor. Five hundred schoolgirls crowded onto the stage to sing excerpts from Wagner's *The Flying Dutchman* and *Greeting to Spring*, arranged to Strauss's *Blue Danube* waltz. The program closed in high spirits with the overture to Rossini's opera *William Tell*. The ensemble went on to perform in Washington's National Theatre at the end of 1899 and began making ambitious plans for a tour of the South. The tour failed to materialize, and the orchestra disappeared abruptly from Baltimore's music scene.

CHAPTER FIVE

My Maryland

THE BEETHOVEN TERRACE ORCHESTRA, perhaps Baltimore's best-known amateur musical group in the late 1880s, grew out of a club that Edwin Litchfield Turnbull had organized at age 16.[1] It rehearsed on Saturday nights at Turnbull's home at 1530 Park Avenue (in the Bolton Hill block known as Beethoven Terrace),[2] and kept busy performing benefit concerts in Baltimore and nearby cities, including an event in Pennsylvania that featured the two-hundred-voice York Choral Society. After graduating from Johns Hopkins in 1893, Turnbull went to Europe to study music. Returning to Baltimore two years later as a skilled violinist, conductor, and composer, he resumed work with the Beethoven Orchestra. He also organized the Johns Hopkins Musical Association, which in turn sponsored the Johns Hopkins Orchestra. The group performed at university events, gave benefit concerts for local hospitals, and took music into the community. In about 1914 the university moved from Monument Street to the new campus at Charles and 34th Streets, Homewood, where the orchestra began rehearsing in the old Carroll family barn under the baton of the Peabody faculty member Charles H. Bochau.[3]

Far away from the sedate parlors and evening musicales that took place in select Baltimore homes, wasp-waisted beauties in purple tights scandalized and delighted masculine audiences behind the gaslights of the Odeon Theatre at 3 South Frederick Street. The show starred "Mlle. Ordlar," a dreamy-eyed young woman who made history when she became the first performer to strip off her clothes on a Maryland stage. The mademoiselle's act reached either its zenith or its nadir when she tossed her garters into the audience. The show ended in February 1904, when the Odeon and its neighbors literally went up in smoke in the Great Baltimore Fire.[4]

But the city boasted plenty of like establishments. The Monumental Theater stood on the south side of Baltimore Street beside the Jones Falls. Built in 1874 on the site of the recently incinerated Washington Hall, it was known at various times as the Casino, the Baltimore Opera House, the Central, and finally, the Folly. A streetcar ran past its door. The hall hosted burlesque-circuit performers like Sliding Billy Watson, Dave

Marion (as Snuffy the Cabman), and Billy Arlington, the Happy Hobo. James L. Kernan, the owner, had such success at the Monumental that he could afford to purchase a truly legitimate venue, the Holliday Street Theatre. Just before curtain time, the Monumental orchestra would assemble on the sidewalk outside the theater and play a march to attract patrons. The pit musicians, who received a princely fifteen dollars a performance, played outside even during the winter months, when the temperatures dipped so low that fingers turned blue and the valves on their cornets nearly froze.[5]

For decades, visiting sailors, Maryland farm boys, and otherwise respectable businessmen from out of town found their way to the Gayety Theatre, the centerpiece of the city's lurid "Block" on Baltimore Street, for an evening of risqué entertainment. The Gayety was built on the ashes of the Great Baltimore Fire of 1904. A brand-new, one-thousand-seat establishment with a gilded interior and a sixty-light chandelier, it began as a venue for legitimate vaudeville shows, featuring first-rate comedians and beautiful chorus girls touring on the Columbia Circuit. It had its own ten-piece orchestra, Charles Weber's Gayety Harmonists.

Adding more color to this musical tapestry, far more respectably, the Arion Singing Society of Baltimore participated in all the great singing festivals of the North Eastern Saengerbund, winning prizes in Philadelphia and Brooklyn. In 1863 the Arion sang for Abraham Lincoln at Gettysburg in a memorial service for the dedication of the National Cemetery.[6]

Resuscitating the Conservatory; Envisioning an Orchestra

Following Asger Hamerik's painful departure in 1898, the Peabody trustees drew from the ranks of the faculty and named as his successor Harold Randolph, a pianist from Theodore Thomas's chorale-supporting orchestra in Baltimore. Thomas invited Randolph to tour with him in 1888 after hearing his performance of Beethoven's "Choral Fantasy." Two years later, in 1890, he became a member of the Conservatory faculty, making him the first American-trained musician to serve as a full-time instructor at the Peabody. Randolph toured

with the violinist Franz Kneisel's quartet, performing in Philadelphia, New York, Boston, and elsewhere. Kneisel described Randolph as "the best ensemble player I have ever played with."[7] Randolph had appeared as a soloist with the Boston Symphony Orchestra under Emil Pauer in 1897.

Randolph's credentials as a musician were impressive, but perhaps even more important to the trustees was his patrician manner and the ease with which he moved in Maryland society. He epitomized traditional southern gentility; he strengthened his social standing by marrying Emma Gary, the daughter of James A. Gary, a member of President William McKinley's cabinet.

Randolph was intimately familiar with the strengths and shortcomings of the Peabody. When his appointment became permanent, he initiated a series of changes that broadened and strengthened the curriculum, including a program designed to train musicians to become teachers (the first in a conservatory of music). He brought the Peabody Graduates School, founded in 1894 by May Garrettson Evans, under the banner of the Conservatory, renaming it the Peabody Preparatory. Randolph organized a touring series that took Conservatory musicians to towns throughout Maryland, from Chestertown to Emmitsburg, and to Delaware, Pennsylvania, and West Virginia.

Such regional ambitions happened to coincide with the appointment of the pianist Ernest Hutcheson to the Conservatory faculty in 1900. Twenty-nine years old and fresh from a triumphal tour of England, Germany, and Russia,[8] Hutcheson accepted responsibility for the piano department, bringing with him his exotic bride, Baroness Irmgart Senfft von Pilsach Hutcheson. Hutcheson's extraordinary abilities surfaced in dramatic style when he opened the 1901–2 concert season. His varied program included his stunning transcription of Wagner's "Ride of the Valkyries." Within moments after the opening measures, the lights went out, plunging the hall into darkness. A flash of alarm surged through the audience until they realized that Hutcheson, without missing a beat, was sailing through the work in an exhibition of virtuosity.[9]

In addition to his popular performances, Hutcheson

Ernest Hutcheson, ca. 1900. The performer, teacher, and composer Ernest Hutcheson, a native of Australia who studied and then worked in Germany before coming to the United States, wrote concertos for piano and violin and solo piano works, including his transcription of Wagner's "Ride of the Valkyries." Hutcheson joined the Peabody faculty in 1899. At his New York debut, with the New York Symphony Orchestra in 1919, he performed three concertos—Beethoven's Third, Fourth, and Fifth. He went on to teach at Juilliard in 1926 and became its president in 1937. Archives of the Peabody Institute of the Johns Hopkins University.

played hour-long weekly programs, always from memory, in a small, out-of-the-way recital hall for students and colleagues during the Peabody's eight-month season. During his twelve years at the Peabody, he played the thirty-two sonatas of Beethoven, all two-hundred of Chopin's piano works, and countless works by Bach, including the entire *Well-Tempered Clavier*. Randolph often joined him, playing works for four hands. On one of these occasions a local music critic happened to hear one of their performances and urged them to appear together publicly.

The two men embarked on an obliging schedule of joint appearances, and they won high praise from Baltimore to Boston. Audiences adored them; critics praised them. Well matched temperamentally and musically, Hutcheson and Randolph even wore the same size in clothes. Once, their similarities proved unusually helpful. Off on tour, the distinguished Randolph discovered that he had left behind the trousers to his formal attire. No matter: while Hutcheson performed, Randolph waited in the dressing room in black tie and boxer

shorts. While the audience applauded, Hutcheson dashed back stage, shucked off his pants, and passed them on to Randolph.

The renewed vigor of the Peabody Conservatory, however welcomed, did not make up for the fact that the city lacked a resident professional orchestra. Ross Jungnickel's struggle to keep his Baltimore Symphony afloat and the need for city funding reached the pages of the *Baltimore Sun* on March 3, 1898: "Why should Baltimore not support such an organization? Would not such an organization add to the fame and reputation of the city?" The article went on to point out that the Cincinnati Symphony Orchestra enjoyed a guaranteed fund of seventy-five thousand dollars and that the Boston Symphony received substantial support as well. The plea went unheeded.

In 1901, just as the Conservatory's concert season ended, Randolph received a letter from John Work Garrett, the President of the B&O Railroad, offering ten thousand to support such a group at the Peabody. With Garrett's check in hand, the trustees envisioned a season of ten concerts, four of them devoted to light fare, beginning with the 1901–2 season. In 1905 the trustees admitted failure, and the remains of the once grand Symphony Concert Fund went quietly into a Conservatory emergency account.

A year later, the violinist Abram Moses recruited twenty musicians to form what he hoped would become a permanent orchestra. After attempting to wedge the fledgling orchestra into the Charles Street home of one of the musicians, Abrams went to Randolph, who graciously provided space for their weekly rehearsals. When word went out that another attempt to establish a symphony orchestra made up of Baltimore musicians was under way, skeptics thought the whole idea was almost ludicrous. Though short of becoming the city's resident orchestra, it thrived as the Peabody's orchestra class with a membership of gifted amateurs.

Meanwhile, Randolph and Hutcheson played a leading part in founding the Florestan Club, a self-selecting collection of amateur and professional musicians, many of them Peabody men, who devoted themselves to music and socializing. Similar organizations in Maryland towns contributed to their communities by hosting public recitals and lectures. The Florestan was made up of men from Baltimore's musical aristocracy and exerted a strong influence on local music. The clubhouse, on Charles Street near Centre Street, provided a congenial place for musical talk and impromptu chamber music. Charlie Wettig, an old North German Lloyd Line steward, presided over the dining room and saw to it that the club kept ample reserves of beer. Field-night recitals featured performances by club musicians of difficult and esoteric works that one seldom heard in concert halls. On guest nights the club hosted visiting musicians such as Walter Damrosch, Leopold Stokowski, and Mischa Elman. Manuscript nights provided local composers an opportunity to perform their own music.

One of the primary goals of the Florestans was to find a way to organize a resident symphony orchestra in Baltimore. The Boston Symphony had been performing annual seasons in Baltimore since 1890. When it threatened to end its Baltimore appearances, Frank Frick, Frederick M. Colston, and other members of the original Auditorium Company raised funds to continue the concerts.[10] The Peabody Conservatory put up a substantial portion of the subsidy to ensure that its students would have access to quality performances of symphonic music. The Florestan Club also arranged an annual series of concerts by the New York Philharmonia and helped to organize regular visits by the Philadelphia Orchestra. Such positive developments did not mask the absence of a Baltimore symphony.[11]

Between 1913 and 1915 two occurrences highly gratified the Florestans. Many years earlier, the Boston Symphony Orchestra had invited the great Hungarian conductor Arthur Nikisch to move from Leipzig to Boston. Accepting, Nikisch asked Gustav Strube, who had performed under Nikisch in Germany and secured a faculty position at the Mannheim Conservatory, to join him. In the autumn of 1890 Strube became a member of the violin section and the symphony's associate conductor. In 1898 he began conducting the orchestra during the summer months. A gifted and prolific composer and a superb theoretician with a working knowledge of most orchestral instruments, Strube had written major works that the Boston Symphony performed. He wrote marches for the Boston City Band, which drew many of its players from the ranks of the Boston Symphony Orchestra, and premiered several of his major works at the Worcester Festivals, which he conducted after 1909. He wrote many of his lighter works, including his graceful *Elegy and Serenade* and *Berseuse*, for the Boston Symphony's summer concerts, which led eventually to the Boston Pops.[12]

In 1913 Randolph invited Strube to head the Peabody Conservatory theory faculty and to conduct the student orchestra. For Strube it was the dream of a lifetime: he would have the opportunity to devote his time to his three great passions—composing, conducting, and teaching. Strube accepted Randolph's offer knowing that a movement to establish a city orchestra was afoot. The Florestan Club had a conductor.[13]

Like Strube, the cellist Bart Wirtz knew that plans for an orchestra in Baltimore were in the air when he joined the Peabody faculty in 1905. Then, in the fall of 1915, the Cleveland Orchestra offered Wirtz, who was

The Florestan Club, ca. 1916. The club opened its doors at 522 North Charles Street on February 10, 1911. Harold Randolph (1st row, center) served as the club's unofficial director. The membership included men who would become founding members of the Baltimore Symphony Orchestra: J. C. Van Hulsteyn (1st row, far right), concertmaster, and Bart Wirtz (standing, 2nd from left), principal cellist. The club's members met on a regular basis to play chamber music, socialize, and hoist a few beers. The club also arranged an annual series of concerts by the New York Philharmonia and helped to organize regular visits by the Philadelphia Orchestra, but their primary goal was to secure a resident orchestra for the city. Archives of the Peabody Institute of the Johns Hopkins University.

by then the Peabody's premier cellist, a chair. Sorely tempted to accept Cleveland's offer, Wirtz, who had put down roots in Baltimore, went to Strube and told him that he would stay if there was any hope of getting a symphony orchestra under way. Wirtz, Strube, and the violinist Abram Moses approached Randolph on the question, and Randolph finally agreed to provide performance space for a symphony, as well as liberal use of the Peabody's music library.[14]

A prominent member of the Florestan Club, Edwin Litchfield Turnbull, steadfastly supported the effort to found a city-sponsored symphony orchestra. "How can it be," he asked in *Art World*, that "the richest country in the world" had spent "practically nothing for the encouragement of musical organizations?"[15] The movement sought city financial support. The logical person to pitch the idea to Mayor James H. Preston was Frederick Huber, who as a young man had shown talent as a pianist but aspired to a career in law. At the age of 13 he had worked in the offices of William F. Broening,

who would later become mayor of Baltimore. Broening advised Huber to put aside his plans to pursue law and concentrate on music.[16] Huber went on to become a pianist and organist of modest talent who capitalized on his prodigious gifts as a promoter and carved himself a niche as a local impresario. He managed the Lyric Theatre and all the while maintained his contacts in political circles. The ambitious Huber also ran the Peabody summer school, served as its public-relations contact, and organized the city's community-band concerts.

Sensing the prestige that would accrue to Baltimore if the orchestra were established and maintained from the tax rolls, Mayor Preston supported the plan Huber outlined, saying, "The people of Baltimore are entitled to municipal symphony orchestras, municipal opera, municipal organizations which provide for individual atheistic development, just as they are entitled to municipal service in education, sanitation and public safety."[17] Eager to remain at the center of all Baltimore's musical activities, Huber volunteered to serve as man-

ager of the orchestra. "STRUBE TO BE CONDUC-
TOR. Peabody Man to direct the Baltimore Symphony
Orchestra," proclaimed the *Baltimore Sun*.[18] It was the
Christmas season of 1915, and Baltimore would receive
its gift the following February. On December 23, Fred
Huber met with members of the press at the Peabody to
announce a city appropriation of six thousand dollars
for the support of a municipal orchestra. A semiofficial
Municipal Department of Music with jurisdiction over
city-sponsored musical activities formed, with Huber
at its head. A letter to the school board went out the
same day, asking to hold rehearsals in the auditoriums
of City College, the Polytechnic Institute, and Western
and Eastern High Schools. Students would attend the
season's six Friday-morning dress rehearsals.[19]

Apparently for the first time in the history of the
country a city included in its budget an appropriation
for a city orchestra. The orchestra would be committed
to the performance of American music, especially music
of Maryland composers. The Musicians' Association
of Metropolitan Baltimore—American Federation of
Musicians offered the use of its hall for rehearsals and,
more importantly, pledged to supply movie theaters
with substitute musicians on Friday orchestra concert
nights. Theater owners took note, because Friday evenings produced their biggest receipts.[20]

On New Year's Eve, Strube visited Philadelphia,
where the Philadelphia Orchestra performed his
Variations on an Ancient Theme. Soon after returning to Baltimore, he accepted the helm of the city
orchestra. J. C. Van Hulsteyn, a former concertmaster
of the Lamoureau Orchestra of Paris and head of the
Peabody's violin faculty, signed on as concertmaster.
Accustomed to the polished musicians of the Boston
Symphony, Strube had before him a varied crew. The
orchestra's rank-and-file musicians came from dance
bands, movie-house pit orchestras (every downtown
movie theater had an orchestra), and the ranks of the
Peabody. Many of them had never played in a symphony orchestra. They came to rehearsal in dress suits,
straight from a night of ragtime, arriving early enough
to catch a few minutes' sleep before rehearsal. Strube
began the process of turning his assortment of musi-

cians into an orchestra, exhorting, threatening, and
cajoling his musicians in a fractured mixture of English
and German.[21]

America had its first municipally supported orchestra, and Baltimoreans had a bargain. Gallery seats cost
fifteen cents, balcony seats a quarter, and boxes could
be had for a dollar. The city's relatively small allocation
of six thousand dollars provided a limited number of
concerts and wide coverage from national media. The
presence of a large number of highly skilled musicians
at the Peabody Conservatory made this orchestra on a
shoestring possible.[22]

The public response to the announcement of the
opening concert was immediate, and the heavy demand
for tickets forced Huber to move the concert from Al-
baugh's Lyceum Theatre to the Lyric. The people who
made up the majority of the new Baltimore Symphony's
audiences were not the elite subscribers who attended
concerts of the Boston Symphony, the New York Philharmonic, and the Philadelphia Orchestra, but working
men and women—bricklayers, department-store employees, police officers, carpenters, and office workers.[23]

The members of the Florestan Club watched their
hopes become reality on Friday evening, February 11,
1916, when America's first municipal symphony orchestra opened its inaugural concert with a performance
of Beethoven's Eighth Symphony. As a February snowstorm turned Baltimore traffic into a snarl, a standing-
room-only audience packed the theater. In keeping with
the decision to actively promote Maryland composers
and performers, the distinguished Metropolitan Opera soprano Mabel Garrison, a Maryland native, was
engaged as the guest artist of the evening.[24] A week
later, seats sold out for the next concert, on March 10.
Anticipating the demand, tickets for the orchestra's next
concert went on sale the next day.[25]

Great War, Popular Fears

German Americans, for so long a significant and highly
visible part of the population of Maryland musicians,
began to feel the sting of rising anti-German sentiment well before Congress declared war in April 1917.
Afterward, loyalty seemed to correlate with suspicion

of things German. In November 1917 the Philadelphia Orchestra played a program at the Lyric that studiously avoided the works of German composers, playing nothing but Russian music. Harold Randolph, watching the hysteria take hold in Maryland, was keenly aware that his colleagues and friends were vulnerable to attack. *Sun* reporters appeared at Randolph's music-appreciation class to question his own views on German music. Citing Richard Strauss as an example, Randolph explained that he had no quarrel with a ban on the performance of music by living German composers, who might receive royalties. While he supported the Philadelphia Orchestra's decision to program non-German works, he said that banning all German music was going too far. "Suppose Germany had given the world some great invention," Randolph asked. "Is it reasonable to suppose that the Allied countries would forego all its advantages because it had originally come from Germany? The same thing applies in the world of art."[26]

Randolph tried to protect German American colleagues by involving them in patriotic projects like the US Liberty Loan drives. In the spring of 1918 the *Baltimore News American* reported that "one of the most enthusiastic Liberty Loan meetings held in Baltimore . . . took place at the Peabody Conservatory this morning, when, in response to the call of Harold Randolph, director of the Conservatory, many of the musicians of the city, including some who technically are ranked as enemy aliens, gathered in Mount Vernon Place."[27]

Even so, high-profile musicians like Strube suffered the slings and arrows of American patriotism. Anti-German sentiment took a heavy toll on music in Maryland. The pianist Max Landow was forced to resign from the Peabody Conservatory faculty even though nothing in his speech or actions had ever implied any disloyalty on his part. Educated in Berlin and Paris, Landow had come to America in 1903. His appearance as a guest artist at the Peabody Conservatory had made such an impression that he was invited to take the post left vacant by the departure of Ernest Hutcheson. Landow, a quiet and retiring man, had won high respect from his colleagues and students for his artistry and

integrity. Known for discretion, he had been especially careful since the outbreak of the war to avoid statements that could be construed in any way as anti-American. The attack on Landow came solely because he had not taken steps to become a US citizen. To avoid any hint of controversy, Harold Randolph replaced Landow with the pianist Alfred Butler, "a well-known musician, all-American, of Los Angeles."[28]

A plethora of war-related performances were held throughout the state in support of the war effort. Early in 1917, Gregor Paderewski performed a benefit concert at the Lyric for Polish refugees. The audience could not help noticing the toll his patriotic campaigning had taken and wondered aloud if he would ever regain his lofty place in the constellation of concert pianists. After the concert, Madame Paderewski presided over a table in the lobby selling dolls made in Paris by Polish refugee painters and sculptors for the benefit of war victims.[29]

Musicians all over the state were enlisted to promote a statewide draft-registration drive mounted on September 12, 1917, the anniversary of the Battle of North Point. In towns and cities throughout Maryland, military music encouraged able-bodied young men to register for service. Beginning at 8:00 a.m., buglers from Fort Howard and Camp Holabird played at the base of the Washington monument. The musicians crowded into automobiles driven by the women of the Motor Messenger Service to sound bugle calls in every quarter of the city. Members of the bands from Camp Meade and Fort Holabird boarded streetcars to furnish music for Baltimore, while in Annapolis the Naval Academy Band encouraged citizens to take up arms. A huge bell loaned by the McShane Bell Foundry was placed on a flat-bottomed electric car and rung by the Naval Reserves as it toured the city. Church bells and factory whistles added to the din. The cacophony finally ended in the evening, when thirty thousand people gathered in Druid Hill Park for a massed band concert and fireworks.[30]

Weeks later, a band of six hundred musicians blasted away at the new Oriole Park, at Greenmout Avenue and 25th Street, to welcome Colonel Theodore Roosevelt to the Liberty Bond Drive. Baltimore schools joined in

"Baltimore, Our Baltimore" (1916)

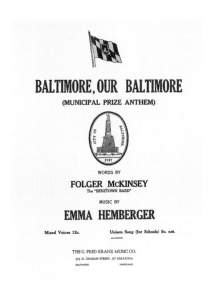

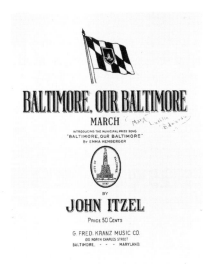

Upon adopting an official Baltimore City flag in 1915, the city council and the incumbent mayor, James H. Preston, decided that the city also should have an official municipal anthem. With the help of Frederick R. Huber, of the Peabody Conservatory, who suggested a prize of $250 for a fitting poem, the city arranged a contest, which more than six hundred contestants from a dozen states entered. Folger McKinsey, the popular Bentztown Bard of the *Baltimore Sun*, took laurels with lines he entitled "Baltimore, Our Balti-more." In a subsequent contest, Mrs. Emma Hemberger, wife of the conductor of the Germania Männerchor, won another $250 for composing the music. With McKinsey's approval, John Itzel, a Baltimore musician, made some minor changes to the verses.

The city scheduled the premiere of its new anthem for the afternoon of Washington's Birthday in 1916 and took pains to make it a memorable event. Hundreds of citizens crowded into the Lyric Theatre, where black-and-gold bunting hung generously and stands of city, state, and national flags added further color. A small orchestra started off the program with the overture to Offenbach's *Orpheus*. Next, a German American singing society, the United Singers, offered a few vocal and instrumental solos. The mayor then rose to emphasize the importance of recognizing the first president on his birthday and expressed a belief that in the near future Baltimore would be "civically" greater but also musically greater. When he noted that the municipal anthem had been the work of two Baltimoreans, the audience erupted in applause. McKinsey and Hemberger mounted the stage to receive their prizes, and applause and cheers again filled the theater. Finally, the audience grew silent, and the orchestra began its introduction.

At this point three hundred schoolgirls, who had rehearsed the anthem many afternoons and who patiently had stood in rows in the front of the theater during the preliminaries, chimed in with the United Singers. Together, triumphantly, the singers gave the city its first performance of "Baltimore, Our Baltimore." The audience cheered mightily, and the day went down as a great success.

Whether by requirement or by tradition, city children for many years—until the 1940s—sang the anthem regularly, at least once a week in school. Many of them still remember its praise for "Baltimore where Carroll flourished and the fame of Calvert grew."

the patriotic display when Dr. John H. Latane, professor of American history and dean of faculty at Johns Hopkins, organized a musical program at the Lyric celebrating British participation in the war. The Lyric Theatre was decorated by Maryland Institute students under the guidance of the sculptor Hans Schuler with British and American flags supplied by the Baltimore Bargain House. Music provided by the Fort McHenry Band and a chorus of four hundred young women from Eastern and Western High Schools alternated with patriotic speeches and a historical tableau honoring the British navy.[31]

The Baltimore Symphony Orchestra played its first "run out" concert in May of 1918 for soldiers at Camp Meade. The musicians, who had volunteered unanimously to play the performance, traveled to the camp aboard special cars on loan from the Washington, Baltimore and Annapolis Railroad. The all-wood Liberty Theater was filled with two thousand young soldiers who had been given the choice between a baseball game and a concert. One of the soldiers stationed at the camp, Gilbert Stange, the orchestra's first clarinetist until his enlistment, rejoined his colleagues for the performance. The Metropolitan Opera soprano Lenora Sparks charmed the soldiers with the gavotte from *Manon* and the waltz song from *Romeo and Juliet*. The men stood up and cheered her performance and listened quietly as the orchestra played Dvořák's Sym-

Olive Drag! Aberdeen Goes to Broadway (1918)

In the summer of 1918, illustrating the military buildup that had followed American entry into the Great War a year earlier, places like Camp Meade and Aberdeen Proving Ground in Maryland and a quartermaster school at Camp Meigs in Washington, DC, hummed with activity. Crowded with recruits, they posed familiar challenges to authorities. Plans in the making would turn them into soldiers, but the army had to give them some time just to be boys. So the colonels and generals hit upon the idea of "soldier shows," musical follies whose most interesting feature may have been some private soldiers playing female parts. These programs had the public-health advantage of keeping men in camp. Outside, the threat of venereal disease and assorted misbehavior prevailed. What better way to titillate the boys and keep them inside the fence than to feature a chorus of sexy "girls"?

So that year the men at Aberdeen and Camp Meigs organized two different shows to benefit war relief and the Soldiers Welfare Fund. The troops at Aberdeen managed to capture the attention of some New York professionals—the well-known director Jack Mason; Will Rogers, who helped his impersonator do rope tricks; Andre Sherri, who furnished expensive gowns for the "girls"; and Al Piantadosi and Jack Glogau, who furnished original music. All expenses lay outside of army appropriations, so the director and cast

had to find sponsors, patrons, and people who would buy tickets. Though rehearsals took place after normal duty hours, the soldiers had a hit show, Who Stole the Hat?, which packed houses at nearby Wilmington, Baltimore, and Philadelphia.

Meanwhile, the production at Camp Meigs carried the title Atta Boy. It enlisted the well-known songwriters Ballard Macdonald and Nat Osbourne, both lieutenants, and in Captain Frank Tinney the show boasted a proven Broadway comedian. It also featured a minstrel show, a bevy of "beautiful girls," and various racy skits about camp life. Like the Aberdeen program, the Meigs review ended with the sudden appearance of "President Woodrow Wilson." So well did the show go off that Wilson himself once went backstage to congratulate his alter ego. Atta Boy was a success wherever it went. But soon the quartermaster-school graduates readied to ship out to France, and then, strange as it may seem, the army decided to combine the best of both productions (Aberdeen furnished the majority of personnel) and take a shot at Broadway.

On Christmas Eve 1918, the new Atta Boy opened on the Great White Way. "With Frank Tinney as a headliner, 'Atta Boy,' a soldier show of the musical type given by the boys at the Aberdeen Proving Grounds, Maryland opened last night at the Lexington Theatre," reported the New York Times. "Like many of

ATTA BOY

ABERDEEN PROVING
GROUND, U. S. A.
COLONEL W. A. PHILLIPS
ORDNANCE DEPARTMENT, U. S. A.
COMMANDING OFFICER

its predecessors, there are the burlesques on camp life and the amusing antics of the male chorus girls. Of course, Frank Tinney was the piece de résistance, and he lived up to his well-deserved reputation as a comedian. The music of 'Atta Boy' is unusually tuneful, and no doubt Broadway will be whistling 'Strolling 'round the Camp with Mary,' which seemed particularly to please the good-sized first night audience."

Despite these compliments, the show lasted only two weeks (and finally lost money), perhaps because after the armistice of November 11, 1918, audiences and most Americans wanted to concentrate on peace and recovery.

Harrison Fisher, famous for his "American Girl" illustrations, designed covers for the official programs for both Who Stole the Hat? and Atta Boy.

phony No. 5, the *New World* Symphony.[32] During the largo movement, the orchestra musicians, seated on the makeshift stage, could hear the voices of the soldiers singing the words of "Goin' Home." The familiar section describing the oncoming cavalry elicited spontaneous cheers and whoops from the soldiers.

As more and more of the state's resident musicians donned uniforms or entered war industries, the symphony management considered introducing women into the orchestra. So many chairs had been vacated

that the 1918–19 season was in jeopardy. While European audiences were accustomed to women symphony musicians, there were few opportunities in professional orchestras for competent American women musicians. Only a few conductors, Leopold Stokowski being one, were strong advocates for the employment of women in symphony orchestras. Strube and Huber not only made it clear that they had no objection to women's being added to the orchestra's ranks but pointed to a ready pool of capable women musicians in the city.[33] The bar preventing women from joining the ranks of symphony musicians would be left high.

After the armistice, in November 1918, Maryland's musicians began to return home. The baritone Eugene Martinet, a favorite of Baltimore audiences since his student days at the Peabody, had served in "Baltimore's Own" 313th Infantry Regiment; in France a blast from a shell had destroyed his wristwatch but miraculously had not damaged his hands. Martinet celebrated his return with a recital sponsored jointly by the Peabody Institute and the Johns Hopkins University. The violinist Frank Gittelson and the pianist Austin Conradi returned from service in France to take on teaching positions at the Peabody. Toward the end of his service, Conradi had been teaching in France at the Army's School of Music established by General Pershing to instruct Army bandmasters. Trading their instruments of Mars for those of the Muse, servicemen enrolling at Peabody broke all attendance records.[34]

Ain't Misbehavin'

Maryland summers deserved their reputation for high temperatures and sometimes unbearable humidity. When a British visitor asked how one could account for the gross discomfort of summers in Baltimore and Washington, a native supposedly replied, "Capitol punishment!" Well-heeled Washingtonians and Baltimoreans took steamboats and then the train to Ocean City or Rehoboth or went out on the B&O Railroad to Western Maryland—Deer Park or Mountain Lake Park. Some lucky Baltimoreans could afford to flee to nearby villages in Baltimore County, places like Mount Washington, Glyndon, Ellicott City, Waverly, Govans, and Towson. Wage-earning families remained at home in their row houses for the most part, shutters drawn to hold out the heat of the day, and then, after sundown, moved to their front steps with pitchers of ice tea or beer to catch the breeze and socialize with neighbors.

Almost anyone could spend a summer night enjoying music and dancing at one of the parks in and around Baltimore. They were only an excursion boat or streetcar ride away, and admission was free. Gwynn Oak Park opened in Woodlawn, in a grove near the city line,

between Liberty Heights and Windsor Mill Road in 1893. Its picnic grounds, carousel, and amusement rides, along with its proximity to the city, drew families and Sunday school groups in the daytime. In the evening, as water bubbled over the Gwynns Falls, local groups and touring artists played in the park's Dixie Ballroom. John Farson boasted that his twenty musicians had the most expensive uniforms in the country (costing about $40 apiece). His band played a mixture of Italian airs and classics for dancers. In contrast, John F. Kurznacher's band at Electric Park, on Belvedere Avenue, achieved renown for letting dancers get really close. It played slow romantic rhythms for the purpose of what participants then called "drag dancing": "They would just hang onto each other and just grind back and forth in one spot all night."[35] In 1907 Signor Vincent Dei Manto's "Electric Park March" was played on special occasions.[36]

Visitors traveled to Bay Shore Park, built on a point of land north and east of Baltimore, either by steamboat or trolley line and there enjoyed the sandy beach, strolled the thousand-foot-long Crystal Pier, which reached out into the Chesapeake, and listened to music. Bands played every night in season in the grand pavilion. In 1906, when Bay Shore Park opened, the cellist Belle Yeaton Renfre led the Bostonia Ladies' Orchestra, which she proclaimed the only orchestra of its kind in the country. At the time touring the East and the Midwest, the twenty Bostonian musicians coped valiantly as fiddle strings and wind-instrument reeds went more or less limp in the damp bayside air. The ladies performed the classics.[37]

Riverview Park, at Point Breeze in East Baltimore, gained a reputation for its spectacular pavilion with its grand staircase, soaring columns, and Moorish twin towers bedecked with lights that shone in the night like stars. In the summer of 1904 the Royal Artillery Band of Italy, led by Signor Euclide Tasca, played there to a crowd that reportedly numbered sixty thousand. The *Baltimore Sun* described Tosca, who was known for his mop of hair, fiery repertoire, and passionate style, as "warm enough to melt an iceberg."[38]

On May 16, 1915, at Riverview Park, Eubie Blake

happened to meet Noble Sissle, and soon after that they formed one of the most successful songwriting teams in American musical history. James Hubert Blake, born in Baltimore on February 7, 1883, began his musical studies in a four-room house at 319 Forrest Street, not far from Belair Market. His father, John Sumner Blake, a Civil War veteran who had endured slavery, was a stevedore. His mother, Emily Johnston Blake, was a laundress. Eubie was the youngest of eleven children, the only one to survive infancy. His teacher, Margaret Purviance, played the organ at Waters's Chapel Church. Young Eubie enlivened the classical exercises he was given to practice with infectious rhythms adapted from black funeral bands and church shouting. Mrs. Blake took a dim view of her son's improvisations. Eubie remembered his mother hearing those rhythms: "And she's standing in the room: 'Take that ragtime out'a my house and don't you ever let me hear that ragtime again.' That's the first time I paid any attention or cognizance to the work 'ragtime.'"[39]

Blake took his church-based training into the streets with a neighborhood vocal quartet that catered to the saloon trade with tunes like "Camptown Races" and "Beautiful Dreamer" and learned buck dancing.[40] At age 12 he mastered the cornet and played for Captain Harris's band until he was pitched out for embellishing his parts with ragtime riffs. By 13 he had picked up the pianist Jesse Pickett's sinewy and seductive style and mastered Jack "The Bear" Wilson's hot piano sound, becoming adept at improvisation. Aggie Shelton, the proprietor of one of Baltimore's best bordellos, hired young Blake as her house musician when he turned 15.

By the end of the 1890s Blake was developing a whole new approach to the piano. Playing the characteristic syncopation with his right hand and a heavier, steady beat with the left, he became one of the virtuosos of ragtime on the East Coast. He teamed up with the cabaret entertainers Madison Reed and Mary Stafford and played in the saloons of Atlantic City. Blake started out earning twenty-five dollars a week and was soon bringing in fifty-five dollars—a fortune in those days. After playing melodeon and buck dancing in a medicine show throughout the Maryland and Pennsyl-

vania countryside, Blake did a stint in a plantation-style review at New York's Academy of Music in 1902. He returned to Baltimore to play piano at Alfred Greenfield's Saloon, an establishment haunted by colorful characters and "working" girls. He immortalized the place in his rag "Corner of Chestnut and Low," named for Greenfield's location.

For a time, Blake's career followed the journeyman's description. After Greenfield's, he played for Annie Gilly's sporting house, at 317 East Street (where the patrons carried knives and brass knuckles). Blake became a star attraction at cafes and clubs and a perennial winner in national piano-playing contests. For a while he teamed up with Preston Jackson and his Uptown Band. In the summers around 1905 Blake headed for the Jersey Shore, playing for the Middle Section Club in Atlantic City. There he met and formed a lifelong friendship with Will Marion Cook, the well-known composer who would become Blake's mentor. Back in Baltimore in 1907, Blake went to work for Joe Gans, the African American prize fighter who owned the newly opened Goldfield Hotel at East Lexington and Colvin Streets. The prestigious hotel became a mecca for wealthy travelers and touring entertainers and inspired a number of Blake's compositions. Encouraged by W. Llewellyn Wilson, he wrote "The Baltimore Todolo," "Kitchen Tom," "Tricky Fingers," "Novelty Rag," and "Poor Katie Redd" between 1907 and 1910. In the years that followed, Blake played in many of the best clubs in Baltimore, Atlantic City, and New York and wrote "Troublesome Ivories," "Fizz Water," "Brittwood Rag," and "Chevy Chase" (after the Washington suburb).

After Blake met Sissle, a singer originally from Indianapolis, the pair landed a job working with Joe Porter's Serenaders that summer at Riverview Park, at Point Breeze, just outside Baltimore City—Blake the pianist, Sissle the lyricist. Their first collaboration, a song entitled "It's All Your Fault," was introduced in 1915, just days after it was written, by Sophie Tucker at the Maryland Theater on Howard Street in Baltimore.

Most artists spent many years and endured much heartbreak trying to reach the stage of the Palace Theatre in New York. Sissle and Blake did it in a couple of

Eubie Blake's "Tricky Fingers," ca. 1980. James Hubert "Eubie" Blake was born on February 7, 1883, in a four-room house at 319 Forrest Street, near the Belair Market. His neighbor, a church organist, gave him his first music lessons. When Blake was still in his teens, he was playing in the city's "sporting district." Later he played at the Goldfield Hotel's nightclub on East Lexington, the first black and tan club in Baltimore, one of the earliest integrated clubs in the United States. Blake claimed that the first time he heard the word *ragtime* was from his mother, who used it in reference to his playing. Archives of the Peabody Institute of the Johns Hopkins University.

weeks. Their hits included "Gypsy Blues" and "Baltimore Buzz." Everything they wrote clicked, and with the opening of *Shuffle Along* in late May 1921, Sissle and Blake made musical and theatrical history. One of the first musicals written, produced, and directed by African Americans, *Shuffle Along* brought African American humor, music, and jazz dancing to Broadway in pure form. The show introduced Paul Robeson and Josephine Baker and featured three hit tunes—"Bamville," "Love Will Find a Way," and "I'm Just Wild about Harry." It created new demand for African American musical and dancing talent.

Even so, the exigencies of travel and the possibility of confrontations with police (or Mounties) continued to hamper African American performers, who had to endure racially motivated slights and indignities. While on tour, Blake had to send his clothes back home to Baltimore to be washed. "SISSLE AND BLAKE

ARRESTED IN TORONTO . . . EUBIE BLAKE CHARGED WITH MAKING A HIGHBALL," read headlines to an article published in the *Baltimore Afro-American* in early May 1925. On tour in Toronto with their musical comedy *The Chocolate Dandies*, Sissle and Blake had been arrested at a mixed-race cast party. The magistrate dropped charges against Blake, but Noble, who had the liquor, paid a fine of fifty dollars and court costs.

Later that month *The Chocolate Dandies* opened a week-long run at Ford's Theatre, where the management reserved the "entire first and second balconies" for its "Colored Patrons."[41] Blake wrung a concession from the theater, however, so his mother and her guests received places of honor in box seats.[42] In 1930 Blake worked with the composer and lyricist Andy Razaf to produce songs for *Blackbirds of 1930*, including the hit song "Memories of You."

Eubie Blake's Big Break (1921)

The first all-black Broadway musical to become a box-office success (with 504 consecutive performances), *Shuffle Along* (1921) made national celebrities out of its writers, the Midwesterner Noble Sissle and the Baltimorean Eubie Blake. James Hubert Blake, born in 1883, played keyboard as a young child and landed his first job, playing piano in a brothel, when he was fifteen.

The show opened the legitimate theater to black performers, who previously had been relegated to minstrel shows or the vaudeville policy of only one black act on a bill. Josephine Baker, Ethel Waters, and Paul Robeson performed with *Shuffle Along*. Pit musicians performed without music, to the amazement of many. However, to their further surprise, many black musicians were classically trained, jumping to their first chance at Broadway. *Shuffle Along* produced two hit songs, "I'm Just Wild about Harry," a tune that such famous singers as Judy Garland, Al Jolson, and Carmen Miranda later performed, and "Baltimore Buzz," which inspired members of the theater audience to get out of their seats and dance in the aisles—a first for Broadway. Such excitement inspired Florenz Ziegfeld and George White to open studios, with girls from *Shuffle Along* to teach their white dancers the jazz steps.

"Harry" almost dropped out of the show because of its lackluster presentation. Lottie Gee sang it with a background of dancing chorus boys. Noble relates: "One night one of the boys was sick and Bob Lee, a singer, was drafted to replace him. Bob couldn't dance so we sent him leading the line so that he would be the last off and not in the way of the others when they made their exit. All of a sudden we heard a roar of laughter. We ran to the wings. Blake flew up out of the pit, wild eyed: 'Keep him in!' he yelled, and disappeared. We thought we had gone nuts, then the encore was on. Bob Lee could not do the steps the other fellows were doing and couldn't get off the stage, so he dropped out of line and with a jive smile and a high-stepping routine of his own stopped the show cold" (*Reminiscing with Noble Sissle and Eubie Blake*, by Robert Kimball and William Bolcom [New York: Cooper Square, 2000], 106).

Just as Irving Berlin used his "Smile and Show Your Dimple" melodic line for "Easter Parade," Sissle and Blake borrowed lyrics and meter from "My Loving Baby" (published in 1916 by H. Federoff's Maryland Music Publishing Company) in writing "I'm Just Wild about Harry."

"I'm Just Wild about Harry" (1921)	"My Loving Baby" (1916)
I'm just wild about Harry And Harry's wild about me. The heav'nly blisses of his kisses Fill me with ecstasy. He's sweet just like cho'late candy, And just like honey from the bee. Oh, I'm just wild about Harry And He's just wild about me.	I'm just wild about Baby, Baby's wild about me. And when I look into his dreamy eyes, His very soul I can see, He's just as sweet as 'lasses candy, Sweeter than the honey from the bee, I'm just wild about Baby Baby's just crazy 'bout me.

American Rhapsody

The Baltimore Municipal Orchestra did reasonably well following World War I, but eventually it illustrated the difficulties of sustained success. In one episode, it nearly fell afoul of the fundamentalism that then gained a grip on the country and produced more than a decade of prohibition of alcoholic drink. Concerts immediately after the armistice sold so well that the management decided to organize an orchestra chorus for the fall season and present a special holiday concert in December featuring George W. Chadwick's "Noel."[43]

When advance tickets sold out, the mayor applied special police-board permission to repeat the performance the following Sunday afternoon. Maryland Sabbath-enforcement law strictly forbade Sunday performances, but the mayor's request had strong editorial support from major newspapers, and the police relaxed the blue laws for the orchestra.

Then city commissioners allowed the orchestra to move its regular performances from Friday evenings to Sunday afternoons. The ruling was a boon to symphony musicians and to theater-house managers. Most of the musicians were dependent on the income they earned playing in jazz bands and dance orchestras on Friday and Saturday nights. Others had regular jobs as pit musicians at movie houses. (In those days even Philadelphia Orchestra musicians made more money playing for silent films than they did from their symphony jobs.) Substitute musicians hired to play on movie houses' biggest night of the week were proving inadequate, and house managers were having second thoughts about their deal with the musicians' union. Movie houses were not allowed to operate on Sundays, clearing the way for orchestra performances, and with Friday concerts free, the musicians could resume their places in the pit orchestras.

This fortuitous solution inflamed the members of the Lord's Day Alliance, who, outraged over this desecration of the Sabbath, pressed the police commissioner to ask the state attorney general to rule on the legality of Sunday orchestra concerts. He decided in favor of the orchestra, wryly observing that if a Maryland jury would not convict the Baltimore Orioles for playing baseball on Sunday afternoons, citizens would hardly indict the Baltimore Symphony for playing Beethoven.

Beginning on January 28, 1920, Madame Olga Samaroff performed all of Beethoven's sonatas at the Peabody (a feat that had not been attempted since von Bülow's performance in 1875). It was thought to be the first time such a feat had ever been undertaken by a woman.[44] That summer Max Landow quietly returned to the Peabody as head of the piano faculty of the summer school.

The Municipal Orchestra continued to operate under its small annual appropriation until 1919, when the rosy glow surrounding it began to fade. While it continued to play to large audiences and attracted major artists, such as the internationally acclaimed violinist Maud Powell and the English diva Maggie Teyte, Baltimore's new mayor, William F. Broening, viewed the orchestra with indifference. Articles questioning the orchestra's future began to appear in the local press and in national music journals. No artists had been engaged for the coming season, and by July there was talk of removing Strube as well as Huber and placing the orchestra in the hands of a committee.[45] Rallying to the defense of the orchestra, Miss Elizabeth Ellen Star, a

musician with strong social and political ties, organized the Permanent Committee for the Promotion of Music in Baltimore. Miss Starr took her arguments for saving the orchestra directly to Broening, citing its contributions to the war effort and the commercial life of the city. The mayor not only backed down; he increased the annual appropriation to the orchestra by five thousand dollars, allowing it to increase its number of concerts.[46]

Shaken by the prospect of loosing control of the orchestra, Huber moved hastily to secure his place with the new administration, submitting articles praising Baltimore's municipal music programs to national magazines and journals. He ingratiated himself and the orchestra with the mayor and city officials. Huber told reporters that he had been asked to manage the orchestra and the school of music endowed by the philanthropist George Eastman in Rochester, New York. Approached by a skeptical reporter trying to substantiate the story, Eastman set him straight: "Rumor not correct."[47]

The orchestra's concertmaster, Joan Van Hulsteyn, repeatedly urged Huber to seek outside support to supplement the city's appropriation. He refused, fearing that an outside subsidy would jeopardize the orchestra's municipal funding. Orchestra members suspected a darker motive, namely, that Huber feared losing control of the orchestra.[48] As the orchestra grew, so did suspicion and distrust of Huber. Salary disputes erupted in the autumn of 1921, when six of the orchestra's first-chair players made modest demands. Huber, who doled out city money for concerts as if it were his own, cast them as villains.[49] With the opening concert cancelled, orchestra members were pilloried in the press, and the six capitulated.

A different controversy swirled around a 1923 guest appearance by Siegfried Wagner, the son of the legendary composer, who was slated to perform with orchestras in New York, Boston, Philadelphia, Chicago, Cincinnati, and Detroit. To underwrite his fee, Huber asked Baltimore's underpaid musicians to forfeit part of their salaries. (In those days symphony musicians had no fixed salaries; they were paid by the performance and the rehearsal.) When the musicians balked, they were

Some Music of the Chesapeake Bay (1923)

The Chesapeake Bay has linked the Eastern and Western Shores from the earliest days of the province of Maryland. It fostered trade between Maryland and Virginia and among all the cities and towns around its shores and up and down its many rivers. It brought goods from around the world to Norfolk and Baltimore. It carried immigrants to Locust Point and enabled tidewater folk to shop and sightsee in Baltimore, self-styled "Queen City of the Chesapeake." Watermen pulled up delicacies from the bay. Sailors loved to sail it. Composers loved to write about it, and examples abounded.

The sheet music for "The Chesapeake March and Two-Step" (E. F. Droop & Sons, 1902), by Edward Bergenholtz, features a sketch of an attractive young woman in a turn-of-the-century bathing suit looking just a little vulnerable. Bergenholtz eventually wrote a ballad celebrating another exotic subject, "Old Hawaii."

"March Tolchester" (R. F. Seitz, 1894), by Charles Henry Bochau, celebrated both Chesapeake Bay steamboats of the period (Bochau dedicated the march to John M. Naudain, vice president of the Tolchester Steamboat Company) and the charms of Tolchester Beach, a popular Eastern Shore

resort dating from 1877 that lay about twenty-seven miles across the bay from Baltimore, in Kent County. The Louise, the Emma Giles, and the Tolchester were among the boats that plied the waters to Tolchester. There family-style attractions included an inviting beach, bath-houses, a hotel, food, saddled ponies, and amusement-park rides with names like "Flying Horses" and "Whirlpool Dips." German born, Bochau had only recently graduated from the Peabody Conservatory when he published this "Great Two Step." He went on to serve as choirmaster of the Madison Avenue Synagogue and to direct the Arion Singing Society and the Johns Hopkins University Orchestra. During his long career in Baltimore, he composed many anthems and orchestral, organ, and piano pieces.

excoriated in the press. Private sources eventually raised the money, and the concert was set.

Siegfried's arrival became a media event. There were reporters waiting on the platform of Mount Royal Station when the maestro stepped off the train with his

wife and his tour manager. Huber whisked them off to Druid Hill Park to see the bronze bust of Wagner before lunching with the mayor at the Baltimore Country Club.[50] The following day, when Siegfried arrived for his first rehearsal with the orchestra, several hundred

Sailing Down Chesapeake Bay

"Sailing Down the Chesapeake Bay" (Jerome H. Remick, 1913), by Jean C. Havez and George Botsford, may be the best-known bay ballad ever written. Havez, the lyricist, was born in Baltimore in 1870. He graduated from Baltimore City College, then joined the reporting staff of the *Baltimore American*, but he left the paper to work with Lew Dockstader's Minstrels, a New York theater group that organized in about 1906. A founder of the Friars Club in New York, Havez eventually wrote more than one hundred songs, including "Everybody Works but Father." He died suddenly in 1925 while working on a Harold Lloyd movie script. His collaborator on "Sailing Down the Chesapeake Bay," a South Dakota native, had become a success as a composer and arranger for the Detroit-based popular-music publisher

Jerome Remick. Botsford's early arrangements included pieces for barbershop quartets on the vaudeville circuit. His "Black and White Rag" and "Grizzly Bear Rag" may have started the craze for animal dances such as the turkey trot and the fox trot. Baltimoreans still recall hearing Bob Scobey's Frisco Band playing "Sailing Down the Chesapeake Bay" as the theme song for *The Harley Show*, Music out of Baltimore on WFBR and WBAL for about twenty years, beginning in 1952.

"Sweet Old Chesapeake Bay" (Walter Donaldson, 1923) never achieved the popularity of the Havez-Botsford song, but it still plucked the heartstrings of many listeners, whether native to the Chesapeake or outsiders. Born in Brooklyn in 1893, Donaldson started out after high school as a clerk on Wall Street, then worked for a music pub-

lisher who fired him for trying to "improve" submissions. Eventually a member of the Songwriters Hall of Fame, Donaldson wrote such perennial favorites as "Carolina in the Morning" and "My Blue Heaven."

---

people tried to force their way into the Lyric. The orchestra cheered when he stepped up on the podium, but enthusiasm quickly diminished as the maestro revealed his ineptitude as a conductor. What little respect the musicians had left for the son of the great composer was lost when Siegfried, nearing the end of the prelude to act 3 of his father's opera *Lohengrin*, suddenly realized that he had been conducting from the score of the prelude to act 1.

The thriving orchestra owed its progress entirely to Strube's masterful guidance. The Municipal subsidy ensured that the orchestra remained accessible to all segments of society, allowing it to become in a very true sense a people's orchestra. Strube regularly performed new American works, including his own. The Johns Hopkins music master Edwin Litchfield Turnbull gave Strube a collection of poems by Sidney Lanier. Struck by Lanier's poem "The Symphony," Strube began working on a musical interpretation of the poem. The following year, he completed the *Lanier Symphony* in four movements for full symphony orchestra. The New York Symphony Orchestra premiered the work on March 17, 1925, with the composer on the podium as guest

conductor. Critics hailed Strube's highly individualistic style and brilliant instrumentation.[51]

Strube's *Symphonic Prologue* won first-prize at the Philadelphia Sesqui-Centennial Exposition of 1926. The work had its Baltimore premiere the following year. The 1928 season opened with the premiere of Strube's *American Rhapsody*, a new work based on American folk songs; Charles Bochau's *Symphonic Fantasy* made its own debut later that same season.

The Pennsylvania Avenue Rag: Jazz in Black Baltimore

"NOW IT IS THE JAZZ AGE," the *Baltimore Afro-American* announced in 1917,[52] remarking on the arrival of a new kind of music and dance that seemed to be taking hold in certain parts of the city and infecting them with the "delirium tremens of syncopation."[53] Jazz, with its fast, freestyle rhythms, had become wildly popular, especially in dance halls, but this new style, sometimes referred to as "novelty music," had its critics.

Musicians at the Peabody debated the worth of the genre. The so-called primitive origins of the form—the prevalence of noise-making devices such as sandpaper, fly swatters, and coconuts, what Louis Cheslock, who witnessed and wrote on the emergence of jazz, called the "pitiful vocal attempts of the instrumentalists"[54]—prompted some of his colleagues to wonder whether jazz actually had anything at all to do with music. What classical musicians probably found most disturbing was statistics showing that most Americans preferred jazz to classical music.

Aesthetic anxieties paled in comparison with fear that acceptance of the new form, with its African origins and imitations of pagan dancing, might actually throw the march of civilization into reverse. Resistance to the new music extended beyond fussy segments of the white community; African American preachers warned their congregations that the heathenish music, a tool of the devil, could lead the weak to depravity.

The seductive new music could be heard at the Galilean Fisherman's Hall, at 411 West Biddle Street, the Richmond Market Armory, Pythian Castle Hall, the Old Fifth Regiment Armory, the amusement parks and bayside resorts outside the city, and small clubs in East and West Baltimore. The genre had its beginnings in the merging of two traditions, ragtime and the brass band. Among Baltimore groups, Charles L. Harris's Famous Commonwealth Cornet Band probably exerted the strongest influence. Many of Maryland's early jazz practitioners got their start as musicians with Harris, who taught organ and cornet at the Baltimore Conservatory of Music, at the Perkins Square Baptist Church. Harris also led the thirty-five-member Baltimore Colored City Band, taking over in 1927 when A. Jack Thomas was suspended from the musicians' union.[55] The band played in black neighborhoods, at Sharp and Hill Streets, Fremont and Myrtle Avenues, and Caroline and Jefferson Streets, and in front of the Mansion House at Druid Hill Park. After playing their formal programs of overtures, waltzes, and marches, the band would shift to music with upbeat tempos and a jazz flavor for dancing. Many of the men who played for Harris also played "hot" jazz in clubs on the East Side and along Pennsylvania Avenue.

The T. Henderson Kerr Orchestra, a band that ca-

tered to society, played for dances and concerts in and around Baltimore from 1902 until about 1920. "We played churches and moonlights, nice kind of places," Kerr told a Sun writer. "No jazz. I never did like that jumpy kind of stuff. I like society kind of music, not the kind the riff-raff would enjoy."[56] Kerr stuck instead with ragtime, the playful forerunner of jazz, and the latest Broadway show tunes. A classically trained violinist and composer, Kerr was born in Cambridge, Maryland, on the Eastern Shore, in May 1888, the eleventh of the twelve children of Charles H. and Mary Jane Lloyd Kerr. His father, a brass player, organized the Merry Concert Band in Cambridge. Edward Kerr, his paternal grandfather, sang spirituals at gatherings during the Civil War. T. Henderson Kerr began studying violin with his uncle, George Owens, a Baltimore violinist, who made regular visits to the Eastern Shore to teach his talented nephew. Sometime around 1905 the Kerr family moved to Baltimore, taking up lodgings near the Owens' home, in West Baltimore. The young Kerr continued his studies on the violin, taught himself piano and flute, and began writing music. Years later, in the 1920s, he enrolled in the Peabody Preparatory Colored Students' Branch, at the Druid Hill YMCA. His compositions ranged from orchestral preludes to ragtime pieces. In 1911 the Equitable Music Company of Baltimore published Kerr's "That Hobble Rag," inspired by the hobble skirts worn by fashionable ladies to ballroom-dancing classes and socials. W. Llewellyn Wilson performed Kerr's unpublished orchestral preludes "Day Dream," "Genee," and "At Evening" at the Douglass High School commencement exercises in the 1920s. In that decade, Kerr collaborated with Wilson and the lyricist Kennard Williams, writing and producing musical shows at the Galilean Fisherman's Hall. Kerr obtained a substantial part of the repertoire for his group from the touring orchestras performing the latest show tunes at Ford's Theatre. High up in the balcony, the musicians playing in the pit far below, he sat with a pile of manuscript paper, furiously transcribing the melodies. The next day, patrons danced to Kerr's new arrangements.[57] For Kerr, music became more than an avocation: it financed his education. After playing his way through graduate school, Dr. T. Henderson Kerr opened his own pharmacy.

After World War I, Baltimore became a hotbed of musical groups. The John Ridgely Jazzers, also known as the Ridgely 400 Society Jazz Band, organized in 1917. Ridgely's was the first Baltimore band proudly to call what it played "jazz." In the 1920s the band played every night in the Maryland Theater's dining room and "Jardin de Danse." The group included the cellist Lewis Flagg, John Tinner on banjo, the clarinetist Carlos Dowsy, and Alfred Hughes on his "moaning" sax. The anchor of the group was the band's young pianist, Rivers Chambers. Two other popular practitioners of the new art form were Joseph T. H. Rochester and Ernest Purviance. Rochester's dazzling piano technique packed Pythian Hall, at Preston and McCulloh Streets. Purviance, who demonstrated the complexities of the latest jazz steps, became Baltimore's "Dance King." In 1917, the two joined forces to form the Drexel Ragtime Syncopators and set off a dance craze called the "Shimme She Wabble She" at St. Mary's Hall on Orchard Street. Two years later, Bee Palmer, hailed as the originator of the twenties rage the shimmy, performed the dance with her band, the Six Kings of Jazzopation, at the Maryland Theater.[58]

Purviance and Rochester dropped *Ragtime* from their group's name, restyling the group the Drexel *Jazz* Syncopators, and rode a wave of popularity well into the 1920s. Rochester introduced jam-session-style contests among his musicians and challenged other bands to compete with his men. Professor Joe Rochester's Orchestra played at some of the biggest events in the African American community, drawing patrons from the surrounding counties and from Washington, DC. The WB&A (Washington, Baltimore, and Annapolis) Dance at St. Peter Clavers' Hall, at Carey and Presstman Streets, and the Darktown Strutters May Ball, at Fisherman's Hall, on Biddle Street, were the main events of the spring season in the late teens. The Drexel Jazz Syncopators spawned a number of smaller groups, including the Pythian Castle Jazz Band, the Hamer and Faulkner Full Jazz Band, Alexander's Jazz Band, and Johnny Bee's Jazz Band. One of Joe Rochester's musicians left the band in 1919 to lead the Washingtonians.

Pennsylvania Avenue, the heart and soul of music in Baltimore's African American community, stood in the midst of a quiet residential neighborhood in Old West Baltimore. In the first decade of the twentieth century, the neighborhoods surrounding Pennsylvania Avenue went from almost 10 percent African American to 60 percent. The large number of African American homeowners in this comfortable and attractive neighborhood prompted Booker T. Washington to comment on the uniqueness of this community. Druid Hill Avenue and its neighboring streets became the center for Baltimore's black aristocracy. To preserve the tranquility of their neighborhood, residents in 1906 established the Colored Law and Order League, which succeeded not only in persuading the Liquor License Board to refuse licenses to bars in the Druid Hill Avenue district but also in getting eleven licenses revoked, though most of the bars continued to operate.[59]

Amid these quiet residential blocks, churches, and schools, Pennsylvania Avenue provided relief from the harsh realities of downtown Baltimore, where black residents were unwelcome in shops, restaurants, and places of entertainment. Until its importance was diminished by desegregation, Pennsylvania Avenue was the major business and entertainment center for the African American community. "The Avenue was ours," recalled the bandleader Tracy McCleary, "and it was a mighty fine place to go."[60] It was a musicians' paradise, stretching from Biddle Street to North Avenue, with three or four clubs in each block, all featuring live entertainment.

Pennsylvania Avenue had it all: theaters, taverns, nightclubs, bookie joints, shops, restaurants, and numbers operations. The lower part of the avenue, close to the white downtown and known as the bottom, stretched from Franklin at the south end and ran northwesterly to Dolphin Street. Plagued by cholera, typhoid, and tuberculosis, it was the haunt of the avenue's lowlife—prostitutes, pimps, con men, and gamblers. If you were looking for trouble, you were guaranteed to find it at the bottom. Uptown, above Dolphin, elegant nightclubs clustered in and around the 1400 and 1500 blocks, attracting the sophisticated crowds that came to listen to the hottest jazz in town. When in 1919 prohibition closed down the bars and taverns, musicians found refuge in private social clubs.

The Regent Theater, at 1629 Pennsylvania Avenue, opened at the beginning of the summer of 1916. It was billed as the largest, coolest, and best-ventilated house in the city. Its immense facade dominated the 1600 block of Pennsylvania Avenue. The theater featured "high-class photo plays and vaudeville" and had its own orchestra, conducted by Ike Thompson; Paul J. Harris took over in 1919. Rivers Chambers was the orchestra's pianist. Cab Calloway, Lena Horne, and Ethel Waters all performed on the stage of the Regent during its heyday. Waters, one of the foremost African American singers in the country, began her career in Baltimore. For her role in Elia Kazan's film *Pinky*, she became the first African American to be nominated for an Oscar. Enlarged in 1920, with a seating capacity of more than two thousand, boxes, and a balcony, the Regent reopened on January 31, 1921, with Ike Thompson back on the podium. The Regent was the first black house in town to show *The Jazz Singer*.

North of Dolphin Street stood the famed Royal Theatre, the most important black theater in town. When it opened in 1921 as the Douglass, it was the only theater in Baltimore built by African American owners for "colored" audiences. Its first show featured the pianist Jerome Carrington on the theater's grand piano. When the Douglass was sold to white operators in 1926, they renamed it the Royal, reopening the theater with uniformed usherettes and a show starring Fats Waller. Whites began flocking to the Royal to see Louis Armstrong, Duke Ellington, Nat King Cole, and Pearl Bailey perform on the grand stage. The Royal was on the same circuit as the Apollo in New York and the Howard in Washington. Playing the New York–Philadelphia–Baltimore–Washington, DC, circuit was referred to as "going around the world." The Royal had a reputation for being tough on its acts. Musicians who

had played both houses agreed that the Royal had been even more discriminating than New York's Apollo.[61]

Originally a black art form, jazz reached the white world in several ways. Some whites simply frequented black establishments; while the practice of racial segregation kept blacks from white hotels, theaters, dance halls, and so on, the reverse did not hold. There were no color bars at the Royal or in the clubs along Pennsylvania Avenue, and whether fully welcomed or not, whites could usually be found in the audiences and sometimes sitting in with the musicians. Jazz also found a wider audience as white bands demonstrated the old saw about imitation being the sincerest form of flattery by playing their versions of the music from Pennsylvania Avenue. Many white patrons learned to appreciate jazz by listening to bands like Felice "Feen" Iula's. Skilled as a violinist and a regular in the pit orchestras of Baltimore-area theaters, Iula formed his own group. Their lively repertoire of popular and classical works played in the style of Guy Lombardo put them in demand for society dances, weddings, and Bar Mitzvahs.[62]

Increasingly in the second and third decades of the twentieth century, anyone could listen to jazz on records. This technology had its origins in late nineteenth-century efforts to build reliable voice recorders for office use and in the early years had relied on tinfoil-covered or wax-coated cylinders. Competition between companies associated with Alexander Graham Bell and Thomas A. Edison led to new devices for cutting and playing recordings. Recorded music soon became big business.

In Baltimore, the Hammann Music Company, a family-owned firm that had been doing business on Liberty Street since 1921, illustrated this success. Two brothers, C. Gordon Hammann and F. Burton Hammann Jr., had worked for their father since he opened the shop, which sold instruments, sheet music, and records. Listening booths filled on weekends with customers eager to hear the latest recordings. The Hammann brothers went on to organize the Townsmen, a popular group that made no bones about replicating the music other groups had made into hits. When published arrangements weren't available, they copied recordings.[63]

The inventiveness and creativity of the musicians performing in clubs along Pennsylvania Avenue stood in sharp contrast. Black musicians, ripe with talent, listened to one another and then pushed on to cultivate and perfect their own distinctive styles and sounds. Their accomplished jazz performances were often based on solid classical training and well-developed technical skills, giving them free rein to create brilliant improvisations and complex rhythmic patterns characteristic of the new style of playing.

Leaving Home for Harlem

One of the most accomplished jazz musicians of his generation, Cab Calloway began his meteoric rise in Baltimore. His seductive charm, musicianship, and inimitable style brought him success in every entertainment realm he entered and every medium he employed. Cab was about 11 in 1918, when his father, Cabell, decided to leave Rochester, New York, and return with his wife and children to his family's home in Baltimore. The Calloway family, well known and highly respected in the city's African American community, lived in a comfortable house on Druid Hill Avenue. Grandfather Calloway was a colorful and jovial man who ran a pool hall. Grandmother Calloway, a stern, God-fearing woman, ruled the family with an iron hand. Sundays were devoted to all-day church services at Grace Presbyterian Church, at Madison and North Avenues, where young Cab's mother, Martha Eulalia Reed Calloway, played the organ. They put the energetic young Cab on the floor under the organ, "and she would pedal the organ, she might take her foot off the pedal and put it on him to hold him in place."[64] During the week, when the children weren't in Bible classes or rehearsing with the church choir, they were expected to sit quietly at home while neighborhood children played outside.[65]

Cab's father died unexpectedly soon after returning to Baltimore, and his grandfather passed away soon after that. Cab's mother left the grief-ridden house and took the children to the home of her parents, Andrew and Anna Credit Reed, just a few blocks away, where the laughter and lively atmosphere of the Reed home seemed like another world. Young Cab pitched in to help with the family income, selling the *Baltimore Afro-American* and the *Sun* on the streetcars to commuters on their way to work in the morning; in the evening he was back on the streetcars with the *News* and the *Star*. When the horses were running at Pimlico, he sold racing forms to the fans coming in to the races and then stayed on to work as a hot walker.

After Mrs. Calloway married John Nelson Fortune, Cab threw himself into sports and his academic studies and began singing in the choir at the church where his mother played the organ. He took private lessons in voice and elocution with Ruth Macabee. Preparing her talented student for a concert career, Mrs. Macabee refused to allow young Cab to sing jazz. At Douglass High School, Calloway studied music and music theory with W. Llewellyn Wilson. Impressed with Calloway's talent, Wilson began teaching him privately after school. Calloway sang every chance he got—at church, at school, in the streets with his friends, and later in clubs around town, like the Arabian Tent and a local speakeasy in a three-story house with a living room converted into a bar and a kitchen that turned out ribs, barbecue, and pigs' feet. Listening to Baltimore performers like Johnny Jones and his Arabian Tent Orchestra prompted Calloway to organize his own band, and Chick Webb, whom he greatly admired, inspired him to take up drums.

Passing himself off as a drummer, he found a job in a pickup band. Calloway went straight to Conn's, on Howard Street, and rented an outfit. After one rehearsal with the group, he was playing rhythms copied from Chick Webb at a roadhouse on the Washington Pike. Calloway sang to draw attention away from his lamentable drumming technique. The band was a success, and Calloway offered to hustle for gigs if the other musicians would let him lead the group. Calloway quickly lined up a job at the Dandy Restaurant, at Gay and Baltimore Streets, playing Dixieland and hot jazz. Before the year was out, Calloway joined Johnny Jones's ten-piece band, playing New Orleans Dixieland, Baltimore style. Singing popular tunes in revues at the Regent and playing in clubs, Calloway earned thirty-five dollars a week, which he took home to his mother with little explanation. Goodbye paper routes and hot walking at the track, hello jazz!

Everyone, it seemed, had plans for young Cab: his mother wanted him to pursue a career in law. Macabee and Wilson were preparing him for a concert career. Eugene Prettyman, a fellow student and musician at Douglass High School, told him to forget about jazz and set his sights on a career in grand opera so he could be somebody.[66] No one—not Cab's mother and stepfather, Miss Macabee, nor his teachers at Douglass— had any idea that he was spending his nights drinking gin and bootleg rye while making music in speakeasies around town.

Blanche Calloway, Cab's older sister, was the first in the family to go into show business. In 1923 she joined the touring company of *Shuffle Along*. In 1927 *Plantation Days* came to the Royal Theatre with an orchestra and cast of about twenty-five, with Blanche as one of the leads. It was during the show's stay at the Royal that Cab realized that he too had to have a career in show business. When one of the singers in the cast fell ill, he talked his sister into arranging an audition for him.

Cab signed on for the show, promising his mother that he would enroll in college when the tour ended. Traveling the circuit was anything but glamorous. The show traveled on the Theater Owners Booking Association circuit, TOBA, or as the performers traveling the circuit called it, "Tough on Black Asses." Shut out of hotels, the cast stayed in rooms rented from black families who would put up theater people for ten dollars a week. Cab loved every minute of it. After the tour ended in Chicago in 1927, Calloway began classes in law at Crane College. By midyear he was singing at the Dreamland Cafe, on State Street. At the end of the academic year Calloway was the house singer and then master of ceremonies at the Sunset Cafe, one of Chicago's most popular clubs. Calloway was twenty-one and still at the Sunset Cafe when Louis Armstrong introduced him to scat singing.

When Louis Armstrong and Carroll Dickerson's band left Chicago for Harlem, the Alabamians replaced them, and Calloway took over as the group's bandleader. When the Alabamians left the Sunset Cafe

bound for New York, Calloway went with them. The band's New York opening at the Savoy in November 1929 ended in disaster. The Alabamians were no match for Cecil Scott's band at the Savoy, and Calloway suddenly found himself out of a job. Armstrong recommended Calloway as a replacement for Paul Bass, a singer in *Hot Chocolates*, one of the biggest hits on Broadway. Calloway got the job and had hits singing "Ain't Misbehavin'," "Sweet Savannah Sue," and "Rhythm Man." While he was on tour with the show, a band then playing at the Savoy in New York, the Missourians, asked Calloway to be their front man. Unwilling to walk out on the show, he postponed his return to New York until *Hot Chocolates* finished its run. In 1930 he took over the band and changed its name to Cab Calloway and His Orchestra.

Calloway and the Missourians were booked into the new Plantation Club, which opened on 126th Street near Lenox Avenue and aimed to compete with the Cotton Club, at 142nd Street. On the day they were to open, thugs (whom Calloway assumed had been hired by the Cotton Club) sacked the Plantation Club. Only the Missourians' music, left on the stands after rehearsal, was spared. Calloway and the band scratched around New York, picking up jobs in smaller clubs to keep the group together. In the 1920s and 1930s the Cotton Club hosted the finest musicians, comedians, singers, and dancers in the business. Calloway was still in his early twenties when he and the Missourians were called to perform at the Cotton Club while Duke Ellington and his band were on tour. By the summer of 1930 the band was playing there regularly, styling itself Cab Calloway's Cotton Club Orchestra. The crowds at the club loved Calloway's flamboyance.

At about the same time, another Baltimore-born musician, a vocalist, began a highly successful yet ultimately tragic career in New York. Eleanora, daughter of Sarah Julia "Sadie" Fagan, née Harris, and a guitarist named Clarence Holiday, was born on April 7, 1915. Her father had worked at Mary's Casino, on Preston Street, with Elmer Snowden, who played banjo, mandolin, and guitar and doubled on saxophone. Holiday confided to Snowden that he had become the father of

Cab Calloway, ca. 1975. Cab Calloway (1907–1994) began his meteoric rise in the world of music in Baltimore. He excelled in every realm he entered: Calloway and his band drew crowds at the Cotton Club. His hit tune "Minnie the Moocher" sold more than a million records. He starred on Broadway in *Porgy and Bess* and *Hello, Dolly!* and toured through Canada, Europe, and across the United States (traveling in a private train through the South). Calloway and his band became one of the greats of the swing era. Photo by James J. Kriegsmann, New York. Archives of the Peabody Institute of the Johns Hopkins University.

a daughter, and Snowden remembered meeting the girl when she was about three years old. The child's indifferent father provided little in the way of financial or emotional support, and later the leader of the house orchestra at the Royal Theatre even heard Holiday deny that he was the child's father after all.[67] After a failed marriage with another Baltimore woman, the guitarist left for Philadelphia, where he became a jazzman in South Philadelphia clubs before joining up with Fletcher Henderson's orchestra. Meantime, the young woman turned to Elmer Snowden as a surrogate father. She would drop in to hear Snowden performing at clubs and halls around town. She discovered her voice, and, having joined her mother in New York and adopted the stage name Billie Holiday, she began singing in small clubs in Brooklyn and Harlem.

The record producer John Hammond heard Holiday singing in a club on 133rd Street in New York City and wrote the first review she ever received.[68] Hammond gave her high marks; he also gave her her first real break when he brought Benny Goodman to hear her

sing. The meeting resulted in three recording sessions with Goodman. In 1933 she won an appearance at the Apollo Theater. Holiday's voice was light, filled with warmth and emotion and tinged with melancholy. Influenced by Louis Armstrong, she used her voice like an instrument. In her 1936 Columbia recording of "Did I Remember?" Holiday demonstrated her own melodic style and unique phrasing. Her recording of "Strange Fruit" (Commodore, 1939), about the lynching of African American men on the Eastern Shore of Maryland, brought her a popular following. A few years later critics voted her the best vocalist in the country, ahead of Ella Fitzgerald.

William Henry "Chick" Webb was born in East Baltimore on February 10, 1907. Shortly after his birth, Webb's mother returned to her father's house at Madison Street and Ashland Avenue, and there Webb grew up. His career became a study in beating the odds: less than four feet tall, a hunchback, crippled by tuberculosis of the spine, uneducated and poor, shy, and sensitive, Webb elected to become a performer in a profession that places great weight on showmanship and good looks. His diminutive size earned him the nickname "Chick." When his fragile health permitted, he attended public school, PS 105, on East Street near Lexington.

On Sunday mornings he would often stray from his family as they made their way to church to follow a parade band. Webb credited one of these drummers with leading him to the drums. When he was 9 years old, Webb began contributing to the family's income by selling newspapers at the corner of Gay and Aisquith Streets. Given to embellishing his stories, he variously claimed that he built up his newspaper business to four hundred or four thousand customers, but he was successful enough to buy himself a secondhand set of drums. Bouts of ill health prevented him from going on to high school and completing his education. Instead, he took on the world of jazz and fought his way to the top. He virtually changed the course of drumming, contributing a series of spectacular hits to the repertoire that included "Stompin' at the Savoy," "Blue Lou," and "Don't Be That Way."

Webb started drumming with anything he could get his hands on to divert himself from his illness and attendant boredom. If he wasn't "rapping bones," he would take a knife and fork or anything that could make a noise and beat on the table or the chairs. He beat out rhythms on garbage cans and on the fences along East Baltimore streets. Elsie Matthews, a neighbor driven nearly to distraction by the sounds emanating from the Webb household, bought Webb his first drum from a store on Gay Street. The respite lasted but a few days, and the rapping started up again. With a broad grin, Webb told his neighbor: "Miss Elsie, I busted my drum."[69]

Replacing that first set of drums with a cheap set he bought with the money he had earned selling papers, Webb joined a local band playing weekend gigs. He teamed up with a small group called the Jazzola Band, working on excursion boats on the Chesapeake Bay, and became friends with the band's guitarist, John Trueheart.

Still in their teens, Webb and Trueheart struck out for New York in 1924. Trueheart landed a job out of town, while Webb played pickup jobs in the city and got to know musicians like Duke Ellington, Sonny Greer, and Coleman Hawkins at the Rhythm Club, at 132nd Street and Seventh Avenue. He became friends with the trumpeter Bobby Stark, who played in Edgar Dowell's band. At Stark's insistence, Webb went to rehearsal with him. Satisfied with his own drummer and possibly put off by Webb's appearance, Dowell flatly refused to hear him. Later, when the band auditioned for a job at the Palace Gardens and its regular drummer failed to show up, Dowell called in Webb to substitute. The Palace Gardens manager was so impressed with Webb's playing that he hired the band on the spot—with the stipulation that Webb stay on as drummer.

Webb's next job came through Duke Ellington, then playing at the Kentucky Club. Ellington got Webb, Bobby Stark (trumpet), Johnny Hodges (alto sax), Don Kirkpatrick (piano), and Johnny Trueheart into the Black Bottom Club. There, despite Webb's hesitation about the pressure and responsibility of leading a group, the young drummer yielded to the persuasion of the others and began his career as a bandleader. Webb and his musicians stayed at the Black Bottom for five months and then, again through Ellington, went on to the Paddock Club, on 50th Street, beneath the Earl Carroll Theatre. No one in the band, which now included Elmer Williams on sax and a trombone player called "Slats," could read music. They worked out arrangements and "woodshedded" until they got them down. Fletcher Henderson offered to buy their scores, unaware that none existed. The Paddock Club sadly having burned down not long after they opened, Webb and his band opened at the Savoy in 1930. Stark, who had been performing with another band, rejoined the group, as did the gifted bass player John Kirby and Taft Jordan, an inspired trumpet player and showman. Edgar Sampson, one of the best arrangers of the era, brought Webb the fabulously successful "Stompin' at the Savoy" and "Don't Be That Way."

In 1934, Webb's band played the Apollo, at about the same time that a teenage singer, Ella Fitzgerald, was performing there in an amateur-talent contest. Chick's front man, Bardu Ali, urged Webb to hear her perform. Jittery about playing for a prom at Yale that weekend (following groups headed by Noble Sissle, Duke Ellington, Benny Goodman, and Tommy Dorsey), Webb needed further prodding but finally gave in and listened to the gawky Fitzgerald sing "Judy" as he packed up for New Haven. Webb, who knew talent when he heard it, sent Fitzgerald out to get her hair done, bought her a couple of evening gowns, and told her to be ready to travel the next day. Afterward, Fitzgerald enjoyed a permanent place with the band. She made her first recording, "Love and Kisses," with Webb and his group that same year and soon celebrated her first recorded hit, "A-Tisket, A-Tasket," which she helped write. Ella and the band recorded 150 sides between 1935 and 1938.

Webb put together a first-rate team of some of the best musicians in the business: the bass player John Kirby, known for his powerful supporting beat and walking bass lines, who could also double on trombone and tuba; the pioneer jazz flutist Wayman Carver; the Cuban-born trumpeter Mario Bauzá, who had been performing with Noble Sissle before joining Webb's band; the pianist Tommy Fulford; Hilton Jefferson, a fine lead alto sax player; the trumpeter Taft Jordan, a gifted mimic who was known for his explosive solo breaks and brilliant improvisations; Garvin Bushell, who could play all the orchestral reed instruments with equal facility and recorded the first known examples of jazz bassoon; the trombonist Nat Story, who started out working on Mississippi riverboats with Fate Marable; the dazzling trumpeter Bobby Stark, acclaimed for his smooth solos and long lines; the trombonists George Matthews and Sandy Williams; and the tenor sax player Teddy McRae. Webb's band recorded his signature tune, the hard-hitting "Let's Get Together," for Columbia, with the trumpeter Reunald Jones as sideman. They played as though they were a single entity. The band's entrances were razor-sharp. Their impeccable ensemble playing and perfect intonation were supported by Webb's fiery and precise rhythms.

The ascent of the Savoy Sultans, the Savoy's house band, coincided with the era of the legendary battles of the bands. Groups led by Basie, Ellington, Lunceford, Goodman, and Webb would come together for a twin bill at dance halls in black communities to see which orchestra could outplay the other. Mounted policemen would be called out to control the crowds when Webb played for the Savoy Ballroom's Battles of the Bands. Two sharp reports from Webb's bass drums heralded the beginning of his act. Crowds would begin to roar before the band played a single note. Webb and his men played opposite Joe "King" Oliver's band. Many of Oliver's men were new, and although he had a number of top musicians in the band, it was not quite up to its best form. Their showpiece tune was "The Cat." Webb and his band had their own arrangement of "The Cat"; after they played through it, Oliver didn't perform it again as long as he stayed at the Savoy.

Nobody wanted to go up against Chick Webb and his men when they were "hot." It was said that Webb could outdrum anyone on the face of the earth. In 1937 Benny Goodman and his band went up against the Savoy Sultans at Harlem's Savoy Ballroom. Afterward, Goodman's drummer, the renowned Gene Krupa, conceded that Webb had cut him "to ribbons."[70] Webb's playing exerted a strong influence on Krupa's style.

Webb was an anomaly in the fast-paced world of jazz. As soon as his work with the band was over, he went home. Considered a hick because he neither smoke nor drank, he stayed away from the fancy women who populated the clubs. He concealed his recurring bouts of illness—even from his band when he could. Occasionally, Webb would leave the band and go to a hospital for a "checkup," but he'd always be present at rehearsals, performances, and broadcasts, drumming, listening, and prodding his men. He returned to the Johns Hopkins Hospital so frequently for treatments and back surgery that one of the rooms in the Halstead Building was named for him. Sensitive about his condition, Webb made it a point to be seated on stage, surrounded by an array of traps, drums, snares, and assorted percussion instruments, when the curtain went up, so that the audience was unaware of his disabilities.

The band was driven by Webb's phenomenal sense of rhythm and virtuoso drumming. He was one of a handful of drummers who broke away from the symmetrical phrasing and four-square bass accompaniments characteristic of the time. His fellow musicians called his drumming style the "power-drive." They admired Webb for his immaculate technique, dynamic control, and the intensity and precision of his playing.

Like many Maryland musicians, including Eubie Blake, Webb never put Maryland behind him. He returned again and again to play for community benefits and to perform at Pennsylvania Avenue's Royal Theatre and in Cambridge, on the Eastern Shore. Recalling his own childhood, he spoke of performing a series of benefits to establish a recreation center for young people in East Baltimore.

Pleasures of the Pit Orchestra

Until "talkies" made their appearance, the sound accompanying the screen at the Rivoli Theatre, on Baltimore Street, was provided by the twenty-five- or thirty-member Rivoli Symphony Orchestra, conducted by Felice S. Iula. On Fridays Iula and his pianist, Edmund Hammerbacher, would preview the films and select the music for the show—mood music for the love scenes, gallops for outlaws chased by posses, light and bumptious music for comedies. The theater hosted visits by Victor Herbert, Fred Waring and his Pennsylvanians, and Cliff "Ukulele Ike" Edwards, who could imitate orchestral instruments with throat sounds. Gene Austin, who began his stage career with the Baltimore Follies, was a frequent guest at the Rivoli. His recordings of "My Blue Heaven," "Ramona," and "Look Down That Lonesome Road" sold millions of records and drew crowds at the theater. It was at the Rivoli that Fred Waring picked up Iula's "In a Little Garden (You Made Paradise)." Waring and the Pennsylvanians recorded it for Victor in 1926 and made it a national hit.[71]

The Stanley Theatre, built at a cost of $2.5 million, opened its doors in 1927. As the largest and most opulent movie house in Baltimore, it of course had the largest theater pipe organ in the city. Opening-night patrons paid sixty cents for a balcony seat and seventy-five cents for a seat in the luxurious boxes on the small mezzanine. The Stanley hosted films, legitimate theater,

and variety shows that employed local and touring musicians.

Some three thousand Marylanders and the incumbent mayor of Baltimore assembled on Eutaw Street to open the new Hippodrome Theatre, designed by the Scottish architect Thomas Lamb, in November 1914. The auditorium showed motion pictures and hosted vaudeville acts. The handsome theater fell on hard times when the stock market collapsed in October 1929. It was rescued in 1931 by Isadore Rappaport, president of a Philadelphia optical firm and a theater owner-operator. He restored and reopened the fabulous entertainment palace, starting off with the director George Archainbaud's feature film *Three Who Loved* and the comedian George Jessel. The Hippodrome offered four shows a day, starting at half past noon. Rappaport ran a tight ship: no off-color material and no dialect jokes. He brought the country's top entertainers to the Hippodrome—Gene Krupa, the Andrews Sisters, Frank Sinatra and Ella Fitzgerald with Chick Webb and his band. He continued to show first-run films and premiered all of the early Disney movies. Cab Calloway, Tommy Dorsey, Paul Whiteman, Guy Lombardo, and Glen Miller all played there during the era of the big bands.

The Hippodrome, like most of the downtown theaters, had its own orchestra for the four daily hour-long stage shows. The shows usually included an acrobatic or juggling act, a famous singer, and a comedian or dancer. When the stage lights were brought down and the movies flashed up on the screen, the pit musicians would find a comfortable place to nap, walk down to the department stores on Lexington and Howard Streets or to Lexington Market, or gather for a game of pinochle. Many of the musicians augmented their salaries by giving music lessons in their off-hours. Some of the Hippodrome's pit musicians had come from touring bands. For them, the routine of a pit musician was a welcome relief from the rigors of touring, especially in the summer months. The Hippodrome had an air-conditioning system—rare in those days—that emanated from a large basement room stocked with dozens of three-hundred-pound blocks of ice set up on end on the concrete floor.

The Parkway Theatre, on West North Avenue,

Here Comes the Showboat!! (1925)

A local writer, Alfred Gough Jr., contributed a piece to the summer 1989 edition of The Chronicles of St. Mary's in which he noted a serious cultural flaw in the St. Mary's County record. "Except for fishing, hunting, drinking, gambling, politics, horse racing, baseball, church dinners, dancing, an occasional jousting tournament, procreation and the grand jury," Gough declared, "there wasn't much going on in the way of entertainment."

Then in 1915 the James Adams Floating Theatre docked at Leonardtown Wharf, and it continued to do so each summer for the next quarter century. This barge, 122 feet in length by 34 feet in beam, could accommodate 850 customers. The company performed a different show each day, and in Leonardtown each performance was a sellout. For this community, commercial travel was mainly by water, and the floating theater, or showboat, was the primary source of entertainment for tidewater residents. Railroads and improved motorways were to come later. For this plantation area, the steamships were the main source of travel and Baltimore and Washington received passengers by way of the steamship routes.

In 1925 a Saturday Evening Post article described the James Adams Floating Theatre as a floating gold mine and the Chesapeake region as the clover patch of showboats. Asking a Leonardtown resident her child's age might prompt an answer like, "Eight years come next floating theater." But the James Adams returned value to the community and to the entertainment world.

Charles Hunter, the director, stage manager, leading man, and later owner of the James Adams, incorporated local personalities and culture into each performance. At the end of each weekly run, Hunter held a special benefit performance for either the St. Mary's Hospital or the local volunteer fire department.

The motion picture and Broadway show Show Boat were patterned after the James Adams. When the idea for a showboat novel struck Edna Ferber, she visited the James Adams as part of her research. Though the book is about a Mississippi showboat, the characters come straight from her experience on the James Adams. The meeting, courtship, and marriage of the Hunters—Charles Hunter and his wife, Beulah Adams, "The Mary Pickford of the Chesapeake"—was the basis of the love story between Ravenal and Magnolia. Two cooks, Joe Gunn of Leonardtown and Aggie Scott of California, Maryland, were embodied in the characters played by Paul Robeson and Hattie MacDaniel. Ferber related that "in those days I lived, played, worked, rehearsed and ate with the company. The food on the James Adams Floating Palace Theater was abundant, well cooked, clean. The negro cook, waiter, man and wife, place the food, sizzling hot on the table all at once. Hot biscuits in the morning, platters of ham and eggs, coffee, jam, pancakes. If you're punctual you got the best and got it hot. Late, you took it as it was, hot or cold. There was no mollycoddling" (Edna Ferber, The Peculiar Treasure [New York: Doubleday, Doran and Co., 1939], 299).

Though the James Adams achieved some notoriety from the book and show, the improvement in the roads, the Depression, and the loss of steamship business reduced the need for the floating theater. Leonardtown still provided it with sellout crowds until its last performance in 1941 (C. Richard Gillespie, The James Adams Floating Theatre [Centreville, MD: Tidewater, 1991]).

just west of Charles Street, opened in about 1915 and underwent redecoration in 1926 under the architectural supervision of John Eberson. The magnificent Parkway, with its curved balcony, box seats, chandelier, and organ, was closely modeled on London's West End Theatre. The Parkway entertained audiences for decades with everything from vaudeville to movies to live musical productions. Herbert Bangs, the Baltimore Symphony Orchestra's principal violin, led its orchestra.

Movie-house jobs were lucrative. Musicians who played in the larger houses received higher salaries than did their colleagues in symphony orchestras (although many musicians earned money in both worlds). Soon after release of the first "talkie," The Jazz Singer, in 1927, most movie-house musicians were fired. Only the Hippodrome, famous for its stage shows between films, kept them on.

The Many Faces of Barbara Frietchie (1927)

A drama Clyde Fitch completed in 1899, *Barbara Frietchie, the Frederick Girl,* loosely followed John Greenleaf Whittier's Civil War poem celebrating the story of Confederate General Stonewall Jackson's troops passing through Frederick in the Maryland Campaign, of September 1862. In Whittier's poem the 95-year-old Barbara Frietchie waves the Union flag from her second-story window, crying, "Shoot if you must this old gray head, but spare your country's flag!" while Jackson admonishes his men, "Who touches a hair of yon gray head, dies like a dog! March on!" The popularity of the poem fed the Barbara Frietchie legend. In Fitch's play, the beautiful young actress Julie Marlowe marries Captain Trumbull, a Union officer. (After a few performances, Marlowe refused to powder her hair gray, so Jackson used a different adjective.) Jealousy so besets one of Barbara's former suitors, Jack Negly, that he joins his father's Confederate unit, hoping to kill Trumbull in action. As the troops pass, Barbara clings to the flag, Jackson directs his men not to shoot, but young Negly fires on and kills Barbara. The play closes with Confederate soldiers holding Jack as his father issues an order with trembling voice: "Carry out your orders! Forward! March!"

Summertime

Anne Brown began her life in a classic West Baltimore row house with white marble steps at 1501 Presstman Street, near Stricker Street. She was the first of four daughters born to Harry Frances Brown, a prominent physician, and Mary Allen Wiggins. She descended from a family of singers. Her mother had studied voice and piano in New York. Anne was named for her paternal grandmother, Annie E. Brown, a gifted singer and powerful evangelist who divided her time between her son's home in Baltimore and her own home in Florida when she was not touring through the Southeast, using her powerful voice to bring souls into the church.[72]

Brown always knew that she would be a performer. She and her sister entertained soldiers home from Europe in 1918, before they attended primary school. Seven-year-old Anne begged her mother to let her take violin lessons at a nearby Roman Catholic convent, which offered music lessons to area children. The nuns, though

My Maryland (1927)

Further embellished by Dorothy Donnelly and Sigmund Romberg, the Frietchie story emerged again as the musical My Maryland, which enjoyed a record-breaking forty-week tryout in Philadelphia before opening on Broadway in September 1927. In true Broadway fashion, Frietchie's modest home became a palatial antebellum mansion that made for a spectacular set. Donnelly and Romberg followed much of Fitch's script but gave the drama a happy ending: Frietchie and Trumbull elope in secret. While the jealous Negley still joins the Confederate army, hoping to kill his rival, Barbara's brother Arthur ends up shooting Trumbull in battle, and the wounded captain is spirited into the Frietchie home. Barbara's father discovers him and demands that he leave, until Barbara reveals their vows and pleads for her husband to remain in his home. As Jackson's troops march through town, Barbara goes to the balcony and waves the Union flag, to which Jackson responds, "Who touches a hair of that woman's head—dies like a dog! March on!"

My Maryland opened the 1927–28 season on September 12, 1927, and ran for a successive 312 performances on Broadway. The New York congressman Emanuel Celler, then serving his third of twenty-four terms, wondered aloud whether the show's lead song, "Your Land and My Land," should replace the "The Star-Spangled Banner" as the (unofficial) national anthem.

impressed with her talent, explained that they would lose their white students if they took a "colored" child.

Frederick Douglass High School was still on Dolphin Street when twelve-year-old Anne Wiggins Brown enrolled (the following year Douglass moved to Baker and Carey Streets). The faculty at Douglass was superb. Anne studied music with W. Llewellyn Wilson and had leading roles in the musical comedies that were mounted at Douglass each year. She also discovered the joy of basketball.

Where to turn after Douglass was another matter. The Peabody Conservatory of Music, with its color bar firmly in place, would not admit her. The solution to this dilemma was provided by Mrs. Harry Black, wife of the chairman of the board of the Sunpapers. The English-born Constance Black learned of the gifted physician's daughter from her chauffeur, who was one of Dr. Brown's patients. Mrs. Black asked him to bring the young woman to her home so she could hear her sing. Mrs. Black, an anesthetist, volunteered at South Baltimore General Hospital. She hosted musicales at her home and often invited Brown to perform. Mrs. Black encouraged her to audition for Juilliard. After Anne graduated from Douglass, she gave her basketball shoes to her sister, Henrietta, and went to New York.

There, while still a Juilliard student, Anne Brown wrote to George Gershwin, hoping to land a role in a new work she had learned the composer had under way—an opera based on DuBose Heyward's novel *Porgy*. Brown asked for an audition, and Gershwin invited her to come to his apartment, carrying lots of music with her. When she arrived, Gershwin put her at ease by asking her about Baltimore and her studies at Juilliard. She was amused to learn that they shared a love of roller-skating.

After hearing Brown sing Brahms, Schubert, Massenet, and "The Man I Love," Gershwin asked her to sing a spiritual. Noting that she had not come prepared to sing spirituals, she softened and then sang "City Called Heaven" unaccompanied. With that, Gershwin knew he had found the perfect Bess. From that time until he finished the opera, Brown visited the composer every week, going through the music, singing all the parts—singing duets with Gershwin or trios with other members of the cast.

While Gershwin had written much of *Porgy* before Brown walked into his apartment, her voice and presence prompted him to make significant changes to the work. Brown loved the hauntingly beautiful "Summertime," which was to have been Clara's song, and

Anne Brown at the launching of the Frederick Douglass, 1943. On May 23, 1943, Anne Brown, who created the role of Bess in Gershwin's Porgy and Bess, christened the Navy's third liberty ship at the Bethlehem-Fairfield Shipyards in Baltimore. She was accompanied by the ship's African American commander, Captain Adrian Richardson. On September 20 the Frederick Douglass was attacked by a German submarine (all hands and one woman, a stowaway, were rescued). Archives of the Peabody Institute of the Johns Hopkins University.

asked Gershwin if it could be Bess's. At first dubious, Gershwin changed his mind. He also surprised Brown with the news that he had decided to call his new work *Porgy and Bess*, so she would share star billing with Todd Duncan.[73] "There's *Tristan and Isolde* and *Romeo and Juliet*," he explained when Brown asked how he had come to make the change. "Why not Porgy and Bess?"

Brown enjoyed great success in the role of Bess despite some early doubts and objections from Baltimore. At first Gershwin had worried that her complexion was too light for the role and that the role was too seedy for her to sing "Summertime." Brown admitted that mastering Bess posed a challenge. "I tried to get under the skin of the role of Bess, which was very difficult for me. I was young and came from a terribly conservative middle-class black family," she observed. In truth, her father disapproved of *Porgy and Bess*. She recalled that he "didn't like the way 'negroes' were portrayed. There was so much drinking and all that sort of thing—killing and fighting. One more stereotype, he thought."

On October 10, 1935, *Porgy and Bess* premiered at the Alvin Theatre in New York. Brown was just 23 years old, and, while Gershwin's opera received mixed reviews, critics unanimously praised her and Duncan. Gershwin never regretted his choice of a leading lady,

and he relied on her judgment when he had to find a replacement for John Bubbles when he left the cast of *Porgy and Bess*. Gershwin asked Brown if she knew anyone who could take his place. As a student at Douglass, Brown had performed with Avon Long. "He was a wonderful dancer," she recalled. "I knew he would be the perfect Sportin' Life."

Porgy and Bess went on tour, and Brown was delighted that the opera would perform at the National Theatre in Washington, DC, just forty miles from Baltimore. Happiness turned to chagrin when she discovered that the National was segregated. "That meant my parents could not attend, nor my sisters, nor high school friends nor any of the people who had known me all my life, and who had been unable to travel to New York." Brown went to Todd Duncan and told him that she would not perform. Horrified cast members pointed out that if Brown refused to perform, her name would be placed on every blacklist in New York. Brown and Duncan persevered and succeeded, however briefly. "The National Theatre admitted African Americans to a desegregated house," she recalled. "But, after our performance, it returned to its original policy of segregation."[74]

CHAPTER SIX

Musical Airs, Aired Music

MAX STRAKOSCH, manager of the exotic Italian Opera and a regular visitor to Maryland's shores, dreamed in the late nineteenth century of music arriving in parlors by means of telephone wires. This new medium, he prophesied, would make high-quality music readily available—as easily obtained as switching on a gas stove or turning a water spigot. It would put a merciful end to what he called the "torment . . . of a million pianos, played upon by the average American girl."[1] Owners of piano factories in Baltimore wouldn't find Strakosch's forecast so rosy.

Radio made its American debut in 1920, when the first commercial radio station aired in Pittsburgh. Two years later Baltimore had its own stations, beginning with WKC and WFBR. WKC broadcast from the home of Calman Zamoiski Sr. Zamoiski had tried to sell radios in a city with no stations and had concluded that he had to stimulate demand. He converted first the garage and then a bedroom at his home at 2527 West Madison Avenue into a radio studio and pressed his wife into service as the announcer. Holding a converted telephone up to a phonograph, Zamoiski catered to a broad range of musical tastes. The station's premiere broadcast, in the spring of 1922, showcased the eight-member Century Roof Dance Orchestra atop Lowe's Century Theater on Lexington Street. The banjo player G. H. McCauley, the flutist Robert Paul Iula, and the members of a group called the Miami Six later made their way into the crowded "studio" to perform (for little or no pay). More radio stations in Baltimore and Washington came on the air in the mid-1920s. Baltimore's self-proclaimed flagship station, WBAL, owned and operated by the Consolidated Gas Electric Light and Power Company of Baltimore, began broadcasting in 1925. On January 2 of that year Marylanders heard the first of the Victor radio concerts broadcast from New York, featuring the popular tenor John McCormack and the Victor Orchestra with Lucrezia Bori, who in 1912 had made her American debut at the Metropolitan Opera opposite Enrico Caruso.[2]

Manufacturers let loose on the public a flood of "radio phones" in a bewildering array of styles and sizes, priced for every budget and decor. As Strakosch predicted, new technology—the radio rather than telephone—began replacing the piano in more and

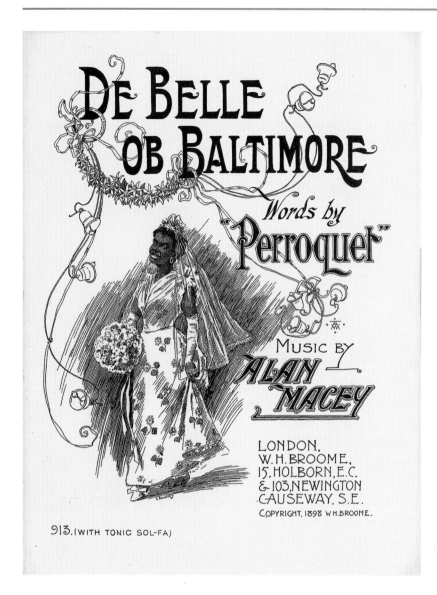

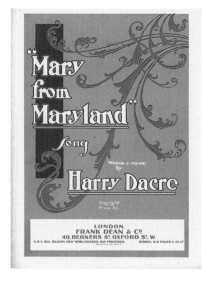

The Lure of Baltimore and Romance of Maryland (1929)

A strong showing of sheet music from London, Australian, and Canadian publishers in the late nineteenth and early twentieth centuries raises the question of what made the names Baltimore and Maryland so popular with English-language songwriters. Was it the trio of syllables? Did these places conjure up appealing, haunting, or romantic scenes? Natives could wonder. A sampling of the songs would include:

"De Belle ob Baltimore" (1898), by Perroquet and Alan Macey (W. H. Broome, Causeway, S.E. London), and "Belle of Baltimore" (1901), by Charles Rawlings (C. Wood, London).

"Mary from Maryland" (1903), by Harry Dacre (Frank Dean & Company, London). Dacre (who changed his name to Henry Decker when he came to the United States) also wrote one of the most famous songs at the turn of the nineteenth century, "Daisey Bell," or "A Bicycle Built for Two."

"When It's Honeysuckle Time in Maryland" (1917), by Dai Jenkins and Jay Whidden (B. Feldman & Company, New Oxford, London). Born in Brooklyn, Jay Whidden went to Britain playing ragtime and became a popular bandleader in London and then Australia before returning to the United States. While in London, he wrote "Honeysuckle Time" with Dai Jenkins, a pseudonym for an unknown songwriter.

"Jericho to Baltimore March" (1919), music by Chev. C. L. Graves, published in London, Canada. Dedicated to the Independent Order of Odd Fellows of America on its one-hundredth anniversary in Baltimore.

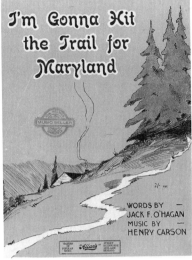

"I'm Gonna Hit the Trail for Maryland" (1920), by Jack F. O'Hagan and Henry Carson (Allan & Company, Australia). It's a long hike from Australia to Annapolis even if you can walk on water.

"I Left My Heart in Maryland" (1920), by Gene McCarthy and Andrew Allen (Lawrence Wright Music, London). Long before Irving Berlin left his heart at the stage-door canteen and Tony Bennett left his own in San Francisco, McCarthy and Allen left their hearts in dear old Maryland.

"Baltimore Vocal Waltz" (1921), by Henry J. Stafford (Cecil Lennox & Company, London). This is a lovely waltz number, easy to learn to play and sing.

"The Midnight Choo-Choo Bound for Maryland" (1922), by J. G. Gilbert (Lawrence Wright Music Company, London). In 1912 Irving Berlin wrote the highly popular "When the Midnight Choo-Choo Leaves for Alabam'." Ten years later Gilbert tried to hop a train for Maryland.

"(I'm Comin') Maryland" (1929), by Haines, Edgar, and Kern (Harmer Music Company, London). According to the lyrics, "Water melons ain't so juicy as that stew of old Aunt Lucy / Gee! I'm hungry, I'm not boasting, I can smell that chicken roasting / Holy smoke! It's worth the strivin', Jes' to see my bed and dive in / When I'm back in Maryland."

more homes across the state. Even the big green tuning-eye cabinet models took up less room than a piano, and anyone could do the tuning. Baltimore Gas and Electric carried a full range of "wooden-cathedral" radios from Philco, Atwater Kent, Zenith, Westinghouse, General Electric, and Crosley in its downtown showrooms. The Eisenbrandt Radio Company, at Paca and Pratt Streets, offered Marylanders the new "Majestic Superheterodyne" compact radio on display, for a princely eighty-six dollars, and a compact receiver, the aptly named Little Giant—a mere thirty-nine inches high. The *Sun* published detailed instructions for a build-it-yourself radiophone, with a detailed parts list, estimating the cost of materials at between six and fifteen dollars.

Best Out-of-Town Feed

Maryland musicians who witnessed the dawn of radio were of two or more minds about the new media. Some took an optimistic view: radio had the potential to bring quality music into homes all across the country. Others, like the composer Louis Cheslock, considered radio as essentially an air pollutant. "Radio programs," he said unhappily, "burst from open windows of homes, explode from advertising trucks, shriek from parked and passing autos, and howl from doorways of shops."[3] For the hundreds of Maryland men and women making their living playing in restaurants and dancing establishments, radio threatened, or seemed to threaten, their employment, just as talkies had spelled the end of most movie-house groups. In this case, however, the outcome was not immediately clear. Harry A. Henkel, the manager of Ford's Theatre, brushed off suggestions that radio would kill musical theater, pointing out that on the night of the broadcast of the first Victor radio concert, he had a full house. The manager of the Lyric reported that the radio program had no effect on his own audience, members of which had come to hear the Paul Whiteman Orchestra during its 1924–25 season. Then at the height of his career, Whiteman could boast of three new Victor recordings at the top of the bestseller charts. In fact, the best of Maryland's musicians found new opportunities at the local radio stations, because early radio made good on its promise to bring quality music to the public. WBAL

adopted a "no jazz" policy and claimed to be the first radio station to specialize in classical musical programs.[4]

In the 1930s many of the best musicians in Baltimore had regular jobs on radio. Stations drew heavily from the Peabody Conservatory and the Baltimore Symphony Orchestra, whose members occupied most of the chairs in the four orchestras WBAL employed (concert, salon, dinner, and dance). In addition to hosting guest performances, the station had its own string quartet and maintained several choral groups. Its music director, Frederick Huber, manager of the Baltimore Symphony and the Lyric Theatre, held programming to high standards. Edmund Cooke, first violinist in the station's string quartet and a member of the Baltimore Municipal Orchestra, was the station's staff arranger. Cooke played violin and viola with equal facility; he led his own string ensemble and made regular appearances over WBAL as a soloist with the station's orchestra.[5]

J. C. Van Hulsteyn juggled symphony and radio careers. The former concertmaster of the Lamoureau Orchestra of Paris was concertmaster of the Baltimore Symphony and head of the Peabody's violin faculty. His wife, Ruth Truitt, was one of his most gifted students. Before coming to Peabody, she belonged to a group called the Snappy Six, a jazz and ragtime band that performed for dances and in theaters on the Eastern Shore. Barred from playing in the all-male orchestra, Ruth played for WBAL and WFBR in the 1920s and 1930s.[6] In 1939 Van Hulsteyn urged her to try out for the Baltimore Symphony. Eventually the bar came down, and Ruth joined her husband in the race after rehearsals at the Lyric to the third-floor studios on Charles Street (and later to the new studios on North Avenue). Her boundless energy well suited these marathons. Her fellow musicians would see her sitting forward in her chair during rehearsals, "like a cat ready to pounce on its prey," before her dash to the radio station.[7]

The Baltimore Symphony Orchestra's first concert over a national radio network was broadcast from the Polytechnic High School auditorium at 3:00 p.m. on January 20, 1945, after Franklin Delano Roosevelt's inauguration as president.[8] For the orchestra's first broadcast concert in NBC's Orchestras of the Nation series, Reginald Stewart opened with his own arrangement of Bach's "Little" Fugue in G Minor.[9]

Radio stations broadcast works by local composers, providing larger audiences than any of the state's concert halls could hold. Cheslock's own distaste for radio subsided when WBAL broadcast an hour of his prize-winning new compositions in 1930. Even after the rise of network radio—with CBS airing the New York Philharmonic with Eric Kleiber, the conductor of the Berlin State Opera, and NBC broadcasts of the Philadelphia Orchestra concerts with Leopold Stowkowski—there were plenty of opportunities for regional musicians. Sunday airwaves abounded with liturgical and inspirational works by Baltimore artists and services from the downtown churches with professional choirs. Appearances on "The Good Time Society," an African American radio review, heightened the popularity of Chick Webb, his band, and his vocalist, Ella Fitzgerald.[10]

Radio made a few local musicians instant celebrities. A recording Dale Wimbrow made of his down-home ballad "The Good Old Eastern Shore" received plenty of air time, especially east of the bay. Wimbrow, called "Old Pete Dale of Whaleysville, Worcester Co.," became a regional favorite. Perhaps even more notably, there were Eugene Martinet and John Charles Thomas, both alumni of the Peabody Conservatory. Martinet, the Baltimore-born baritone and World War I veteran, made his way to Broadway and in 1926 became a regular on the airwaves as host of a show sponsored by the Emerson Drug Company of Baltimore. Broadcast over WCAP in Washington, the show featured so many Baltimore musicians that newspaper reporters began calling it "The Baltimore Hour."[11] The popularity of the show with listeners in the Baltimore-Washington-Virginia area prompted WFBR to hire Martinet as music director in 1931.[12]

Thomas began broadcasting for NBC in 1927, as network radio began a steep ascent in profits and influence. A Pennsylvania native who grew up traveling and singing with his father, a country minister, and mother, a talented singer and voice teacher, Thomas began his professional career as a singer earning fifty cents a night at Howard Hitchen's Opera House in Frostburg, Maryland. As a young man, in 1907, he moved to Baltimore and enrolled

at a homeopathy college. At the same time, beginning at five dollars a month, he played the organ at St. Michael and All Angels Episcopal Church, on St. Paul Street near North Avenue. By the end of the year he was the highest-paid church musician in Baltimore.[13]

Two years later, hearing of the annual Lutheran Reunion encampment at Pen-Mar Park, an old summer resort on a Catoctin mountaintop, Thomas organized a two-hundred-voice choir and presented Sunday afternoon choral concerts there, featuring himself as soloist. The success of the concerts and the applause for his singing were so intoxicating that he began to have doubts about his career choice. After returning to Baltimore the following autumn, Thomas auditioned for a scholarship at the Peabody Conservatory. He came in second. The following year, he auditioned with a Handel aria before faculty members fairly worn down after hearing more than a dozen singers work over the same piece. Thomas's performance made them sit up in their seats and netted him a three-year scholarship. The young singer later flipped a coin and let it decide on music over home remedies.

At the Peabody, Thomas studied with Blanche Sylvana Blackman, a graduate of the Leipzig Conservatory. She had spent twelve years studying and teaching in Europe, including a stint with the Dutch baritone Adelin Fermin, who had only recently come to the Peabody himself. Soon after his arrival, Fermin took on Blackman's star pupil. Thomas sang in organ recitals, composition recitals, student recitals, opera performances—whatever placed him on stage. He made forays into the countryside, appearing in recital in small towns like Sykesville, twenty miles northwest of Baltimore, a few train stops away. At the end of his second year at the Peabody, Thomas and gifted young soprano Grace Morgan were recommended by faculty and invited by the director to sing on the opening night of the Peabody's Exhibition Concerts.

Thomas had everything he needed for a stage career—a voice as rich as a cello, good looks, natural charm, and the physique of an athlete. He soon made a fine early career of stage plays. In Baltimore he took part in *Everywoman*, written by J. M. Barrie, the author of *Peter Pan*, with music by George W. Chadwick, and signed on as an understudy in the touring company. On Broadway he debuted in *The Passing Show of 1913*, produced by Lee and Jacob Shubert at the Winter Garden Theatre, and won a loyal public following. Thomas thereafter auditioned for his friend DeWolfe Hopper, who was organizing a company to perform a series of Gilbert and Sullivan operas. He rattled off the Major General's song in *The Pirates of Penzance* with perfect diction and glorious tone. He danced, sang, and clowned through *The Mikado, The Gondoliers*, and *H.M.S. Pinafore*. His popularity soared.

Eldridge R. Johnson, president of the Victor Talking Machine Company,[14] persuaded Thomas to pursue a career on the concert stage. Thomas presented his debut recital in 1918 at New York's Aeolian Hall and received enthusiastic praise from the New York critics. In the early twenties Thomas signed a contract with Johnson that took him on his first tour of the American West. In 1922 Thomas left Broadway altogether and went to Europe, making his concert debut at Covent Garden, in London, with Luisa Tetrazzini. Two years later, on March 3, 1925, he made his operatic debut in Washington, DC, as Amonasro in *Aida*. He married the heiress Dorothy Mae Kaehler two days later and sailed for Europe with her aboard the *Isle de France*, working on his operatic repertoire. That summer in Paris, Adelin Fermin visited the couple and made arrangements for Thomas to audition at La Monnaie (Royal Opera) in Brussels. After two days of auditions, the opera managers asked Thomas to join the company at once to sing all the principal baritone roles.

Thus, Thomas had already established a career as a radio singer long before NBC was born. Songs he recorded or sang live on the airwaves immediately made their way into the mainstream of American popular culture (a fact not lost on the hundreds of composers who sent him their compositions). Thomas embraced the new media with characteristic enthusiasm. He began recording for the Edison Company and Rex Records in 1914, for Vocalion in 1920, and for Brunswick in 1924. He acquired a mass audience as soon as Victor finally began recognizing and recording American artists. Engaged by Johnson, Thomas embarked on his long and successful association with RCA Victor in 1931, recording on RCA's prestigious Red Seal records. In 1933 Bing Crosby told a *Los Angeles Examiner* reporter that Thomas's recordings were some of his favorites. Victor phonographs became preeminent in the record industry, as the Steinway was among pianos. The Red Seal records were reserved for the aristocracy of the musical world, such as the conductor Arturo Toscanini and legendary opera stars. No "popular" artists recorded on the Red Seal label. They were expensive; there was an unabashed snob appeal attached to the label.

Thomas saw radio and the recording industry to maturity and in the process won the hearts of ordinary Americans who had never entered an opera house or a concert hall. While other singers of his generation made their reputations on the operatic and concert stage, none achieved the broad popularity in opera, concerts, light opera, radio, and recordings that Thomas enjoyed.

Depression

In March 1931, Cab Calloway and his band cut their first record and premiered the song that would become Calloway's signature tune, "Minnie the Moocher." He and Irving Mills composed the song, some of whose lyrics escaped Calloway during a live radio broadcast, forcing him to improvise, or scat, "hi de ho" to cover the lapse. The audience loved "Minnie" and Calloway's sudden inspiration as well. A string of songs followed, including "Lady With a Fan," written for the Cotton Club's fan dancer, Amy Spencer, and "That Man's Here Again." Calloway and Mills wrote "Jitterbug" in 1934, marking the first use of the word. Calloway took the band to Europe that year and went on to make several films, including *The Singing Kid* in 1936 and *Stormy Weather* in 1943. His hit songs were replete with sexual innuendo and references to drugs. His flashy style and ability to attract musicians of high caliber to his band, paying them high salaries and giving them room to demonstrate their talent, made the band one of the greats of the swing years. Calloway rode the crest of the wave as one of the most successful bandleaders of the radio and big-band era.

Following the lead of musicians like Calloway, along with Eubie Blake and Billie Holiday, Rivers Chambers, another Baltimore native, tried the New York music

The Rivers Chambers Orchestra, 1943. Chambers (*seated*) would be succeeded as bandleader by Buster Brown (*far left*) after Chambers's death. Playing for the younger audiences at colleges and high schools prompted changes in their repertoire. In a *Baltimore Sun* interview published on December 28, 1973, Brown stated, laughing: "We play anything. . . . We even like to play a little rock. . . . We try to make the music fit the party. . . . They think there's something wrong with anything their mother and father like." The group officially disbanded on New Year's Eve 1973. The Roy McCoy Collection, Archives of the Peabody Institute of the Johns Hopkins University.

scene. He found regular employment as a theater organist, but the bustle of New York and the frenetic life of a club musician held no allure for him. Besides, the Hudson and East Rivers were no match for the Chesapeake Bay for a man whose second love was fishing. At the onset of the Depression, he left New York to go home and organize his own group.[15]

Chambers had begun his musical studies at home. By the time he was a student at Douglass High School, he was playing with professional bands all over town. The accordion and the piano were his instruments of choice,

but he was equally adept at the organ and the violin. The guitarist Charles "Buster" Brown was playing in a jazz band in Albany, New York, and Leroy "Tee" Loggins was down in Louisiana playing in a traveling musical show when Chambers asked them to come back to Baltimore to form the nucleus of a group that, after 1930, became the house orchestra at the Royal Theatre and possibly the most popular band on Pennsylvania Avenue.

Elmer Addison joined later, bringing his mean saxophone and an outrageous sense of humor. Addison's renditions of "Bill Bailey," which he sang in falsetto voice, wearing a kerchief and clutching a rose, and "Good Mornin' Judge" were guaranteed to bring down the house. Behind the scenes, the serious-minded Addison managed the band's finances.

The Rivers Chambers Orchestra created a sound all its own. It was elegant, smooth, and sometimes, when the atmosphere was just right, a little wild. No one could remain seated when the air was filled with the music of Rivers Chambers. To a remarkable degree, the Chambers sound appealed to white listeners who may not have been comfortable visiting the Royal. Such popularity and the frequency of his outside jobs eventually put him at odds with the owners of the Royal. When Chambers decided to leave Pennsylvania Avenue and go independent in 1937, he recommended the bandleader Tracy McCleary to take his place on the podium.

An Oklahoma native, McCleary, had attended Alabama State College before catching the big-time music bug and trying his luck in Harlem, where he worked with Dusty Fletcher at the Old Harlem Opera House, just down the street from the Apollo Theater. Once the Depression began to dampen nightlife (and noting that gangsters "had Harlem locked up" in the 1930s), he decided to return to college. "I was on my way back to Alabama to school," he later remembered, "when I stopped in Baltimore to collect a debt. I'd written some charts for a bandleader in Atlantic City called Banjo Bernie. Bernie had the band at a place called the Plantation Club at Pennsylvania Avenue and Greenwillow Street." "Greenwillow Street," McCleary explained, "was famous for being the street where the ladies of the evening hung out and transacted their business. I got there in the afternoon and went to the Plantation. It was a big place, probably seating about 250 to 300 people." McCleary learned from the owners that Bernie usually came in the afternoon, hours before the eight-o'clock show. But eight o'clock came, and no Bernie. Nine o'clock came, and no Bernie. McCleary and the owners went to the second floor of the club, where the band was staying, and found all of the band's equipment gone. Bernie and his band had split.[16]

Downstairs, the club's patrons were banging on the tables, demanding that the show begin. The club owners, seeing McCleary's saxophone in its corduroy sack, asked him to step in for Bernie. Taken aback, the erstwhile student replied, "Look, I'm by myself. I don't know anybody—I'm just passing through." He had been in and out of Baltimore as a performer, but never long enough to form ties with local musicians. Desperate, the club's owners offered to pay him top dollar and rounded up a couple of guys off the street to sit in with him for the show. McCleary relented and played what he later claimed was the worst musical performance of his life. The crowd nonetheless loved it, and the club's owners asked him to stay. McCleary was adamant: "I'm on my way to Alabama, I'm in school—in college!" But when they upped the ante, McCleary succumbed and agreed to cover the club until they could hire another band. He stayed at the Plantation for about a year and a half.

After a while, the hustling and vice at Greenwillow began to get to him, so McCleary moved up the avenue to work for Isaiah "Ike" Dixon, one of the few African American entrepreneurs on Pennsylvania Avenue. Ike Dixon's Comedy Club was one of the most sophisticated clubs along the avenue. "Ike Dixon's Comedy Club New 1936 Orchestra," McCleary explained, "wasn't my band. It was Ike Dixon's band . . . in the fine lines underneath in the ads it said: 'Directed by Tracy McCleary.' He made me the leader of the band when he found out I could arrange music."

Then opportunity beckoned. Around 1937 Milton Babbage, a black radio announcer for WCBM radio in Baltimore and a local impresario, recruited McCleary and the musicians in Dixon's band to fill in at Carlin's Park for the Royal Kentuckians, a white band from Louisville that had failed to turn up for its engagement. When word got around that Babbage had recruited McCleary to take Ike's group to Carlin's Park, Dixon refused to pay the band, holding up its salaries to make sure McCleary and his company would return to work the following Monday. The musicians appeared punctually, but they had decided on a promising new career in radio at Carlin's Park.

The band members parked a car and a truck outside Dixon's stage door, in the rear of the building. After getting paid, they went straight out the back, heading for Carlin's. The truck drove off, as McCleary relates the story, but his car would not start. Frantically looking over his shoulder, expecting Dixon to appear at any moment, McCleary finally got away after his musicians returned and pushed the car, jumpstarting the engine.

The story did not end as McCleary and his musicians had expected. They made it to Carlin's Park, but Babbage had forgotten to tell the proprietors that the members of the band were black. No African American musicians had ever played at Carlin's, and although the group played its two-week engagement, McCleary and the band were fired at its end. Their new name, Tracy's Kentuckians, stuck. McCleary and his band clearly could not return to the Comedy Club. Luckily, Babbage wrangled a deal with WCBM: for a modest stipend, Tracy's Kentuckians played on the radio Wednesday nights and Sunday afternoons.

Rivers Chambers's departure having opened up the number-one spot at the Royal, McCleary happily stepped in, playing the second half of the 1937–38 theater season and through the 1938–39 season. McCleary then took his band on the road. Tracy's Kentuckians played a circuit that went from Western Maryland to Virginia, North Carolina, Pennsylvania, and then Baltimore, where they played the twice-weekly dances at the New Albert Auditorium's Strand Ballroom. McCleary also led a twelve-piece band at Joe Gans's Goldfield Hotel in East Baltimore (named for the 42-round fight he won in Goldfield, Nevada, in 1906), where, he recalled, all of the chorus girls were aspiring starlets.

Yet a third major musical figure emerged from the Pennsylvania Avenue scene during the Depression. Roy McCoy was then a kid living on the corner of Dolphin and Division Streets in black Baltimore, where local churches, parochial schools, and fraternal organizations offered musical training. A friend, William Harris, took McCoy to a rehearsal of the *Baltimore Afro-American*'s drum and bugle corps. The newspaper company provided instruments for its newsboys and even hired a German cornet player to teach them how

to play. McCoy joined up and went home carrying a bugle. A bright but indifferent student with a talent for improvisation, he focused all his attention on his newly acquired bugle. McCoy's parents, eager to provide direction for their son, had enrolled him in Preston Street School (near Druid Hill Avenue) in the hope that he would find a trade. Young McCoy—after somehow getting tickets to the Royal Theatre, on Pennsylvania Avenue, to hear Louis Armstrong—instead found his vocation in music. Seated in that darkened theater, listening to Armstrong play, he found himself overwhelmed by the sound of Satchmo's horn. McCoy would never forget the moment when he decided "I had to get me a trumpet."[17]

McCoy knew that his parents could not afford to buy him an instrument, so he marched down to the offices of the *Afro-American* and got a job selling papers. Every day McCoy took the streetcar downtown to the corner of Howard and Franklin Streets to sell the news, and every night, on his way home, he walked up Howard Street, pausing at Conn's Music Store to gaze at the trumpet in the window. One evening McCoy discovered a fourteen-dollar trumpet in a pawn shop on Eutaw Street. He began saving every penny he could get hold of. When he'd saved up two dollars, he went straight to the pawn shop and made the down payment. In the meantime, the resourceful youngster improvised. He took the slide and keys out of his grandfather's alto horn and fixed it onto the bugle he had on loan from the drum and bugle corps to extend the range of the instrument. "Since I had the keys, I could play all the notes," McCoy later explained. "I'd study, practicing hard every day. I wanted to play . . . it was my dream." He took a plain copy notebook and made his own manuscript book, copying down and memorizing the names of the notes. He talked to the musicians who visited his school and listened to their advice about taking care of his teeth so they wouldn't go bad and interfere with his playing. Twelve dollars and some weeks later, McCoy finally brought home the gleaming trumpet from the pawn shop window. He persuaded Clarence "Babe" Bright, who played trumpet in the City Colored Park Band and in clubs around town, to give him lessons.

McCoy progressed so quickly that Bright sent him on to study with A. Jack Thomas, one of the finest music teachers in Baltimore, black or white. Thomas taught him theory, harmony, and counterpoint.

McCoy continued his musical education with the men who played in the clubs along Pennsylvania Avenue, sitting in with them whenever he could. At the time, musicians would go from one club to another, playing their horns. Many young jazz musicians got their start in those clubs and continued their music training there, honing their skills under the watchful eyes of older, seasoned musicians, who would pass along advice and critique their playing. The famed drummer Max Roach, who often visited Baltimore as a young man, observed that "playing in the clubs on Pennsylvania Avenue was like going to school."[18]

Through the Pennsylvania Avenue grapevine McCoy heard that the trumpet player in Sammy Louis's band had quit. McCoy flew into action. Though only 16 years old and still struggling to master his instrument, in 1937 he joined the musicians' union. Louis took him on to play at the Ritz, the largest club on the avenue. His towering height and size-14 shoes prompted his fellow musicians to dub him "Tanglefoot" ("Tango" for short), after the rangy, big-footed horse in the Mickey Mouse cartoons. The older musicians in the band took the young trumpet player under their wing, teaching him the routines and sharpening his technique.

McCoy loved playing at the Ritz, one of the hottest spots on Pennsylvania Avenue. Beautiful chorus girls danced on the tables, and comedians livened up the audience. On Sunday afternoons patrons would come straight from church. The band would start playing at 2:00 p.m. and keep going into the night. The management served the musicians sandwiches so they wouldn't have to leave the club to eat. The band danced as they played on stage at the Ritz, their rhythms making it all but impossible to sit still.

When Sammy Louis took his band on the road with a traveling carnival, McCoy went along. The group started out in High Point, North Carolina, making their way north to Pennsylvania through small towns. They traveled by bus and spent nights in rooming houses listed in *The Negro Traveler's Green Book*.[19] When it wasn't possible to find a decent place to stay, the men slept on the bus. Well aware of the harsh conditions African American musicians faced on the road, McCoy packed a tent and followed the group on the train. He learned how to save his money and cooked his own meals, camping style.

McCoy's playing was attracting attention. Soon after joining the union, he was called to sit in with the band at the Royal Theatre for a performance featuring Louis Armstrong. McCoy never told Armstrong that he had bought his first trumpet and made it to the stage of the Royal Theatre because of him.

In the late 1930s McCoy stepped in for his first teacher, Clarence Bright, when Bright left Bubby Johnson's group, then the house band at the Royal Theatre, to join up with the Rivers Chambers Orchestra. The Royal's band played in the pit for variety shows featuring both black and white performers (music in the latter shows ranged from German and Italian classical repertoire to jazz), for groups like the original Ink Spots, made up of musicians who got their start in Baltimore, and for headliners like Lionel Hampton. It was at the Royal that McCoy found himself playing a solo in front of Count Basie's Big Band. The shows at the Royal always opened with a number by the house band. That night the show was opening with Duke Ellington's "Boy Meets Horn," a work entirely for trumpet, and McCoy was out in front of the band. Everyone knew that Count Basie and his band were in town, and when the curtains opened, there they were, in the front row. McCoy, who enjoyed performing under pressure, never played this work better.

Like so many of the musicians who worked on the avenue, McCoy would play half the night and then get up Sunday morning to play in church, in his case at the Enid Baptist Church and for the Union Baptist Sunday School Orchestra, led by violinist James Young.

McCoy never stopped perfecting his playing. Everyone on the block knew when he was home at his Madison Avenue apartment, because he played his horn all day long. McCoy juggled club jobs with City Park Band concerts and rehearsals under Edward Prettyman and the Maryland State Guard Band. McCoy's solo performances with the City Park Band were lauded in the press and talked about in city music circles. In 1939, McCoy hooked up with a nine-piece band called the Harlem Dictators. The Dictators played at Club Orleans, on Gay Street, through the early forties. Duke Ellington, Benny Carter, and other headliners at the Royal would sit in with the Dictators after finishing their own performances at the Royal.

Meantime, the musical stylings of Rivers Chambers found a welcome just about everywhere, from Dundalk to My Lady's Manor. The Chambers orchestra played for the annual Flower Mart on Mount Vernon Place, for ship launchings in the harbor, for lawn parties in the Green Spring Valley, and for proms at both black and white high schools. Chambers played for legislators in Annapolis and for plain folks dancing at downtown Baltimore hotels. He and his band became almost synonymous with Maryland hospitality. Few matrons thought of scheduling an important party until they were assured that Chambers and his musicians could be there. At the height of the social season, Chambers felt obliged—to accommodate white patrons but also for obvious business reasons—to divide his twenty-five or thirty musicians into smaller groups. In spring and early summer one might find three or four Chambers groups playing on a single night.

At one memorable event, a dinner in October 1941, when General Henry M. Warfield hosted a gala at his country house, Salona Farm, the original Rivers Chambers Trio—Chambers, Charles "Buster" Brown, and Leroy "Tee" Loggins—was hired for a private dinner party honoring the Duke of Windsor and his wife, the former Wallis Warfield Simpson, General Warfield's niece, on one of their visits to Baltimore. Chambers's trio was asked to sing a few quiet spirituals after dinner. To play it safe, Chambers packed a set of drums in the back of his car and left them outside the house, just in case. "I couldn't help thinking those people might want to do a little dancing later on," he remembered; "big people like to enjoy themselves about the same as anyone else."[20] After dinner, the trio hummed and sang their way through two or three spirituals. The duke

paid his compliments and confided to Chambers that he had always wanted to be a musician but had only played a little on the drums. Rivers dashed to the car, set up the drums, and sat the duke down. The carpet was rolled back, and the dining room became a dance floor. The guests danced as the musicians played— Chambers on the accordion, Brown on guitar, Loggins playing saxophone, and the Duke of Windsor on drums.

At one point in these years, playing at the Wilkins Tavern on Harford Road, Chambers and his men discovered the signature tune that practically all their listeners eventually learned to sing. Someone asked Brown, much admired for his low-pitched voice and slow enunciation, to sing a hillbilly standard called "They Cut Down the Old Pine Tree," about a lover mourning for his deceased sweetheart. Brown found the lyrics depressing, so he made up catchy new lines on the spot, substituting "cottage" for a "coffin of pine" and interjecting "They Cut Down the Old Pine Tree" once or twice for the graveside scene. He also upped the tempo. Within minutes everybody in the place had joined in, repeating "Oh, cut it down, and they hauled it away to the mill. . . ." The tune was perfect. Anyone could sing it; it sounded just as good shouted as sung, and it never ended. No one let the Chambers Orchestra forget the new arrangement. Whenever and wherever it played, a reveler would shout, "They Cut It Down," and the clapping and shouting would begin.

Amateur Hour: H. L. Mencken and the Saturday Night Club

In the first half of the twentieth century, several of Maryland's most prolific composers created works in response to the prompting of an unlikely muse. Baltimore's muse was no sandal-shod, gossamer-clad goddess, but a stoop-shouldered, cigar-smoking newspaperman named Henry Louis Mencken. Born and raised in West Baltimore, Mencken loved the city. The Lyric Theatre, Peabody's concert hall, and art galleries were familiar haunts, and he knew most of the city's best musicians and writers. Mencken successfully resisted publishers' attempts to move him out of Baltimore—beginning in 1900 when

Henry Louis Mencken at the piano, ca. 1935. In a 1925 letter to Isaac Goldberg, the Baltimore newspaperman H. L. Mencken described his taste in music as "very orthodox." He put Beethoven first, ahead of Bach. On September 15, 2007, the Maryland Historical Society presented the world premiere of The Artist, an opera written by Mencken in 1912. In 1949, it was scored for piano by Louis Cheslock, the last surviving member of the Saturday Night Club (of which Mencken had also been a member), using music by Beethoven. The opera was based on an experimental play that was a satire on American audiences. Papers of Louis Cheslock, Archives of the Peabody Institute of the Johns Hopkins University.

Frank Leslie's Illustrated attempted to lure Mencken to New York.[21]

Mencken's great fondness for music was fostered by his father, August Mencken Sr., who had been forced to give up the violin when it was discovered that he was tone-deaf. The elder Mencken's unshakable belief that no respectable German household could exist without music prompted him to acquire a brand-new Stieff square piano for his family. On Sundays and holidays, he would gather up his children for outings at the Western Schützen Park or the German beer gardens in West Baltimore, where Henry could hear the city's best German music teachers and musicians.

Young Henry's formal schooling began in a private school opposite city hall. The school was run by Friedrich Knapp, who began each day with German *Volkslieder*, leading the students with his violin. Arrangements were made for young Henry to begin piano lessons with a kindly, bewhiskered gentlemen known as Professor Maass. Charles Maass was a bookkeeper in August

Mencken's cigar factory on Baltimore Street. After the professor's death, Henry's musical education was placed in the hands of a series of neighborhood music teachers, who doled out such uninspired fare that he nearly gave up music altogether. Young Henry quit taking lessons as soon as he was able to perform well enough to entertain guests in the Mencken home, but his love affair with the piano continued unabated.

Without the benefit of instruction, Henry tried his hand at composing, dashing off waltzes and a few piano sonatas. At 15 he produced a musical comedy at his high school, Polytechnic Institute. In 1892 he wrote *Two-Step*, and the following year he wrote the *Easy Waltz*, a trio flavored by the music of the German beer gardens. Later, he created a setting for William Watson's poem "April" and the beginnings of a red-blooded setting for his own book *Ventures Into Verse*.[22]

Mencken was passionate about music as an avocation. Journalism had captured his imagination, but family duty exerted a tighter hold on young Henry, who was put to work in the August Mencken & Brother cigar factory. Henry had neither the talent nor the patience for ledgers and bookkeeping, and he consoled himself with correspondence courses offered by the Cosmopolitan University.[23] The death of his father during the Christmas season of 1898 liberated Mencken from the cigar factory once and for all.

Henry managed to land a job as a reporter for the *Baltimore Herald* just a fortnight after his father's death. He resumed his piano lessons for a while and fell in with an amiable group of amateur and professional musicians that included the music critic W. G. Owst and Theodore Hemberger, who taught violin at the Peabody Conservatory and conducted the Männerchor. Mencken attended concerts, reviewed performances, and wrote extensively about music and musicians. Musical references permeated his writing. (The greatest praise Mencken could give to an author was to compare his writing to music.)

Mencken, like many Maryland music lovers, made an annual pilgrimage to Bethlehem, Pennsylvania, often in the company of his friend and publisher Alfred A. Knopf. It was in Bethlehem in 1924, during the dark days of prohibition, that Mencken demonstrated the power of Bach's music. Mencken had come armed with a fifth of Scotch to enhance their first evening. But Scotch, Mencken claimed, was unsuitable for the music of Bach, which he said called out for beer as an accompaniment. After trying without success to get the appropriate brew from hotel employees, Mencken and Knopf collared a taxi driver, who took them to a dollar-a-day hotel near the railroad station. The proprietor eyed them doubtfully when they said they were New York musicians. But when Mencken, determined to get his brew, whipped out his score of the B Minor Mass, the proprietor recognized the score, invited them into the bar, and served up five glasses of beer—two for Knopf and three for Mencken—and sixty-five-cent ham sandwiches. Mencken and Knopf spent an agreeable afternoon discussing local politics with the bartender and a local politician.

Mencken held strong views on the subject of music. The arts, he declared, "are not for crowds, but for selected individuals, mostly with bad kidneys and worse morals."[24] The select individual music lovers Mencken habitually

associated with were the members of the Saturday Night Club. The Saturday Night Club had no officers, no dues, no constitution, and no membership lists. Club regulars gathered together to make music solely for their own pleasure.[25]

Membership in the club constantly changed. In its heyday in the 1930s, club membership included Henry Mencken's brother, August; Max Brödel, the director of the Department of Art as Applied to Medicine at Johns Hopkins (considered the greatest anatomical artist of his time);[26] the pianist George Boyle, a member of the faculty of the Peabody Conservatory; Maxwell Cathcart, a passable pianist for whom participation in the Saturday Night Club provided a bit of gaiety and relief from a dispiriting job as a bank clerk; H. E. Buchholz, pianist; Louis Cheslock, who taught theory at Peabody, and Isreal Dorman, violinists in the Baltimore Symphony; the physician and violist Dr. Franklin Hazelhurst; the bass player W. Edwin Moffett, also from the Baltimore Symphony; the Hopkins physician Dr. Raymond Pearl, who played French horn and basset horn; Adolph Torovsky, director of the Naval Academy band, cello; and H. L. Mencken, pianist and arranger. All of the major teachers of the Peabody violin faculty played with the Saturday Night Club at one time or another. The venerable and versatile Gustav Strube, the founding conductor of the Baltimore Symphony Orchestra, was also a regular, filling in on whatever instrument was needed. Mencken rarely missed an evening. Even when he had to be out of town, he'd take the train back to Baltimore in time to be in his usual place on Saturday night.

In its early years, the Saturday Night Club met in the violin maker Albert Hildebrandt's shop on Saratoga Street (and later on Charles). With its ready supply of fiddles and pianos, the shop was an ideal location. After a long evening of music, the participants would retire to a private room in the basement of the old Rennert Hotel, at Saratoga and Liberty Streets, famous for its turkey wings with oyster sauce. Good food, camaraderie, and quantities of good beer were as much a part of their gatherings as the music. During prohibition the Saturday Night Club gave up its meetings at Schellhaus's, on Howard Street. Members took turns meeting at their homes after performing together in Albert Hildebrandt's violin shop. Home brewing became a popular hobby, and Marylanders had a new reason to be thankful for the bountiful Chesapeake Bay, with its multitudinous tributaries and public landings which provided convenient landing places for bootleggers. Maryland was one of the wettest states in the Union. The members of the Saturday Night Club all brewed their own beer—dark, amber, and light—and enjoyed a friendly rivalry over who concocted the best and most potent brew (the alcohol content was reportedly way over the levels of the old commercial beers). Max Brödel, taught to brew by Mencken, became the acknowledged master.

The club maintained an extensive library of piano duets, provided by Albert Hildebrandt and Max Brödel; classical symphonies, mostly bought by Mencken from G. Fred Kranz's music store on Charles Street; and contemporary works. The club's library contained prodigious quantities of chamber works by Beethoven and Mozart, and the surprising number of contemporary works, many of them American, included works by Jerome Kern, Victor Herbert, and John Powell, an English composer best known for his film scores.

Club members played ambitious arrangements from large works (changing the titles and the directions for their performance): Mendelssohn's *Fingal's Cave* became *Finkelstein's Cafe*,[27] and in works calling for two pianos, the primo and seconda became *Primo Carnera* (Primo Carnera was the world heavyweight boxing champion in 1933 and 1934), with Max Brödel and Mencken working over the keys. Mencken conceded that his touch was on the heavy side, and he acknowledged that Brödel's technique was superior. The two, dubbed the Big Berthas by their cronies, made a prodigious noise together. With shirts unbuttoned and sleeves rolled up, Mencken and Brödel played four-hand piano, Brödel seated on the right playing Primo and Mencken on the left playing seconda. In the heat of their performances Mencken was often forced to shout over the din as Brödel, hair tousled, pounded furiously away: "Not so loud, Max," Mencken would implore. "The mark is pp. [pianissimo]. The idea . . . was to make it sound like the flutter of angels' wings—or the sweet tinkle of angels' piss."[28] Then, having caught Mencken playing a pianissimo passage forte, Brödel would retaliate with a howl.[29]

When the club's modest forces fell short of the required instruments, Mencken would sing the part of the missing instrument without missing a beat at the piano. He loved fortissimos, which he dubbed "the purple passages," where he could plunge in with lusty abandon. Though he claimed to be tone-deaf like his father, Mencken was a gifted sight reader, and despite his lack of training, he could keep up with the best of the professionals in the group. Louis Cheslock attributed Mencken's dexterity on the piano to the hours he spent at his typewriter. Evenings customarily ended with a waltz (usually by Strauss), Brödel's yearning for a beer, and the banging of the piano lid, signaling that it was time to retire to the beer table.[30]

The club often devoted evenings to new compositions by members of the club. Cheslock wrote several works for the club, including "Valse Vodka," written when the United States granted official recognition to the Soviet Union. There were collaborative works like the Theme and Variations for French Horn, with Dr. Raymond Pearl,[31] who played the french horn, supplying the theme and Cheslock providing the variations, giving each of the members an opportunity to murder the theme. Mencken furnished the libretto for a chamber opera entitled *The Artist*, which Louis Cheslock set to music.[32] The premiere of a new work would inevitably call for extra rounds of beer, and Mencken, with a great flourish, would present the composer with a gaudy medal or "genuine" diamond-studded belt. The club took a rare night off to attend the premiere of Cheslock's ballet *Cinderella* (written at Mencken's suggestion) at the Peabody.

Mencken's musical circle was far from provincial and reached well beyond Maryland's borders. He regularly attended Boston Symphony concerts, lunched with the music critic Philip Hale, and dined with Olga and Serge Koussevitzky at their home in the Jamaica Plains neighborhood.[33] Mencken himself described his taste in music as "very orthodox." He put Beethoven first, ahead of Bach, and firmly believed that Beethoven's Eighth Symphony was the best thing he ever wrote. Mencken called Beethoven a "musical scientist par excellence" who worked his magic "by sheer brain power." Next to Beethoven was Brahms. Mencken put Brahms's *Deutsches Requiem* in the first rank of choral works, "beside Bach's *B minor Mass*. Compared to it, all the familiar oratorios are shabby stuff, fit only for Methodists."[34]

Mencken rarely went to the opera. Opera, for Mencken, was "to music what a bawdy house is to a cathedral." Yet he thought Puccini was underestimated: "He was," said Mencken, "the best of the wops." Verdi, he believed, "was not to be heard sober, but with a few whiskies under my belt I enjoy the last act of *Il Trovatore*." Jazz, he declared, was "the sort of music that the persons who go to the opera really like." "Someday," Mencken confidently predicted, "a composer of genuine talent will put a jazz scherzo into a symphony. A hundred years hence that is all that will be remembered of jazz." Vitally interested in new works and fond of experiments in the arts, Mencken declared that he'd rather read new music than hear it. He liked Russian music but abhorred Stravinsky, who, he believed, "never had a musical idea in his life."[35]

In 1940 the club membership began to dwindle, as age and infirmity began taking its toll. Max Brödel, who had sat beside Mencken at the piano on Saturday nights for thirty years, died in the autumn of 1941. The lifelong agnostic was buried from the Cathedral of the Incarnation, near his home in Guilford. Max Cathcart, the retiring bank clerk who entertained members of the club with rousing performances of songs from old musical comedies, died in 1943. His death deeply affected Mencken, whose own health was beginning to fail.

"Straight Americanese" from East Baltimore

As network radio began dominating the airwaves, New York emerged as the capital of the broadcasting world. One of the men who stormed radio at the height of its popularity started his musical career in East Baltimore at a Peabody settlement school on South Wolfe Street.[36] The solo performance of Sylvan Levin, the son of a paperhanger, at a 1915 school recital attracted the attention of a local music critic, who wrote that the "delightful little kiddie," who was so small that his feet scarcely reached the pedals of his baby grand piano, gave a bravura perfor-

mance of the florid first movement of the Haydn Piano Concerto in D Major.[37] A year later, at the age of 11, Levin received his second review, this time for his debut performance with the Detroit Symphony: "Levin scored heavily in the last two movements from Saint-Saens' *Second Concerto in G minor*."[38] The director of the Peabody, Harold Randolph, hastily moved Levin to the Conservatory, took charge of his piano instruction, and arranged for him to study harmony with Gustav Strube. The world of music had no boundaries for him.

Small in stature, five years younger than most Conservatory students, and overfilled with confidence, Levin emerged a bit of brat. Alice Garrett, who hosted performances by gifted musicians, invited Levin to perform at Evergreen House, her elegant home on Charles Street, and he joined members of the Hutzler family at their Reisterstown home for their informal musicales. Short of money, he became a regular in Baltimore saloons, and like Eubie Blake, he played in the occasional bawdy house. Not yet 12, he was too young to become a member of the American Musicians' Union until the president bent the rules. When Levin began playing Sunday-evening concerts at the Wardman Park and Shoreham Hotels in Washington, DC, he and a fellow Peabody student who also studied with Strube, Colin McPhee, boarded at a chicken farm outside Towson. After graduating, McPhee like Levin sailed into another realm, writing *A House in Bali*, published in 1947, the first comprehensive analysis of Balinese music published in English, which critics hailed as a musical masterpiece.[39]

After the Peabody, Levin went on to Philadelphia to continue his studies at the Curtis Institute with Moritz Rosenthal. A Curtis faculty member who had taught at the Peabody greeted the cocky youngster: "If you open your face up here you're going to be thrown out in less than twenty-four hours."

Levin lost no time in carving out his own turf. He was 26 and still a student at Curtis when he made his conducting debut with the Philadelphia Grand Opera. Less than two months later, he made his debut as a pianist with the Philadelphia Orchestra under Leopold Stokowski. Never short of nerve, he had the temerity to point out to Stokowski four errors in the horn parts in the original score of *Boris Godonuv*. Stokowski subsequently hired him to conduct the Philadelphia Orchestra Chorus. In 1932 Stokowski planned to perform the premiere performance of a new Ravel piano concerto. Ravel, a close friend of Koussevitzky's, decided that the premiere should be given simultaneously in Boston and Philadelphia. Stokowski asked Levin to play the Philadelphia performance and gave him three weeks to learn the new work. Drawing heavily from his days as a jazz pianist in Baltimore saloons for the Gershwin-reminiscent passages, Levin devoured the work. The audience loved it, and the reviews were enthusiastic. After the two Philadelphia performances, Stokowski and Levin premiered the work at Carnegie Hall.

Levin continued his studies in conducting when Fritz Reiner arrived at Curtis in 1932. "Reiner's way of teaching was tyrannical in the extreme," recalled Leonard Bernstein, who studied with him at Curtis.[40] During his tenure at Curtis, Reiner was the principal conductor of the Philadelphia Grand Opera and appeared frequently with the Philadelphia Orchestra as guest conductor. Levin served as assistant conductor at both. A dramatic confrontation with the Philadelphia Orchestra's guest conductor erupted at a dress rehearsal when Reiner, who arrived after rehearsal had begun, heard Levin rehearsing parts that he had cut from the score. Incensed, he shouted at Levin, "You're excused—for the rest of the season." The five-foot-three conductor shot back, "Suits me," and stormed out the door.[41]

Without missing a step, in 1933 Levin founded the York (Pennsylvania) Symphony Orchestra and introduced outdoor opera at Robin Hood Dell (now the Mann Music Center), the summer home of the Philadelphia Orchestra. In 1938, with David Hocker, he founded the Philadelphia Opera Company and served as its chief conductor and artistic director for six years.

Levin wanted to make the company's productions accessible to American audiences. He rewrote librettos using what he called "straight Americanese." The company musicians and singers were all Americans, most of them still in their twenties. Levin abhorred musical snobbery. During the 1943–44 season the Sylvan Levin troupe departed on a critically acclaimed nationwide tour. At the end of the season, however, Levin quit the company, left Philadelphia, and began work in New York as music director and conductor of NBC's "Jackie Gleason–Lee Tremayne Show." *Radio Daily* praised the first broadcast and called Levin "radio's new genius." Maintaining his career as a composer and concert pianist, he recorded for both RCA's prestigious Red Seal label and the Silvertone label, produced by Sears and Roebuck for its record club. In 1945 he took over the music directorship of New York's WOR-Mutual Radio, succeeding the conductor Alfred Wallenstein.

Through the 1940s and 1950s, Levin was concertizing, teaching, and directing Broadway musicals. He took Gershwin's *Porgy and Bess* on a US State Department tour through Europe and South America from 1954 to 1956 and conducted national road-company performances of Lerner and Lowe's *My Fair Lady* in 1957. After retiring from conducting, Levin returned to Curtis as a member of the music faculty.[42]

Home, Home on the Shore

When the geese are returning to the meandering creeks and fields of tidewater Maryland in the autumn, a distinctive song rings out above the water and grasses that goes straight to the heart of every Eastern Shore native. The interval is a major ninth, harsh and discordant but hauntingly beautiful. It is the song of Canada geese returning for the winter. In 1934 another remarkable bird alighted on the Eastern Shore, settling on the banks of the Miles River in Talbot County: the incomparable musical personality John Charles Thomas, who could sing "Boots and Saddles" and Beethoven's "In questa tomba oscura" with equal grace and ease. He had placed his parents comfortably in Towson. His material success then suggested to him the life of a country squire and conspicuous sailor.

Thomas's triumphs had made him a truly international celebrity. In Brussels in 1925, poised and ready to begin his engagement at the Royal Opera, Thomas had proved such a success that the house extended his contract for three seasons—in fifteen roles. In 1928 he made his operatic debut at Covent Garden as Valentin in *Faust*. Invitations to sing at opera houses in Berlin and Vienna

The Del-Mar-Va Songster (1928)

Born in Whaleyville, Worcester County, on June 6, 1895, Peter Dale Wimbrow dropped out of Western Maryland College to enlist in the army in 1917. Discharged after service in Europe, he pursued a musical career as a radio personality in New York, singing and playing some of his own compositions and recording for Columbia and Decca. Unhappy with the sound of his ukulele, Wimbrow invented what he called the Wimbrola, a six-string instrument that supplied a mellower sound. His musical compositions reflected the sentimentality of his day—"Old Fashioned Locket" (1927), "Wife O' Mine" (1927), "Country Bred and Chicken Fed" (1928), "Every Moon's a Honeymoon" (1929), "O My Eskimo Pie" (1930), and "First Girl I Met Was the Last Girl I Loved" (1931).

East of the Chesapeake, Wimbrow doubtless is best remembered for "The Good Old

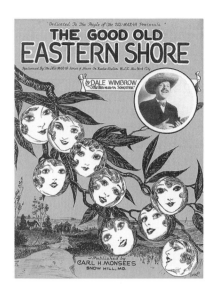

Eastern Shore" (1928), recordings of which played for many years in Delmarva homes and on local radio stations. Equally or more evocative, "When Old Pete Daley Plays His Ukelele Down in Whaleyville" never quite achieved the same popularity, but as "Old Pete Daley," Wimbrow staged a concert that benefited an African Methodist Episcopal (AME) church near Whaleyville in 1926.

Wimbrow's exposure to mustard gas in the Meuse-Argonne campaign affected his lungs and eventually ended his singing career. He and his wife moved to Florida, where he took up photography and writing. In 1934, at the request of a magazine editor, he answered a young man's inquiry whether it really paid to be honest. Wimbrow's answering poem, "The Guy in the Glass," was widely read over the radio, reproduced in advice columns, and read into the *Congressional Record*.

The poem read, in part: "You can fool the whole world down the pathway of years, / And get pats on the back as you pass, / But your final reward will be heartaches and tears / If you've cheated the guy in the glass."

followed. Thomas had firmly established his reputation in Europe; he did not mind being known as America's Singing Ambassador.

After his return to America in the early 1930s, his debuts at major houses followed in quick succession. He devoted his time to concerts and sang roles for opera companies in Philadelphia, San Francisco, and Los Angeles. His debut as Tonio in the 1930 Chicago Opera production of *Pagliacci* was a resounding success, causing the biggest demonstration at the house since the debut there of the famed Italian coloratura soprano Galli Curci. Thomas virtually stopped the show as the house erupted in applause after his first aria. For a full ten minutes, shouts of "Thomas, Thomas," rang through the hall. Thomas's performance prompted one critic to claim that his presence in the cast raised the status of the company "as high as it can be raised, and to make it as truly an American opera company as possible."[43] That same year, Thomas signed a two-year contract with the Philadelphia Grand Opera.

Thomas made his Metropolitan debut in 1934 as Germont in *La Traviata* with the legendary opera star

Rosa Ponselle. Also that year, he was made a cavaliere of the Order of the Crown of Italy. For the next decade, Thomas's career was at its peak. In addition to his opera performances and frequent radio broadcasts, he sang more than seventy recitals a year in towns and cities all across the country, touring nine months out of each year.

During the height of his career, even during his Metropolitan years, Thomas maintained strong ties to Maryland. In 1933 he began giving annual benefit concerts in Easton, on Maryland's Eastern Shore, for local charities and raised thousands of dollars for the Children's Aid Society and the Easton Memorial Hospital. The hospital, which served the communities of Talbot, Caroline, Queen Anne's, and Kent Counties, had sunk deeply into debt during the Depression, taking on many patients who were unable to pay for treatment. Thomas and his accompanist, Carroll Hollister, offered to perform a benefit concert at the New Theatre in Easton. Uniformed hospital nurses volunteered as ushers and ably handled the standing-room-only audience. The event raised twenty-three hundred dollars, enough to put the institution out of immediate financial danger, and for more than two decades John Charles Thomas concerts were important social events on the Eastern Shore.

The impresario returned again and again to Baltimore to perform at the Peabody Conservatory, at the Lyric with the Baltimore Civic Opera, and at benefit concerts. In 1935, fifteen thousand persons jammed every available inch of standing room in the Fifth Regiment Armory to hear Thomas sing at the Community Fund's "Town Party." Loudspeakers carried the performance to the thousands forced to stand outside after all available spaces indoors were filled.

The outbreak of the war in Europe in September 1939 put an end to plans for a concert tour. Beginning in October, Thomas performed a monumental series of five song recitals in New York's Town Hall, in which he presented the vocal literature of France, England, Italy, Germany, and America. The final program, presented on March 24, was devoted entirely to American songs, arousing particular notice and praise. The songs, chosen by Thomas and his accompanist, Carroll Hollister, from some four hundred works by American composers, included spirituals, Virginia folk songs, and songs by Edward MacDowell, Virgil Thomson, and Charles Ives. A Texas cowboy song arranged by David Guion received its New York premiere in this recital. Sung in broad prairie dialect by Thomas, it brought an enthusiastic response from the audience. The song was "Home on the Range," which became a Thomas standard.

For many years, John Charles and his wife, Dorothy, lived aboard their one-hundred-foot yacht *Masquerader*, skippered by the Eastern Shore waterman Harry O. Lowrey and a crew of seven local hands. Boaters nearby could hear Thomas singing "Home on the Range" when he entertained friends aboard the yacht. Tales about the colorful singer's exploits became Shore legends.

Music on the Home Front

Talk of war and America's possible involvement filled the pages of newspapers and dominated radio broadcasts in 1940. Military marches and patriotic airs dominated summer band concerts. Marylanders looking for a new piano could order the "Victory Vertical," built by Steinway & Sons in response to a request from the US Army.

Stepped-up production at Maryland's defense industries and a growing military presence stimulated the local economy. Peabody's trustees, striking while the iron was hot, launched a fundraising campaign—the first in many years—for their cash-strapped institution. The drive was timed to coincide with the announcement of a Carnegie Corporation grant to support a three-year program that would provide instruction in instrumental music in the Baltimore City public schools in 1939. In all but a few of them, resources for music had been limited to songbooks and a few worn pianos. The Carnegie grant put instruments into the hands of students who otherwise could not have afforded them and provided free lessons.[44]

In the early summer of 1940, Eugene Martinet, director of the Baltimore Civic Opera, was recruited to organize a patriotic rally, dance, and concert for the American Red Cross in Easton.[45] He rounded up his Baltimore Opera principals and headed for Talbot County, joining forces with local artists. Martinet's wildly eclectic offering ran the gamut of musical taste, encompassing the Dorchester Bugle and Drum Corps, operatic arias by Marylanders home from the Metropolitan, *tableaux vivants*, and the haunting music of the theramin played by Frederick Philip Stieff Jr., grandson of the founder of the Stieff piano factory in Baltimore. Stieff's performance provided Eastern Shoremen with an introduction to the strange new world of electronic music.[46] Originally the product of research sponsored by the Russian government on proximity sensors, the theramin was embraced by musicians who were sent on tours of Europe by Lenin to herald the Russian invention of electronic music. Leon Theramin, the instrument's inventor, secured a US patent in 1928 and granted production rights to RCA.

The Baltimore Symphony Orchestra optimistically celebrated its silver anniversary season in 1940–41. Its conductor, Howard Barlow, was beginning his second season with the orchestra; he had ceased thinking of his association with the orchestra as temporary. Anticipating a future with an extended orchestra season of twenty-six weeks, better salaries for his musicians, and tours to Reading, Richmond, Washington, and Philadelphia, Barlow fully intended to build a major symphony orchestra, ideally with the cooperation of the Peabody Institute.[47]

I'll Overcome Some Day

Charles Albert Tinley, 1901

The Eastern Shore's Gift to Gospel Music (1933)

In the late nineteenth and early twentieth centuries a new type of sacred music evolved in America, known simply as "gospel." Merging spiritual texts and colorful imagery, this form of religious singing emerged from long traditions of African American worship and owed much to the peculiar conditions of slavery.

An inspired composer who began writing gospel music as early as 1901, Charles Albert Tindley was born in Berlin, in Worcester County, Maryland, in 1851 to a slave father and a free black mother. Forbidden as a slave to learn to read, he collected scraps of paper from the woodbox and in the evening hours tried to make out the patterns of the words. After Emancipation, Tindley worked as a laborer and put every penny he could into reading lessons and books. Through correspondence courses with the Boston Theological Seminary and a friendly rabbi, he learned Greek and Hebrew and studied for the ministry. At his examination for the min-

istry the other candidates made light of him by asking what he had to prepare himself for a religious career. "Nothing but a broom," Tindley replied.

A gifted preacher who stood six feet, two inches tall, with ramrod posture, Tindley drew crowds wherever he preached. He circulated through New Jersey, Maryland, and Delaware as an itinerant clergyman until 1902, when he became pastor of a Philadelphia storefront church, the Bainbridge Street Methodist Church, where he once had worked as a janitor.

Music occupied a central place in worship services at the Bainbridge Street Methodist Church. Tindley's gospel hymns, with their messages of comfort and hope for a better life in heaven, made masterly use of the chorus-and-refrain tradition of "Negro" spirituals. Many of his melodies followed the pentatonic scale, which left room for melodic and harmonic interpolations. He also left space for the inevitable improvisation of text, rhythm, melody, and harmony that marked

African American folk music. Tindley wrote some foundation pieces of twentieth-century African American sacred music—"Stand By Me," "Let Jesus Fix It for You," and "The Storm is Passing Over." Tindley's collection of sacred music, *Soul Echoes*, appeared in 1905. *New Songs of Paradise* came out in Philadelphia in 1916. Five years later the National Baptist Convention published *Gospel Pearls*, a compilation of old and new gospel hymns and spirituals expressly for use in black churches. Owing to Tindley's established position in the African American community and the popularity of his new gospel-style hymns, *Gospel Pearls* contained 7 songs by Tindley out of a total of 162 songs.

Meanwhile, Tindley's flock in Philadelphia grew to almost ten thousand persons, one of the largest Methodist congregations in the world. The Tindley Temple United Methodist Church, seating some thirty-two hundred, opened in 1924. It had twelve doors, like the twelve gates to the heavenly city. When Tindley died in 1933, some five thousand people crowded into the church to hear tributes.

One of Tindley's compositions, "I'll Overcome Someday" (1901), became the inspiration for the anthem of the African American civil rights movement: "We Shall Overcome."

King of the Pipe Organ (1935)

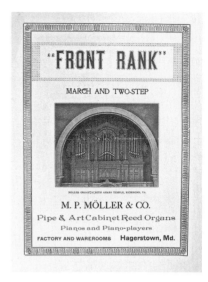

Born on a humble Danish farm, Mathias Peter Möller began working as a carriage maker's apprentice when he was 14, acquiring a reverent love of wood. Within a few years, he migrated to America, where a friend had assured him that fine carriages jammed the byways. With just seven dollars in gold, he landed in southwestern Pennsylvania and took a job in a furniture factory. Later he moved to Erie to work for an organ manufacturer—a fateful encounter, because he fell in love with the craft. In 1875 he built his own organ, which he sold to the Swedish Lutheran church back in Warren, Pennsylvania. Moving to Greencastle in 1877, he produced pump organs, then pipe organs. When he failed to find financing to expand from local banks, he approached Hagerstown, Maryland, whose investors welcomed him. He settled there and never moved. When in 1895 his first factory burned, Hagerstown lent him further support, and Möller reopened.

From 1881 until its close in 1992, Möller's Hagerstown plant, on North Prospect Street, produced eleven thousand or more pipe organs, making it the national, if not world, leader in the industry. Keeping more than a million board feet of lumber in stock at all times, the company produced new organs and restored old ones. It built more than eighteen hundred new tracker-action organs (in which all parts are mechanically connected) and then, after about 1920 and the advent of electromagnetic parts, adopted the new technology. Möller employees manufactured all parts for new organs. In addition to being the major supplier for many small churches in Maryland, the Hagerstown firm produced organs for all of the major service academies; many churches in New York City; the Cathedral of Mary Our Queen in Baltimore; and the National Shrine of the Immaculate Conception in Washington, DC. Möller made the "Might Mo" theater organ at the Fox Theatre in Atlanta and built the fourteenth-largest pipe organ in the world at Calvary Church in Charlotte, North Carolina.

During his career in Hagerstown, in addition to manufacturing organs, Möller built a hotel; opened Möller Apartments; manufactured cars and taxis by means of his M. P. Möller Auto Company; opened music stores under his name selling pianos, organs, radios, records, and later TVs; and helped build a YMCA.

Two pieces connected Möller, who died in 1937, to the world of sheet music—"Front Rank," a march and two-step published by Möller, and the "Dagmar Waltz" (1911), with a picture of the organ maker's young daughter Dagmar on the cover.

The initiative couldn't have come at a more inopportune moment. The Conservatory's director, Otto Ortmann, who was completely absorbed in his research projects at Peabody, scarcely had time to respond to the needs of the Conservatory, nor did he have any interest in forging a relationship with the Baltimore Symphony and its new conductor.[48] Ortmann happily left the Conservatory to the aging band of Hamerik and Randolph appointments; he sought replacements only when forced to do so by deaths or departures.

The Peabody Conservatory was not simply adrift; it was heading rapidly toward the shoals. A visiting composer observed that it had come to resemble "an institution such as one might expect to find on the lower Volga."[49] William Marbury, a prominent Baltimore attorney and chairman of the Peabody's board of trustees, tried in vain to work out a solution that would allow Ortmann to continue his research but lift the administrative burden from his shoulders. Responding as if besieged, Ortmann objected. Marbury enlisted the aid of Ortmann's longtime friend Ernest Hutcheson. Finally, having after failing to find a face-saving resolution for him, the trustees called for Ortmann's resignation. He complied just before the beginning of the 1941 academic year.

In contrast, Howard Barlow and the Baltimore Symphony succeeded in bringing aboard a number of fine new players, including an oboist named Mitchell William "Mitch" Miller,[50] but often could not keep them. Orchestras with longer seasons and more realistic salaries still lured away the symphony's best musicians. One of the violinists in the once-proud orchestra complained, perhaps harshly, that its first-violin section during those years "wouldn't have made second violin section in the St. Louis Symphony."[51]

While Barlow was trying to patch up the orchestra, Frederick R. Huber, the architect of the orchestra's anniversary celebrations, boasted to reporters that the Baltimore Symphony, the first municipal symphonic organization and the only major orchestra financed wholly from a city's tax funds, was about to begin its second quarter century of consecutive seasons.[52] Behind the glowing report was an orchestra that was not growing and was vulnerable to criticism from every direction.

A Haydn performance calling for fewer musicians in the orchestra provoked howls that taxpayers weren't getting their money's worth.[53] Critics upbraided the orchestra for bringing in out-of-town soloists. Huber's refusal to seek private support and the Conservatory director Ortmann's refusal to cooperate with the symphony reduced Barlow's optimistic plans to fantasy. The crisis reached a climax when members of the American Federation of Musicians succeeded in blacklisting Huber. All this wrangling led to the cancellation of the 1941–42 season and the dismantling of the Baltimore Symphony Orchestra. On January 11, 1942, the orchestra played its final concert under Barlow, with the pianist Reginald Stewart performing Tchaikovsky's Piano Concerto no. 1, the work von Bülow had performed in Baltimore in 1875, prior to its Moscow premiere. Huber resigned.

Until the Japanese attack on Pearl Harbor on December 7, 1941, Marylanders had been preparing for war and yet hoping somehow to escape it. As the state and nation mobilized for a full and sustained effort, Pearl Harbor had two immediate effects on Baltimore music lovers, one ironic and the other deflationary. As luck would have it, the Gilbert and Sullivan Opera Company had scheduled a week of repertory at Ford's Theatre to begin on Monday, December 8, with, of all things, *The Mikado*. That day, under a headline reading, "Far Eastern Attacks Give Timely Setting for Opera," the *Sun* announced that the performances would go on as planned, observing, "The opera is all in fun, anyway." Despite the Baltimore Civic Opera's being in desperate financial straits, Martinet had scheduled Sigmund Romberg's *Blossom Time* for December 15 at the Maryland Theater to mark the twentieth anniversary of the show, with Thomas in the lead role.[54] His acceptance meant canceling his scheduled performance with the Chicago Opera.

The diva Rosa Ponselle began her long association with the Baltimore Civic Opera at this point, working with Martinet on casting and helping to coach singers. After the events of December 7, Martinet breathed a sigh of relief that his company wasn't performing *The Mikado*, and Thomas swept in the next day from the West Coast to begin rehearsals. Surprisingly, a large audience turned up for the opening, taking refuge from the stream of war bulletins. But a pall fell over the city, and *Blossom Time* soon closed, a victim of shock.

Blackouts, air-raid drills, and ration books became the stuff of everyday life. Evening dress for concerts changed. For the first time, coatless men were allowed into the Lyric. Ford's Theatre admitted women patrons in slacks. Even proprietors of the clubs on Baltimore's "Block" relaxed dress standards. Max Cohen, proprietor of the Oasis, even allowed patrons clad in undershirts into his establishment: "We don't put them up front, but we don't keep them out."[55]

From Whaleysville in Worcester County to Pennsylvania Avenue to Frostburg in Western Maryland, church choirs and glee clubs lost young tenors, baritones, and basses to the war. Many careers were put on hold or made a sharp turn. A. Russell Slagle, one of the Baltimore Civic Opera regulars, had just made his way to Carnegie Hall, playing in *The Chocolate Soldier*, when he was called up to become a real soldier at Fort Meade. Like many of Maryland's best musicians, Slagle spent much of his time in the military producing and directing US Army shows. Both music critics for the *Sun*, Robert Cochran and Weldon Wallace, were sent off as war correspondents. Flora Murray, a former Peabody student and Goucher College graduate assigned to cover women's clubs, fashion, and the society columns for the *Sunday Sun*, took over for both men, signing her articles "FM."

A few artists benefited from the turmoil. Lionel Hampton was playing at the Royal in 1942 and looking for a trumpeter to replace Joe Newman, who had been drafted. Cat Anderson, one of Hampton's musicians, told his boss about a fine musician who could make a trumpet growl in the old blues tradition or play a classic so well that it sang. Heeding Anderson's advice, Hampton recruited Baltimore's best trumpeter, Roy McCoy.

A member of the Maryland State Guard, the state

Appreciating Appalachian Music (1944)

In 1936 an Illinois-born graduate of the Sherwood School of Music in Chicago with a master's degree in music education from Columbia University, Maurice Matteson, joined the faculty at Frostburg State Teachers College in Allegany County. He soon made his energy felt. As a former resident and student in New York, he knew many artists who had either fled oppression in Europe or simply struggled in the depressed times. He pointed out to them that as they traveled to concerts, especially if they rode the Baltimore and Ohio, it would be easy to stop off at Frostburg. The Matteson family home became a welcome place for many of these artists, who included Percy Grainger and Charles Wakefield Cadman.

Matteson developed the college and community musical culture, but his most important contribution stemmed from his love of folk music. He and his wife, Augusta Lofton Matteson, had spent summers at the Southern Appalachian Music Camp in

Banner Elk, North Carolina. He and others in this group pioneered in transcribing the folk music of the region, paying special attention to the singing and dulcimer playing of Nathan Hicks (one of whose songs, "Tom Dooley," later surfaced in 1958 as a Kingston Trio hit). Matteson learned to play original instruments—the dulcimer, the salmodicum, the melodin, and the zither. Many times his wife, a concert artist, accompanied him on the piano. At Frostburg, Matteson organized a group of students who as the Maryland Singers carried the rich music of Appalachia to audiences throughout the country. In 1944 Matteson received an invitation to attend the prestigious MacDowell Colony in New Hampshire. That year another folklore enthusiast, Dorothy Howard, joined him at Frostburg. She became a leading collector of children's folklore.

Later, when Matteson's son, himself a faculty member at the University of Maryland, College Park, asked how he would like to be remembered, the elder Matteson replied, "Just say, I'm a little mouse in the corner" (interview by William Biehl, 2010). The Maurice Matteson Music Collection is an important holding at the University of South Carolina Library, Columbia. The American Folklore Collection of the Library of Congress houses many of Matteson's research papers and recordings.

defense force, McCoy escaped active military duty. At Anderson's urging, he auditioned and went on tour with Hampton's band. Hampton liked McCoy's playing and his exuberant showmanship. For a while the playing and the tours were exciting. The band would play in New York, then board a train for Norfolk and be on stage for a broadcast at nine o'clock the next morning. The men played at army bases along the tour routes. McCoy had been with the band for almost a year when it played the Apollo in New York. Then disaster hit. Booked into the Capital Theatre in New York, the band was suddenly laid off when another act was held over. Broke, out of work, and facing a huge bill for his newly acquired uniform, McCoy decided to go back to Baltimore. He eventually had his own band at the Club Orleans in East Baltimore.

Pennsylvania Avenue bustled. People waited in long lines to get into the Royal Theatre to hear Nat King Cole, Louie Armstrong, Billie Holiday, Count Basie, Stan Kenton, and Pearl Bailey (once a Royal chorus girl). The clubs were filled with servicemen from Fort Meade, Aberdeen Proving Ground, and the Edgewood Arsenal. Tracy McCleary's Kentuckians played the clubs on Pennsylvania Avenue at night, and McCleary worked at Bendix Radio during the day. When he lost musicians to the draft, he replaced them with players stationed at Aberdeen and Fort Meade.

Supporting the war effort, Maryland's Works Progress Administration orchestra programmed an all-American program at the Baltimore Museum of Art. The orchestra's conductor, Lucien Odend'hal's son Emile, programmed works by Jerome Kern, Victor Herbert, and two Maryland composers, Katherine Lucke and Louis Cheslock. The WPA orchestra took its programs throughout the state, providing for many Marylanders their only opportunity to hear symphonic music.

The Wranglers, a popular group led by Tom and Jimmy Finn, played "hillbilly" (later "country") ballads on

The Roy McCoy Band at the Club Casino, ca. 1942. After performing at the Royal Theatre, touring musicians would make their way to the Club Casino, at 1517 Pennsylvania Avenue, to sit in with Roy McCoy and his band. Archives of the Peabody Institute of the Johns Hopkins University.

the Baltimore radio station WFBR and on weekends performed at dances held at Pine Grove School, at Cub Hill and Old Harford Roads. Their rendition of a traditional nonsense song, "A Hole in the Bottom of the Sea," was a favorite. An admirer claimed that their "playing improved with prodigious amounts of alcohol."[56]

Too old for military service, John Charles Thomas spent the war years singing at war-bond rallies, military bases, and hospitals. In 1943 Westinghouse signed him for a prestigious new Sunday-evening network-radio production that originated in Los Angeles, the *Westinghouse Hour*. The show soon registered some of the highest ratings in the history of radio. Carroll Hollister, Thomas's accompanist since 1933, joined the program, and the Academy Award–winning composer and arranger Ken Darby agreed to direct the chorus.[57] The *Westinghouse Hour* had a full symphony orchestra under the direction of the composer and conductor Victor Young. Though the radio audience could not have known, there were a good many women musicians in the orchestra, an innovation that reflected the wartime shortage of males. Armed Forces Radio beamed the *Westinghouse Hour* to American troops stationed around the world.

Meanwhile, in early 1943 Thomas sang seven performances with the Metropolitan Opera, starting with *Faust* in January and ending with *La Traviata* at the end of February, with *Aida* and the *Barber of Seville* in between—all the while commuting between New York and the West Coast. In February alone, despite travel restrictions, Thomas made eight coast-to-coast trips. After a final performance as Valentin in *Faust* with Helen Jepson, Charles Kullman, and Ezio Pinza in Cleveland the following April, Thomas never went back to the Metropolitan. He admitted to a colleague on the *Westinghouse Hour* that the schedule was killing him. He sang his last major operatic role in the San Francisco Opera's production of *Rigoletto* in late October 1943.

With the vicissitudes of travel eased, the Westinghouse show moved along smoothly. Dedicated fans reportedly shushed friends who had the temerity to interrupt the program. At the studio, any differences about repertoire or show scripts that may have arisen stayed off the air, including differences between Thomas and his accompanist. Hollister, whose Communist Party ties brought him under FBI surveillance, and Thomas, a conservative Republican, performed together peaceably for more than a decade. Hollister's tolerance ran out, however, in mid-April 1945, when news broke of President Roosevelt's death. "Glad the S.O.B. is dead," quipped Thomas. Hollister quit, and his FBI files recorded both the incident and the date of his effective resignation—May 1, International Labor Day.[58]

War Work: Rebuilding the Peabody and the Symphony

In early 1941 the Peabody trustees consigned the job of righting the course of the Conservatory to Reginald Stewart, a Scots-born pianist and founder-conductor of the Toronto Philharmonic Orchestra.[59] With the grace that would become the hallmark of his tenure, Stewart praised his predecessor as director, Otto Ortmann, and began restoring the Peabody's faded luster. He soon made a series of stellar appointments to the faculty that included the theorist Nadia Boulanger, the pianist Harold Bauer, and the composer Henry Cowell.

Reaffirming the Peabody's commitment to American music and musicians, Stewart inaugurated annual contemporary-music concerts featuring works by American composers. At the same time, Stewart had to contend with the loss of the younger men on his faculty to the war. Among the first to go was the head of the Organ Department, Virgil Fox. The organist who had performed at Carnegie Hall and on the great organs of Westminster Abbey and the cathedrals of Europe was now playing for sailors on an electric organ at Bolling Naval Air Station in the District of Columbia. Fox, who had graduated from Peabody in 1932, had joined the Conservatory faculty immediately after his return from a successful four-month European tour in 1938. He had been playing there to packed houses until the night Adolf Hitler delivered his famous declaration of intentions in the Berlin Sports Palace.[60]

Stewart had expressed an interest in a dual appointment as Peabody director and conductor of the Baltimore Symphony Orchestra. With Barlow firmly in place as conductor of the symphony at the time, such an arrangement could not even be contemplated. Now settled in as director of the Conservatory, with most of the orchestra's first-chair players on his faculty and the symphony in hopeless disarray, as well as Barlow's departure, Stewart considered taking matters into his own hands. When the academic year ended, the Stewart family headed to Falmouth, on Cape Cod. While the family settled in to enjoy the summer, Stewart fretted. Realizing that the situation in Baltimore would continue to gnaw away at him, his wife, Ruby, put her foot down. "Go back to Baltimore Reggie," she said. "You know how to start an orchestra, so for heaven's sake, go back and fix that one!"[61] Reginald Stewart took a train back to Baltimore.

After spending months studying other orchestras, Stewart devised a plan for the total reorganization and revival of the Baltimore Symphony Orchestra. The plan called for joint funding from the City of Baltimore for an initial season of twenty weeks (Stewart had hoped for twenty-four weeks), private subscriptions, and income from ticket sales. Mayor Jackson enthusiastically advocated the plan. On July 10, 1942, the Board of Municipal Music issued a statement announcing that Stewart's proposal had been approved with the understanding that he take over as conductor.

First you buy a pound of tea, began Stewart's recipe for a symphony orchestra, and then you send invitations to twelve of the town's outstanding women, and then it all depends upon how much support you get from the women. To help put a women's committee in place, he called on Mrs. Richard N. Jackson, the mayor's wife and Rosa Ponselle's mother-in-law.[62] The organization of the Baltimore Symphony Orchestra Women's Committee got under way at a tea given the afternoon of Tuesday, October 7, 1942, in the Peabody Conservatory's North Hall (now the Leith Symington Griswold Hall). They raised funds for membership drives, called on radio-station officials, organized ticket sales, sold box seats, ran the Young People's Concerts, conducted a speaker's bureau, and performed a host of other tasks. Reginald Stewart gave much of the credit for building and maintaining Baltimore's symphony orchestra to the several hundred women who formed the Women's Committee.

With union backing and the assistance of J. C. Van Hulsteyn, the orchestra's first concertmaster, and Edmund Cook, its personnel manager, Stewart promptly reauditioned every member of the orchestra. The orchestra's least competent musicians simply departed, but many of the players returned to their accustomed chairs, and a number of other city musicians joined their ranks. Some were old-timers, such as the cellist Henry Ditzel, who had played in the pit orchestra at Ford's Opera House before joining the old Baltimore symphony, and W. Edwin Moffett, one of the stalwarts of the Saturday Night Club. But the old guard was in the minority. Newcomers included Henry Bloch, a young refugee who had fled Nazi Germany. Bloch was playing in a Baltimore nightclub when word went out that auditions were being held. Felix Robert Mendelssohn, a grandnephew of the composer, who fled the Nazis and left behind a successful career in Europe, joined the ranks of the BSO.[63] Stewart added the Musical Arts Quartet to the Peabody faculty and enlisted three of its members for the orchestra.[64] After the auditions, Stewart went back to the union and got permission to import fifty players from out of town. Stewart raided the Detroit, Pittsburgh, NBC, and New York City symphonies, the Philadelphia Orchestra, the Kansas City Philharmonic, and the Pasdeloup Orchestra of Paris. He brought in young players just out of Peabody, Curtis, and Juilliard. His dual position as both conductor of the BSO and director of the Peabody Conservatory enabled him to lure quality principal players to Baltimore by offering them faculty positions. Under Stewart's plan, the close association between the two institutions made it possible to undertake a series of major music festivals.

The newly formed Baltimore Symphony Orchestra announced its 1942–43 season proclaiming that it was now "a full-time orchestra of 90 musicians" with a season of fifteen weeks, instead of the hoped-for twenty, and a roster of guest artist that included Risë Stevens, one of the great voices of the Metropolitan Opera, the pianist Harold Bauer, the virtuoso violinist Joseph Szigeti, and Lily Pons, the legendary French American coloratura soprano (a village in Frederick County, Maryland, is called Lilypons in her honor). Stewart hired C. C. Cappel, a seasoned professional with a nine-year track record as manager of the National Symphony Orchestra, as manager of the orchestra and the violinist Walter deLillo, well known and respected by musicians, as personnel manager. Stewart, the dignified Scot with a wit, thus embarked on

a remarkable triple career as a conservatory director, conductor, and concert pianist and gave Maryland's classical-music scene a flair it had never known before.

The ninety-five-member orchestra assembled on the stage of the Lyric Theatre for its first rehearsal in early November 1942. A *Sun* reporter covering the orchestra's first rehearsals proclaimed Stewart "almost a Superman."[65] The emergence of a full-time professional orchestra in the darkest hours of the war was a welcome sign of hope. Despite blackouts and wartime gas rationing, Baltimore rejoined the ranks of American cities with full-time symphony orchestras on November 19, 1942. The symphony office arranged carpools for subscribers, and the Baltimore Transit Company posted inspectors near the Lyric stops to ensure that there were enough trolleys and busses to handle the crowds. Women arrayed in silks and furs and men in evening dress alighted from streetcars and buses. An hour before the inaugural concert, the lobby of the Lyric was packed with people waiting to hear their new orchestra. Precisely at 8:00 p.m. ushers opened the door and watched the Lyric's 2,564 seats fill. The opening concert, with the Metropolitan Opera star Risë Stevens, was a triumph. Stevens was called back for six curtain calls, and Stewart for twelve. After the concert, Arthur Judson, general manager of the New York Philharmonic, told a *Sun* reporter: "It's a damned good orchestra, and it's been a long time since Baltimore had anything like that."[66]

Among the first to extend congratulations to Maestro Stewart was the orchestra's founding conductor, Gustav Strube.[67] The French composer and world-famous professor of music Nadia Boulanger, Glenn L. Martin, an aviation pioneer and founder of the aircraft company that bore his name, and the Metropolitan Opera diva Rosa Ponselle were part of the excited backstage crowd who had gathered to offer their congratulations to Stevens and Stewart. Stewart's audacious new enterprise was a brilliant and unqualified success. Days later, the Philadelphia Opera Company and the National Symphony Orchestra performed *The Marriage of Figaro* to a mostly empty house.

Stewart maintained the BSO's commitment to promoting American music, programming the works of a

Gustav Strube and Reginald Stewart, 1942. At the premiere performance of the newly organized Baltimore Symphony Orchestra, on November 19, 1942, Gustav Strube, the orchestra's founding conductor, passed his baton to Reginald Stewart, who created the present-day orchestra. Archives of the Peabody Institute of the Johns Hopkins University.

number of Maryland composers. Foremost among them was Strube's *Der Harz*, a symphonic poem in three movements, which received its world premiere in the autumn of 1943.[68] Strube, who for a second time had watched the country of his youth descend into the inferno of war, had begun the work in the summer of 1940 and completed it in April 1941, dedicating it to Stewart. *Der Harz* offered a reminder that Germany had once contributed to a saner and lovelier world. The work, for full symphony orchestra, reveals Strube's deep knowledge of the orchestra and its instruments (he could play every one of them). It pays homage to the legend-filled Harz Mountains, stretching across Northern Germany, near Strube's birthplace in Ballenstedt. The first movement, "Das Gelb Haus," evokes an image of a gabled tollhouse: "I would trudge past it late at night, walking home from playing at a late dance, with my fiddle case under my arm," recalled Strube. In the second movement, "Selke Tal," Strube revives memories of Sunday excursions to the beautiful Selke valley, with its murmuring brooks, turreted palaces, and forests. The last movement, "Der Broken—Walpurgisnacht—Hexen Orgie," is a bacchanal, replete with a devil, witches, and wild dancing, which brings the work

to a dramatic conclusion. The movement conjures up the familiar medieval legend of the witches' Sabbath.

The Baltimore Symphony gave Franz Bornschein's tone poem *The Earth Sings*, portraying the coming of spring in Guilford's Sherwood Gardens, its world premiere on November 19, 1943, and it gave the first performance of Howard Thatcher's *Military Echoes* the following year. Bornschein's work became part of the war effort when it was chosen for live rebroadcast to American troops overseas and for use by the Office of War Information to counter German propaganda claiming that Americans were "culturally insufficient."[69]

Despite the praise, good press, and innovative programming, money problems continued to plague the orchestra. Rosa Ponsell and her father-in-law, Mayor Jackson, pitched in to help with the fundraising. Orchestra players continued to take outside jobs to compensate for their small orchestral salaries. Most of the principal players were drawn from the Peabody Conservatory's faculty. Others taught privately or squeezed in outside jobs that would not conflict with their symphony schedules. Many of the orchestra's members added war-related work to their already crowded schedules. The violinist Ruth

Reginald Stewart conducting the Baltimore Symphony Orchestra from his silver podium, ca. 1945. Archives of the Peabody Institute of the Johns Hopkins University.

Van Hulsteyn, already juggling two full-time jobs, added a third when she began working at Bendix, inspecting military radios on the night shift.[70] The violinist Ken Creamer supervised a crew of inspectors on the night shift at the Glenn L. Martin plant. Like their World War I predecessors, BSO musicians played for the servicemen stationed at Fort Meade and programmed special concerts for defense workers at the Lyric. These concerts, intended as morale builders and gestures of goodwill, ended up building audiences and attracting new subscribers.

By the 1944–45 concert season the orchestra was in full stride, presenting five national radio broadcasts in NBC's Orchestras of the Nation series. In January 1945 Stewart appeared with the orchestra as soloist, performing Rachmaninoff's Second Piano Concerto in C Minor. At intermission, Mayor Theodore R. McKeldin lauded Stewart for "raising the status of the orchestra, and for Baltimore music in general."[71]

In February 1945, for the first time in its twenty-eight-year history, the orchestra went on tour. On February 9, the night before their departure, their concert at the Lyric featured *Military Echoes*, by Howard R. Thatcher, with the Maryland composer on the podium. The opening notes, Thatcher explained, reflect the musings of a veteran of World War I: "He remembers a trip across the ocean in the blacked-out convoy; the alarms of attempted submarine attacks, the arrival overseas . . . and the hurried trip to the fighting front . . . and [wondering] whether he would survive the terrible dangers of war and return to the life he once knew." On the same program were three eminent Marylander pianists: Austin Conradi, who had been raised in Baltimore and had spent most of his life there; Alexander Sklarevski, who had left Russia in 1918; and the Italian-born Pasquale Tallarico, who had settled in Baltimore after joining Peabody's faculty. Ifor Jones conducted the Peabody Chorus in four choral works, ending with *Alleluia*, by the American composer Randall Thompson. Jones, a member of Peabody's faculty, was also conductor of the Bach Festival in Bethlehem, Pennsylvania.[72]

"Reginald Stewart and the Baltimore Symphony Orchestra." This full-page ad was drawn from "Almost a Superman," by Allen W. Harris, which appeared in the *Evening Sun* on November 12, 1942. Archives of the Peabody Institute of the Johns Hopkins University.

On Saturday, February 10, 1945, the orchestra played in Dahlgren Hall at the US Naval Academy in Annapolis. On February 13 it performed at Constitution Hall in Washington, DC, and on the following day it repeated the concert at the Lyric in Baltimore. The concert opened with "The Star-Spangled Banner," arranged for orchestra by Nicholas Nabokov, director of music at St. John's College in Annapolis, from the first printed copy of the words and music, dated 1814.[73] Jascha Heifetz joined the orchestra as soloist in Beethoven's Concerto in D Major for Violin and Orchestra, opus 61.

In late February 1945, Stewart folded his six-foot-two-inch frame into a Pullman berth and headed south with his orchestra. The orchestra played its first concert in Danville, Virginia. After the concert, Stewart and the orchestra's concertmaster, Ilya Skolnik, found the only restaurant in Danville that was open until midnight. When it became apparent that the staff was not equipped to serve a large group of hungry musicians, Stewart put a napkin over his arm and turned waiter to help get his orchestra fed. After Danville, Stewart jollied his musicians through four-hour bus rides across the Appalachian Mountains to Athens and Augusta, Georgia; Winthrop College in South Carolina; and Newport News, Virginia.

Baltimore Symphony musicians backstage before a concert on their 1945 tour of the South. With their train from Danville, Virginia, pulling into Gainesville, Georgia, at 6:02 p.m., and transported by bus to their hotel in Athens, Georgia, the musicians had little time to change before sprinting several blocks to the auditorium at the University of Georgia for a concert at 8:30 p.m. Double bass and harp cases served as makeshift dressing rooms. George Schaun Papers, Archives of the Peabody Institute of the Johns Hopkins University.

The BSO played to good houses, winning praise along the way. "Mr. Stewart was like a magician drawing out one lovely passage after another," proclaimed the *Washington Evening Star*.[74]

Back home, Stewart took the orchestra to Essex, Dundalk, and Sparrows Point—to Marylanders who had never heard a symphony orchestra. Ensuring that it would have future audiences, the symphony played concerts for seventeen thousand children in high schools throughout the city and broadcast Saturday-morning concerts for young people. The orchestra's concert schedule was at an all-time high, offering nearly seventy performances a season (several world premieres among them) with first-rank soloists.

The Baltimore Civic Opera in Peace and War

During the war, Maryland's musical organizations, large and small, faced the shortage of men, restrictions on wartime travel, blackouts, paper shortages, and a host of related problems, but opera suffered most. Male roles were hard to fill; tickets to performances tended to go begging until the last minute. A *Sun* reporter speculating on the reasons why Marylanders waited to buy their opera tickets suggested that it was because they feared that performers might be arrested as enemy aliens.[75] That same edition of the paper reported Ezio Pinza's arrest by the FBI at Ellis Island, precluding his appearance at the Lyric in the role of Toreador in the Metropolitan Opera's production of *Carmen*.[76]

For the Baltimore Civic Opera and its director, Eugene Martinet, the war years were a time of prolonged struggle. There were not enough available men to field a decent chorus, and many of the company's principals had enlisted in the services. Then Martinet's health began to fail. Mary and Eugene Martinet talked about disbanding the company, but concluding that opera was more important for the morale of the city during wartime than ever, they decided to keep the company together. The following spring, the company did a week of performances of *The Merry Widow*. Hochschild-Kohn Department Store, in Baltimore's premier shopping district, stocked up on recordings of *The Merry Widow* in their mezzanine record shop. Martinet had Ernst Lert, head of the Peabody's opera department, revise the libretto of the original opera and change the conclusion.[77]

With his own son in the military, Martinet made sure that servicemen knew they would be welcome guests at any Baltimore Civic performance. Four hundred seats were set aside for servicemen for every performance. The day of the opening, the *Evening Sun* announced the sale of the Maryland Theater, on West Franklin Street. Emblazoned across the marquee in the *Evening Sun* photograph was "*The Merry Widow* with Bartlett and Mercer."[78]

Eugene Martinet Presents, a popular Lyric Theatre series, debuted at the end of March 1941. Many of the artists, such as the pianist Shura Dvorine and the harmonica virtuoso Larry Adler, had their roots in Baltimore and had studied at the Peabody. Adler's talent on the harmonica was lost on the imposing women who listened in horror to his raucous rendition of "Yes! We Have No Bananas" at his Peabody Preparatory examination. Adler had the satisfaction of showing his former teachers just what he could do with the instrument when he returned to play Jean Berger's *Caribbean Concerto*, the first major classical work written for harmonica. The Baltimore Civic Opera veteran Elwood Gary appeared in the series after becoming one of the four winners of the 1942 Metropolitan Opera Auditions of the Air, bringing Baltimore representation at the Metropolitan up to five (with John Charles Thomas, Hilda Burke, Robert Weede, and Lansing Hatfield, who had won the Met auditions the preceding year).[79]

The life of an impresario was infinitely simpler than that of the struggling opera producer. Martinet could fill vacancies in the pit orchestra with women musicians, but coping with the shortage of tenors and basses in the chorus was another matter. The Baltimore Civic Opera Chorus was all but stripped of its men. Martinet enlisted the war workers' glee club at the Glenn L. Martin plant to fill the breach. The young singers rehearsed at the Sears

Community House under their own director, Jack Cary, and Martinet, taking in stride opera rehearsals after the long hours building the B-26 Marauder bombers, PBM Mariners, and other war planes. By 1944 Martinet's declining health forced him to rely on familiar repertoire. In January the company staged *Carmen* with Winifred Heidt, a New York Opera star who had appeared in the leading role all over the world. The night of the opening performance at the Lyric, the full house suffered what seemed an interminable delay (actually only fifteen minutes). At last the house lights dimmed and the curtain rose on what would be one of Martinet's most memorable wartime opera productions.

After V-J Day, in August 1945, Martinet and his company waited until the following spring to celebrate the return of peace and the survival of the Baltimore Civic Opera with a surefire winner, *H.M.S. Pinafore*, the opera that had launched it. Its star was Maretinet's lifelong friend John Charles Thomas, whose appearance returned a favor Martinet had done the previous January by performing in a lavish *Pinafore* that Thomas had organized at his winter home in Palm Beach. Martinet was in the middle of rehearsals for *La Traviata* when Thomas asked him to take the part of the Boatswain's Mate. The opera has only one aria, "For He Is an Englishman," but Martinet could wring every last ounce out of it. An offer from an old friend that included escape from January cold in Baltimore (and guest quarters aboard a yacht moored in Palm Beach) was too tempting to refuse. Martinet suspended rehearsals and hopped a train to Florida.

For the Civic's production of *Pinafore* the Opera Chorus mushroomed to 110 singers. Mindful of the press, Martinet enlisted Maryland socialites for minor roles. Alice Whitridge Garrett, a Bachelors' Cotillion debutante, made her debut with the company as Cousin Hebe, garnering for the company a lengthy article on the *Baltimore American*'s society page. Garrett juggled opera rehearsals with practice flights and studying for a private pilot's license. Elizabeth Ridgely, Mrs. Richard Shackelford, and Mrs. W. W. Lanahan donned bonnets for their supporting roles as "sisters, and his cousins, and his aunts." Mary Lida Bowen was cast as Josephine, and Elwood Gary was the devious Ralph Rakestraw. Elwood

Hawkins returned to Baltimore as the Captain after his recent performance as Silvio in the Chicago Civic Opera Company's production of *Pagliacci*.

Presiding over the ship and its colorful crew behind the scenes, Mrs. Frederick P. Stieff, the company's production manager, supervised the scenery, the lighting, and the costumes. Ruth Stieff, a gifted singer and guest artist on Baltimore radio stations, was well equipped to work with *Pinafore*'s colorful crew. Leigh Martinet, just completing service in the Army Air Forces Band, became his father's rehearsal conductor and began the process of taking over the reins of the company.

Newspaper coverage was extensive. Having exhausted the cast for articles, reporters interviewed the star's mother, Mrs. Milson Thomas, a resident of Towson, about her son's favorite dinners and published her recipes. Even Thomas's schnauzer, Tony, got his picture in the paper with an article by the *News-Post* writer and dog-show judge Roslyn Terhune. Local radio stations played excerpts from *Pinafore* in the weeks leading up to the production. Everything was positioned for success, with Charles Thomas in the lead role, his Sir Joseph Porter costumed as Winston Churchill, complete with a cigar, cap, and gestures. The production became a company reunion, as old cast members headed back to Baltimore. The role of Captain's Daughter went to Joann Mastracci, a key member of the company who took on supporting roles and appeared as soloist while also working at the medical clinic of the Rustless Iron and Steel plant in Baltimore and appearing as soloist on the broadcast of the Baltimore Sunday American Variety Show for the US Army. Mastracci's unaffected manner and sense of humor made her a terrific match for Thomas (and would keep him from upstaging her).

On opening night the "Standing Room Only" sign went up early in the evening, and as many standees as the fire marshal would allow packed themselves into the 2,564-seat hall. Another thousand who had lined up outside in spring rain showers were turned away. The audience got its money's worth. The show, which included not only a rousing *Pinafore* that ended with a storm of applause but also a between-acts recital that lasted nearly ninety minutes, complete with encores at

the insistence of the audience, and a mini-ballet, did not end until almost midnight. Thomas brought the house down with his outrageous clowning in "Never Mind the Whys and Wherefores." During the trio, when prim Miss Bowen opened her mouth in preparation for a high note, Thomas turned impulsively and stuffed a handkerchief into her mouth. The ensuing outburst in the audience literally stopped the show.[80] The onstage hi-jinks and the spirited performance of the chorus, with its full complement of men, combined to make an evening that Baltimoreans remembered for decades.

The success of the production inspired Martinet to take *Pinafore* on tour the following season. Because most of the young singers had full-time jobs outside the company, he arranged performances in nearby cities so that the cast could return to Baltimore each night. Disaster struck twice on this modest venture. The tour opened auspiciously on February 14 at Dickinson College in Carlisle, Pennsylvania, with the proceeds from the performance going to the Dickinson scholarship fund. A few days later the company gave two performances of *Pinafore* at Zembo Mosque in Harrisburg, Pennsylvania. On the way back to Baltimore, Martinet was severely injured in an automobile accident with a Harrisburg Railways passenger bus. *Pinafore* was slated for a performance in Hagerstown before opening at Constitution Hall in Washington, DC, with performances on February 18 and 21, 1947. Patrick Hayes was making his own debut as an impresario with his Hayes Concert Bureau, presenting the Baltimore Civic Opera as his first offering in the city.

The Washington opening became the object of press attention when word leaked out that Margaret Truman, who was celebrating her twenty-third birthday on February 18, would take her parents, President and Mrs. Truman, to the performance. Washingtonians clamored for tickets, and the opening-night audience numbered around four thousand. Leigh Martinet, who had never conducted a full-length opera, stepped in for his injured father. The performance, with Thomas in high form, was a smash hit from start to finish. Thomas mugged and camped for all he was worth, introducing bits of operatic arias and, at one point, a comic pop tune, "Open the Door Richard." Thomas repeated his between-acts recital, dedicating the songs to Miss Truman. Fastening his gaze on Margaret, Thomas sang, "There Is A Ladye Sweet and Kind."

The young Martinet repeated his father's success with the operetta, and Thomas excited the audience to a frenzy. Audience reaction was so wild that "Never Mind the Whys and Wherefores" had to be repeated several times, and each time Thomas's clowning was more outrageous. At the end of the performance he led the cast in a spirited "Happy Birthday to You." The Washington papers published enthusiastic reviews, lauding Thomas and praising the young singers in supporting roles and his leading lady, Joann Mastracci, who won over the Washington critics.[81]

Next the company set out for Richmond, Virginia, but found itself caught in a massive snowstorm. Instead of traveling down with the cast on the bus, Thomas stayed behind for a party hosted by his friends in Washington, intending to follow by car. The exhausted cast finally arrived in Richmond, only to learn that Thomas was stranded and the performance had been canceled. The Richmond hosts, the Civic Musical Association, who had arranged a large cast party, graciously welcomed the dispirited singers just the same and offered to reschedule the performance. So the company performed *Pinafore* in late March, with Leigh Martinet on the podium and Thomas in his Churchillian garb, repeating earlier successes. The perpetually cash-strapped company donated the proceeds from the Richmond performances to Greek War Relief.

Overture to Equality

Reginald Stewart and the Baltimore Symphony marked the end of the war with a thirtieth-anniversary celebration. Stewart again turned to the man whom he regarded as the most brilliant and versatile figure in the musical history of Baltimore, Gustav Strube, who, at Stewart's invitation, conducted his newest work, *Peace Overture.*

During the war years, Stewart dramatically improved Maryland's two most important performing-arts organizations, the Peabody, whose tarnished reputation he restored, and the Baltimore Symphony Orchestra,

creating a real professional orchestra and bringing it into national prominence. Stewart had yet another hurdle to surmount: the sorry tradition of rigid segregation, which had so appalled him when he arrived in Baltimore. The process of change began slowly. Stewart integrated the audiences at the Lyric by devising a contest that would inevitably be won by African American children, with tickets to the Lyric as a prize.[82] At the Peabody, he continued to press the Institute's trustees to open the doors of the Conservatory and the Preparatory to African American musicians. The chairman of the Peabody's board of trustees, William L. Marbury, proved a strong ally.[83] Marbury had been in Europe at the end of World War II; he had seen the horror of the concentration camps and learned all too well where the dark paths forged by racism and bigotry lead. He knew that many Peabody faculty members were teaching African American students privately, though they could not attend classes or earn degrees. The baritone Todd Duncan was barred from attending the Peabody Conservatory despite having made a successful Town Hall debut in 1944 and winning a starring role with the New York City Opera. (He was the first African American member of the opera company, appearing as Tonio in its 1945 production of *Pagliacci*.) Duncan, like so many African American musicians before him, simply made arrangements to study privately with a Peabody faculty member, in his case Frank Bibb, outside the Conservatory.

After the war, with Marbury's support, Stewart invited the dean of the Baltimore African American musical community, the composer A. Jack Thomas, to conduct the BSO in a performance of his own tone poem, *Etude en Noir*. Thomas had served in the army from 1903 to 1919 and had been one of the country's first African American army bandmasters. After his discharge from the military, he established the Aeolian Conservatory in Baltimore, open to aspiring musicians of all races. Beginning in 1924, he directed the music department of Morgan College. Thomas quietly built a reputation in the music world that extended far beyond the city and state. A gifted composer, conductor, and teacher, Thomas composed works in jazz and classical idioms. He also wrote the poetry upon which he based *Etude en Noir*. In it, he employed American dance rhythms, blues, and spirituals. Composed in 1939, the composition placed in a contest sponsored by the National Composers Clinic at the University of Akron in 1942. The Cleveland and Chicago Symphonies and the National Symphony Orchestra later performed Thomas's *Etude*.

Thomas accepted Stewart's invitation, and on January 26, 1946, Mayor McKeldin introduced him to a capacity audience at Douglass High School. After the performance, Thomas and the Baltimore Symphony received a long standing ovation.

Once More, with Feeling

At midcentury, time and circumstance took a toll on the leading Maryland musical personalities of the radio age. In July 1946, NBC suddenly interrupted John Charles Thomas's *Westinghouse Hour* to announce that an atomic bomb was about to be tested at Bikini Atoll. Though he toured extensively in the near term, that show marked Thomas's last as host of a network broadcast. After the war, as fewer Americans spent time and money dancing at pavilions, big bands began to disappear. In 1947 Cab Calloway let most of his musicians go.

During the 1947–48 concert season, Thomas embarked on a concert tour that covered forty thousand miles and had him singing in 110 concerts. Crisscrossing the country, he took midnight trains, slept in Pullmans, and spent practically all of his time in railroad stations, hotels, and concert halls. Popular memory of the *Westinghouse Hour* helped pack the halls to capacity.

In late November 1948 a stroke left H. L. Mencken a passive participant in the world of music. Instead of taking part in boisterous musical gatherings with cronies, pounding away at the piano into the night, Mencken listened to evening programs of classical music and Saturday-afternoon radio broadcasts from the Metropolitan Opera. With his brother August, he continued to venture out to symphony concerts and took as much pleasure in the efforts of the youngsters in the Peabody Preparatory's orchestra as he did in the Baltimore Symphony Orchestra. Louis Cheslock, one of the last survi-

vors of the club, who had spent most of his life among musicians at the Peabody and in the Baltimore Symphony, claimed that he never met a man who loved music more than Mencken did.

After World War II, with Stewart at the helm, the BSO performed with first-rank soloists, among them Byron Janis, Gregor Piatigorsky, Vladimir Horowitz, Jascha Heifetz, Lily Pons, Percy Grainger, Kirsten Flagstad, Artur Rubinstein, and Isaac Stern. Stewart's reputation as a conductor and the growing prestige of the orchestra drew first-class musicians to Baltimore. The orchestra's wind section became legendary. With players like Ray Still, Albert Genovaise, Wayne Raper, Ignatius Genusa, Britton Johnson, and Arthur Weisberg, BSO sections could stand up against any in the country.

BSO musicians became virtual ambassadors for the state of Maryland. In early 1947 the orchestra performed before a capacity audience in Washington's Constitution Hall with Jascha Heifetz. It followed this performance with performances in Newport News, Virginia, and—after traveling by bus, train, and a boat over choppy waters in February winds across the mouth of the Chesapeake Bay—at the Maryland State Teachers College in Salisbury. Exhausted by performances and grueling travel but euphoric in anticipation of playing at Carnegie Hall, the musicians boarded a train for New York.[84] They arrived the next morning to find that their rehearsal time in the hall would reduced to a few brief minutes because the train carrying their instruments had been delayed.

That night, William R. Steinway was among the New Yorkers who braved winter winds and icy sidewalks to hear the Baltimore Symphony Orchestra perform the world premiere of Lukas Foss's *Pantomine* and the Brahms Violin Concerto with Georges Enesco as soloist. Enesco was making his first major appearance since the war. The performance was broadcast live over WBAL. After the performance, Steinway exclaimed to one of the Marylander's present: "Your orchestra is really going places. It's one of the fine symphonies of this country." The *New York Times* critic Olin Downes wrote glowingly of the orchestra's performance and gave solid credit to Stewart. The *New Yorker* proclaimed,

Members of the Baltimore Symphony Orchestra preparing to board for their southern tour, 1948. George Schaun Papers, Archives of the Peabody Institute of the Johns Hopkins University.

"Baltimore is equipped with an organization and a leader that can provide substantial music in solid, satisfying fashion and music with bounce and glitter."[85]

The next day, the travel-weary musicians returned home for a short rest. In late February they set out on a tour of the southern and southwestern states. Afterward, the orchestra toured in Pullman cars for two weeks every year—from Toronto, Quebec, and Ottawa to Key West, Florida. While they were treated as visiting celebrities in towns from New England through the Deep South, touring conditions often were deplorable. There were no union regulations prohibiting travel on days off or when road conditions were hazardous. Worse than the heat or harrowing ice storms was the tedium of bus travel. On a trip through Pennsylvania, the French horn player Tom Kenney got so frustrated that after a coffee break, he paid fifty dollars for a gold-painted 1937 Packard he spotted on a used car lot and drove off with his fellow horn players.

After the war, Eubie Blake was thinking of retiring when, in 1948, an unexpected turn in politics gave new life to a hit tune from *Shuffle Along*. Harry Truman, the incumbent president, adopted "I'm Just Wild about Harry" as his campaign song, putting the songwriting team of Blake and Noble Sissle back in the spotlight. After Truman's somewhat surprising victory, the Truman inauguration team called Blake down to Washington, DC, to work with Fletcher Henderson on a new arrangement of the song that played repeatedly during Inaugural Week. Though Sissle and Blake were scheduled to sing the song at one of the inaugural balls, at the last minute administration officials asked a white singer, Alice Faye, to do the honors.

When Cab Calloway's career was at its peak, he had

That Barbershop on North Gay (1959)

In 1939, Doc Kilduff's Bar, at 1530 North Gay Street in Baltimore, became a gathering place for men anxious to try singing in four-part harmony. Without any professional guidance, they attempted to "woodshed" their way to success. It nonetheless became obvious to everyone that a little guidance would help if they were to progress to something other than a gang sing-a-long. The Society for the Preservation and Encouragement of Barber Shop Quartet Singing in America (SPEBSQSA) had organized a year earlier in Tulsa, Oklahoma, and begun publishing The Harmonizer, a magazine that found its way into the hands of one of the songsters at Kilduff's, John C. Bell. In May 1944, Bell and others formed Baltimore Chapter No. 1 of the preservation society. The following summer, as World War II came to an end and veterans streamed home, membership in the chapter grew steadily.

The barbershop craze extended far beyond Gay Street, of course, in this era of painted screens and duckpin-bowling clubs.

In November 1947, perhaps a bit grudgingly, the management of the normally operatic Lyric Theatre agreed to host an "Annual Parade of Barbershop Quartets" concert. The Lyric sold all of its seats (about 2,700) and then sold tickets for standing room. Needless to say, the theater welcomed the singers back each year. Dundalk formed a SPEBSQSA chapter in 1957, and within a year its membership had grown to more than 150 members. Its first music director, Bob Johnson, taught music at Patterson Park High School and also made appearances on the Johns Hopkins File Seven television show, which WJZ TV aired, beginning in 1959. There his enthusiasm and understanding of barbershop helped to fuel its popularity in Baltimore. The challenges and joys of barbershop singing did not escape the notice of women. The Sweet Adelines International formed in Tulsa, Oklahoma, in 1945, and in Baltimore Helen Seay and Louise Leonard, whose husbands sang in the Chorus of the Chesapeake, formed the Dundalk Sweet Adelines in 1958.

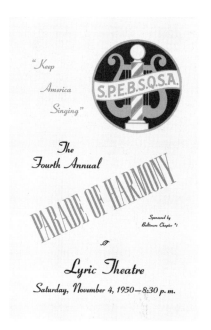

"Keep America Singing"

S.P.E.B.S.Q.S.A.

The Fourth Annual

PARADE OF HARMONY

Sponsored by Baltimore Chapter #1

at

Lyric Theatre

Saturday, November 4, 1950—8:30 p.m.

With a chorus of 156 men, Dundalk captured the coveted SPEBSQSA Chorus championship trophy in 1961. Under the longtime direction of Fred King after 1959, the ladies earned many regional championships, placing second in their first international competition, in Washington, DC, in 1973.

turned down the chance to play the role of Sportin' Life in *Porgy and Bess*—opposite his former Douglass High School classmate Anne Brown. Gershwin, a frequent visitor to the Cotton Club, had modeled Sportin' Life on Calloway. When producers revived the opera in 1953, they persuaded Calloway to join the ensemble and play himself. Fully enjoying the part, Calloway appeared with Leontyne Price as Bess and William Warfield as Porgy. The memorable show ran for three and a half years, including a year in London, putting an older Calloway back on stage.

Immediately after the war ended, Billie Holiday appeared with Louis Armstrong and Kid Orey in a film entitled *New Orleans*. Thereafter, one of the foremost female singers in jazz history lived a nightmare of encounters with police, trouble with agents and club owners, and scrapes with drug-dealing lovers. Despite her deteriorating health, she made two successful European

tours, but after her 1958 tour, police arrested her on drug charges. She died on July 17, 1959, in her hospital room under armed police guard and was buried in an unmarked grave in St. Raymond's Cemetery in The Bronx.

Sylvan Levin adapted well to the postwar musical scene. New York and studio work suited him perfectly. He thrived on the frantic pace of broadcasting, sleeping four hours a night and chain-smoking four packs of cigarettes a day. Radio background music required flexibility and an uninhibited attitude toward music. His musical background as a "hot" piano player in Baltimore movie houses and nightclubs, opera coach, composer, and symphony conductor with a thorough grounding in theoretical studies all gave him the tools he needed. He composed and arranged background music for weekly comedies, dramas, mysteries, and melodramas, each requiring a new score each week.

Levin scoffed at the idea of radio as an educational medium but castigated studio executives for regarding serious music as a luxury item.[86] He conducted WOR's Sinfonietta, which achieved a reputation as a trailblazer for fine instrumental music. The Sinfonietta was a full-time professional ensemble, unlike the pickup orchestras made up of part-timers that frequently performed on radio. In the spring of 1946 Levin conducted the world premiere of the Maryland composer Hugo Weisgall's first full-length opera, *Six Characters in Search of an Author*, with the New York City Opera Company and a cast headed by Adelaide Bishop, Patricia Neway, and Beverly Sills.

When radio began losing ground to television, Levin in 1954 lit out for Broadway, conducting Sigmund Romberg's *The Girl in Pink Tights* at the Mark Hellinger Theater. After the show closed, he went on the road with the European tour of *Porgy and Bess*, and later the American tour of Lerner and Lowe's *My Fair Lady*.

In the mid-1950s, the sexy, pulsating music that young listeners who loved it and those older observers who derided it called rock 'n' roll first appeared. The sound owed a debt to the doo-wop vocal harmony that a singing group from Baltimore, the Orioles (originally the Vibra-Naires), had developed to a high level.

Their first hit, "It's Too Soon To Know," recorded in 1948, had been one of the first successful recordings in this rhythm-and-blues genre. Led by Earlington Carl "Sonny Til" Tilghman, the group included George Nelson, Alexander Sharp, Johnny Reed, and Tommy Gaither. The highly individualistic style of this group, whose popular recordings included "Tell Me So" (1949), "Crying in the Chapel" (1953), and "In the Chapel in the Moonlight" (1954), made them a sensation at Harlem's Apollo Theater.

In May 1957, Rivers Chambers made an appearance at the Odd Fellows Hall, at the corner of Cathedral and Saratoga Streets as a thunderstorm raged outside. Less than a block away, R. Warren Hammann was teaching an organ class at the family's music store on Saratoga Street. A bolt of lightning and a deafening crash of thunder brought the class to a stunned silence. Minutes later he heard a siren approaching. The next day Hammann learned that when that thunder clap split the air, Chambers had collapsed on the podium. After more than four decades of performances, Rivers Chambers was gone. He died as he lived, making music. With Buster Brown keeping that special sound alive, the band pleased Baltimoreans for yet another generation.

Coda

SEVERAL STELLAR PLAYERS from the days of live performance, records, and radio became the closest thing to living legends in Maryland. The incomparable Rosa
Ponselle settled into a home in the Greenspring Valley, northwest of Baltimore, and
supported local opera until her death in 1981. Eubie Blake put his music to work at benefit
performances for the NAACP, the Urban League, and African American youth groups
and schools. He continued to play the piano as if age did not matter. In 1973 he performed
at the Peabody during an event marking his ninetieth birthday. He died a decade later, a
few days after his one hundredth birthday. Ruth Van Hulsteyn continued to perform with
the Baltimore Symphony, under half a dozen conductors, well into the 1990s.

Maryland music clearly suffered cultural losses in the era of "urban renewal," and listening closely, one can hear some mixed reports about broader changes in Baltimore at least.
Tracy McCleary returned to the Royal Theatre as permanent conductor of the house
band about four years after the war. "That was a momentous occasion, I can tell you,"
McCleary recalled.[1] He put together the Royal Men of Rhythm, a band made up of
some of the best musicians in Maryland. (A sign of the changing times was that he began hiring white musicians.) Charlie "Bird" Parker played for McCleary for a time. He
and the Royal Men of Rhythm played it all—jazz, swing, and, later, rock 'n' roll—and
they played it all well. Then in the early sixties Pennsylvania Avenue started to deterio-
rate. No one saw the trend more clearly than McCleary. "I could see the signs that the
whole area had gone by the wayside, partly because places in other parts of town opened
up to blacks." The civil rights movement of the 1960s made movie houses, clubs, taverns, and public accommodations in other parts of the city legally accessible to African
Americans. Television kept people home in the evenings. Growing crime reflected and
affected life on the streets surrounding.

On January 6, 1965, the Royal staged its last major show, ending a grand tradition
of presenting African American artists and musicians for mostly black audiences, with
Count Basie himself. "I don't know which died first," McCleary later mused, "Pennsylvania Avenue or the Royal Theatre." The destruction of the most important cultural

icon of Baltimore's African American community was, paradoxically, part of the Upton Renewal Project. The Royal came down in 1971, leaving behind a vacant lot and fading memories of Pennsylvania Avenue during far better days. "The Royal had a lot to do with the evolution in music in this country," noted McCleary. "A lot of blood, sweat and tears went into that theater and a lot of people put their lives into it."

At the time, for better and worse, civic leaders in the city struggled to "renew" and reinvigorate Baltimore as their counterparts in nearby cities like Pittsburgh and Washington were trying to do. In terms of musical culture, urban renewal produced the wrecking of the Royal, but it had the unexpected effect, by force of repulsion, of encouraging a lively musical counterculture. It thrived in the places urban-renewal efforts overlooked or left alone, and thus small bistros, Irish music halls, and popular nightclubs sprung up in places like Fells Point, the West Baltimore neighborhood around the B&O Museum, and a shopping center not far from Morgan State University. Urban renewal also made space for an ambitious new venue for the BSO, thanks in large measure to Joseph Meyerhoff, who in 1965 became president of the orchestra's board of trustees. While also contributing to classical music as a member of the Peabody Institute board, Meyerhoff led the drive to build a hall that would be a permanent home for the Baltimore Symphony. Opened in mid-September 1982, with Leon Fleisher at the piano, Joseph Meyerhoff Symphony Hall quickly captured attention for its beauty and acoustical excellence. Responding to a music lover who thanked him for making possible the hall that musicians had long dreamed of (and referring to the BSO conductor at the time, the celebrated Sergiu Commissiona), Meyerhoff replied simply, "It was Comissiona's dream. He had the dream and I had the money."[2]

Years earlier, an eighteen-year-old tidewater Virginian, Charlie Byrd, had been drafted, trained, and marched onto a troop ship out of Newport News. He never forgot the passage and the musicians he met onboard. "We got together and we used to play with nothing else to do. We learned a lot and kept ourselves from thinking too much about what we were facing."[3] The young soldier landed in Naples and marched off to Livorno. During the Battle of the Bulge he was ordered to join a division in Alsace. "When I found myself in combat I remember saying to myself, 'My friends and my neighbors have drafted me and sent me in this mess. The rest of the big decisions in my life are mine. I'm going to be a musician. That's what I'm going to do. Whoever thinks they're going to talk me into anything else is going to stand aside because the rest of the decisions are mine. I don't care what kind of trouble it gets me into or not. I could not be in more trouble than I am right now!'"

The postwar career of Charlie Byrd illustrates changes that made the story of music after about 1950 so varied. Byrd epitomized the complicated, multilayered soundscape of late twentieth-century music. In 1961, under the aegis of the United States Information Agency, he toured South America with the bassist Keter Betts and the percussionist Buddy Deppenschmidt. They traveled more than fifty thousand miles, visited sixteen countries, and performed some two hundred concerts. On a night when no performances were scheduled, Byrd visited a nightclub in Recife, Brazil. "I was completely amazed," he recalled. "I found myself playing pure jazz against their authentic bossa nova and it worked beautifully." He spent the remainder of his free time there gathering material and integrating it into his repertoire.

After returning home, Byrd and his quartet began playing the music he had brought back from South America at the Showboat Lounge in the Adams-Morgan section of northwest Washington, DC. The sound quickly became locally popular. Byrd soon introduced the bossa nova to the jazz saxophonist Stan Getz, and together they recorded one of the great jazz record albums ever made, *Jazz Samba*. With Getz and guitarist Antonio Carlos Jobim—and thanks to warm support the music received from Felix Grant, an evening-jazz radio host at WMAL in Washington—Byrd helped create a musical craze in the United States. He also made memorable recordings with the jazz greats Herb Ellis and Barney Kessel. Demonstrating the lasting importance of concert music in his repertoire, he recorded with the guitarist Laurindo Almeida and won rave reviews for

Poster for the Annapolis Fine Arts Festival, June 1968. The festival featured Louis Armstrong and Charlie Byrd. Archives of the Peabody Institute of the Johns Hopkins University.

sophisticated performances. Philip Elwood, the music critic for the *San Francisco Examiner* called them "guitar royalty."[4] Byrd's State Department tours eventually took him to Britain, the Middle East, Africa, and Asia.

In 1972 Charlie Byrd moved to Annapolis, where he could indulge his three great loves—music, sailing, and cooking. Charlie took a shine to the Maryland Inn and performed there regularly. If one were lucky, and hap-

pened to be in Annapolis during those years, one might have found a table at the King of France Tavern on a night when Charlie was playing.

In September 1997 Byrd was declared the first Maryland Art Treasure. Another honor followed when the Brazilian government proclaimed him a Knight of the Rio Branco, an honor accorded to foreign individuals for services of exceptional merit.

Prelude

1. Meredith Janvier, *Baltimore in the Eighties and Nineties* (Baltimore: H. G. Roebuck & Son, 1933), 49.

Chapter 1. Drawing Rooms, Taverns, Churches, and Tobacco Fields

1. Vestry minutes, All Hallow's Parish, St. Anne's Parish, Anne Arundel County, microfilm 1156-P, 178, Maryland Hall of Records, Maryland State Archives, Annapolis (hereafter MSA).

2. Kate Van Winkle Keller, *Dance and Its Music in America, 1528–1789* (Hillsdale, NY: Pendragon, 2007), 249, 213. Keller has traced Kellom Tomlinson's *The Art of Dancing Explained . . .* (London, 1735) to two female subscribers in Maryland (see sidebar, page 25), and Playford's *The English Dancing Master* (London, 1651) to Pennsylvania (1743) and Virginia (1734).

3. Anne Arundel County inventories, book 2, folio 134, Maryland Hall of Records, MSA.

4. William Black et al., "The Journal of William Black, 1744," *Pennsylvania Magazine of History and Biography* 1, no. 2 (1877): 131.

5. David K. Hildebrand, "Musical Life in and around Annapolis, Maryland (1649–1776)" (PhD diss., Catholic University, 1992).

6. Ann Faris, quotation from "The Will of William Faris," an anonymous poem circulated in Annapolis in 1791. Whether lighthearted or malicious, this document provides a glimpse of family life at the time. See William Faris, *The Diary of William Faris: The Daily Life of an Annapolis Silversmith*, ed. Mark B. Letzer and Jean B. Russo (Baltimore: Maryland Historical Society, 2003), 23–28.

7. Charles Carroll of Carrollton Letter-Book, Arents Tobacco Collection, New York Public Library, New York, microfilm edition at Charles Carroll Papers Office, Maryland Historical Society, Baltimore (hereafter MHS), order dated February 7, 1785. Carroll had owned a spinet as early as the 1760s, and he might have ordered the grand harpsichord sooner had it not been for trade embargoes, economic uncertainty, and later hostilities.

8. Hildebrand, "Musical Life in and around Annapolis," 60–61.

9. Information in this and the following two paragraphs is from ibid., 52–56.

10. "Itinerarium, An Electronic Edition: Dr. Alexander Hamilton (ca. 1667–ca. 1732)," entry for September 18, 1744, 638, http://eada.lib.umd.edu/text-entries/itinerarium/.

11. Hildebrand, "Musical Life in and around Annapolis," 305–49. Regarding the Faris music copybook, a diary entry of November 16, 1800, explains some markings in a hand other than Faris's: "Billie Gott Tipsey and in the Evening he told Mrs. Faris that he wanted a candel to transcribe some musick." Faris, *Diary of William Farris*, 346–47. This might explain the appearance of "The Annapolis March," with the name McParlin scrawled under it, in the copybook.

12. *Maryland Gazette* (Annapolis), December 19, 1771.

13. Benson J. Lossing, "Records of the Homony Club of Annapolis. Instituted the 22nd of December, 1770," in *American Historical Record, and Repertory of Notes and Queries*, ed. Lossing, vol. 1 (Philadelphia: Chase & Town, 1872), 302–3. Glenn Campbell, of Historic Annapolis, has done considerable research on the Homony Club.

14. This and the following paragraphs are based on John Barry Talley, *Secular Music in Colonial Annapolis: The Tuesday Club, 1745–1756* (Urbana: University of Illinois Press, 1988), 45–47, 41n34. Audio recordings of some Tuesday Club music include *Maryland's Baroque Composers*, Towson University Early Music Ensemble, dir. H. Gene Griswald; and *Over the Hills and Far Away, Being A Collection of Music from 18th-Century Annapolis*, performed by David and Ginger Hildebrand, Albany Records, TROY042, 1990, reissued by Colonial Music Institute, CMI H103, 2006.

15. A handful of psalm tunes were copied in two-part harmony in a Maryland manuscript begun in 1729. Account Book of Robert Pinkney, MSA SC 435, SCM 217 Carroll County Historical Society Collection, MSA. For a fuller description of this manuscript, along with a full listing of its contents, see Hildebrand, "Musical Life in and around Annapolis," 272–74.

16. Quoted from Elaine G. Breslaw, ed., *Records of the Tuesday Club of Annapolis: 1745–56* (Urbana: University of Illinois Press, 1988), 386–87. As if by way of recompense, Middleton was invited as a guest to the next Tuesday Club meeting, at somebody else's house.

17. *Maryland Journal, and Baltimore Advertiser*, December 10, 1782.

18. Hildebrand, "Musical Life in and around Annapolis," 170–86.

19. Nicholas Cresswell, *The Journal of Nicholas Cresswell, 1774–1777*, ed. Lincoln MacVeagh (New York: Dial, 1924), 19.

20. Ibid.

21. Edward Kimber, quoted in Joseph Towne Wheeler, "Reading and the Recreations of Marylanders, 1700–1774," *Maryland Historical Magazine* 38 (1943): 1, 38.

22. Hildebrand, "Musical Life in and around Annapolis," 90, 103, 177–78.

23. *Maryland Gazette*, February 23, 1769. A year later, in ibid., November 22 and 29, this violinist sought subscribers in a scheme to publish "Six elegant Pieces of Musick." Those named from Maryland included Mr. Adam Steuart at George-Town; Mess. William Sydebotham, Richard Thompson, and Andrew Leitch, at Bladensburg; Mess. Christopher Richmond and George Digges, at Upper Marlborough; Mr. Thomas Clagett, at Piscataway; Mr. John Barnes, at Port-Tobacco; and Mr. Charles Peale, at Annapolis.

24. Norman Arthur Benson, "The Itinerant Dancing and Music Masters of Eighteenth Century America" (PhD diss., University of Minnesota, 1963), 231.

25. *Maryland Gazette*, April 17, 1760. The account of the Homony Club procession that follows is from Hildebrand, "Musical Life in and around Annapolis," 109–10.

26. In October 1773, the Continental Congress banned theater in anticipation of war. Despite this decree, George Washington and ranking officers seem to have encouraged musical and theatrical presentations during the Revolutionary period, thinly disguising them as "lectures" and "moral discourses."

27. Jane McWilliams, *The Progress of Refinement: A History of Theatre in Annapolis* (Annapolis: Colonial Players, 1776), 3.

28. Letter to the editor, *Maryland Gazette*, June 1, 1769.

29. Benjamin Franklin, *Experiments and Observations on Electricity Made at Philadelphia in America* (London: David Henry, 1769), 475.

30. *The Diaries of George Washington*, ed. Donald Jackson, vol. 3 (Charlottesville: University Press of Virginia, 1978), 56.

31. Andrew Burnaby, *Burnaby's Travels through North America, reprinted from the third edition of 1798*, ed. Rufus Rockwell Wilson (New York: A. Wessels, 1904), 80.

32. Located halfway down Duke of Gloucester Street and at Charles Street by the water, respectively, one was used for the 1752 season, and the second was in operation in 1760 and 1769–71.

33. *Maryland Gazette*, September 12, 1771; Hildebrand, "Musical Life in and around Annapolis," 117–18.

34. All these poems appeared in the *Maryland Gazette*. Hildebrand, "Musical Life in and around Annapolis," 144.

35. Talley, *Secular Music in Colonial Annapolis*, 11–14. An excellent study of Dr. Hamilton outside the context of his Tuesday Club is Elaine G. Breslaw, *Dr. Alexander Hamilton and Provincial America: Expanding the Orbit of Scottish Culture* (Baton Rouge: Louisiana State University Press, 2008).

36. David Ritchey, *A Guide to the Baltimore Stage in the Eighteenth Century: A History and Day Book Calendar* (Westport, CT: Greenwood, 1982), 57.

37. Hildebrand, "Musical Life in and around Annapolis," 133–35.

38. These are just two of the titles advertised in Stephen Clarke, *Catalogue of the Annapolis Circulating Library . . . (near 1500 volumes)* (Annapolis: F. & S. Green, 1783). Among other holdings were works by Shakespeare, Addison, and Garrick, as well as numerous collections of plays and ballad operas, for example, *Love in a Village, Cymon, Maid of the Vale, The Golden Pippin, Maid of the Mill, Midas, Lionel and Clarissa*, and *The Village Opera*, many of which were performed in Annapolis.

39. *Maryland Gazette*, October 1, 1772. A single, nearly intact copy survives in the Archives of the Peabody Institute of the Johns Hopkins University (hereafter API). Green's version is based upon *Lionel and Clarissa* (I. Bickerstaffe and C. Dibdin, 1768).

40. Similarly *Love in the Village* (Bickerstaffe, 1762) and *Maid of the Mill* (Bickerstaffe, 1765) served as titles of comic operas presented in Annapolis and also the names of country dance tunes.

41. Alexander Hamilton, *The History of the Ancient and Honorable Tuesday Club, by Dr. Alexander Hamilton*, ed. Robert Micklus, 3 vols. (Chapel Hill: University of North Carolina Press for the Institute of Early American History and Culture, 1990), 1:227.

42. The *Maryland Gazette* of April 20, 1769, includes a lengthy, enticing description of these entertainments.

43. Talley, *Secular Music in Colonial Annapolis*, 15–16; Faris, *Diary of William Faris*, 204. This was in the spring of 1795.

44. Elihu S. Riley, *"The Ancient City": A History of Annapolis in Maryland, 1649–1887* (Annapolis: Record Printing Office, 1887), 80.

45. William Eddis, *Letters from America*, ed. Aubrey C. Land (Cambridge, MA: Belknap Press of Harvard University Press, 1969), 20.

46. Orlando Ridout IV, "The James Brice House in Annapolis" (MA thesis, University of Maryland, 1978), 37.

47. Hildebrand, "Musical Life in and around Annapolis," 90, 178.

48. John Barry Talley transcribed all of Ormsby's minuets and included a brief biography as well. Talley, *Secular Music in Colonial Annapolis*, 26, 31, 33, 279–305. Other Maryland manuscripts, such as those of Johannes Schley of Frederick and William Faris in Annapolis, also include dance tunes.

49. Hildebrand, "Musical Life in and around Annapolis," 90; Keller, *Dance and Its Music in America*, 246–88.

50. *Maryland Gazette*, October 1, 1767.

51. Robert Saladini, "American Catholic Church Music: The Baltimore Cathedral" (MA thesis, Catholic University of America, 1984), 4.

52. Hildebrand, "Musical Life in and around Annapolis," 8–10, 187–92; Ethel Roby Haydn, "Port Tobacco, Lost Town of Maryland," *Maryland Historical Magazine* 40 (1945): 268.

53. Saladini, "American Catholic Church Music," 9–12, 16–17. John Aitkin's *A Compilation of the litanies and vespers hymns and anthems as they are sung in the Catholic Church adapted to the voice or organ* (Philadelphia, 1787), America's first published music for the Catholic service, was the main source for music at St. Peter's. Several later compilers of sacred music, such as Benjamin Carr and Baltimore's Jacob Walter, issued successful collections of Catholic music soon thereafter. These included compositions by the influential English composer Samuel Webbe and Baltimore composers like John Cole and Christopher Meinecke.

54. Many editions of *The Whole Booke of Psalmes, Collected into English Meter* (London, 1562) went to print over the next forty years. As the seventeenth century unfolded, more complex musical settings by Playford, Tan'sur, and Ravenscroft were published in England. Yet while copies of all made it to the New World, they were at the time beyond the musical capabilities of most colonial singers and players.

55. The library was that of Henry Callister (ca. 1716–ca. 1766), a merchant and musician active on Maryland's Eastern Shore; Joseph Towne Wheeler, "Reading Interests of Maryland Planters and Merchants, 1700–1776," *Maryland Historical Magazine* 37 (1942): 27, 31, 41.

56. The Reverend Thomas Craddock of Baltimore, an honorary member of the Tuesday Club, translated his own *New Version of the Psalms of David*, and Jonas Green published it in Annapolis in 1756. (Henry Callister, mentioned in the previous note, also owned one of these psalters.) American psalm collections of the 1760s, such as those

compiled by Francis Hopkinson and James Lyon in Philadelphia, seem to have been rare in Maryland, which, unlike the colonies to the north, remained closer to mother England in its practice of church music.

57. Clifton Hartwell Brewer, *A History of Religious Education in the Episcopal Church to 1835* (New York: Arno, 1969), 21.

58. Anne Arundel County inventories, book 10, folio 371.

59. Talley, *Secular Music in Colonial Annapolis*, 73. These lines appeared in response to a poem mocking George Whitefield, written by Baltimore ministers Thomas Craddock and Thomas Chase.

60. Another minister of questionable repute, the Reverend Bennet Allen, served both St. Anne's and All Saints parishes. He left his bass viol behind in Frederick when he fled back to England before the Revolution. Allen became known as "the fighting parson of Maryland" after he killed Lloyd Dulaney in a duel. See *Inland and American Printer and Lithographer* 22, no. 1 (1898): 575, in *The Inland Printer: A Technical Journal Devoted to the Art of Printing, Volume XXII, October, 1898, to March, 1899* (Chicago: Inland Printer, 1899), https://babel.hathitrust.org/cgi/pt?id=hvd.hb2or0;view=1up;seq=323;size=125.

61. Talley, *Secular Music in Colonial Annapolis*, 57; James R. Heintze, "Alexander Malcolm: Musician, Clergyman, and Schoolmaster," *Maryland Historical Magazine* 73 (1978): 226–35.

62. See Hildebrand, "Musical Life in and around Annapolis," esp. chap. 5.

63. Ibid., 212–13. These men included Mayor John Bullen, the Tuesday Club leader Dr. Hamilton, and the chief clerk of the Maryland Land Office, Thomas Jennings, who also owned a harpsichord in the early 1750s.

64. Ibid., 214–16.

65. Jane McWilliams, letter to David Hildebrand, December 1994. Stadler, a popular itinerant music instructor of the day, taught children of the Carter and Washington-Custis families in Virginia.

66. *Maryland Gazette*, September 5, 1771.

67. Hildebrand, "Musical Life in and around Annapolis," 230–32; St. Anne's Parish Register and Vestry Minutes, Microfilm M 1012, roll 2, pp. 97, 99, Maryland Hall of Records, MSA.

68. Francis Hopkinson, *The Miscellaneous Essays and Occasional Writings of Francis Hopkinson, Esq. Volume I[–III]* (Philadelphia: T. Dobson, 1792), 119.

69. This was Mr. James Small, of Somerset County. Also in Philadelphia, Francis Hopkinson in 1763 issued *A Collection of Psalm Tunes, with a Few Anthems and Hymns* (Philadelphia: Printed by William Dunlap, 1763), and four years later, *Psalms of David* (New York: James Parker, 1767).

70. Hildebrand, "Musical Life in and around Annapolis," 221–23, 272–73.

71. *Maryland Gazette*, April 26, May 3, 10, 17, 1764. The remainder of this paragraph is based upon Hildebrand, "Musical Life in and around Annapolis," 225–29.

72. "The price to each scholar will be 30 shillings per annum, seven shillings and six pence to be paid at entrance." *Maryland Journal, and Baltimore Daily Advertiser*, May 10, 1775. Digins's advertisement three weeks later specifies a different location and the teaching of "Psalmody" per se and suggests that students attend three mornings and three

evenings each week. The better-known and better-trusted singing master Andrew Law was active out of Baltimore and Bladensburg for some time after the Revolution, although he was plagued by mishaps and frustrated by lack of copyright protection. He composed a church tune entitled "Maryland" and printed another entitled "Baltimore." Noah Webster also tried his hand at teaching sacred music in Baltimore. Richard Crawford, *Andrew Law, American Psalmodist* (Evanston, IL: Northwestern University Press, 1968), esp. chaps. 3 and 4.

73. *Maryland Journal, and Baltimore Daily Advertiser*, October 4, 11, 18, 1775.

74. Robert J. Brugger, *Maryland: A Middle Temperament, 1634–1980* (Baltimore: Johns Hopkins University Press in association with the Maryland Historical Society, 1988), 67–70.

75. This paragraph and the following one are based on Historical Society of Frederick County, MS0008, The Schley Family Papers, "Biography/History," https://hsfrederickco.wordpress.com/finding-aids-2/ms0008-the-schley-family-papers, with analysis by David Hildebrand. See also John Thomas Scharf, *History of Western Maryland. Being a history of Frederick, Montgomery, Carroll, Washington, Allegany, and Garrett counties from the earliest period to the present day; including biographical sketches of their representative men*, vol. 1 (Philadelphia: Everts, 1882), 509, 1199. The Schley manuscripts have been described and cataloged in Anne Louise Shifflet, "Church Music and Musical Life in Frederick, Maryland, 1745–1845" (MA thesis, American University, 1971), 7–8, 12–20, 102–8; and James J. Fuld and Mary Wallace Davidson, *18th-Century American Secular Music Manuscripts: An Inventory* (Philadelphia: Music Library Association, 1980), 53–61.

76. Dieter Cunz, *The Maryland Germans: A History* (Port Washington, NY: Kennikat, 1948), 63, 77, 94–109.

77. This paragraph is summarized from Richard Crawford and Larry Hamberlin, *An Introduction to America's Music* (New York: W. W. Norton, 2013), 40–42.

78. James I. Warren, *O for a Thousand Tongues: The History, Nature, and Influence of Music in the Methodist Tradition* (Grand Rapids, MI: F. Asbury, 1988), 45–46, 87.

79. Frederick Emory, *Queen Anne's County, Maryland: Its Early History and Development* (Queenstown, MD: Queen Anne Press, 1981), 230.

80. *Maryland Gazette*, December 1, 1757. This melody, which dates from 1744, continued to be widely popular and in 1831 was used for "My Country 'Tis of Thee." The melody has long served for the national anthem of the United Kingdom, "God Save the Queen."

81. Dickinson's song appeared on July 14, 1768, in Annapolis (*Maryland Gazette*) and on January 23, 1776, in Baltimore (*Dunlap's Maryland Gazette; or, the Baltimore General Advertiser*). The original melody, "Hearts of Oak," appears in "The William Faris Musical Notebook?," 1764, microfilm M 948, Maryland Hall of Records, MSA, original unlocated. The question mark is part of the Hall of Records catalog listing. This rich collection, comprising seventy-five pages, is described in great detail in Hildebrand, "Musical Life in and around Annapolis," 264–71.

82. *Maryland Gazette*, July 11, 1782. More fully, "The day was

spent in perfect mirth; the entertainment, which was in a pleasant grove, well adapted for the purpose, concluded with a dance on the green of thirteen couple of the younger ladies and gentlemen, and the joy expressed in every countenance clearly shewed."

83. A later, standardized version entitled "New Yankee Doodle" shows up in Mary Dorsey's music copybook of 1799, MSA, SC 5879. And a rare English version appears in an Annapolis merchant's account book penned around 1812:

> Then in tar and Feathers drest
> You'll march so neat and handy
> With the tune which you detest
> Yankee Doodle Dandy

From Nathan Hammond Account Book, MS 429, H. Furlong Baldwin Library, Special Collections, MHS.

84. David K. Hildebrand, "Musical Instruments: Their Implications Concerning Musical Life in Colonial Annapolis" (MA thesis, George Washington University, 1987), 83, 98, 132, 136.

85. "God Save the Thirteen States" is one of many wartime parodies of "God Save the King." When playing indoors, bandsmen often played instead on flute, violin, or bass violin (cello).

86. This and the following two paragraphs are from Raoul Camus, *Military Music of the American Revolution* (Chapel Hill: University of North Carolina Press, 1976), 29–34.

87. Cunz, *Maryland Germans*, 51–53.

88. *Maryland Gazette, and Baltimore General Advertiser*, November 23, 1778.

89. *Dunlap's Maryland Gazette; or, the Baltimore General Advertiser*, April 2, 1776. Initially, the Continental army excluded African American soldiers, but once the British lured runaway slaves to join their ranks, the policy was changed.

90. Ibid., January 27, 1778. Regarding the myth of "The World Turned Upside Down," see Arthur Schrader, "'The World Turned Upside Down': A Yorktown March, or a Music to Surrender By," *American Music* 16, no. 2 (Summer 1998): 180–215.

91. Ray Eldon Hiebert and Richard K. McMaster, *A Grateful Remembrance: The Story of Montgomery County, Maryland* (Rockville, MD: Montgomery County Government and Montgomery County Historical Society, 1976) 54. They had just finished playing in Frederick. Maryland was outside the mainstream of presurrender military concerts, many of which were given near Philadelphia and in New Jersey.

92. In 1798, about a decade after Phile composed "The President's March," Joseph Hopkinson wrote the lyrics "Hail, Columbia!" to it. How ironic that the composer of this march melody, intended apparently to be played at George Washington's first inaugural, originally came to America to help subdue her, but was captured at Trenton by Washington himself.

93. MS 2415, Theater Playbill Collection, 1781–1796, H. Furlong Baldwin Library, Special Collections, MHS. Handwritten upon the Annapolis playbill of September 20, 1781, is a note reading, "The Band of Musick that was provided for this night's performance belong'd to the Regiment of the Count de Chalour, who with the French Army were on their March to Virginia, to attack Lord Cornwallis, posted at Yorktown."

94. As published in London, from a letter by a foreigner in America, later reprinted in *Dunlap's Maryland Gazette; or, the Baltimore General Advertiser*, February 11, 1777.

95. Preface to *A Pill to Purge State-Melancholy, or a Collection of Excellent New Ballads* (London: n.p., 1715), viii.

Chapter 2. Something for Everyone

1. Saladini, "American Catholic Church Music," 41, 46; for the following paragraph, see ibid., 23, 37, 52–53.

2. Raphael Semmes, *Baltimore as Seen by Visitors, 1783–1860*, Studies in Maryland History, No. 2 (Baltimore: Maryland Historical Society, 1953), 144; J. Bunker Clark and David Hildebrand, "Meinecke, Christopher," in Charles Hiroshi Garrett, ed., *The Grove Dictionary of American Music*, 2nd ed., vol. 5 (Oxford: Oxford University Press, 2013), 434.

3. The constitution, bylaws, and rules of the orchestra survive in the Baltimore Harmonic Society Record Book, 1809, MS 78, H. Furlong Baldwin Library, Special Collections, MHS. A print version of this constitution was issued the same year in Baltimore by G. Dobbin and Murphy, suggesting that club leaders sought a high profile. Detailed descriptions of the 1821 concert appeared in the *Federal Gazette & Baltimore Daily Advertiser* of May 3 and June 7, 1821. The *Baltimore American and Commercial Daily Advertiser* of January 9, 1808, includes notice of a "Miscellaneous Oratorio by the Handelian Society. On Monday Evening Jan. 11th, Will be performed In Christ Church . . . a grand collection of Sacred Music, with In-strumental Accompaniments. . . . Tickets of Admission at one dollar, with a pamphlet containing the arrangements and the words to be performed, may be had." Mr. J. Cole was to conduct. See also Saladini, "American Catholic Church Music," 39, 46.

4. MS 93, H. Furlong Baldwin Library, Special Collections, MHS. The libretto to the Mendelssohn oratorio is in the same collection, PAM 1500.

5. Regarding Webster, see John H. Gardner Jr., "Presbyterians of Old Baltimore," *Maryland Historical Magazine* 35 (1940): 150–51. Regarding Law, see Crawford, *Andrew Law*, 84.

6. *The Seraph* bears the inscription "Mr. Rinaldo Pindell West River AA County Maryland." Cole, mostly active in Baltimore, had it printed in Philadelphia, and it sold in other cities as well. It includes works by European as well as American composers, along with standard chants and doxologies. This compilation of psalms, hymns, and anthems bears a dedication to Christopher Meinecke, whose compositions are included, and recommendations by the Baltimore organists Frederick Darmish at Christ Church and George Schminke at First Presbyterian. Mrs. Worth B. Daniels Collection, MSA, MdHR MSA SC 557.

7. *Sacred Harp* has become a generic name for shape note singing. It derives from the title of Benjamin Franklin White and Elisha J. King's *The Sacred Harp* (Philadelphia, 1844), which has gone through multiple editions, with hundreds of thousands of copies sold, and remains in print today. Always issued in shape notation, it remains an extremely successful publication. For an excellent discussion of shape-note music, see Stephen A. Marini, *Sacred Song in*

America: Religion, Music and Public Culture (Urbana: University of Illinois Press, 2003), 68–99.

8. Cole eventually conceded and in 1829 published *Union Harmony or Music Made Easy* in shape notes (Baltimore: William & Joseph Neal, n.d.). Perhaps he thought he was losing business to Wyeth in Harrisburg.

9. Charles A. Johnson, "A Baltimore Circuit Camp Meeting, October, 1806," *Maryland Historical Magazine* 44 (1949): 269, 273–74. The description concludes: "To see the people runing yes runing, from every Direction to the stand weeping. Shouting, and shouting for Joy, Pray[er] was then made—add every Brother fell upon the neck of his brother and wept and the Sisters did likewise—then we parted. O! glorious day they went home singing and Shouting."

10. In the early 1990s, such singing and praying bands were recorded in Severna Park, Baltimore, and in several churches on the Eastern Shore. See *On One Accord: Singing and Praying Bands of Tidewater Maryland and Delaware*, Global Village, 1995, compact disc; and Jon Michael Spencer, "The Hymnody of the African Methodist Episcopal Church," *American Music* 8 (Fall 1990): 274. Regarding the establishment of the Bethel A.M.E. church, see Kathryn E. Lofton, "Coker, Daniel," in Leslie M. Alexander and Walter C. Rucker, eds., *Encyclopedia of African American History*, 3 vols. (Santa Barbara, CA: ABC-CLIO, 2010), 2:341.

11. MS 2415, Theater Playbill Collection, 1781–1796, H. Furlong Baldwin Library, Special Collections, MHS; Hildebrand, "Musical Life in and around Annapolis," 138–40; Susan L. Porter, *With an Air Debonair: Musical Theatre in America, 1785–1815* (Washington, DC: Smithsonian Institution Press, 1991), 502–42.

12. St. Anne's Parish Register and Vestry Minutes, 2:97; Porter, *With an Air Debonair*, 9.

13. Oscar Sonneck, *Early Concert-Life in America (1731–1800)* (Leipzig: Breitkopf & Härtel, 1907), 44–59. Quotation from Semmes, *Baltimore as Seen by Visitors*, 13. Regarding the renovated theater, see Hewitt, *Shadows on the Wall*, 66–67, 77, 106.

14. Robert Hopkins and Kate Van Winkle Keller, "Alexander Reinagle," in Garrett, *Grove Dictionary of American Music*, 7:84–86.

15. John Durang, *The Memoir of John Durang, American Actor, 1785–1816*, ed. Alan S. Downer (Pittsburgh: University of Pittsburgh Press and Historical Society of York County, 1966), 22–23, 26–28, 118, 127–28, 135–36.

16. Porter, *With an Air Debonair*, 384; John Pendleton Kennedy, quoted in Raphael Semmes, "Baltimore during the Time of the Old Peale Museum," *Maryland Historical Magazine* 27 (1932): 120.

17. Francis included pieces "as danced at the Theatres, Philadelphia & Baltimore" and catered to locals by composing dances like "The Maryland Hornpipe" and, honoring the frigate built in Baltimore during the 1790s, "The Constellation." In 1800 Bonsal & Niles published a manual with some one hundred dances with instructions and thirty-two songs.

18. Robert L. Alexander, "Nicholas Rogers, Gentleman-Architect of Baltimore," *Maryland Historical Magazine* 78 (1983): 85–90.

19. Duport's "New Sett of Cotilions" also honored the USF *Constitution*, the USF *President*, and other ships of the US Navy.

20. Keller, *Dance and Its Music in America*, 280; Faris, *Diary of William Faris*, 241; Latrobe-Vinton Collections, MS 2009.1, H. Furlong Baldwin Library, Special Collections, MHS.

21. Frederick Damish, organist at Baltimore's Christ Church, dedicated his "March of the Marion Corps" to Benjamin Cohen, who served as first captain of the elite militia unit when it organized in 1823. Damish also composed a march and a waltz for President and Mrs. John Quincy Adams.

22. Alan Jabbour and Christopher Jack Goertzen, "George P. Knauff's 'Virginia Reels' and Fiddling in the Antebellum South," *American Music* 5, no. 2 (Summer 1987): 121–44.

23. John Hill Hewitt, *Shadows on the Wall; or, Glimpses of the past. A retrospect of the past fifty years. Sketches of noted persons met with by the author. Anecdotes of various authors, musicians, journalists, actors, artisans, merchants, lawyers, military men, &c., &c., met with in Baltimore, Washington, Richmond, and other southern cities. Also the historical poem of De Soto, or The conquest of Florida, and minor poems* (Baltimore: Turnbull Brothers, 1877), 74–75.

24. This paragraph and much of the next are based on "Anacreontic Society of Baltimore, 1820–26," MS 1793, H. Furlong Baldwin Library, Special Collections, MHS. Included in this record book are the organization's constitution, lists of members and guests, and several rules, including the following, rule no. 2: "[Members shall] have the right to call for glees, catches, songs, recitation, etc. and it is understood that when called on, no member shall refuse to comply."

25. John Pendleton Kennedy, quoted in Charles H. Bohner, "The Red Book, 1819–1821: A Satire on Baltimore City," *Maryland Historical Magazine* 51 (1956): 181.

26. "The Diary of Robert Gilmor," *Maryland Historical Magazine* 17 (1922): 254, 265. The Grand Harmonicon was a specially designed set of musical glasses filled to various levels with water, played with moistened fingers. Smith patented it in Baltimore around 1820, and he also issued an instruction book. The Maryland Historical Society owns a Grand Harmonicon built by Smith in Baltimore around 1825. People also enjoyed musical clocks, intricate alarm clocks, and music boxes. Gilmore's diary dates suggest the Society lasted beyond 1826.

27. See "Aanacreontic Society of Baltimore, 1820–26."

28. Hewitt, *Shadows on the Wall*, 67–68. "Of course, with all these enviable qualities, he was very popular, particularly with the ladies, whose hearts he won by his touching delivery of tender melodies on his favorite instrument" (68).

29. Elliott W. Galkiln and N. Quist, "Baltimore," in Garrett, *Grove Dictionary of American Music*, 1:311.

30. Ibid.; Elwyn Arthur Wienandt, *The Bicentennial Collection of American Music*, vol. 1 (Carol Stream, IL: Hope, 1974), 175.

31. Considerably more detail can be found in Kate Van Winkle Keller, *Music of the War of 1812 in America* (Annapolis: Colonial Music Institute, 2011), as well as in "Broadside to Anthem: Music of the War of 1812," a public radio program initially broadcast on WWFM—The Classical Network in 2012, published on the compact-disc set *Music of the War of 1812*, written, recorded, and narrated by David K. Hildebrand, Colonial Music Institute, Annapolis, 2012.

32. Nearly a decade before 1814, in 1805, Key had employed the melody of "To Anacreon in Heaven" for lyrics he wrote to honor

Stephen Decatur as an American hero returning from the war in Tripoli. See Keller, *Music of the War of 1812*, 103–8. Key had long been interested in music and theater. Writing to his mother around 1790 as a student at St. John's College in Annapolis, he names *Love in a Village* as one of the works he enjoyed, and he quotes at length the opening lines to a song within it, "A Plague on those Wenches." "Letter of Francis Scott Key," *Maryland Historical Magazine* 44 (1949): 283. Jacob Englebrecht, a professional musician active in Frederick, Maryland, noted in his diary in 1876 the singing of Key's hymn "Before the Lord We Bow" at the city's centennial celebration. He also recalls singing Key's most famous song as a much younger man in October 1814. "Musical References in Diaries of Jacob Engelbrecht, Frederick, Maryland, 1818–1878," 5, typescript, Historical Society of Frederick County.

33. Daniel Spillane, *History of the American Pianoforte: Its Technical Development, and the Trade* (New York: D. Spillane, 1890), 127. The Annapolis silversmith and clockmaker William Faris claimed in a diary entry of 1795 to have built a piano. See Faris, *Diary of William Faris*, 216, 226. Whether he actually did build a piano is unclear, but if he did, it was likely the first constructed in Maryland and among the very earliest in America.

34. Spillane, *History of the American Pianoforte*, 127–28. The story of building pianos in Baltimore continues later in this chapter.

35. The called-for tune to "Adams and Liberty" was that of "To Anacreon in Heaven." The Dorsey music copybook is in MSA, MSA SC 5879.

36. The *Baltimore Musical Miscellany or Columbian Songster* was published in Baltimore by Sower & Cole and Samuel Butler in 1804–5, one volume each year. Now quite rare, it includes an essay on vocal music and many nautical ballads; each volume ran a full two hundred pages. Copies now at the Maryland Historical Society were owned by men in Dorchester County, Maryland, and Alexandria, Virginia.

37. Margaret Law Callcott, ed., *Mistress of Riversdale: The Plantation Letters of Rosalie Stier Calvert, 1795–1821* (Baltimore: Johns Hopkins University Press, 1992), 150. Rosalie's letters also describe with relish the swirl of social life in Annapolis during the late eighteenth century, when she lived in the Paca house and danced frequently. "I have been to three dancing parties which have completely reconciled me to America . . . Society here is really delightful" (11). Sophie Gough is mentioned in Edith Rossiter Bevan, "Perry Hall: Country Seat of the Gough and Carroll Families," *Maryland Historical Magazine* 45 (1950): 39.

38. Callcott, *Mistress of Riversdale*, 185.

39. David Bailey Warden, "Journal of a Voyage from Annapolis to Cherbourg on board the frigate *Constitution*, 1 Aug. to 6 Sept., 1811," *Maryland Historical Magazine* 11 (1916): 132, 134. Perhaps the Carroll daughters also performed pieces known to be in the family music library and recorded on *Music of the Charles Carroll Family, from 1785–1832*, performed by David and Ginger Hildebrand, Albany Records, Troy056, 1991.

40. Semmes, *Baltimore as Seen by Visitors*, 157.

41. Several important sheet-music collections are currently maintained in Baltimore, notably the Lester Levy Collection, Special Collections, Eisenhower Library, Johns Hopkins University (also available online at levysheetmusic.mse.jhu.edu/); the Diehlman Collection, Maryland Historical Society; and that of the Enoch Pratt Free Library. When one adds to these the Music Division, Library of Congress, much of the surviving sheet music from nineteenth-century America is convenient for study in and near Maryland.

42. The phrase "Bard of Baltimore" is derived from the subtitle of Hewitt's own composition "Song of the Hungarian Exile." This and the following paragraph draw upon Fred W. Hoogerwerf, *John Hill Hewitt: Sources and Bibliography* (Atlanta: Emory University, 1981), esp. 5–6.

43. Hewitt dedicated published pieces to 45 individuals, 32 women and 13 men.

44. Hewitt, *Shadows on the Wall*, 71.

45. Clifton's "March for Lafayette," published in full band parts in 1824, is a notable exception.

46. The July 4, 1728, parade is described colorfully in Hewitt's *Shadows on the Wall*, 132–33. Clifton was not the man's given name, as he had left his native London because of a scandal concerning his wife, giving up an established musical reputation as well as his birth name, Philip Corri. He was the son of England's famed Domenico Corri. Clifton's "Carrollton March" is recorded on Hildebrand and Hildebrand, *Music of the Charles Carroll Family*.

47. Hewitt, *Shadows on the Wall*, 66–67. A solid, current biography of Corri/Clifton, plus a bibliography and finding aid to primary sources, can be found at "Philip Antony Corri / Arthur Clifton," http://www.unk.edu/academics/music/buckner_corri.php.

48. Semmes, *Baltimore as Seen by Visitors*, 105.

49. By around 1900, banjos, along with mandolins and guitars, were being popularized through college clubs and used by wealthier white amateurs. Baltimore became somewhat of a center of banjo manufacturing. According to Robert Winans, "William Boucher is the earliest known commercial manufacturer of banjos, starting around 1845. His shop (along with others in the musical trades) was in the same central Baltimore district as the theaters, in which minstrel performances were frequent." http://www.appalachianhistory.net/2014/01/making-music-banjo-baltimore-beyond.html.

50. "De Boatmen's Dance. An Original Banjo Melody, by Old Dan D. Emmit; Leader of the Virginia Minstrels" (Boston: Chas. H. Keith, 1843). Recent scholarship has called into question Emmit's authorship of this and other popular hits; indeed, they were likely taken directly from slaves and free blacks and claimed as Emmit's own work. See Howard L. Sacks and Judith Rose Sacks, *Way Up North in Dixie: A Black Family's Claim to the Confederate Anthem* (Champaign: University of Illinois Press, 2013).

51. Albert G. Emerick, ed., *Songs for the People, Vol. 1: Comprising National, Patriotic, Sentimental, Comic and Naval Songs* (Philadelphia: G. B. Zieber, 1848), 189.

52. Brugger, *Maryland*, 803. The China trade began with John O'Donnell's arrival at Baltimore with cargo from Canton, China, in August 1785.

53. See *National Songster* (Hagerstown, MD: John Gruber & Daniel May, 1814), 28–30. Key's lyrics and those of "The Battle of Baltimore" are compared in David K. Hildebrand, "Two National

Anthems? Some Reflections on the Two Hundredth Anniversary of 'The Star-Spangled Banner' and its Forgotten Partner, 'The Battle of Baltimore,'" *American Music* 32, no. 3 (Fall 2014: 253–71.

54. Captain Alex Kellum, interview by David Hildebrand, Queenstown, MD, July 1982.

55. Roy Palmer, comp., *The Oxford Book of Sea Songs* (Oxford: Oxford University Press, 1986), xvii–xxix.

56. Richard J. Wolfe, *Early American Music Engraving and Printing: A History of Music Publishing in America from 1787 to 1825 with Commentary on Earlier and Later Practices* (Champaign: University of Illinois Press, 1980), 51.

57. Henry Stockbridge Sr., "Baltimore in 1846," *Maryland Historical Magazine* 6 (1911): 31.

58. Interestingly, when George Gershwin researched *Porgy and Bess* in Charleston in 1934, he noted actual street cries and used them in his opera.

59. "July 4th. When shall we learn to celebrate this great national festival as becomes rational beings! . . . The husband . . . had already begun to keep the fourth of July, and was lying drunk on the floor." *Walks of Usefulness—Reminiscences of Mrs. Margaret Prior*, 13th ed. (New York: Am. F.M.R. Society, 1848), 241.

60. David Grimstead, *Melodrama Unveiled: American Theater and Culture—1800–1850* (Chicago: University of Chicago Press, 1968), ix. This paragraph draws heavily on Hewitt, *Shadows on the Wall*; and John Ford Sollers, "The Theatrical Career of John T. Ford" (PhD diss., Stanford University, 1962).

61. On the early circus, see Robert C. Toll, *On with the Show: The First Century of Show Business in America* (Oxford: Oxford University Press, 1976), 50–58; and J. Thomas Scharf, *History of Baltimore City and County, from the Earliest Period to the Present Day: Including Biographical Sketches of Their Representative Men* (Philadelphia: L. H. Everts, 1881), 689. On the Peale Museum, see Baltimore Museum Account Book of Rembrandt Peale, Peale Museum Library, MS 92, H. Furlong Baldwin Library, Special Collections, MHS.

62. Toll, *On with the Show*, 10–11; Sollers, "Theatrical Career of John T. Ford," 57–65; Hewitt, *Shadows on the Wall*, 107.

63. Katherine K. Preston, *Opera on the Road: Traveling Opera Troupes in the United States, 1825–60* (Urbana: University of Illinois Press, 2001), 118–21, 397. This book is the source for the following paragraph as well.

64. This and the following paragraph draw upon Paul Charosh, "'Popular' and 'Classical' in the Mid-Nineteenth Century," *American Music* 10 (1992): 117–35.

65. Similar in purpose to *Dwight's Journal of Music*, which flourished from 1852 to 1881 in Boston, the most opinionated article in Peters's *Olio, and American Musical Gazette*, entitled "Musical Taste in Baltimore," appears in volume 5 (May 1850). Most of the printed music included in this journal was by Peters himself, although a song and a dance piece by Stephen Foster appear as well.

66. MS181, API.

67. Nancy Newman, "The Germania Musical Society and Other Forty-Eighters," *Institute for Studies in American Music Newsletter* 33 (Fall 2003): 2–3.

68. This and the next two paragraphs are largely based on Spillane, *History of the American Pianoforte*, 127–36. Variant spellings of *Hartye* include *Hartge* and *Hartje*. On Stewart and Meyer, see Gregory R. Weidman, *Furniture in Maryland, 1740–1940* (Baltimore: Maryland Historical Society, 1984), 147–48; on Hartye, 89.

69. Hewitt, *Shadows on the Wall*, 73–74.

70. Spillane, *History of the American Pianoforte*, 135–36. A detailed listing of Knabe's Baltimore addresses from 1840 to 1856 is in Weidman, *Furniture in Maryland*, 296. For more on Stieff and Hartye, see ibid., 209–10, 241.

71. Hewitt, *Shadows on the Wall*, 68.

72. Brugger, *Maryland*, 249–52.

73. Cunz, *Maryland Germans*, 222.

74. Ibid., 237–38. At an *Eisteddfod* (a German version of a Welsh festival of literature and music) held in Frostburg in 1871, a prize of forty dollars was offered for the chorus of twenty-five or more members who best sang "The Heavens are Telling" from Haydn's *Creation*. Katherine A. Harvey, *The Best-Dressed Miners: Life and Labor in the Maryland Coal Region, 1835–1910* (Ithaca, NY: Cornell University Press, 1967), 120.

75. Cunz, *Maryland Germans*, 245.

76. Ibid., 243, 246–48, 277; Jörg Echterncamp, "Emerging Ethnicity: The German Experience in Antebellum Baltimore," *Maryland Historical Magazine* 86 (1991): 11–14.

77. Preston, *Opera on the Road*, 7–9.

78. Ibid., 214–15; Barnard Hewitt, "'King Stephen' of the Park and Drury Lane," in Joseph W. Donohue Jr., ed., *The Theatrical Manager in Britain and America: Player of a Perilous Game* (Princeton, NJ: Princeton University Press, 1971), 101.

79. Published in 1823 in Boston in Heinrich's collection of songs and instrumental works entitled *The Sylviad, or Minstrelsy of Nature in the Wilds of North America*, Heinrich's "The Yaeger's Adieu" comprised six verses in German. Heinrich dedicated it to the Baltimore Yaegers.

80. Preston, *Opera on the Road*, 26–32.

81. Ibid., 64.

82. Barnum, whose name survives today in the circus world, also promoted a woman professing to be 161 years old. He made the dwarf known as Gen. Tom Thumb a household name. Perhaps ironically, Barnum claimed to prefer opera and fine concert music to the more plebeian offerings that made his name.

83. Charles G. Rosenberg, *Jenny Lind in America* (New York: Stringer & Townsend, 1851), 84–86.

84. W. Portter Ware and Thaddeus C. Lockard Jr., *P. T. Barnum Presents Jenny Lind: The American Tour of the Swedish Nightingale* (Baton Rouge: Louisiana State University Press, 1980), 50–52, 184–85.

85. The movement enjoyed widespread support, often voiced in ideologically charged antidrinking songs at large public meetings, from the 1830s through midcentury. The Hutchinson family's temperance songs enjoyed widespread popularity. Even today the many so-called temperance halls constructed for meetings serve as concert halls. Other singing groups imitated the Hutchinsons' approach, for example, The Alleganians, who in 1847 appeared at the Belvedere Hotel in Cumberland.

86. Scott Gac, *Singing for Freedom: The Hutchinson Family Singers and the Nineteenth-Century Culture of Reform* (New Haven, CT: Yale University Press, 2008), 168–69, 175.

87. Hewitt, *Shadows on the Wall*, 74–75.

88. Ibid., 172–73. Hewitt describes Ford as popular, gregarious, politically active, and quite successful.

89. *Baltimore Olio* 6 (June 1850).

Chapter 3. Intermission

1. Both Deems and Holland are characterized in Hewitt, *Shadows on the Wall*, 69. Deems composed numerous pieces of local interest, such as "The Baltimore March," a "5th Regiment March," and most notably, "Col. Geo. Armistead's Grand March—Performed at the Dedication of the Armistead Monument, Baltimore, September 12th, 1882." These were published by Geo. F. Cole, F. D. Benteen, and Deems himself, respectively. William Smythe Babcock Matthews, ed., *A Hundred Years of Music in America: An Account of Musical Effort in America* (Chicago: G. L. Howe, 1889), 298–300. On Holland's career, see S. E. Lafferty, "Names of Music Teachers, Musicians, Music Dealers, Engravers, Printers and Publishers of Music, Conservatories of Music and Music Academies, Manufacturers of Pianos, Organs and Other Musical Instruments appearing in the Baltimore City Directories from 1798–1900," unpaginated typescript, n.d., PA.

2. John P. Kennedy, Navy Department, to Com. Chas. Morris, November 10, 1852, Letters Received by the Superintendent, 1845–87, box 1, folder 3, US Naval Academy Archives, Annapolis. By 1865 the Navy band had twenty-eight players.

3. Michael Mrlik, "Some Facts and Assumptions Relative to the Origin and History of the U.S. Naval Academy Band," 8, typescript, n.d., US Naval Academy Archives. For impressive work on Pfeiffer, see R. Bruce Horner, "A History of the United States Naval Academy Band" (draft, uncompleted PhD diss., Syracuse University, collection of David Hildebrand), 24–25, 32, 35–41, 166n42.

4. Thomas G. Ford MS, US Naval Academy Archives, chap. 12, p. 5, lyrics from chap. 10, p. 4. Ford's chap. 27, entitled "Nautical Songs," includes lyrics to a rich trove of unique music, such as the "Song of 'The Wasp' by W. F. Davidson U.S.N., U.S. Prize Schooner Wasp at sea, June 9, 1849."

5. Ibid., chap. 10, p. 10.

6. Hollywood picked up and effectively used Hewitt's sentimental favorite of 1864, "Somebody's Darling," in the movie *Gone with the Wind* (1939).

7. Cunz, *Maryland Germans*, 296–99. The eighth national *Sængerfest* had been held in Baltimore two years earlier.

8. Spillane, *History of the American Pianoforte*, 132–33; Thomas S. Eader, "Baltimore Organs and Organ Building," *Maryland Historical Magazine* 65 (1970): 276.

9. For an excellent discussion of this and the following song, plus many others, see Raphael Semmes, "Civil War Song Sheets: One of the Collections of the Maryland Historical Society," *Maryland Historical Magazine* 38 (1943): 205–29. Couplet quoted from "The Exiled Soldier's Adieu to Maryland. Air—'Bertrand's adieu to France.' Camp near Manassas, July 5, 1861," ibid., 208.

10. As recently as February 2016 the Maryland General Assembly was considering legislation to remove or replace "Maryland, My Maryland!" as the state song because its pro-Confederate message is insulting to many. David Hildebrand sat on the appointed advisory group, which unanimously recommended repealing all but Randall's original third verse.

11. Thomas G. Clemens, ed., "The 'Diary' of John H. Stone, First Lieutenant, Company B, 2d Maryland Infantry, C.S.A.," *Maryland Historical Magazine* 85 (1990): 116.

12. Ibid., 131. According to Stone, Steuart also did various gymnastics, all the while whistling the tune to "My Maryland."

13. Hewitt, *Shadows on the Wall*, 31.

14. MSA, SC 930. Another song in this manuscript is entitled "A.D. 1862, Or How They Act in Baltimore, by a volunteer Zouave."

15. Ibid.

16. Semmes, "Civil War Song Sheets," 212. The titles were "Marshal Kane" and "Oh, Jeff! Why Don't you Come?"

17. Ibid., 229.

18. *The Soldier's Companion, Dedicated to the Defenders of their Country in the Field* (Boston: American Unitarian Association, 1865), 19.

19. Hewitt, *Shadows on the Wall*, 70.

20. William Harrison Lowdermilk, *History of Cumberland (Maryland)* (Washington, DC: James Anglim, 1878), 399.

21. Roger Keller, *Roster of Civil War Soldiers from Washington County, Maryland* (Baltimore: Genealogical Publishing, 2008), 101, 169–70.

22. Stephen R. Bockmiller, *Hagerstown in the Civil War* (City of Hagerstown, 2011), 59. Details on Joseph, Perry, and Robert Moxley and their military service are in Keller, *Roster of Civil War Soldiers*, 169.

23. The original edition was issued in New York by A. Simpson.

24. Journal of John Pendleton Kennedy (August 1, 1855–March 14, 1857), entries for February 6 and 7, 1857, 318–24, API.

25. Minutes of the Board of Trustees of the Peabody Institute in the City of Baltimore, April 1859, API.

26. Vertical Files, Maryland Room, Enoch Pratt Free Library, Baltimore.

27. The Maryland State Office Building now stands on Preston Street in the area once known as Baltimore's Latin Quarter.

28. Louis Moreau Gottschalk, *Notes of a Pianist* (Philadelphia: J. B. Lippincott, 1881), 245.

29. "The Wednesday Club Room," 2, H. Furlong Baldwin Library Special Collections, MHS. Sutro, a native of Aachen, Germany, had studied under Mendelssohn at the Royal Conservatory of Music in Brussels, graduating with honors.

30. "Early Days At The Wednesday Club," undated newspaper clipping, ibid. An illustration by J. R. Robertson accompanied the article and portrayed members of the group: Courleander, E. S. Sutro, Robertson (the artist, with bell), Noyes (bottle), Emil Sutro, Jim Gibson (fire shovel), Dr. Volck (tongs), John Allman, Theodore Sutro, Martin (tea kettle), Walker, Dr. Steuart, Frank Gibson (violin), Prescott Smith, A. B. Coulter (coal scuttle), Davis, and Colston.

31. Born in Augsburg, Germany, in 1828 and educated at the University of Munich, Volck migrated to the United States after the political unrest of 1848. One of the founders of the Baltimore College of Dental Surgery, Volck also helped found the Charcoal Club of Baltimore. Adalbert J. Volck MS. Collection, 1878–1948, MS 867, MHS.

32. The group included J. R. Kenly, A. Weidenback, Aug. Hoffman, E. Harrington Jr., A. M. Mayer, James H. Meredith, Edward M. Keith, Hugh Sisson, W. W. Richmond, W. C. Waite, George B. Coale, J. C. Kraft, J. W. Richards, J. Sudsburg, Hugh Newell, William T. Walters, E. G. Mc Dowell, H. G. McCann, and Andrew John Henry Way.

33. A reprint of Volck's cartoon of Abraham Lincoln as Don Quixote and Ben Butler as Sancho Panza appeared in the *Baltimore Sun* on April 22, 1934.

34. See "Memories of the Old Wednesday Club—A Famous Social Organization of Baltimore," Adalbert Johann Volck Scrapbook, MHS.

Chapter 4. Toward Union and Concord

Note: It has proven difficult to research much of what appears in this and the following chapters, even more difficult to document the sources. The most interesting and revealing stories are often the ones whose significance was not recognized at the time and thus went unrecorded. Much of the information came from conversations Elizabeth Schaaf had with the musicians who played with the Baltimore Symphony in its early years, those who entertained in Baltimore theater orchestras, elderly members of Mencken's Saturday Night Club, and those who enlivened the music scene on Pennsylvania Avenue.

1. Innes Randolph, *Poems by Innes Randolph*, ed. Harold Randolph (Baltimore: Williams & Wilkins, 1891). Innes Randolph dedicated the collection to his son, Harold, director of the Peabody Institute. Innes was also held in high regard as a sculptor. His marble bust of William Pinckney, ca. 1870, is in the art collection of the Peabody Institute.

2. Minutes of the Wednesday Club, 1869–1885, MS 885, H. Furlong Baldwin Library, Special Collections, MHS.

3. Undated clipping, Papers of Rose and Otto Sutro, MS1867, ibid.

4. *Baltimore Sun*, May 7, 1852, 1; "The Old Germania Orchestra," *Scribner's Monthly* 11, no. 1 (November 1875): 98. Charles Lenschow, trombonist, violinist, vocal coach, and administrator, came to America with the Germania Orchestra. Publishers issuing his work included Henry McCaffrey and G. Willig Jr. of Baltimore, John F. Ellis of Washington, DC, and Lee & Walker of Philadelphia. Lubov Keefer, *Baltimore's Music: The Haven of the American Composer* (Baltimore: J. H. Furst, 1962), 115–17.

5. "The Founder's Letters and the Papers Relating to Its Dedication and its History Up to the 1st January, 1868," *Address of the Trustees of the Peabody Institute of the City of Baltimore* (Baltimore: William K. Boyle, 1868), 103, API.

6. By the end of the Civil War, Peabody had invested three-fourths of his assets in US and Union-state securities. "George Peabody: Founder of the Peabody Institute," http://msa.maryland .gov/msa/stagser/s1259/143/ghexhibit/onlinebio.html.

7. Deems received the rank of brevet brigadier general for gallantry at Gettysburg. Ray E. Robinson, "A History of the Peabody Conservatory of Music" (PhD diss., Indiana University, 1969), 122.

8. Catherine Pierre, "To the Letter: Peabody Turns 150," *Johns Hopkins Magazine* 59, no. 1 (February 2007).

9. *Dwight's Journal of Music* 26 (February 16, 1867): 398.

10. Wounded in battle, Southard had been honorably discharged in 1865. Robinson, "History of the Peabody Conservatory of Music," 122.

11. Annual Report to the Chairman, June 1, 1871, Records of the Board of Trustees, Committee on the Academy of Music, API.

12. For accounts of the problematic early years of the Peabody, see Record Groups II, Board of Trustees, and III, Office of the Provost, API.

13. Courlaender was a close friend of Hans Christian Anderson, the composer Liszt, and the Danish sculptor Bertel Thorvaldsen.

14. Annual Report of the Provost of the Peabody Institute, June 3, 1875, 17, API.

15. Annual Report of the Provost to the Trustees of the Peabody Institute of the City of Baltimore, June 1, 1878, and Report of the Director of the Conservatory of Music to the Committee on Music, May 27, 1878, 43–44, API; Keefer, *Baltimore's Music*, 5.

16. *Baltimore Saturday Night*, April 15, 1871.

17. Concert program for event at the Baltimore Masonic Temple, March 28, 1873, API.

18. The St. Petersburg Conservatory, the earliest school of music in Russia, opened on September 20, 1862. Piotr Tchaikovsky was a member of the first graduating class.

19. See "Death of Rubinstein Lyric Opera House," newspaper clipping, November 21, 1894, Clipping Books, vol. 1, API.

20. Von Bülow was critical to the success of several major composers of the time. He conducted the premieres of two Wagner operas, *Tristan und Isolde* and *Die Meistersinger von Nürnberg*, in 1865 and 1868, respectively.

21. The Venezuelan pianist, singer, composer, and conductor Teresa Carreño was called the "Valkyrie of the Piano" for the strength and virtuosity of her playing. She toured internationally, often giving more than seventy recitals and concerts a year. In 1863 she played for Abraham Lincoln at the White House (ending her performance with improvisations on "Listen to the Mockingbird," the president's favorite song).

Carreño made her debut as an opera singer in New York in January 1876, when she appeared in the role of Zerlina in Mozart's *Don Giovanni*. She composed works for voice and piano. During her lifetime, more than thirty of her compositions, mostly for solo piano, were published by Heugel in Paris and Ditson in Boston. Carreño's *Possibilities of Tone Color by Artistic Use of Pedals* (Cincinnati, OH: John Church, 1919) continues to be held in high regard.

22. Seventh Annual Report of the Provost to the Trustees of the Peabody Institute of the City of Baltimore, June 4, 1874, 44, API.

23. *Music in Baltimore*, circular distributed in April 1892, Vertical Files, Maryland Room, Enoch Pratt Free Library, Baltimore; *Dwight's Journal of Music* 36 (June 24, 1876): 253.

24. The memory of Lanier's music stayed with his fellow prisoner John B. Tabb long after the end of the war. Lanier played one of the compositions he had written at Point Lookout, *A Melody from Lanier's Flute*, with Edwin Litchfield Turnbull, who arranged it for piano (Leipzig: Breitkopf & Härtel, 1902).

25. Sidney Lanier to Mary Day Lanier, September 22 and November 26, 1873, in *The Centennial Edition of the Works of Sidney Lanier*, ed. Charles B. Anderson and Aubrey H. Starke, vol. 10 (Baltimore: Johns Hopkins Press, 1945), 416.

26. Sidney Lanier to Mary Day Lanier, Dec. 2, 1873, in ibid., 8:424.

27. *Baltimore Sun*, December 8, 1873.

28. Sidney Lanier to Mary Day Lanier, Dec. 25, 1873, in Lanier, *Centennial Edition*, 8:444.

29. Edwin Mims, *Sidney Lanier* (Boston: Houghton Mifflin; Cambridge, MA: Riverside, 1963), 160.

30. Jefferson Davis to Sidney Lanier, January 24, 1875, Papers of the Lee Family, box 4, M2009.413, Archives of the Robert E. Lee Memorial Foundation, Montrose, VA.

31. "Lanier Defends His Cantata," *New York Tribune*, May 22, 1876, 2.

32. Lanier, *Centennial Edition*, vol. 8.

33. *Baltimore Saturday Night*, April 22, 1871.

34. Jacob Frey, *Reminiscences of Baltimore* (Baltimore: Maryland Book Concern, 1893), 359.

35. Morris Mechanic maintained Ford's Theatre (formerly Ford's Grand Opera House) until the early 1960s, when he sold it to the Hecht-May Company. The building later was torn down to make way for a parking garage.

36. *Baltimore Sun*, October 3, 1871.

37. Ibid., December 28, 1878.

38. Frances F. Beirne, *The Amiable Baltimoreans* (New York: E. P. Dutton, 1951), 183.

39. *Nightingale Echo* 2 (June 14, 1934): 2; *New York Times*, September 6, 1983.

40. The 1870s were tempestuous years for Carreño, whose Maryland audiences warmly received her throughout her long career. Marta Milinowski, *By the Grace of God* (New Haven, CT: Yale University Press, 1940).

41. *Dwight's Journal of Music* 38 (November 9, 1878): 336.

42. Vertical Files, H. Furlong Baldwin Library, Special Collections, MHS.

43. *Dwight's Journal of Music* 38 (August 3, 1878): 280.

44. Brugger, *Maryland*, 357.

45. Keefer, *Baltimore's Music*, 199.

46. The Festival Grand Orchestra performed Beethoven's Seventh Symphony; "In questa tomba oscura," with the soloist Franz Remmertz; and "The Calm of the Sea," a four-voice glee (an English type of part song), for massed choirs and orchestra. The pianist Nanette Falk-Auerbach performed the Concerto in G Major and played the piano part in the "Choral Fantasy." A chorus of three hundred spirited amateurs singing the "Hallelujah Chorus" from the oratorio *Christ on the Mount of Olives* ended the dress rehearsal.

47. The *Jewish Trilogy* was composed in Paris in 1868 for Mrs. Hester Rothschild, of London. The work received its first performance in its final (and lengthened) form at the festival.

48. Undated clipping, Vertical Files, H. Furlong Baldwin Library, Special Collections, MHS; *Dwight's Journal of Music* 38 (June 8, 1878): 247.

49. Elliott N. Galkiln and N. Quist, "Baltimore," in Stanley Sadie, ed., *New Grove Dictionary of Music and Musicians*, vol. 2 (New York: Macmillan, 2001), 611–12; Annual Report of the Provost to the Trustees of the Peabody Institute of the City of Baltimore, June 1, 1880, 13, and June 1, 1884, 20, API. Fincke, professor of vocal music, also played violin in the Peabody Symphony. He conducted the chamber music program and the Peabody chorus.

50. Handel's *Messiah* was first performed during Lent in 1742 as a benefit to help free men from debtors' prison, Mercer's Hospital, and the Charitable Infirmary in Dublin.

51. Their ranks included A. S. Abell, Charles J. Bonaparte, Thomas Deford, Robert Garrett, Daniel Coit Gilman, Edward Greenway, Reverdy Johnson, J. I. Middleton, Enoch Pratt, C. Morton Stewart, Severn Teackle Wallis, and William T. Walters. Lyric Opera Collection, API.

52. The festival concluded on the following Saturday with a Wagner Night with Thomas on the podium. After opening with the *Overture to Tannhaeuser*, the orchestra cut loose with a spirited *Ride of the Walkyries* from Act III of *Die Walkure*. Frau Friedrich-Materna sang *Brunnhilde's Supplication* and Herr Scaria *Wotan's Farewell*. The orchestra had the last word with *the Magic Fire Scene*. The assembled forces of the Festival closed the program with excerpts from *Die Meistersinger*, ending with the *Finale* with chorus. Two thousand music lovers, exhausted and satisfied, made their way out into the spring night, their hands stinging from prolonged applause.

53. President's Report of 1884, Oratorio Society of Baltimore, Vertical File, API.

54. Galkiln and Quist, "Baltimore."

55. *New York Times*, October 1, 1899, 18.

56. The building was designed to be constructed in two stages. The lecture hall, now the Miriam A. Friedberg Concert Hall, would be built in the first stage, and the library, in the second. When the second building was completed, the library was moved to its present quarters, making room for the Gallery of Art and the Conservatory of Music.

57. *Dwight's Journal of Music* 38 (October 26, 1878): 326.

58. Fifteenth Annual Report of the Provost to the Trustees of the Peabody Institute of the City of Baltimore, June 1, 1878, API.

59. *Philadelphia Times*, May 15, 1879.

60. Fifteenth Annual Report of the Provost, June 1, 1876.

61. *Baltimore Sun*, May 10, 1877, 4.

62. The movements were "Childhood," andante, with its skips of alternate fifths and fourths; "Youth," adagio-maestoso, which opens with the melody in the bass clef; "Manhood," allegretto, opening in C Major; and "Old Age," a sober march scored for timpani.

63. *Dwight's Journal of Music* 39 (February 4, 1879): 16.

64. *Baltimore Sun*, May 14, 1893.

65. *New York Times*, April 16, 1891.

66. Ibid., September 6, 1893.

67. President's Report of 1884, Oratorio Society of Baltimore.

68. The committee was enlarged to thirty members: B. N. Baker, Frank Frick, R. C. Davidson, Ernest Knabe, Richard S. Albert, J. LeRoy White, Alex. Frank, Geo. H. Sargeant, Chas. A. Martin, J. Guggenheimer, Alfred Dohme, F. M. Colston, A. H. Hecht, Henry Lauts, Henry Smith, Blanchard Randall, Edward Leyth, A. K. Shriver, G. M. Shriver, F. H. Gottlieb, Nelson Hill, W. A. Hanaway, Louis Schneider, George Savage, J. F. Supplee, Ross Jungnickel, Geo. Blummer, W. H. Love, D. L. Bartlett, W. Graham Bowdoin. From Elizabeth Schaaf, "Lecture for the Baltimore Symphony Associates," January 1999, Schaaf's personal collection.

69. Undated clipping, Personal Scrapbook of Frank Frick, API.

70. Ford's Grand Opera House had opened in 1871, the Academy of Music in 1875.

71. *Baltimore Sun*, October 16, 1894.

72. Ibid., November 1, 1894, in personal scrapbook of Frank Frick, API.

73. *Baltimore Morning Herald*, May 3, 1896.

74. *Baltimorean*, June 13, 1896, Lyric Theatre Clipping Books, 1:65, API.

75. Frederick Innes formed his band in 1887, when he went to San Francisco to accept a solo engagement at the exposition being held in Golden Gate Park. Innes was to perform with a local band sponsored by the Market Street Railroad Company. The company's comptroller absconded with the money, scuttling the band. After an appeal to the president of the exposition, Innes formed a concert band to play at the exposition.

76. Lyric Theatre Clipping Books, API.

77. Photocopy of a letter Jungnickel signed as director of the Baltimore Symphony Orchestra, reprinted in *Music in Baltimore*.

78. Ross Jungnickel, Retrospect and Prospect. Advance Announcement, Sixth Season, 1898–1899, Baltimore Symphony Orchestra, 5, API.

79. *New York Times*, January 14, 1890.

80. Ibid.

81. Howard R. Thatcher, "Notes on Music in Baltimore," *Peabody Notes* 5, no. 1 (Fall 1950): 1.

82. "Jungnickel to Play in Washington," *Baltimore Sun*, December 12, 1899.

83. Thatcher, "Notes on Music in Baltimore," 1.

84. Baltimore Symphony Orchestra Advance Announcement, 1898–1899, API.

Chapter 5. My Maryland

1. Bernard Christian Steiner, *Men of Mark in Maryland . . . biographies of leading men of the State*, vol. 2 (Baltimore: B. F. Johnson, 1910), 310.

2. Gen. Henry C. Evans, "I Remember The Beethoven Terrace Amateur Orchestra," unpublished manuscript, API.

3. John C. French, *A History of the University Founded by Johns Hopkins* (Baltimore: Johns Hopkins Press, 1946), 312. Now called

the Merrick Barn, the barn was built by Charles Carroll in the early nineteenth century to house dairy cattle; it is now used for theater productions.

4. "Baltimore Theaters," Ephemera and Advertising folder, Vertical Files, H. Furlong Baldwin Library, Special Collections, MHS; Marshall Winslow Stearns and Jean Stearns, *Jazz Dance: The Story of American Vernacular Dance* (1968; reprint, New York: Da Capo, 1994), 21.

5. Frank Fink, "I Remember . . . The Old Monument Theatre," *Baltimore Sun*, March 24, 1957.

6. Randall Donaldson, "German-American Social Organizations in Baltimore, Part I," *Journal of German-American History* 42 (1993): 23–29.

7. Quoted by Denoe Leedy, in *Harold Randolph—The Man and Musician, Musical Quarterly* 26, no. 2 (April 1944): 202.

8. A native of Melbourne, Australia, Hutcheson began his career at the age of 5 as an "Infant Phenomenon." At 14 Hutcheson was sent to the Leipzig Conservatory to study with Reinecke and Zwinstscher. After completing his studies at Weimar, he went to Berlin, where he was acclaimed as a composer of promise and a pianist second to none. Inez Bull, *The Immortal Ernest Hutcheson: A Biography* (Elmira, NY: Elmira Quality Printers, 1993).

9. Thatcher, "Notes on Music in Baltimore." Peabody's new electrical lighting system had been designed by Johns Hopkins professors. Ibid.

10. Members of the committee were involved with plans to convert James Lawrence Kernan's Auditorium, a vaudeville theater on North Howard Street, into a concert hall.

11. Records of the Florestan Club, Vertical Files, H. Furlong Baldwin Library, Special Collections, MHS.

12. Born in Ballensted, Germany, in 1867, Gustav Strube received his early music training at home. His father, Friedrich Strube, the town musician, conducted a youth orchestra that was made up of his students and three of his six children, including Gustav. After becoming a student at the Leipzig Conservatory, Gustav supported himself by composing music for local orchestras and performing, playing for a time under Johann Strauss. After completing his studies, he performed in the Gewandhaus Orchestra under Carl Reinecke and in the Municipal Opera House orchestra under the baton of Arthur Nikisch.

13. Papers of Gustav Strube, API.

14. Abram Moses, "The Baltimore Symphony Orchestra," *Community News* 19 (November 1923), quoted in Richard Alan Disharoon, "A History of Municipal Music in Baltimore" (PhD diss., University of Maryland, College Park, 1980); Kenneth S. Clark, *Municipal Aid to Music in America* (New York: National Bureau for the Advancement of Music, 1925).

15. Edwin Litchfield Turnbull, "The Domination of American Music by Trade Unions," *Art World* 2, no. 6 (September 1917): 525.

16. Ibid. On Huber, see Programs and printed material, BMS20-10, and Clippings, 1890–2007, BMS20-12, Records of the Baltimore Symphony Orchestra, Vertical Files, H. Furlong Baldwin Library, Special Collections, MHS.

17. Kenneth S. Clark, Baltimore, *Cradle of Municipal Music* (Baltimore: City of Baltimore, 1941), 10, API.

18. "Strube to be Conductor," *Baltimore Sun*, December 24, 1915.

19. Ibid.

20. This information is based on conversations Elizabeth Schaaf had ca. 2005 with musicians who performed in Baltimore theater orchestras.

21. This information is based on conversations Elizabeth Schaaf had from 1965 to 2000 with Baltimore Symphony Orchestra musicians who performed under Strube.

22. For decades the conductor and most of the principal players would depend on Peabody salaries for a substantial part of their income.

23. Stephen Wigler, "The Forgotten Conductor," *Baltimore Sun Magazine*, February 10, 1991, 5.

24. Garrison, a Peabody Conservatory graduate with an artist diploma, made her Metropolitan Opera debut on November 27th, 1914, singing the role of Frasquita in *Carmen*. Robinson, "History of the Peabody Conservatory of Music," 64.

25. Clipping Book, 1917, Record Group VII, Academy of Music / Conservatory of Music, API.

26. "Mr. Randolph Would Bar Works of Living German Composers," *Baltimore Sun*, November 15, 1917.

27. Scrapbook, Peabody Conservatory of Music, 1917–1919, API.

28. "Alfred Butler to Get Landow's Place," *Baltimore News*, June 20, 1918.

29. Lyric Theatre Clipping Books, API.

30. Ibid.

31. Records of the Baltimore Symphony Orchestra, Vertical Files, H. Furlong Baldwin Library, Special Collections, MHS.

32. Concert Programs, Programs and Printed Material, Records of the Baltimore Symphony Orchestra, Baltimore City Archives.

33. *Baltimore Evening Sun*, August 13, 1918.

34. Enrollment records, Record Group VII, Academy of Music / Conservatory of Music, API.

35. Stearns and Stearns, *Jazz Dance*, 21.

36. Mary K. Zajac, "Wild Ride," *Style* (Baltimore), April 7, 2010.

37. "Rollercoaster Ride," ibid., June 19, 2007; John P. Coleman, *Historic Amusement Parks of Baltimore: An Illustrated History* (Baltimore: McFarland, 2014).

38. *Style* (Baltimore), January 7, 2010; *Baltimore Sun*, June 17, 1909. Riverview Park opened in 1890 and closed during Prohibition in 1929.

39. Eubie Blake, interview by Robert Hebb at Blake's home in Brooklyn, NY, August 2, 1972, Maryland Historical Society Oral History Project, Oral History #OH8473, ed. Elizabeth Schaaf, H. Furlong Baldwin Library, MHS. Information on Blake in the next several paragraphs is from this interview.

40. Buck dancing was a routine popular with minstrel and vaudeville performers portraying African American men, called "Bucks."

41. *Baltimore Afro-American*, May 9, 1925, A6.

42. Lucille Brooks, interview by Elizabeth Schaaf, Baltimore, August 8, 2002, MHS.

43. The net cost of the orchestra's first three concerts was $2,037.

44. Samaroff performed the sonatas in eight recitals, from January 28 to April 28, 1920. Peabody concert programs, API.

45. *Baltimore Evening Sun*, July 9, 1919.

46. Papers of Reginald Stewart, Clipping Books, API.

47. *Baltimore Star*, February 3, 1920.

48. Ruth Van Hulsteyn, telephone interview by Elizabeth Schaaf, summer 1994, API.

49. Tracy McCleary, interview by Elizabeth Schaaf, August 11, 1995, API. The group of six included J. C. Van Hulsteyn and Bart Wirtz, who had served as mentors to Huber when he was attempting to gain a foothold in the Baltimore music world.

50. The Druid Hill Park statue of Wagner was erected in celebration of the first-prize performance of the United Singers of Baltimore at the 1900 Saengerfest in New York.

51. "Wild Gyrations and Lusty Rhythms," in "The Storm is Passing Over: Celebrating the Musical Life of Maryland's African-American Community from Emancipation to Civil Rights," API, http://music library.peabody.jhu.edu/content.php?pid=599119&sid=4940847.

52. *Baltimore Afro-American*, October 6, 1917, 2.

53. Ibid., September 29, 1917.

54. Otto Ortmann, "Notes on Jazz," *Peabody Bulletin*, December 1931, 11.

55. *Baltimore Afro-American*, May 7, 1938.

56. Undated *Sun* article by Isaac Rehert, ca. 1978, Baltimore music folders, Vertical Files, H. Furlong Baldwin Library, Special Collections, MHS.

57. Thomas Henderson Kerr, interview by Andrew Field, API.

58. *Baltimore Evening Sun*, November 1, 1919.

59. James H. N. Waring, "Work of the Colored law and order league, Baltimore, Md.," Library of Congress, https://memory.loc.gov/service/gdc/lhbcb/02097/02097.pdf.

60. McCleary interview, August 11, 1995.

61. Mike Giuliano, "The Royal Theatre in Review," *Baltimore Sun*, August 10, 1986.

62. Jack Hook, president of the Musicians' Association of Metropolitan Baltimore, provided information in 2006–7 on Baltimore ensembles.

63. F. B. "Burt" Hammann, who founded the Townsmen, a society dance band, with his brother C. Gordon Hammann, conversations with Elizabeth Schaaf ca. 2006.

64. Camay Calloway Murphy, oral history interview by John Spitzer, February 7, 2002, API.

65. Camay Calloway Murphy recounted many of these stories about Cab and Blanche Calloway in conversations with Elizabeth Schaaf, 2001–6.

66. Eugene Prettyman, conversation with Elizabeth Schaaf, February 4, 1999, Enoch Pratt Free Library, Baltimore.

67. Tracy McCleary, conversation with Elizabeth Schaaf, spring 1999.

68. Hammond spoke about Holiday and her career at length when he lectured at the Peabody Conservatory in the late 1970s.

69. "She Gave Chick His First Drum," *Baltimore Afro-American*, July 1, 1939.

70. Gilbert Sandler, "Baltimore Glimpses: The Chick Webb Funeral," *Baltimore Sun*, March 12, 1985.

71. Much of the information on the theater orchestras is based on the recollections of senior members of the Musicians' Association of Metropolitan Baltimore who played in them. Descriptions of the theaters are drawn from the vertical files of the MHS and the Enoch Pratt Free Library, Baltimore.

72. Much of the information here on Anne Brown is from Eugene Prettyman, conversations with Elizabeth Schaaf, late 1990s.

73. Todd Duncan's playing Porgy led to his London debut at the Drury Lane. He was awarded the George Peabody Medal of Music by the Peabody Conservatory on May 24, 1984.

74. Anne Brown, interview by Elizabeth Schaaf, spring 1998. This interview took place when Brown was in Baltimore to receive the George Peabody Medal for Outstanding Contributions to Music in America from the Peabody Institute—the institution that had denied her music education seventy years earlier. She was made an honorary citizen of Baltimore in 1999.

Chapter 6. Musical Airs, Aired Music

1. "The Telephone Revolution in Music," *Dwight's Journal of Music* 37 (April 28, 1977): 16.

2. The information in this paragraph is drawn from the Andrew S. Pope Collection, API.

3. Louis Cheslock, quoted in *Baltimore Evening Sun*, August 25, 1937, reprinted in *Peabody Bulletin*, December 1937.

4. "Paul Whiteman 'The King of Jazz' (1890–1967)," redhotjazz .com/whiteman.html. WBAL Radio acquired a sister, WBAL-TV, channel 11, which began broadcasting on March 11, 1948, from WBAL's original Charles Street studios in downtown Baltimore.

5. Edmund Cooke Collection, API.

6. The Fifth Regiment of the Maryland National Guard purchased WEAR's equipment and applied for new call letters and a license. They went on the air in 1924 as WFBR (World's First Broadcasting Regiment), transmitting from the Fifth Regiment Armory, on Howard Street.

7. Fred Rasmussen, "Ruth van Hulsteyn, 91, Long Time BSO Violinist," *Baltimore Sun*, November 30, 1996.

8. "Symphony Gives First Concert Over National Radio Network," ibid., January 21, 1945.

9. Baltimore Symphony Orchestra program for Saturday, January 20, 1945, API.

10. "Early Baltimore 'Wireless Telephone' (Radio) Stations," *Charm City History* (blog), April 20, 2013, http://charmcityhistory .blogspot.com/2013/04/early-baltimore-wireslls-teleph9one.html.

11. Baltimore *Sunday Sun*, December 12, 1926.

12. Leigh Martinet, conversation with Elizabeth Schaaf, 1989.

13. Michael J. Maher, *John Charles Thomas, Beloved Baritone of American Opera and Popular Music* (Jefferson, NC: McFarland, 2006). Also on Thomas, see Papers of John Charles Thomas, API.

14. Johnson, inventor in 1901 of the Victor Talking Machine, afterward become the driving force behind Victor Records, America's most influential music and recording company.

15. Camay Calloway Murphy, conversations with Elizabeth Schaaf, 1989–2004. On Chambers, see the countless articles in Verti-

cal Files, H. Furlong Baldwin Library, Special Collections, MHS, and Vertical Files, Maryland Room, Enoch Pratt Free Library, Baltimore.

16. McCleary interview, August 11, 1995. Information on Mc-Cleary in this section comes from conversations with Elizabeth Schaaf, 1999–2003.

17. Roy McCoy, interview by Elizabeth Schaaf, at the McCoy residence, 1832 Moreland Avenue, Baltimore, August 12, 1996, API.

18. Max Roach, conversation with Elizabeth Schaaf, February 13, 1999, at Coppin State University, Baltimore, API.

19. *The Negro Travelers' Green Book*, popularly known as the *Green Book*, was a travel guide for African American travelers published from 1936 to 1964 by Victor H. Green, a New York City mailman, that listed hotels, boardinghouses, barbershops, restaurants, and other services.

20. James K. McManus, "Memory Lapses, Guitarist Improvises, and Social-Function Tradition is Born," *Baltimore Evening Sun*, October 23, 1947.

21. A faculty member of the Peabody Conservatory of Music for sixty years and a charter member of the Baltimore Symphony Orchestra, Cheslock was the last surviving member of the Saturday Night Club. He and his wife, Elise, were frequent guests at Mencken's home at 1524 Hollins Street and a ready and reliable source of stories. Over the years the Cheslocks shared many of them with Schaaf. Many of Cheslock's stories would appear in his book *H. L. Mencken on Music, Selected by Louis Cheslock*, published by Macmillan in 1975, and in Elam Ray Sprenkle's "The Life and Works of Louis Cheslock" (DMA diss., Peabody Institute, 1979).

22. "And what were all the joys that bide / In meadow, wood and down, / To me, if I were at your side / Within the joyless town?" H. L. Mencken, "Madrigal," in *Ventures Into Verse* (1903).

23. The Cosmopolitan University, one of the earliest correspondence schools in the country, was founded by John Brisben Walker, the editor of *Cosmopolitan* magazine.

24. Henry Louis Mencken, "From Reflections on the Drama," in *Prejudices*, 3rd series, quoted in Isaac Goldberg, *The Man Mencken* (New York: Simon & Schuster, 1925), 155.

25. *Baltimore News-Post*, May 11, 1946.

26. Henry Walters endowed the Department of Art as Applied to Medicine in 1911.

27. *Finkelstein's Café* took its name from Arnold Finkelstein's bargain clothing store, a landmark in Towson, north of the city, from its opening in 1920 until the 1990s.

28. Henry Louis Mencken, *The Diary of H. L. Mencken*, ed. Charles A. Fechter (New York: Alfred A. Knopf, 1989), 167.

29. Unrecorded anecdote told by Louis Cheslock to Elizabeth Schaaf, among others.

30. Louis Cheslock, unrecorded conversations with Elizabeth Schaaf, 1966–78.

31. The renowned Johns Hopkins biologist Dr. Raymond Pearl was the first American biologist to publicly rebuke eugenics. Mencken published Pearl's critique in the *American Mercury* in November 1927.

32. Compositions by Mencken can be found in Papers of Louis Cheslock, API.

33. Serge Koussevitzky was music director of the Boston Symphony Orchestra from 1924 to 1929.

34. Mencken to Isaac Goldberg, May 6, 1925, Papers of Louis Cheslock, API.

35. Ibid.

36. Sylvan Levin recounted stories from his student years and his career in an interview by Ned Quist and Elizabeth Schaaf at Levin's home in New York in the mid–1990s, when they accepted his personal papers for the Archives of the Peabody Institute.

37. Undated newspaper clipping, Papers of Sylvan Levin, API.

38. "Sylvan Levin Makes Notable Debut with Detroit Symphony Orchestra," *Detroit Free Press*, undated clipping, ibid.

39. Matthew Gurewitch, "Celebrating a Gift from Bali: Delicious Confusion," *New York Times*, October 8, 2010.

40. Leonard Bernstein, quoted in Philip Hart, *Fritz Reiner: A Biography* (Evanston, IL: Northwestern University Press, 1994), 65.

41. Sylvan Levin, unrecorded conversation with Elizabeth Schaaf, New York, 1994.

42. "Sylvan Levin, 93; Championed Music In Philadelphia," *New York Times*, August 16, 1996.

43. *Baltimore Sun*, November 16, 1930.

44. Record Group VII, Records of the Peabody Institute Conservatory of Music, API. The Carnegie grant also provided a matching gift of sixty thousand dollars to support the regular operations of the Peabody Conservatory of Music.

45. Mrs. George Dobyne, mother-in-law of the baritone John Charles Thomas, was the driving force behind the concert. Governor Herbert R. O'Conor, Senator and Mrs. Millard E. Tydings, and Senator and Mrs. George L. Radcliffe headed the list of patrons.

46. The theramin is the electronic instrument that is heard at the conclusion of the 1948 film *The Red Shoes*. Stieff's theramin is now in the collection of early electronic instruments in API.

47. "Barlow Foresees 26-Week Symphony Season and Tour," *Baltimore Sun*, November 12, 1940.

48. Howard Barlow to William L. Marbury, October 14, 1940, Records of the Trustees of the Peabody Institute of the City of Baltimore, API.

49. Marbury to Reginald Stewart, March 14, 1951, ibid.

50. Mitch Miller went on to become one of the most influential figures in American popular music during the 1950s and early 1960s, both as the head of Artists and Repertoire at Columbia Records and as a bestselling recording artist with an NBC television series, *Sing Along with Mitch*.

51. Irving Cooperstein, interview by Scott Gregg, April 20, 1990, API.

52. *New York Musical Courier*, December 1, 1940.

53. Letters to the editor, *Baltimore Evening Sun*, January 1, 1941.

54. Letters to the editor, ibid., January 1, 1940.

55. "Coats—To Wear Or Not To Wear Them," *Baltimore Sun*, September 15, 1944.

56. Betty Littleton, unrecorded conversation with Elizabeth Schaaf at Littleton's home in Glenarm, MD, April 20, 2011. Littleton attended weekend dances at the schoolhouse in the 1940s.

57. The conductor and composer Ken Darby did not work with Thomas until he became involved with the Westinghouse Hour. Darby sang backup for Bing Crosby on the original 1942 studio recording of *White Christmas*, portrayed one of the Marx Brothers in a musical spoof in *Honolulu*, was a conductor and composer with Disney Studio's film *Song of the South*, and coached Marilyn Monroe for *Gentlemen Prefer Blondes*. He shared an Academy Award with Andre Previn for scoring *Porgy and Bess*.

58. David Hollister (Carroll Hollister's son), unrecorded interview by Elizabeth Schaaf, New York, 1995.

59. An advisory committee chaired by Ernest Hutcheson first offered the directorship to the pianist and composer Rudolph Ganz.

60. "Peabody Organ Department Head Now is Private in Army," *Baltimore Sun*, July 12, 1942.

61. Delphine Stewart recalled the exchange in an informal, unrecorded conversation with Elizabeth Schaaf in the summer of 2008.

62. Ella Jackson, a native Baltimorean, was a descendant of the Bond family, whose home, Mount Royal, was located at Park Avenue and Reservoir Street. Her family settled in Baltimore during the American Revolution and entertained Lafayette when he visited the city. Mrs. Jackson astutely chose the best-connected women in the city to serve on the symphony steering committee. Mrs. Jack Symington, representing Baltimore society's old guard, asked to chair ticket sales; Mrs. Howard M. Kern, president of the Baltimore Music Club; Mrs. Arthur Deute, director of the Baltimore Music Club's chorus; Mrs. Carle Jackson (the former Rosa Ponselle); Mrs. Charles Fisher, a resident of fashionable Ruxton, asked to chair the committee arranging for the attendance of private schools and colleges; Mrs. John Cyrus Distlere, called upon to enlist support from the Guilford and Homeland area; Mrs. Louis Hutzler; Mrs. William Ellis Coale; and Mrs. Hamilton Owens (the violinist Olga von Hartz). From Schaaf, "Lecture for the Baltimore Symphony Associates," January 1999.

63. *Baltimore Sun*, February 21, 1943.

64. The Musical Arts Quartet, one of the leading chamber-music organizations in the United States, served as quartet in residence for music festivals held at the Garrett home, Evergreen House, on North Charles Street.

65. *Baltimore Evening Sun*, November 12, 1942.

66. *Baltimore Sun*, November 20, 1942.

67. Stewart invited Strube to return to the podium as guest conductor later in the season, when the orchestra played the premiere performance of Strube's *Der Harz*. Baltimore Symphony concert programs, Baltimore City Archives.

68. The score and parts for *Der Harz* are in the Gutav Strube Collection, API.

69. *Baltimore Sun*, November 20, 1943.

70. Ruth Van Hulsteyn would become the orchestra's elder stateswoman. She continued playing in the BSO into her eighties. Her insight, frank opinions, and good judgment made her a valued adviser to the trustees and administrators of the symphony. Rasmussen, "Ruth van Hulsteyn, 91, Long Time BSO Violinist."

71. *Baltimore News Post*, January 18, 1945.

72. Mencken knew Jones, loved Bach, and regularly attended the festival. Convinced that Bach's music went wonderfully with beer, regardless of prohibition, Mencken set out to find appropriate libations. At the door of a local speakeasy he was met by the proprietor, who was convinced that Mencken was a revenuer. The resourceful Mencken protested, explaining that he was a musician in town for the festival. Asked to prove it, Mencken held up his score of Bach's Mass in B Minor. The proprietor let him in, and Mencken left with his beer. Dan Hartzell, "How Mencken Escaped Death in the Desert in Bethlehem," *Allentown (PA) Morning Call*, May 21, 1989.

73. Nicholas Nabokov became a US citizen in 1939. He wrote his arrangement of "The Star-Spangled Banner" in the early 1940s, while a student at St. John's College.

74. Alice Eversham, *Washington, DC, Evening Star*, February 21, 1947.

75. *Baltimore Sun*, March 13, 1942.

76. Sarah Goodyear, "When Being Italian Was a Crime," *Voice*, April 11, 2000.

77. Ernst Lert came to the United States from La Scala to stage-direct at the Metropolitan. He joined the Peabody faculty in 1937, staying on until 1955.

78. *Baltimore Evening Sun*, April 13, 1942.

79. Other Baltimore singers to reach the Met include Roberta Glanville, a student of Lucien Odend'hal's, and Mabel Garrison, also a student of Odend'hal's as well as of the late Pietro Minetti, at the Peabody Conservatory of Music.

80. William McCloskey, "The Baltimore Opera: An Unobjective Look at Fifty-plus Seasons," *Peabody News*, September–October 1982.

81. Glenn Dillard Gunn, "John Charles Thomas Sings Superbly as Trumans Listen," *Washington, DC, Times-Herald*, February 18, 1947.

82. Johanna Zacharias, "Reginald Stewart, the 'Real Thing'—The BSO, 1942–1952," *Overture* 75, no. 2 (1991): 11.

83. William Marbury was one of the organizers of Maryland's Legal Aid Bureau, which offered legal services to the poor. A prominent Maryland lawyer, Marbury represented Alger Hiss in the early stages of Hiss's suit against Whittaker Chambers. See *Harvard Crimson*, April 10, 1952.

84. Weldon Wallace, "City's Symphony Applauded In Concert at Carnegie Hall," *Baltimore Sun*, February 6, 1947.

85. Olin Downes, "Reginald Stewart Conducts the Baltimore Symphony in First Program at Carnegie Hall," *New York Times*, February 6, 1947, 27; *New Yorker*, February 1947.

86. WOR is one of the oldest radio stations in New York. The call letters have no meaning but indicate that the station dates from the 1920s.

Coda

1. Quotations from McCleary are from *Baltimore Sun*, August 10, 1986.

2. Joseph Meyerhoff, conversation with Elizabeth Schaaf, September 1982.

3. Quotations from Byrd are from an oral history interview by Elizabeth Schaaf, May 29, 1997, H. Furlong Baldwin Library, Special Collections, MHS.

4. Undated music review, Papers of Charlie Byrd, API.

<BMH>Index

INDEX